UNSETTLING NATIVE ART HISTORIES ON THE NORTHWEST COAST

NATIVE ART OF THE PACIFIC NORTHWEST

A Bill Holm Center Series

This series fosters understanding and appreciation of the dynamic cultural and artistic expressions of the Indigenous peoples of the Pacific Northwest.

In the Spirit of the Ancestors: Contemporary Northwest Coast Art at the Burke Museum, edited by Robin K. Wright and Kathryn Bunn-Marcuse

Return to the Land of the Head Hunters: Edward S. Curtis, the Kwakwaka'wakw, and the Making of Modern Cinema, edited by Brad Evans and Aaron Glass

Northwest Coast Indian Art: An Analysis of Form, 50th Anniversary Edition, by Bill Holm

Unsettling Native Art Histories on the Northwest Coast, edited by Kathryn Bunn-Marcuse and Aldona Jonaitis

Unsettling Native Art Histories on the Northwest Coast

EDITED BY

KATHRYN BUNN-MARCUSE
ALDONA JONAITIS

BILL HOLM CENTER FOR THE STUDY OF NORTHWEST NATIVE ART
Burke Museum, Seattle

in association with

UNIVERSITY OF WASHINGTON PRESS
Seattle

Bill Holm Center
for the Study of Northwest Native Art
BURKE MUSEUM

Unsettling Native Art Histories on the Northwest Coast was made possible in part by a grant from the Quest for Truth Foundation.

This publication was also supported by a generous gift from Jill and Joseph McKinstry.

www.tulalipcares.org

Additional support was provided by the Tulalip Tribes Charitable Fund, which provides the opportunity for a sustainable and healthy community for all.

First paperback edition 2022

Designed by Katrina Noble
Composed in Noto, typeface designed by Google Fonts

26 25 24 23 22 5 4 3 2 1

Printed and bound in the United States of America

Bill Holm Center for the Study of Northwest Native Art
Burke Museum of Natural History and Culture
www.burkemuseum.org/bhc

UNIVERSITY OF WASHINGTON PRESS
uwapress.uw.edu

LIBRARY OF CONGRESS CATALOGING-IN-PUBLICATION DATA ON FILE

ISBN 978-0-295-74713-2 (hardcover)
ISBN 978-0-295-74714-9 (ebook)
ISBN 978-0-295-75070-5 (paperback)

∞ This paper meets the requirements of ANSI/NISO Z39.48–1992 (Permanence of Paper).

The contributors to this volume come from and work in many distinct Indigenous territories. Kathryn Bunn-Marcuse and the University of Washington Press stand on the land of the Coast Salish peoples, which touches the shared waters of all tribes and bands within the Duwamish, Suquamish, Tulalip, and Muckleshoot nations. Aldona Jonaitis lives and works in the Athabascan/Northern Dene land of the Tanana. We would like to acknowledge the long history of teaching and learning in each of these territories and express our gratitude for each nation's stewardship of the lands in which we make our homes.

CONTENTS

UNSETTLING NATIVE ART HISTORIES ON THE NORTHWEST COAST

Introduction

Kathryn Bunn-Marcuse

"We have no word for art in our language." This oft-repeated phrase has been used by Indigenous community members and scholars to push back against the ways in which Indigenous creations have been presented in museums and analyzed in scholarship as "art" according to frameworks and scholarly methodologies that were developed outside of the original cultural paradigms. To put "art" in quotation marks notes how that term has been contested as one imposed by outsiders and applied in a manner that erases cultural function, kinship connections, or the spiritual power of cultural creation or belongings. Academic and museum frameworks have at times contributed to the alienation of Indigenous artworks both literally, when they were removed from communities, and conceptually, when they are subjected to scholarly analysis that ignores or dismisses Indigenous understandings, concepts, and contexts for those creations. Moreover, the perils of language translation and epistemological translation are equally dire. As Tlingit scholar Ishmael Hope points out in chapter 14 in this edited volume: "While Tlingit people never had a word for art, Europeans never had a word for at.óow, either."

Throughout this book, contributors discuss Indigenous creations as *artworks* with full understanding that this term, while still an English gloss for culturally specific Indigenous vocabulary, has the potential to carry the relational, aesthetic, and performative functions of these creations within a cultural network. Such robust and Indigenously informed interpretations demonstrate Chickasaw curator heather ahtone's definition of an Indigenous aesthetic that proposes broad roles for Indigenous arts, including expressing identity within a complex sociocultural community, creating didactic materials and mnemonic references to traditional cultural cosmology and values, and providing instruments for intergenerational transmission of cultural knowledge.[1]

Unsettling Native Art Histories

This book presents new scholarship in the field of Northwest Coast art studies. As editors, Aldona Jonaitis and I were struck by the inflections in this work—in both process and outcome—that reflected new directions in our field, including work to "unsettle" the field of Northwest Coast studies in particular and cultural museum practices in general.[2]

What does it mean to "unsettle" art history, and why has this term appeared at this moment in time? "Unsettling" emerges in concert with studies that examine the particular historical and social formations of colonialism characterized by outsiders claiming Indigenous land as their own.[3] Cherokee scholar Alicia Cox explains settler colonialism as "an ongoing system of power that perpetuates the genocide and repression of indigenous peoples and cultures. Essentially hegemonic in scope, settler colonialism normalizes the continuous settler occupation, exploiting lands and resources to which indigenous peoples have genealogical relationships."[4] In a conversation on "Unsettling Settler Colonialism," political scientist Jeff Corntassle (Cherokee) asserts that if you want to "unsettle" and you are a settler, you have to change the relationship and take direction from Indigenous nations themselves.[5]

To "unsettle" might take a variety of forms in terms of reexaminations of previous scholarship or questioning current academic or institutional practices as the essays in this book exemplify. While bringing new questions to past histories is an established part of scholarly practice, at its core "unsettling" requires work that is actively aware of both past and ongoing effects of settler colonialism; commits to listening, learning, and acting in ways that respect and uphold Indigenous priorities; and calls for or demonstrates new practices based in this awareness and accountability to the impacts of scholarly work. Corntassle suggests that part of this process is reflected in the Tsalagi (Cherokee language) saying "Live in a longer now," understanding how our current moment is part of the longer history that surrounds us, connecting past to present to future with awareness of our responsibilities across these generations.[6] The authors in this volume reflect the current ethics in our field, which recognize that:

- Native artists have shaped the record of Native history with their creations, which constitute recorded history through various media.
- The histories recorded in artistic creations belong to the communities from which they come.
- Indigenous artists, scholars, and communities are the experts on their own histories.
- Scholarship and museum practice have obligations to Indigenous communities and thus must respect these ethical tenets.[7]

This edited volume brings forward voices demonstrating how Indigenous priorities can shape or enhance the understanding of Northwest Coast art. The writers in this book often use archival and published information gathered from Native experts and filtered through earlier generations of non-Native scholars, bringing them into conversation with current issues and inquiries, at times reading against the grain of what was previously published. Colonial conceptions of "great art" focused on the painted and sculptural pieces, most often produced by men. This focus led to investigations that ran counter to or overshadowed community values—discounting the role of women, or of art made for sale, or following queries that stemmed from anthropological or aesthetic concerns adrift from the communities under consideration. Previous scholarship often elided the institutional and social structures that lead to the theft, collecting, or other removal of material culture from communities. As Jonaitis notes in her conclusion, the 1980s rise of postcolonial studies set the stage for questioning these structures. In much recent scholarship, Indigenous priorities are front and center, sparking inquiries into how aesthetic creations embody survivance and demonstrate connections to family, to land, to sovereignty—in essence, to all the tangible and intangible cultural heritage from their communities. As those priorities have reshaped scholarship and museum practice, so too have they informed a set of common themes that run through the essays collected here.

A number of the contributions unsettle Northwest Coast art histories by examining historical artworks and previous scholarship to expose the colonial biases that unfairly discounted women's artwork and the cultural resilience it embodies; overlooked the performative power of artistic creations; and underestimated the expertise of Indigenous knowledge holders about their own artistic heritage. Part I, "Cultural Heritage Protection: Questions of Rights and Authority," discusses cultural heritage protections and the long-standing defense of natural resources and territory by Tlingit and Haida artists. This section of the book addresses histories of non-Native artists' use and production of Native art in the context of rights and ownership. Part II, "Women's Work: Stories, Art, and Power," recenters women and the critical role they play in transmitting cultural knowledge across generations through materials, techniques, and creations. Although Megan A. Smetzer's chapter 6, on Tlingit textile artist Shgen George, is the only essay that directly deploys the framework of unsettling settler colonialism, this work runs through the book as a whole. It is reflected in the decolonization work being undertaken in museums and discussed in Part III, "Changing Museums." Part IV, "Beyond Art," illustrates art as *living* history in which oral histories and archival materials are examined through current artistic knowledge to reveal new understandings of the contemporary and historical artworks.

Unlearning and Relearning

"Research" has long been a part of the colonial project.[8] Steeped in Euro-American knowledge hierarchies, university lecture halls and dissertation committee meetings are most often *not* the place to learn Indigenous values and protocols. While research methodologies such as CBPR (community-based participatory research) and ethics based in what Cree scholar Shawn Wilson calls the three Rs of Indigenous methodologies—respect, reciprocity, and relationality—are taught within some classes in certain disciplines, exposure and consistency to these methods are quite variable.[9] The chapters in this edited volume reflect knowledge gained both within and outside academic realms, often in combination with lessons stemming from the actual experience of collaborative research and the unlearning of certain academic values that conflict with the cross-cultural relationships built through experience, including research experiences.

Values that disenfranchise Indigenous knowledge or conflict with true collaborative work are still at large in the academy, including the unequal power relationships in research, the discounting of knowledge or expertise gained outside of the academy, the valuation or compensation for only certain kinds of labor, and continued structural and systematic biases against Indigenous people and histories. While challenges to these started a generation ago (see Jonaitis's conclusion) and despite positive improvements, Indigenous scholars continue to point out how the academy centers Western knowledge systems and how "Indigenous knowledges and forms of cultural expressions are transformed in academic and public spaces into resources and property sustaining colonial production of knowledge about Indigenous peoples."[10] "Unlearning" provides the opportunity for authors and readers "to deconstruct what they 'know' about Indigenous people and Indigenous state-relations in order to 'clear space' for new, more accurate knowledge regarding both Indigenous peoples and settler colonialism."[11] Within this framework a combination of established academic practices and Indigenous perspectives and methodologies can give rise to new methods in knowledge-making, a convergence demonstrated by much recent scholarship in Native studies and the related field of Indigenous history, literature, and art history.[12]

To unlearn these values, to unsettle the hierarchies of power and privilege within academia, involves making deliberate choices to listen to other voices and to learn what is offered. While we as scholars may need to unlearn or learn "extracurricularly," this need not imply a wholesale condemnation of educational training but an awareness of ongoing structural and methodological issues.[13] The lessons learned outside of the academy are foundational to many of the approaches exemplified in this book, including the respect for deep histories as recounted by tribal historians; the knowledge that artworks communicate about people, relationships, land, and materials; and the responsibilities that accompany a sharing of knowledge and the reciprocity that is a part of those responsibilities. While some of these lessons can be gleaned through the essays in this collection, others are not revealed and exist as part of the working methodologies that remain off the pages and behind the scenes.[14]

We Have Words for Art

The contributors in this edited volume draw out examples of broader trends in Native American and First Nations art and Indigenous art studies, acknowledging how current work shapes the field and future conceptions of Indigenous art. The book brings together voices that are integral to the field, highlighting perspectives that have been marginalized or filtered by others. The diversity of approaches and writing styles presented, including what preconceptions each author brings to their subjects and which artworks they chose to study, all affect not only our understanding of past histories and art production but also impact future artistic creations as published images and information are redirected into new creations and understandings.[15]

To that end, the choice of contributors was intentional—bringing people together with academic or artistic and community-based training (or both). The authors reflect the fact that expertise can be gained through many different paths.[16] Some chapters fit firmly within the history of academic exegesis in the field even when turning the gaze to previously underrepresented subjects. Others bring approaches grounded in genealogical or artistic kinship, Indigenous language insights, and community-based knowledge. The poems that start each part of the book reflect on art forms, art-making, place, and sovereignty through creative expressions whose emotive impact is quite distinct from the chapters. All together, the contributions—especially the poems but also the reliance on oral history, personal recollection, and the visual complement of extensive illustrations—underline that knowledge is expressed in many ways, scholarly traditions being only one mode. Of course, no single publication can claim comprehensiveness in a field; we certainly don't suggest this is the case here. There continue to be underrepresented areas of research in Northwest Coast art studies, and we unsuccessfully endeavored to find contributors for these areas. Most critically, the field needs much more work on historical and contemporary Salish art as well as creative practices from Southern regions (including the Columbia River, which has seen a recent flourishing of contemporary art by artists thinking through historical aesthetic traditions). In addition, while there are synergies throughout the book, the distinctiveness of approach and style are not intended to blend together but rather to illuminate the varied paths into the material.

As coeditors, we are aware that the inclusion of a diverse set of voices is not decolonization or unsettling in and of itself. Scholars Adam Gaudry and Danielle

Lorenz call inclusion "the low-hanging fruit of indigenization"—a critical first step but not transformative to institutional practice.[17] Our hope is that this book goes a step beyond inclusion to better reflect Indigenous methodologies of knowledge-making and sharing, pushing against constraints around who is considered an expert and how that information is filtered or not filtered. As these essays engage with both current practice and previous scholarship, they set the stage for imagining future histories that move us away from settler colonial frameworks that have shaped the understanding of Northwest Coast art and toward healthier foundations led by Indigenously informed priorities for understanding through the work of both the Native and non-Native contributors.

As we imagine future historians turning to the published record of Native art and finding increasingly more works written directly by Indigenous artists and historians, we can imagine a much more robust bibliography than what was available to twentieth-century scholars looking back across a historiography dominated by non-Native (often male) historians (for more on this, see Jonaitis's conclusion).[18] Artist contributions to publications have often been limited to artist statements or pieces narrowly focused on their own productions. The contributions in this book by Tlingit poet Ishmael Hope, Haida weaver Evelyn Vanderhoop, Kwakwa̱ka̱'wakw artist Lou-ann Neel, and Haida curator Jisgang Nika Collison demonstrate the expertise conferred by years of training in community with elders, through language lessons, at the loom, in the studio, or in the historical archives of institutions and in the deep histories known by community historians. This expertise merits recognition and publication in scholarly texts.

Voices and Themes

This edited volume reflects a number of interventions into how art and artists have been framed in past scholarship or in museums. Organized in four parts, the book highlights a number of themes under consideration. Part I, "Cultural Heritage Protection: Questions of Rights and Authority," includes wide-ranging queries by Kaitlin McCormick, Emily L. Moore, and Christopher Green on who has the rights to Indigenous imagery, natural resources, and the telling of histories through public monuments. Janet Catherine Berlo and Aldona Jonaitis examine histories of appropriation and reappropriation of forms and titles. In Part II, "Women's Work: Stories, Art, and Power," Lou-ann Neel, Megan A. Smetzer, and Jisgang Nika Collison recenter women's artwork as embodying deep historical connections while addressing current realities through a variety of forms and media. Their work helps to remediate the invisibility of women's creations in the scholarly record of Northwest Coast art.

Part III, "Changing Museums," features six curators—myself, Sharon Fortney, Lucy Fowler Williams, Karen Duffek, Peter Morin, and Karen Benbassat Ali—who discuss the historical traumas inflicted by museums and the making of collections based on Eurocentric (and patriarchal) conceptions of what "art" is; also explored is subsequent work to form more appropriate relationships between museums and Indigenous people.[19] The curators provide distinct stories about how their own institutions have confronted these histories and are developing practices that move toward healing. Each case study reveals more than just working toward healing—which implies acknowledging and dealing with the past; each museum is thinking about how current changes will help to create a different future of healthy relationships supporting Indigenous priorities for the institution. In Part IV, "Beyond Art," Evelyn Vanderhoop, Ishmael Hope, and Denise Nicole Green look at how artworks function well beyond previous scholarly framings of them, foregrounding Indigenous world views, language, and functions intrinsically embedded in intangible connections to song, ceremony, and power.

Part I. "Cultural Heritage Protection: Questions of Rights and Authority"

Who has the right to tell a story? How do artistic creations represent certain moments and perspectives in history? Part I looks at the positionality of the artist and what it means to bring history, relationships, or heritage to their aesthetic creations. As McCormick postulates for Haida argillite, the materials and knowledge that are the foundation of Northwest Coast art production often stem from cultural patrimony. The examples in her essay query whether those without cultural heritage should be able to shape the product, to be creators of Northwest Coast art. McCormick moves the question from who has the right to be an artist, to cultural rights over the natural resource protections for the argillite and if it should be exclusively reserved for Haida expression. This reveals both new and old tensions, two centuries of entanglement with economic and commercial exploitation as well as the power that "Euro-American notions of authenticity and expectations of aboriginality" wield over Haida artists. She examines strategies of keeping while giving and how to both produce and protect this "inalienable" commodity.

A similar question lies at the center of Berlo and Jonaitis's examination of "artifakes" and "surrogates" querying how stories and histories are told and by whom—issues that lie at the heart of concerns around the participation of non-Indigenous artists in the creation of Northwest Coast art. They discuss questions of replication, both sanctioned and unsanctioned, and the spectrum of acceptance and rejection for historical persons, including Duane Pasco, Bill Holm, and Lelooska, and extending into overseas fakes and tribally sanctioned 3-D replicas. One of the key contributions of this historically grounded examination is the positionality of the authors who speak from personal experience with Northwest Coast art in the 1960s and 1970s; their chapter reveals the generational changes that have occurred with regard to the question of authority.

Storytelling through monumental public artworks has been a part of Tlingit history for centuries. Moore, in her chapter, considers how totem poles and bronze statues of William Seward are public history, monuments of both Tlingit history and Alaskan colonial history, asserting control over territory and over storytelling. She posits the 2017 Seward Shame Pole by Stephen Jackson as a "countermonument" steeped in long-held Tlingit practices of public history. Her essay addresses Tlingit histories of activism, refusals of "reconciliation," and implications for the larger national debate around the removal or rehabilitation of historical monuments.

Christopher Green looks at the appropriation and reappropriation of forms and titles in his discussion of Tlingit artist James Schoppert. Fascinated by the centuries-old practice of Tlingit aesthetics as well as the appropriation of these forms by the Surrealists, Schoppert refused the "expected" aesthetic narrative that allowed for oversimplified readings of Northwest Coast art in the past as "an enclosed visual system." Instead, Schoppert asserted his autonomy as a Northwest Coast modernist. This essay is critical to building up the history of late twentieth-century artists—those who set the stage for the current generation.

Part II. "Women's Work: Stories, Art, and Power"

A number of essays in this book touch on the fact that women's artistic creations are highly treasured and valued within First Nations communities on the Northwest Coast and yet long discounted by collectors and scholars. Fortunately, these biases are starting to be addressed in current scholarship, public art commissions, and recent exhibitions that highlight women's artistic creations and their critical role in community survivance.[20] Analyzing the impact of historical biases against women is critical to recentering women's contributions to arts in this region and is a growing subject across Indigenous art studies; these changes reflect the growing number of women scholars and curators in the field. Recentering women in artistic histories is critical to painting a more robust and balanced image reflecting the full spectrum of art production in this region. It serves to unsettle the colonial story through recognizing the invisibility of women in that story. As Smetzer explores in her essay, Indigenous women "have been an invisible presence in the center, hidden by the gendered logics of settler colonialism."[21]

Haida artist Freda Diesing (1925–2002) acknowledged that women "were always planning in advance; right from the time a child was born," taking into consideration the ramifications of various decisions for future generations.[22] In other words, women created and shaped the cultural framework upon which the public aspects, often expressed by men and their arts, were based.[23] Smetzer's chapter on the Tlingit textile artist Shgen George examines how scholars, primarily male, were likely unaware of this power-sharing balance between genders, and their ignorance contributed to a skewed understanding of this history. This book discusses many contemporary women artists whose work addresses these issues and speaks to their ongoing engagements with deep history and with innovation through employing not only long-standing, customary materials and techniques (weaving and textile arts) but also new platforms such as light installations, printmaking, and glass that are less entrenched in calcified gendered expectations. Smetzer notes the resiliency of artists and how George's octopus bags, both in materiality and design, reinforce Tlingit ways of knowing despite the impacts of settler colonialism on cultural inheritance.

Collison, Haida Gwaii Museum curator, discusses how her institution's exhibition history reflects the roles and responsibilities of women in Haida society. This is a strong contrast to the lack of exhibits featuring women's artwork in most Northwest Coast art venues over the past century. Women's participation in the predominantly male-dominated arts of carving or tool-making is attested by early (and often overlooked) writings of visitors to the Northwest Coast. Collison (and Vanderhoop in Part IV of the book) cites the journals of eighteenth-century visitors as well as transcriptions of Haida oral histories that document women's roles that were unexpected or unrecognized by European and American visitors.

New scholarship is correcting the balance in the published record, and women artists and scholars are activating the archive and their current artworks in ways that foreground Indigenous ways of knowing, particularly in terms of women's roles within and between generations and communities. Lou-ann Neel's chapter looks at how gender biases were exacerbated by patriarchal expectations of women's abilities and contributions. While her grandmother, Kwagu'ł carver Ellen Neel, did not receive the recognition she deserved at the time, nevertheless she persisted in carving monumental poles and was foundational to the Northwest Coast commercial market, even though that market was biased against women as carvers and the concept of art-for-sale. Lou-ann Neel's circular journey as a woman artist away from and back to carving is created in part by her own growing knowledge of her grandmother as relation and as formidable inspiration.

Part III. "Changing Museums"

While Indigenous communities have long acknowledged that artworks are embedded in kinship, and sometimes considered kin themselves, this knowledge is just starting to inflect the work of museums.[24] The essays in Part III demonstrate how institutions—and more specifically the people in institutions—are changing both policy and practice as a result of witnessing the kinship relations with historical collections that Indigenous researchers, artists, curators, staff members, and other community members bring to collections. These chapters reflect the belief that artists and communities must take the lead in guiding interpretation and stewardship of their artistic creations.

Museums have a responsibility to the communities whose cultural treasure they care for and to the traditional territories on which they stand. A part of unsettling is to reexamine institutional histories to reveal the previously hidden community impacts of the separation of artworks.[25] For example, Fortney discusses the Museum of Vancouver's partnership with the Musqueam First Nation to host the exhibition *c̓əsnaʔəm, the city before the city*. The Museum of Vancouver acknowledged their position on unceded Coast Salish territory and questioned the "museumification" of cultural belongings into "artifacts." This case study addresses how museums have excluded local Indigenous people from earlier displays of and access to their collections.

Relationality and reciprocity are central to the work of fruitful collaborations. Across the continent, and especially on the West Coast, museums have collaborated with Indigenous communities for several decades.[26] Increasingly, partnerships with Indigenous scholars, artists, and researchers are used to "develop strategies for upending the power relations" between institutions and Indigenous communities. These changes are demonstrated by Tahltan artist Morin's collaboration with curators Duffek and Ali at UBC's Satellite Gallery. Morin reminds us that museums can be places of trauma as well as healing, and their exhibit modeled the relationality between artistic creations and the people who are their kin. This collaboration demonstrated that as curators, scholars, or museums visitors, our roles and the roles of these artworks are coconstituted by our relationships with others: when we act, it is not in a vacuum adrift from the effects and expectations of our relations but in concert (or in conflict) with others.

My own chapter discusses the Burke Museum's *Here & Now: Native Artists Inspired* exhibit in which artists, in their own words, described their work with historical collections. The essay explores how work in collections can be revealed in exhibits and, moreover, how that work can affect larger changes within an institution. Curators and others at the museum are implementing lessons learned from Indigenous values of relationality and reciprocity to ensure that those principles guide policies and care for historical collections. My chapter and others in this part of the book speak to how particular moments can move a museum forward. As museum personnel change processes and protocols, it is critical to document not just the theoretical methodologies behind those processes but also the specific moments of change that give rise to them.

Williams provides a view of Tlingit curator Louis Shotridge from her perspective as the current curator of his collection for the University of Pennsylvania Museum (Shotridge collected for the museum from 1912 through 1932). Shotridge's description of the Tlingit T'akdeintaan clan's Lituya Bay Robe demonstrates what Ishmael Hope (in his chapter in Part IV of the book) outlines as Shotridge's strengths—genealogy and clan knowledge. This information undergirds the recent

Native American Graves Protection and Repatriation Act (NAGPRA) process for the Snail House Tlingit clan treasures at the museum. Williams's personal story of her own learning and her growing relationship with Tlingit clans—reflected in her adoption and honorary naming during the repatriation ceremonies—demonstrates how the experience of protocol and relationships, enacted both within the colonial spaces of the museum and in traditional territory, can be transformative to museum personnel. This is often the first step in changing institutional policy.

The essays in this part of the book attest to the importance of storytelling by the people involved in moments of significant institutional change. The scholarship around decolonizing museums is only about a decade old but is rapidly growing, and the term itself is spreading out into the mainstream, so much so that it threatens to become a buzzword signifying more heat than light in certain institutions. "Decolonizing" as terminology is being contested and questioned in some circles, not because the work that this connotes is unnecessary but because of a fear that the term is becoming a metaphor for certain kinds of liberal reforms that don't engage in the truly hard work of addressing calcified structural inequities and redressing issues of stolen land, polluted waters, and stolen property. As Nitasha Dhillon and Amin Husain of the MTL Collective put it: "It could very well become an ossified or empty formality with no teeth."[27] While terminology is always changing, the original issues remain.[28] Whether we call it "decolonizing the museum" or "Indigenizing the museum" or "unsettling our practices," acknowledging colonial histories and centering Native and First Nation community priorities, people, and voices within institutions is key.

Part IV. "Beyond Art"

In this section the authors push back, either directly or through differing interpretations, on how Northwest Coast art has been framed in the past. Most notably, the contributors demonstrate how past creations are living documents carrying information critical to today's inquiries. Their knowledge of Indigenous languages, artistic techniques, materiality, protocols, and ceremonial practices undergird the work in these essays. Denise Nicole Green's discussion of how Nuu-chah-nulth thliitsapilthim (*ceremonial curtains*) "perforate" the boundaries of time and space resonates with Vanderhoop's connections to the lessons and protocols embedded in ancient Haida weavings. Hope's essay explores his insights into how early twentieth-century Tlingit curator Louis Shotridge's writings reflect Tlingit linguistic structures of communication—"bending English to mirror Tlingit"—which inform Hope's own reading of the artworks and their histories.[29]

Green explores thliitsapilthim as an example of a living document that (unlike artworks captured in the time capsule of a museum) can grow and change with family needs over time. She argues that thliitsapilthim connect recent events to deep histories of land, family, and territory. The creation and use of these pieces is inextricably embedded in their performative context. When hung across the hall at a potlatch, the curtain intersects with bodies, memory, regalia, and other material culture to create "a site of creative, spiritual, cultural production." The curtains are visual representations of memory that work as "didactic materials and mnemonic references" in communicating cultural knowledge across generations; they exemplify the deep web of connections often instantiated in Indigenous artworks.[30]

Vanderhoop, a Haida weaver, discusses in her essay how women's artwork, as seen in eighteenth-century Haida weavings, had the power to embody the intangible forces in the environment, including not only natural forces like weather and clouds but also supernatural beings. Through her insights as a cultural historian and particularly as an accomplished weaver, Vanderhoop connects the artworks back to these intangibles by reading meanings obscure to non-Haida scholars who lack her expert technical understanding of Ravenstail and Naaxiin weaving materials and processes. She and other contributors elsewhere in the book (Collison, Hope, Neel, Smetzer) tell the implicit stories in the artworks through "clues tucked within the language of the ancestors in story and song" that connect past creations and knowledge to current art and knowledge-making.

Hope, a Tlingit and Iñupiaq poet and scholar, provides in his essay another view of Shotridge, who is also discussed in Lucy Fowler Williams's essay. Hope's work foregrounds Tlingit structures of understanding and how they are embedded in Shotridge's work. Hope's honest assessment—that he was "bewildered" at times by Shotridge's stories because the "cues, gestures, and trailmarkers" were so culturally embedded—hints at what can be missed when approaching artworks without understanding culturally specific contexts in relation to linguistic or aesthetic structures. He asserts that only those aspects of "common ground"—ideas that can resonate within Western contexts (and institutions)—are given attention and are privileged in those circles. He shows that Shotridge himself understood some common-ground interests in both Tlingit and museum contexts: aesthetics, attribution, history. Hope, like Chickasaw curator heather ahtone more broadly, makes the case that to truly understand Tlingit aesthetics, one must first connect to their deep cultural context.

Reweaving, New Weavings

"Unsettling Native art history" not only signifies the disruption of outdated practices or biases. It can, as Smetzer explains, create new productions woven from fragments of older work, weaving continuous threads from long-held beliefs and practices into contemporary forms that have never existed before. Weaving knowledge through the "warps of settler colonialism," Smetzer evokes current activism, including moves toward and refusals of reconciliation on the part of current and past artists and communities. Similar trends are found through this book: Moore highlights these strategies in Jackson's 2017 Seward Shame Pole; Morin questions "the museum"; and McCormick discusses Haida assertions of control over argillite as cultural patrimony. Unsettling can recenter women, balancing gendered expectations with their ongoing engagement with both deep history and innovation and recognizing their roles in intergenerational knowledge sharing (see Smetzer and Collison essays). Shotridge wrote in 1921 that despite the hopes of settlers that "native customs and habits have about disappeared," he believed that "could the lid of the true Tlingit woman's mind be thrown wide open there would be seen the mystic veneration of her art still alive and active."[31] The women artists featured in the chapters of Collison, Neel, Smetzer, and Vanderhoop, as well as my own essay illustrate the innovative ways that women have always woven knowledge through their creations—knowledge about land, materials, protocols, techniques, and creativity. Their artworks hold lessons for future generations.

The contributors to this edited volume all have many different kinds of teachers in our lives. Duffek, Morin, and Ali in their contribution discuss how art engages collective knowledge, and they acknowledge that "survival is collective knowledge." The critical role of art itself as a teacher is exemplified by Vanderhoop's learning from nineteenth-century Haida weavings; through their construction and design, they prompted questions that lead her back to Haida oral histories. The weavings and the histories informed each other, particularly when explored through Vanderhoop's own knowledge of the rhythms and materials as a skilled Naaxiin weaver herself. Collison, in her chapter, emphasizes the treasured status of living knowledge and the gift and responsibility of teaching that lies with master artists such as Haida basketweaver Delores Churchill, who has had a lifetime of embodied practice and is training both the hands and hearts of the next generation. As Tsimshian artist David R. Boxley said of the old pieces, "They are my teachers" (quoted in my own chapter). When artists and community gather around creations from the past, the artworks serve as "a pebble to generate ripples of dialogue within the stream of Indigenous consciousness."[32]

This edited volume represents certain commonalities in practice—careful attention to the artworks themselves, a recognition of the specificity of the historical moment and how that informs interpretation, methodologies that prioritize Indigenous knowledge, and a recognition of artists and cultural historians as experts in their own fields. Throughout this book, we see how relational models effect change—relationships between researchers and the artists or communities they work with, relationships between the historical artworks themselves and the contemporary artists who engage with them often in a mentor-apprentice kinship relation, and the genealogical or artistic relationships between current Indigenous artist-scholars and their subjects.[33] Changes in museum practice germinate from personal relationships and grow into ethics and practice that shift institutional policy. These relational models in scholarship or artistic practice demonstrate how direct genealogical, artistic, or even linguistic and epistemological relationships are at the core of insights into artistic practices.

Neel's consideration of her grandmother Ellen Neel's role as a successful carver, entrepreneur, educator, and activist reflects her direct genealogical relationship but also larger considerations of relationality—where we are all coconstituted by others. In situations where non-Indigenous scholars or curators are working with artists or communities, they have integrated parts of their academic training into customized methodologies for both historical analysis and museum practice shaped by both rightfully persistent demands for Indigenous protocols as well as generous knowledge-sharing of community histories. Methodologies and anecdotes throughout the book demonstrate the impact of work that is done face-to-face and in spaces that call for accountability. Research methodologies or systems of accountability are not uniform across these essays—these are contingent on each situation, each set of relationships.[34] The examples of each author's unique position with regard to their subject unfolds in their contributions. For some non-Indigenous scholars this came through working with Indigenous communities on exhibits or research projects; for Indigenous scholars or artists within their own communities, they often combine deep historical research with current community knowledge and protocols taught to them over a lifetime, melding both implicit and explicit academic or cultural training.

The essays here represent a variety of viewpoints, legacies of training and institutional biases, international and disciplinary boundaries. As editors, Aldona Jonaitis and I are examples of generational viewpoints in the field—each reflecting issues that were key to our training and shaped our trajectories and visions of how the field has come to be. We come together in our engagement with the field as it stands today and our anticipation for where it is going. Historicity is reflected in the first-person recollections of generational differences in hopefulness and cultural revitalization. Berlo and Jonaitis, in their chapter, reflect in part on the zeitgeist of the Northwest Coast artwork in the 1960s and 1970s, following up with the hopefulness of subsequent decades as underlined in Jim Schoppert's collaged metaphors for reassembling the shattered fragments of culture in the 1980s (in Christopher Green's chapter). Collison, for her part, parallels the artistic revitalization of those decades with current language revival efforts: "I hope (that one day) my daughters marvel, in Xaayda kil, at the thrill of growing up during the revival of their language, the same way I marvel at my luck of having grown up during the revival of our artistic and cultural practices."

Collectively, as artists and authors, subjects and writers, we all depend on what came before, drawing on the past to create change for the future. Each of us brings our own methods to this practice. This looking both backward and forward means recognizing what past generations of scholars, artists, elders, or mentors have created and how it contributes—either negatively or positively—to the current moment and to future generations. This book is a small part of weaving together past and present as we look to the future, to recognize how to live in a "longer now."

NOTES

I would like to thank Aldona Jonaitis for being a patient and generous coeditor of this edited volume. Her enthusiasm brought all of these contributors together. Megan A. Smetzer turned her talented editorial eye to all my writing, as usual. Ashley Verplank McClelland's tireless work pulling together all the illustration, permission, and citation details was invaluable. I also want to thank the members of the University of Washington Indigenous Studies Writing Group, especially Jean Dennison, Josh Reid, Sara Gonzales, and Radika Govindrajan, who provided critical feedback on this introduction in particular and who provide a productive forum for discussing all aspects of academic labor.

1 heather ahtone, "Designed To Last: Striving toward an Indigenous American Aesthetic," *International Journal of the Arts in Society: Annual Review* 4, no. 2 (2009): 373–77.

2 This book emerged in part out of sessions that took place at the 2017 Native American Art Studies Association conference in Tulsa, Oklahoma, and includes other scholars and artists working in communities, museums, and universities. These are just some of the many people contributing to Northwest Coast art studies today.

3 Linda Tuhiwai Smith, Eve Tuck, and K. Wayne Yang, *Indigenous and Decolonizing Studies in Education: Mapping the Long View* (New York: Routledge, 2019), xii.

4 Alicia Cox, "Settler Colonialism," in *Oxford Bibliographies in Literary and Critical Theory* (Oxford: Oxford Universty Press, 2017); and Corey Snelgrove, Rita Kaur Dhamoon, and Jeff Corntassle, "Unsettling Settler Colonialism," *Decolonization: Indigeneity, Education & Society* 3, no. 2 (2014): 1–32.

5 In Snelgrove, Dhamoon, and Corntassle, "Unsettling Settler Colonialism," 17, the authors make the case for this critical framework of unsettling. Scholarship on settler colonialism dates back to the 1990s, before the term was coined, with foundational work by such scholars as Winona Laduke, Lee Maracle, and Paula Gunn Allen and extending to recent critical work by Maile Arvin, Eve Tuck, Angie Morrill, Patrick Wolfe, Kēhaulani J. Kauanui, and others. See Winona Laduke, "The Struggle for Cultural Diversity," *Race, Poverty & the Environment* 1, no. 2 (1990): 1–13; Lee Maracle, *I Am Woman: A Native Perspective on Sociology and Feminism* (Vancouver, BC: Press Gang Publishers, 1996); Paula Gunn Allen, *The Sacred Hoop: Recovering the Feminine in American Indian Traditions* (Boston: Beacon, 1986); Maile Arvin, Eve Tuck, and Angie Morrill, "Decolonizing Feminism: Challenging Connections between Settler Colonialism and Heteropatriarchy," *Feminist Formations* 25 (2013): 8–34; Patrick Wolfe, "Settler Colonialism and the Elimination of the Native," *Journal of Genocide Research* 8 (2006): 387–409; and Kēhaulani J. Kauanui, "'A Structure, Not an Event': Settler Colonialism and Enduring Indigeneity," *Lateral* 5, no. 1 (2016), https://csalateral.org/issue/5-1/forum-alt-humanities-settler-colonialism-enduring-indigeneity-kauanui/.

6 Snelgrove, Dhamoon, and Corntassle, "Unsettling Settler Colonialism," 227.

7 These ethics are shared broadly across Native American studies with parallel variations specific to many fields, including literary studies, history, anthropology, and other fields. See Alyssa Mt. Pleasant, Caroline Wigginton, and Kelly Wisecup, "Materials and Methods in Native American and Indigenous Studies: Completing the Turn," *William and Mary Quarterly* 75, no. 2 (2018): 207–36; Chris Andersen and Jean M. O'Brien, *Sources and Methods in*

Indigenous Studies (London: Taylor and Francis, 2016), 1–4; and Robert Innes, "Introduction: Native Studies and Native Cultural Preservation, Revitalization, and Persistence," *American Indian Culture and Research Journal* 34, no. 2 (2010): 1–9.

8 Eve Tuck and K. Wayne Yang, "R–Words: Refusing Research," in *Humanizing Research: Decolonizing Qualitative Inquiry with Youth and Communities* (London: SAGE Publications, 2014), 1–29; Linda Tuhiwai Smith, *Decolonizing Methodologies: Research and Indigenous Peoples* (London: Zed Books, 1999); and Jane Anderson and Kimberly Christen, "Decolonizing Attribution: Traditions of Exclusion," *Journal of Radical Librarianship* 5 (2019): 113–52.

9 Shawn Wilson, *Research Is Ceremony: Indigenous Research Methods* (Black Point, Nova Scotia: Fernwood Publishing, 2008). One example of Indigenous methodologies on the Northwest Coast is set out by the Sealaska Heritage Institute (www.sealaskaheritage.org/about), which specifically calls for people and organizations to follow the Tlingit concepts of Wooch Yax̱ calling for balance, reciprocity, and respect.

10 Aileen Moreton-Robinson, *Critical Indigenous Studies: Engagements in First World Locations* (Tucson: University of Arizona Press, 2016); and Anderson and Christen, "Decolonizing Attribution," 117.

11 Adam Gaudry and Danielle Lorenz, "Decolonization for the Masses? Grappling with Indigenous Content Requirements in the Changing Canadian Post-Secondary Environment," *Indigenous and Decolonizing Studies in Education* (2018): 159–74, 164, 167. See Eve Tuck (Unangax) and K. W. Yang ("R-Words: Refusing Research," 4, 17) on research, refusals of research, and the ethical stances that humanize research. These concerns echo pivotal questions about authority and authorship posed by Gayatri C. Spivak, "Can the Subaltern Speak?" in *Marxism and the Interpretation of Culture*, edited by Cary Nelson and Lawrence Grossberg, 271–313 (Urbana: University of Illinois Press, 1988).

12 Gaudry and Lorenz ("Decolonization for the Masses?" 218) investigate the challenges and limits that accompany efforts to "decolonize" or "Indigenize" the academy: "Conceptually, indigenization represents a move to expand the academy's still-narrow conceptions of knowledge, to include Indigenous perspectives in transformative ways (Kuokkanen, 2008, p. 2). What exactly this transformation looks like in practice is still a matter of debate." See R. Kuokkanen, *Reshaping the University: Responsibility, Indigenous Epistemes, and the Logic of the Gift* (Vancouver, Canada: University of British Columbia Press, 2008).

13 Jonaitis's conclusion illustrates her personal story of changing values in the field of Native art studies and her own support for Indigenous artists and priorities.

14 Tuck and Yang ("R-Words: Refusing Research," 14) explicate the relationships of trust that develop between researcher and members of community and advocate for the refusal of research (or publication) when stories shared with you are not yours to tell. See also Gaudry and Lorenz ("Decolonization for the Masses?," 225) for Indigenous protocols for knowledge-sharing and knowledge boundaries.

15 Anthropologist Solen Roth has written on how the products of anthropology and written scholarship can be consumed by the members of communities under consideration and how these written works might contribute to what is subsequently produced by artists. Solen Roth, "Répercussions des publications et des expositions sur la création en art autochtone de la côte Nord-Ouest," *Recherches Amérindiennes au Québec* 48, no. 1–2 (2018): 101–12.

16 This book includes the contributions of seventeen authors, including six Indigenous authors, fourteen women, and ten PhDs. See Jonaitis's conclusion on the history of contributions in Northwest Coast art anthologies and exhibition catalogs from Indigenous experts who were not academics.

17 Gaudry and Lorenz, "Decolonization for the Masses?," 220. For an overview of the growing body of literature on this, see Anderson and Christen, "Decolonizing Attribution," 115–16, 133.

18 Robert Warrior's call in the 2007 *Early American Literature* journal for literary scholars "to broaden their archives to include tribal repositories and oral histories and to consider texts written by Native people themselves" echoed a similar moment in Northwest Coast art studies when the historiographical anthology *Native Art of the Northwest Coast: A History of Changing Ideas,* edited by Charlotte Townsend-Gault, Jennifer Kramer, and Ki-Ke-In (Vancouver: UBC Press, 2013), presented an epic selection of archival writings by Native authors from throughout the twentieth century. Also see Pleasant, Wigginton, and Wisecup, "Materials and Methods in Native American and Indigenous Studies," 209.

19 Major changes in museums' relationships with Indigenous communities began in earnest with the Native American Graves Protection and Repatriation Act (NAGPRA) (1990) in the United States and the Task Force Report on Museums and First Peoples in Canada and has been growing steadily ever since.

20 The 2019 exhibit catalog *Hearts of Our People: Native American Women Artists,* edited by Jill Yohe and Teri Greeves (Minneapolis: Minneapolis Institute of Art, 2019), is one of few Native art publications written entirely by women scholars and artists. See also Lara Evans, Cynthia Chavez Lamar, and Sherry Farrell Racette, *Art in Our Lives: Native Women Artists in Dialogue* (Santa Fe: School for Advanced Research Press, 2010); and Jaune Quick-to-See Smith, *Women of Sweetgrass, Cedar and Sage: Contemporary Art by Native American Women* (Phoenix, AZ: Gallery of the American Indian Community House, 1985). Recent high-profile exhibits of women artists include Susan Point (2016) and Dana Claxton (2018) at the Vancouver Art Gallery and Musqueam artist Debra Sparrow's "Blanketing the City" murals in Vancouver in 2018.

21 Arvin, Tuck, and Morrill, "Decolonizing Feminism," 14.

22 Mary Ann Slade, "Skilquewat: On the Trail of Property Woman the Life of Freda Diesing," PhD diss., University of British Columbia, 2002, 122.

23 Kathryn Bunn-Marcuse and Megan Smetzer, "Working To Change the Tide: Women Artists on the Northwest Coast," in *Hearts of Our People,* edited by Yohe and Greeves, 258–72.

24 Martha Black and Caitlin Gordon-Walker discuss this same concept, though they choose the word "family" over "kin": "The objects that museums hold are not just artefacts and collections. . . . Images and objects are not simply representative of an ethnographic group or style; they depict, signify, and sometimes are family members" (Caitlin Gordon-Walker and Martha Black, "Indigeneities and Museums: Ongoing Conversations," *BC Studies* (2018): 11–22, 11.

25 See Jonaitis's conclusion in this edited volume. As a part of the reflexive turn in anthropology, scholars have responded to issues raised in postcolonial studies by scrutinizing museum collection practices.

26 Gordon-Walker and Black, "Indigeneities and Museums," 119.

27 See Jasbir K. Puar, "The Land of the Lost," *Art Forum* 56, no. 10 (2018); and Siobhan Burke, "On This Land: Dance Presenters Honor Manhattan's First Inhabitants," *New York Times,* August 1, 2018. The term "decolonization" now appears regularly in the press, from the *New York Times* coverage of the activist group Decolonize This Place to *Yes! Magazine* and *Teen Vogue*'s articles on decolonizing national holidays.

28 Eve Tuck and K. Wayne Yang, "Decolonization Is Not a Metaphor," *Decolonization: Indigeneity, Education & Society* 1, no. 1 (2012): 1–40.

29 Indigenous language terms are presented throughout this volume in regular (roman) font with their English translation in italics. This practice marks the Indigenous term as the natural term for that artwork or concept and English as the foreign imposition on the Indigenous creation or concept.

30 ahtone, "Designed to Last," 375.

31 Louis Shotridge, "Tlingit Woman's Root Basket," *Museum Journal* 12 (March 1921): 161–78, 163.

32 ahtone, "Designed to Last," 375.

33 On the relationships between researchers and the artists or communities they work with, see Marge Bruchac, *Savage Kin: Indigenous Informants and American Anthropologists* (Tucson: University of Arizona Press, 2018).

34 Indigenous studies professor Robert Inness (Cowessess First Nation) discusses the importance of variability in the modes of accountability; see Innes, "Introduction." Smith, Tuck, and Yang note that Indigenous research methodologies are always "people and place-specific" (Smith, Tuck, and Yang, *Indigenous and Decolonizing Studies in Education*, xi).

A BEAR IN THE CEDAR

Duane Niatum

After dinner while sitting in my rocking chair gazing out the patio window at a red cedar, I caught something forming from a branch. Within five to ten seconds a creature settled on the branch the wind slowly blew from side to side. My eyes sang to the visitor: "Bear, you're welcome." The image soon changed to a bear mask and stared straight at me for a few seconds more, then faded. The mask was cedar with distinct carved planes with edges like the ones of our ancestors. His muzzle pointed toward me and his open mouth shined like a passing moon. Dusk shifted to a grizzly bear face. He had a rough texture and approaching night revealed brownish-black hair. I saw the bear as a friend. Fear was as far away as the Salish Sea on our green rambling coast. I spun around in my head like a gyroscope; joy mirrored the moment for the two of us: brothers in a land of disappearances. I pulled my chair closer to the patio; the cedar branch swept back into focus as if no one had been there. The swinging branch shot my breath higher than the North Star. The cedar spoke as a carrier of a guardian who would take me beyond myself. The blue flow beyond signaled a mask that came from a time the forest rippled in our blood like a river of evergreens, stones, and salmon. The bear took me to an open field. His eyes possessed mine for the duration of his presence. The bear talked to me in his own way, at a silent space I may never comprehend but should value like our breath of life. The tree and Bear gave me a story to pass on to you.

PART I

Cultural Heritage Protection

QUESTIONS OF RIGHTS AND AUTHORITY

CHAPTER 1

The Seward Shame Pole

A TLINGIT COUNTERMONUMENT TO THE ALASKA PURCHASE

Emily L. Moore

ON JULY 3, 2017, A CROWD GATHERED IN FRONT OF THE STATE CAPITOL BUILDING in Juneau, Alaska, to dedicate a new bronze monument of William H. Seward, the US Secretary of State who bought Alaska from Russia 150 years earlier (Figure 1.1). The bronze monument, designed by Alaskan artist David Rubin and his sister Judith Rubin, depicts a full-length Seward holding the Treaty of Cession that he signed on March 30, 1867, transferring ownership of Alaska from Russia to the United States. Speeches at the dedication ceremony praised Seward for his "masterstroke" in obtaining Alaska, and the monument visually cemented this reputation: framed between the Alaskan and American flags, with his feet firmly planted on a plinth of Tokeen marble (from the same Alaskan quarry that supplied the marble for the famous columns of the Alaska State Capitol behind him), Seward appears integral to Alaskan and American history.

The Seward Monument was dedicated in the midst of a national debate about monuments and the "civic landscape of white dominance that they . . . annotate and ornament."[1] But while other cities were removing monuments to white males with contested histories, the Seward Monument in Juneau was unveiled with little mention of his own controversial legacy. A few speakers at the Juneau dedication acknowledged Alaska Native sensitivities about Seward and about the Alaska sesquicentennial's celebration of the sale of Native lands. Alaska lieutenant governor Byron Mallott, who is Tlingit, described Seward's purchase of Alaska from Russia as "selling our land out from under our feet," since neither the United States nor Russia made any acknowledgment of Indigenous claims to the lands they were trading.[2] Historian Stephen Haycox noted that it would take another century—until the 1971 Alaska Native Claims Settlement Act (ANCSA), which paid Alaska Natives $963 million to extinguish Native title to 363 million acres of their ancestral lands—for aboriginal claims to be recognized and compensated (even then there remain many questions about the adequacy of ANCSA).[3] But these nods to a more contested narrative of the Alaska Purchase faded after the dedication ceremony, when the

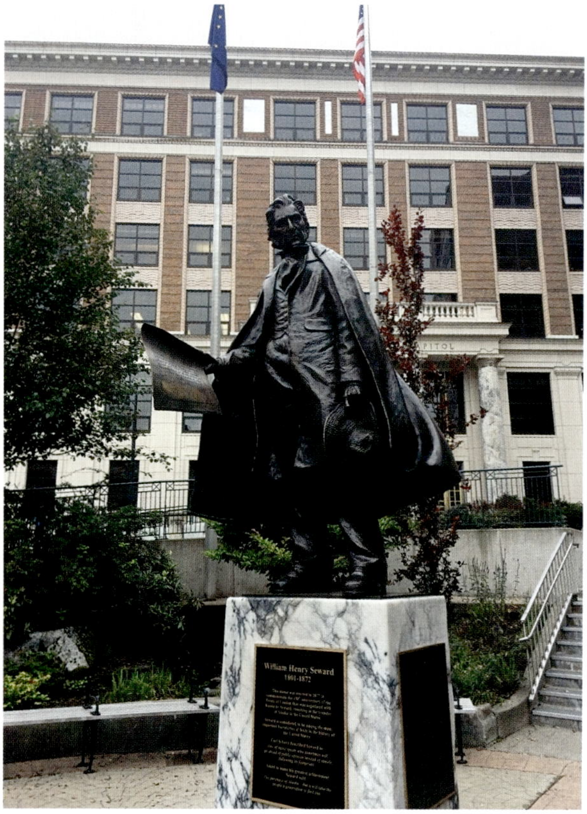

1.1. The Seward Monument, dedicated July 3, 2017, outside the State Capitol in Juneau, Alaska. Monument designed by David and Judith Rubin. Photograph by Craig Moore.

bronze monument and its accompanying signage once again commanded the small park that had been built for the Seward statue in front of the State Capitol. Of the four signs framing the monument, only one offers a paragraph acknowledging Seward's failure to "consider Alaska Natives' ownership of land or resources." There is little record here of the enormous impact that Seward's purchase had on Alaska Natives, nor any mention of a very different monument to Seward that one Alaska Native community had erected a few weeks earlier.

On April 29, 2017, in a Tlingit community three hundred miles south of Juneau, the City of Saxman dedicated a new version of the secretary of state pole, a totem pole that is also known as the Seward Shame Pole (Figure 1.2). The new pole, carved by Tlingit artist Stephen Jackson, replaced an older, deteriorated version, which itself was a replica of a nineteenth-century pole first erected at Tongass Village, some forty miles south of Saxman. The original Tongass pole was a shame pole, erected sometime in the 1880s to ridicule Seward for failing to repay the honors he had received during a visit to Tongass Village in 1869, two years after he had arranged the purchase of Alaska for the United States. According to the Taant'a k̲wáan Tlingit of Tongass, Chief Ebbets, the leader of the Teik̲weidí Brown Bear clan and the most high-ranking clan member at Tongass Village at the time, treated Seward to a lavish potlatch, honoring his guest with all the gravitas and gifts befitting a high-ranking government official. But after several years went by, and Seward "did not repay either the courtesy or the generosity of his hosts," in the words of Tlingit people who were later interviewed about the event, "the Seward shame pole [was erected] to remind the Tongass people of this fact."[4]

The renewal of the Seward Shame Pole in 2017 is significant, not only because it continues a Northwest Coast practice of publicly shaming individuals for unpaid debts but also because it works to counter the Alaska sesquicentennial and its celebration of settler narratives on Indigenous lands. As several Taant'a ḵwáan Tlingits have noted, the Seward Shame Pole has come to stand for more than the specific 1869 potlatch that remains unpaid in terms of dollars or stacks of furs. Instead it is—and perhaps always was—more about Seward's failure to recognize the status and sovereignty of Chief Ebbets and his Taant'a ḵwáan people as well as the United States's failure to recognize their claims to the land and waterways that Seward had claimed to buy. As Tom Harris, a member of the Tongass Teiḵweidí clan, stated in an interview: "No individual can straighten this out . . . the totem is actually a legal claim against the [US] government."[5] Dan Montieth, an anthropologist who interviewed several Taant'a ḵwáan elders in the 1990s, wrote that "the potlatch and the subsequent story about the Tongass people receiving nothing in return has become a significant discourse. . . . The Tongass people continued to wait for a return potlatch from the Secretary of State William Seward, or his clan, the United States."[6] The Seward Shame Pole has come to represent the wider debts of the American government to Taant'a ḵwáan people—a very different sort of legacy for Seward and the United States than the one celebrated by the Alaska sesquicentennial.

In fact, as this chapter argues, the three versions of the Seward pole—the first erected in the 1880s, the second in 1941, and the third in 2017—were each intended to counter settler claims to land ownership and control of resources in Alaska and to assert Taant'a ḵwáan sovereignty to the American public. The debts of Seward's "clan" are particularly salient for the Taant'a ḵwáan Tlingit, who remain one of the "landless" communities that was never granted territory under the Alaska Native Claims Settlement Act of 1971 and whose rights to subsistence privileges were revoked under the Alaska National Interest Land Conservation Act of 1980 (ANILCA).[7] These acts of the federal government have continued to ignore the status and claims of Taant'a ḵwáan people, just as Seward did in the 1860s. Thus the Seward Shame Pole has continued to publicly proclaim the Taant'a ḵwáan Tlingit's fight for federal recognition. In this sense the Seward Shame Pole works not only as a ridicule pole on the Northwest Coast, but as a "countermonument," which scholar James Young asserts is a monument that works against its traditional role as "a self-aggrandizing locus for national memory." Rather than attempting to cast in bronze a triumphant, hegemonic narrative of the state, countermonuments seek to "commemorate . . . the

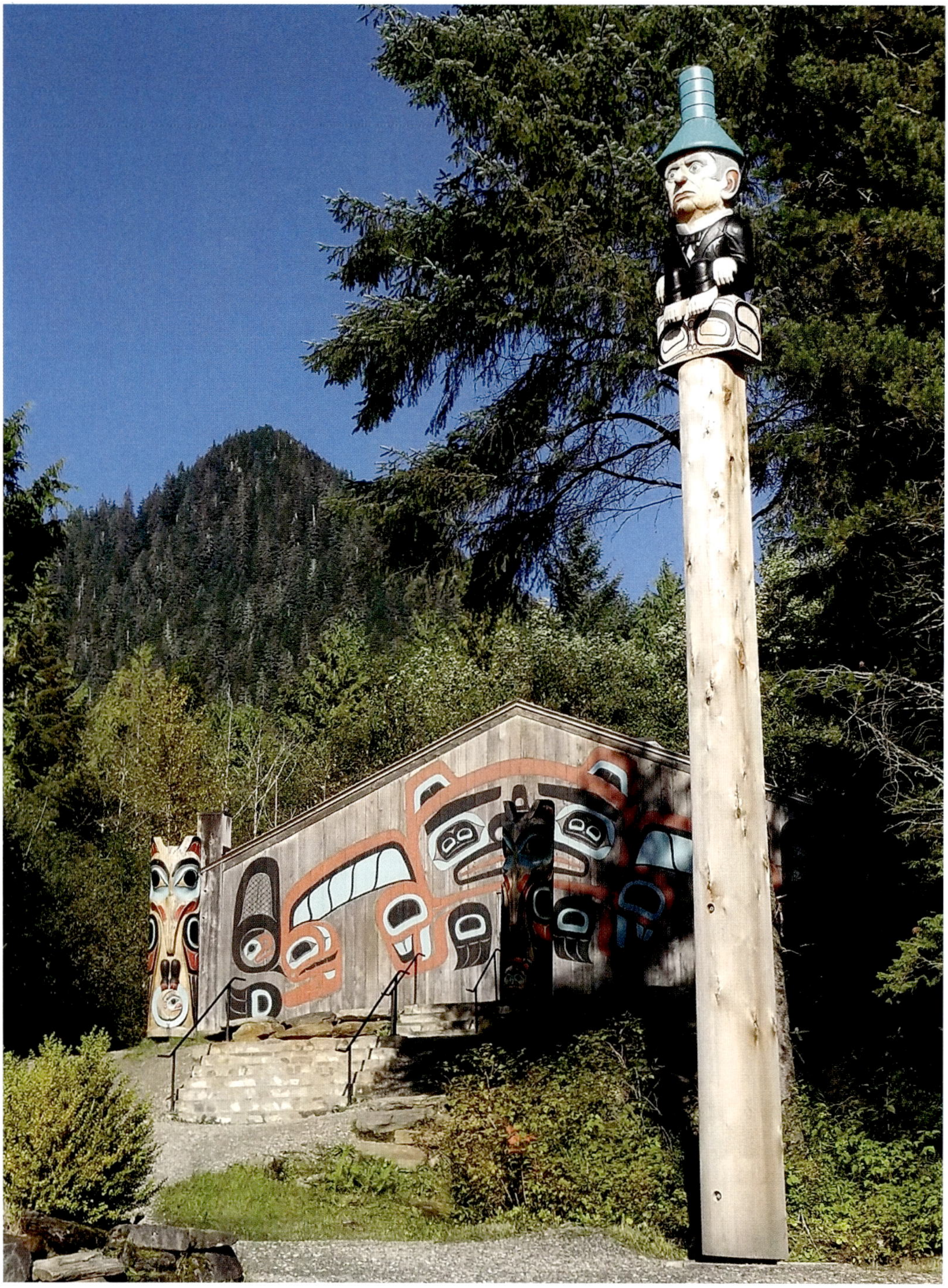

1.2. The third iteration of the Seward Shame Pole, dedicated April 2017 in the Saxman Totem Park, Saxman, Alaska. The pole was designed and carved by Stephen Jackson (Tlingit). Photograph by Hans Holum.

litany of [the state's] misdeeds, making them part of its reason for being."[8] The Seward Shame Pole works in a similar way: as a Tlingit countermonument to settler narratives told in Alaska for 150 years.

Seward's Folly

Every school child in Alaska learns the story of "Seward's Folly," the derisive phrase critics used for Seward's decision to buy the "icebox" of Alaska from Russia for $7.2 million in 1867. As secretary of state under President Abraham Lincoln, Seward had been instrumental in the international negotiations supporting the Union through the Civil War, and he remained a close confidante to Lincoln until the president's assassination in April 1865 (the same night that Seward was targeted for assassination, although he survived his stabbing with scars and a disfigured jaw). As secretary of state under President Andrew Johnson, Seward dedicated himself to expanding American landholdings, pursuing a "ravenous expansionist" credo that made him, as one historian wrote, an "apostle of Manifest Destiny."[9] He purchased Alaska and Midway Island in the Central Pacific in 1867; he was also working to buy islands in the Caribbean. None of these transactions considered the claims of Indigenous people to their lands.

The Alaska Purchase is a case in point. Neither Seward nor Edouard de Stoeckl, the Russian ambassador to the United States, acknowledged Alaska Native claims when they signed the Treaty of Cession in 1867. The treaty explicitly excluded Native people from citizenship, allowing for Russians and Russian-Native "creoles" already living in Alaska to become US citizens but not the "uncivilized native tribes" indigenous to the land.[10] Moreover, because the Alaska Purchase coincided with the end of treaty making between tribes and the US government, Alaska Natives were never acknowledged as sovereign nations within the United States.[11] Without citizenship in any nation, Alaska Natives like the Tlingit would have to spend fifty years fighting for the right to vote and to organize as tribal governments, and more than a century to have their land claims recognized by the US government.

Haycox has argued that it would be "unreasonable and anachronistic" to expect that any nineteenth-century Euro-American would take seriously aboriginal title, as many believed that Native people did not have a concept of property ownership, and most "dismissed indigenous people as yet incapable of managing such affairs."[12] But many Alaska Natives did have systems of property ownership—in particular, the Tlingit, who fiercely defended their right to property that was both tangible (hunting grounds, salmon streams, berry patches, and carved and woven depictions of clan crests) and intangible (songs, names, stories, and clan prerogatives). When Tlingits learned of Russia's plans to sell their lands in what is now Southeast Alaska, they convened meetings in a dozen of their villages to argue that Russians did not "own" Alaska, and that they had only been allowed to live in Tlingit territory for the trade that was mutually beneficial.[13] When the Russians sold the land anyway, Tlingits cried foul. As an official from the US Treasury Department wrote in 1868: "The dissatisfaction among the tribes on account of the sale of the territory did not arise from any special feeling of hostility, but from the fact that it had been sold without their consent."[14] Violent encounters ensued between Tlingits and American officials, but the "gunboat diplomacy" of American military ships that bombed Native villages in 1869 and 1882 soon convinced the Tlingit that they would have to pursue diplomatic rather than military measures to address their claims to the US government.[15]

Chief Ebbets was an early proponent of such diplomacy with his 1869 overtures to Seward. Although it is unclear if Chief Ebbets attended any of the Tlingit meetings about the Alaska Purchase, he was certainly aware of the Americans' arrival: he courted an American military fort for Tongass Island, probably for the trade and status it would provide the Taant'a ḵwáan Tlingit.[16] Ebbets actively sought out encounters with US officials, impressing on them his status and his peoples' claims to Taant'a ḵwáan territory in southern Southeast Alaska. The opportunity to meet with the former US secretary of state who had driven the Russians and the British out of Alaska must have seemed a tremendous diplomatic occasion for Ebbets. Montieth has written that "the Tongass potlatch for Seward is an epitomizing event for [the Tongass people]. . . . They were seeking recognition and interaction with the government of the United States."[17]

Accounts differ of Seward's visit to Tongass Village in 1869. After retiring from the State Department that year, Seward traveled to San Francisco on the new transcontinental railroad (which he had supported as part of his project of American expansionism); he then learned of an opportunity to travel north on the *Active* and seized the chance to finally see the northern territory he had worked so hard to buy. He went first to Sitka, the capital of the US military district in 1869, and then to the northern Tlingit community of Klukwan, where his statesmanship (and stabbing scars that he bore from the 1865 assassination attempt) greatly impressed the G̱aanax̱.teidí Tlingit leader Koh'klux.[18] At the end of his trip, on his return south to San Francisco, Seward stopped at the US military fort at Fort Tongass, where Ebbets invited him to his clan house in the nearby Tlingit community.

Taant'a ḵwáan oral tradition holds that Ebbets treated Seward to lavish gifts of furs, bentwood boxes, and Tlingit regalia—gifts befitting an exchange between two high-ranking leaders.[19] Curiously, however, Seward made no mention of a potlatch at Tongass Village in his own autobiography. He noted meeting an "intelligent chief" at Tongass and going into "his spacious house," but there was no remark of any major gathering. Whatever diplomatic favors he received, Seward must have felt were repaid by inviting Ebbets to dine with him on the *Active*. Seward noted several "curiosities" that he took home with him from Tongass Village, including bear skins and a live bald eagle, the latter which he kept for many years in his home in Auburn,

New York, as "a fine specimen of the emblematic bird, whose portrait adorns the American arms and coins."[20]

The First Seward Shame Pole

If Seward had not registered the diplomatic importance of his visit to Tongass Village, however, Chief Ebbets had, and he was offended when Seward did not reciprocate the honors. After several years went by and it was clear that Seward had no intention of repaying the ceremony he had received—nor of recognizing Taant'a ḵwáan rights to their lands—Chief Ebbets commissioned a ridicule pole, as was custom on the northern Northwest Coast for publicly shaming an individual or clan with unpaid debts (Figure 1.3). The pole depicted Seward at the top, wearing a

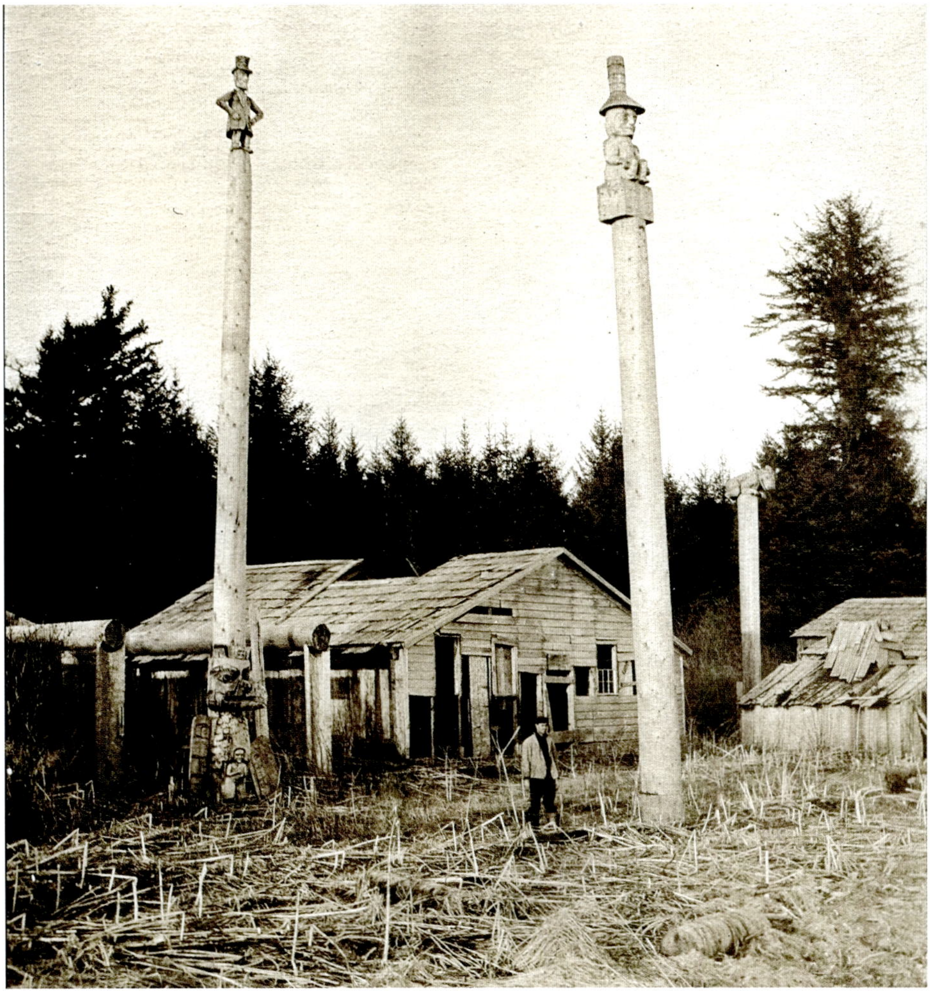

1.3. The first version of the Seward Shame Pole (right) as it appeared at Tongass Village at the turn of the twentieth century. William A. Langille Photograph Collection, Alaska State Library, P123-36.

"potlatch" hat piled with four woven discs, sitting on a rectangular object that has been interpreted as a bale of furs or as a bentwood box—either one serving as a pointed symbol of the valuable gifts he had received as Ebbets's guest.[21] According to most accounts, Seward's face was painted white, and his ears and nostrils red as a mark of shame.[22]

The Seward Pole stood at Tongass Village for the next fifty years, waiting for the offense it indexed to be recognized—and resolved—by the offending party. But resolution did not come. Seward himself died in 1872, three years after the Tongass potlatch; Chief Ebbets died in 1892. A few years later, as more American settlers encroached on Taant'a ḵwáan lands that Seward had claimed to buy, the Taant'a ḵwáan Tlingit agreed to relocate their village to another site within their territory at Kich.x̱áan Creek, where the Episcopal church promised a mission and permanent school. These relocations began in 1894, and because of promises to the church missions not to partake in "heathen customs," few new totem poles were erected in the new villages.[23] The Seward Pole was left to deteriorate on Tongass Island, with a handful of elders who lived in Ketchikan and nearby Saxman remembering the debt it recorded.

The Second Seward Shame Pole

It was not until the Great Depression that Tlingits had the opportunity to carve a second version of the Seward Shame Pole—again with the express intention of reminding the US government of its debts. Ironically, the opportunity to renew the Seward Shame Pole came via a federal program during the New Deal, the Civilian Conservation Corps (CCC), which hired Native men to restore nineteenth-century totem poles for "totem parks" for tourists.[24] At first, the US Forest Service, the federal agency in charge of the CCC program in Alaska, passed over the Seward Pole for restoration because its relatively plain shaft did not recommend it as a tourist attraction; however, after an anthropologist alerted the Forest Service that the pole was "apparently of exceptional interest" for local Tlingits, the agency decided to replicate it for the new totem park in Saxman.[25] Even then, the Forest Service did not understand the full story of the "secretary of state" pole and expressed frustration that local Tlingits "were reluctant to tell the real history. . . . It makes one suspect that there is more to the story behind it than the natives want to divulge."[26] It was only after the pole was completed in 1941 that the Forest Service learned they had paid Tlingits to replicate a pole that ridiculed a representative of the US government![27]

The CCC version of the Seward Shame Pole was carved by Charles Staast' Brown, the lead carver at the CCC camp in Saxman and a man who wanted the US government to rectify its debts to Tlingit people (Figure 1.4). Charles Brown was the son of William Brown, a Taant'a ḵwáan Teiḵweidí man who had been born at

Tongass Village around the time of the American Purchase.[28] William Brown belonged to the same clan as Chief Ebbets, and he almost certainly knew the story of the Seward Shame Pole. The opportunity to renew the pole in the CCC carving shed must have been significant to both William and Charles Brown. At the same time that they were employed by the CCC, they were active in local efforts to develop a Tlingit and Haida lawsuit against the US government for aboriginal claims to Southeast Alaska. In 1935, just a few years before the start of the CCC program, and after years of continued efforts by Tlingit and Haida people to have their rights to lands and fisheries recognized by the federal government, the US Court of Claims had ruled "that the Tlingit and Haida Indians exclusively used and occupied most of Southeast Alaska at the time of purchase of Alaska in 1867, that the land had not been abandoned by the Indians prior to the dates of taking," and that they should be allowed to bring a lawsuit against the federal government.[29] *Tlingit and Haida Indians of Alaska v. the United States* became the focus of Tlingit and Haida leaders in the late 1930s and 1940s—the exact period of the CCC totem pole restoration program.

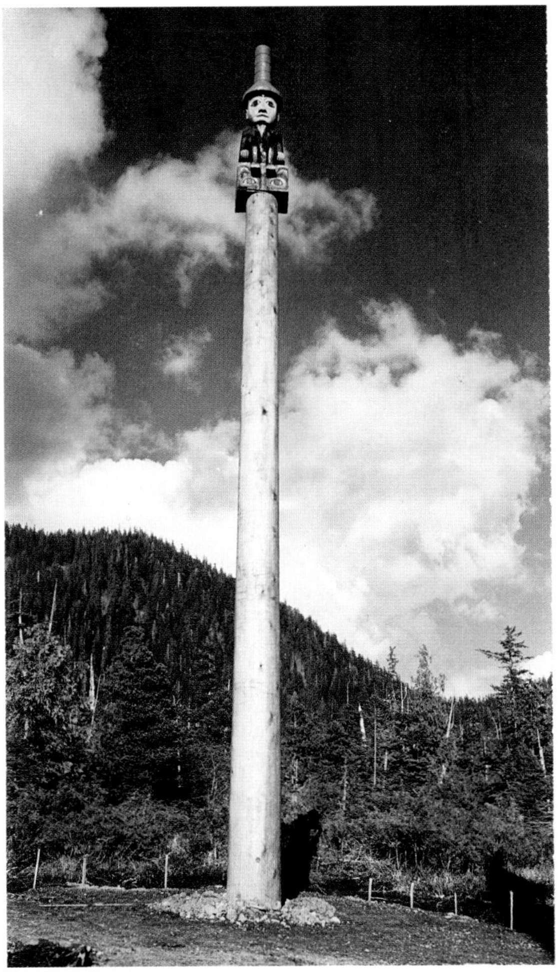

1.4. The second version of the Seward Shame Pole carved for the Civilian Conservation Corps totem pole restoration program by Charles Staast' Brown (Tlingit), 1941. USFS Historical Photographs, Ketchikan Ranger District.

Charles Brown's version of the Seward Shame Pole repeated the depiction of Seward sitting atop a bale of furs, wearing a potlatch hat, with a face painted white and ears painted red as a mark of shame. His version stood in Saxman for the next seventy years, as the Tlingit and Haida lawsuit against the federal government cleared numerous hurdles. It would take until 1959 for the US Court of Claims to rule that the Tlingit and Haida deserved compensation for the lands the US government had taken from them, and until 1968 for the court to decide a price—$7.5 million for seventeen million acres of land, less than 10 percent of the $80 million the Tlingit and Haida had requested.[30] If the settlement was disappointing, however, the lawsuit succeeded in forcing the federal government to recognize aboriginal title in Alaska; many scholars credit the Tlingit and Haida lawsuit for establishing a precedent for the larger Alaska Native Land Claims Settlement Act in 1971.[31] Due in part to the paltry sum of the 1968 settlement, the Tlingit and Haida were included in the larger settlement of ANCSA in 1971, which established a profitable regional corporation for the Tlingit and Haida, Sealaska Corporation, as well as several village corporations. Significantly, the Taant'a k̲wáan Tlingit were left out of the ANCSA settlement, in part because they were judged to be "modern and urban in character."[32] Members were allowed to enroll in the regional corporation of Sealaska, but they did not receive a village corporation or any ancestral lands.

The Third Seward Shame Pole

In 2014, after nearly seventy years of standing in the Saxman Totem Park, Charles Brown's replica of the Seward Shame Pole had to be taken down. A Saxman resident noticed that half of Seward's face had slipped several inches below the other, and city officials found that carpenter ants had destroyed the interior of the pole. Because the debt had still not been resolved, however, the Native-run City of Saxman decided to commission a third version of the pole to keep its message standing in the totem park. City officials initially had hoped the pole could be completed by the 2016 tourist season; they had not yet anticipated the Alaska sesquicentennial celebrations scheduled for 2017.[33] As it turned out, the pole was not finished until the spring of 2017—by which point Tlingits in Saxman had become well aware of the sesquicentennial celebrations and their role in countering the legacy of Seward.

The City of Saxman commissioned Stephen Jackson, son of the renowned Tlingit carver Nathan Jackson, to carve the replica of the Seward Shame Pole. Although Jackson had not previously been interested in replicating other poles, the complex story of the Seward pole offered an opportunity to "do several things at once," he said, and he agreed to take the commission.[34] Jackson, who earned an MFA from Columbia University and is well known for pushing Northwest Coast art in new directions, chose to create a different kind of portrait for Seward (Figure 1.5).[35] He said that close study of the original pole seemed to suggest some aspects of caricature, like the fact that Seward leaned forward slightly on his seat, perhaps in his eagerness to "get the goods."[36]

Caricature was common in nineteenth-century portraits of Euro-Americans by Native artists on the Northwest Coast (think of the famous Haida argillite sculptures of English sailors, with their giant eyeballs and arms akimbo). Jackson incorporated caricature into Seward's portrait: the secretary's neck bulges out of a too-small neckline, and his eyes gleam with a miniaturized gold pick painted in one pupil and a map of Alaska in the other. But Jackson also honored the realist

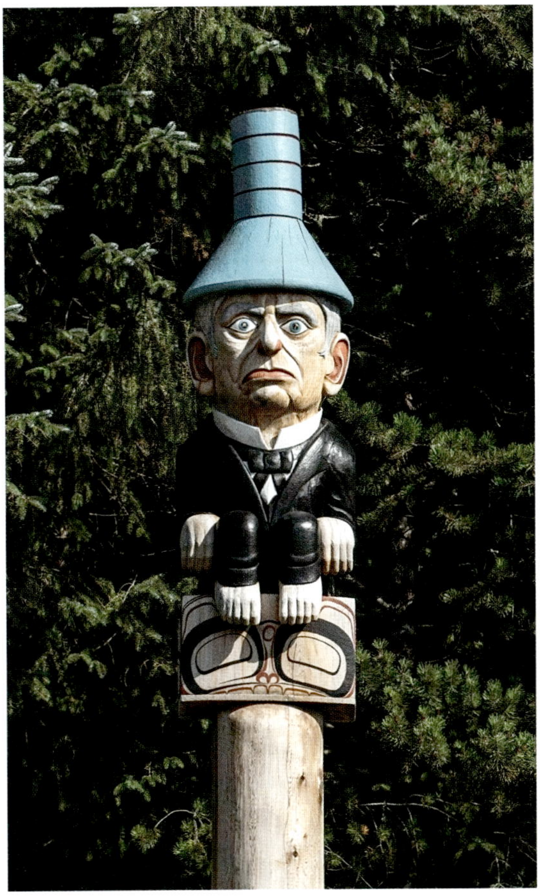

1.5. Detail of the Seward Shame Pole by Stephen Jackson. Photograph courtesy of Hall Anderson.

tendencies of many nineteenth-century Northwest Coast portraits. After studying photographs of Seward's face, Jackson chose to portray the famous stabbing wounds and broken jaw that Seward bore after his attempted assassination.

The totem pole raising for Jackson's version of the Seward Shame Pole, held in Saxman on April 29, 2017, was not widely publicized, in part because of local controversies surrounding the pole. Beginning in 2015, a non-Native woman who had worked as a tour guide in the Saxman Totem Park circulated a petition (complete with a three-ring binder of travel plans and deadlines) urging local Tlingits to invite descendants of the Seward family to Saxman to "repay" Seward's debts and remove the shame from the pole. The woman had gone so far as to contact Seward's descendants in New York, the Messenger family, who were initially interested in the idea of the "pay-back potlatch" but who rejected the idea when they learned it had not originated with the Tongass Tlingit. The woman's proposals were explicitly timed to remove Seward's shame before the Alaska sesquicentennial and the dedication of the new bronze monument in Juneau. As she wrote in a public petition: "If the Seward-Tlingit potlatch was held July 1, 2017, the [Seward] family could continue onto Juneau for the July 4th celebration. With the debt paid in full and peace offering accepted, the burden is lifted. The dedication of the W.H. Seward bronze statue is a new beginning—for everyone!"[37]

The refusal of Taant'a k̲wáan Tlingits to participate in this woman's prescription for "reconciliation" is notable, as they resisted settler pressures to "get over" colonial history or to "move on" after a single ceremony that was supposed to make things right. Stephen Jackson has spoken of the "incommensurability of desires" in these calls for reconciliation, suggesting that while Native people may seek reparations on their own terms, they do not want settler societies to forget the enduring impacts of colonization.[38] For what does reconciliation allow people to silence rather than remember, to set aside rather than spur toward justice? Jackson suggested that it might be better for the Seward Shame Pole to remain standing as a continued reminder of the debts of the United States to Indigenous people.[39]

Some Taant'a ḵwáan Tlingits may agree with Jackson's sentiments. Willard Jackson, one of the elders of the Taant'a ḵwáan Teiḵweidí Bear Clan (and unrelated to Stephen Jackson), told me that another branch of the Seward family in Nebraska is very serious about repaying their great-great-great-great-grandfather's debt to the Taant'a ḵwáan people.[40] But while Willard Jackson would welcome a potlatch instigated by the Seward family themselves, he was not sure it would mean the pole would be chopped up and burned down as would be the custom after the debt had been repaid. As he said, "There are other things that are still not resolved." These include the fact that the Taant'a ḵwáan were never recognized under ANCSA as well as the decision of the Federal Subsistence Board not to include the Taant'a ḵwáan on the list of groups having "rural status" required for subsistence privileges under ANILCA.[41] Willard Jackson suggested that if the potlatch were performed, the "shame" might be removed from the particular figure of Seward by painting over the red on Seward's ears and nostrils; still, the pole might remain standing to tell a story of the healing that can take place through treating other human beings—and their property—with dignity and respect. But he's not sure yet what will happen if the Seward family actually does repay this historic potlatch. Those are decisions Jackson's older brother, Milton Jackson, head of the Taant'a ḵwáan Teiḵweidí Tlingit, will decide when the time comes, so this story is to be continued.

Heroic Pasts

This question of what we commit to—and erase—from public memory is part of the Seward Monument debate. The bronze monument in Juneau was dedicated in the thick of heated national debates about Confederate monuments that still stand in US cities—once again rallying points for white supremacist groups, revealing that supposedly "inert" statues remain active forces in the social values and memories of the public.[42] Certainly the Seward Monument in Alaska differs from Confederate monuments—for one thing, Seward was an ardent abolitionist who housed fugitives from the Underground Railroad in his basement; for another, the artist siblings who designed the bronze monument are sensitive to many Alaska Native concerns (Dave Rubin, who lives in Ketchikan and who is a friend of Stephen Jackson, even helped do some of the painting on the Seward Shame Pole).[43] Still, a bronze monument to a white male in front of a State Capitol cannot be said to be a fresh approach to representing the complexities of history. As one journalist wrote, the debate about erecting a Seward monument in Juneau was a debate about "literally putting a 19th century imperialist on a pedestal," and about the fact that many Alaskans do not view Seward—or his historic purchase—as part of a "heroic past."[44]

It was for these reasons that non-Native historian Ross Coen objected to the Seward Monument's very presence in Juneau, arguing that any monument to a single white male was too simplistic to really "honor" Alaska's history.[45] Rosita Worl, a Tlingit anthropologist who is head of Sealaska Heritage, the nonprofit research arm of Sealaska Native corporation, stated that she could understand why people wanted to remember Seward's role in Alaska. However, she wished other narratives were equally present: "I don't object to that statue up on the Capitol. What I object to is that the story of Alaska Natives is not there adjacent to that statue."[46] Both Worl and Coen agreed that the "Indigenous voice needs to come forward in a much bigger way" in any public commemoration of the Alaska Purchase.[47]

For a few months in the fall of 2017 the Tlingit counternarrative represented by the Seward Shame Pole did appear "adjacent to" the Seward statue in Juneau. In October of that year, Lieutenant Governor Mallott hosted a photographic exhibition of the Seward Shame Poles in his offices in the Alaska State Capitol, just behind the Seward Monument. Photographs of all three versions of the pole—the original carving from the 1880s in Tongass Village, the 1941 version by Charles Brown, and Stephen Jackson's 2017 iteration—hung in a hallway open to the public, along with wall text explaining the history of the pole. Around the same time, the Alaska State Library, Archives and Museum invited Stephen Jackson to Juneau to speak about the Seward Shame Pole in an hour-long public lecture. Appearing under his nom de plume of Jackson Polys, the artist was careful to begin with a territorial acknowledgment of the Áak'w ḵwáan Tlingit on whose lands he stood—something Seward had not done and something that settlers often ignore. He spoke of the "origin story" that Seward's Purchase had come to represent for many non-Natives in Alaska and reminded his audience of origin stories of Alaska Native people that long predated Seward. Referencing the "unpaid debts" inherent to a shame pole, Jackson emphasized that it was "significant to think about that in relation to William Seward—and to the United States."[48]

As powerful as these talks and exhibits were, however, their temporary appearance could not compete with the 24/7 presence of the bronze Seward Monument in front of the State Capitol. It is regrettable that the permanent signage surrounding the Seward Monument did not include a section dedicated to the Seward Shame Pole and to images of the three iterations of the pole that have countered Seward's legacy since the 1880s. Such signage could have provided a powerful counternarrative to the history of the Alaska Purchase and offered clear evidence that Indigenous peoples have resisted settler colonialism all along. As Stephen Jackson said at the raising of the Seward Shame Pole in April 2017: "It's an honor to keep the complexity of this story alive."[49] It is this complexity that we must acknowledge in the monuments we commit to public memory, and it is this complexity that countermonuments like the Seward Shame Pole help to tell.

NOTES

Thanks to Willard Jackson, David Rubin, Wayne Jensen, and especially Stephen Jackson for speaking with me about the various Seward monuments. Thanks also to Jacob Resneck at KTOO-Juneau and Scott Bowlen at the *Ketchikan Daily News* for sharing their audio recordings of the dedications of the two Seward monuments in 2017.

1 Dell Upton, "The *#HimToo* Movement," *Panorama: Journal of the Association of Historians of American Art* 4, no. 1 (Spring 2018), http://journalpanorama.org/upton-bully-pulpit/.

2 Byron Mallot, public speech at the dedication of the Seward Monument, Juneau, Alaska, July 3, 2017, recorded by KTOO, the local TV/radio station in Juneau.

3 For an in-depth analysis of Alaska Native critiques of ANCSA, including its controversial establishment of Native corporations with profit responsibilities, see Thomas Berger, *Village Journey: A Report from the Alaska Native Claims Commission* (New York: Hill and Wang, 1985). See also Eve Tuck, "ANCSA as X-Mark: Surface and Subsurface Claims of the Alaska Native Claims Settlement Act," *Alaska Native Studies* 1, no. 1 (2014): 240–72.

4 Viola E. Garfield and Linn A. Forrest, *The Wolf and the Raven: Totem Poles of Southeastern Alaska* (Seattle: University of Washington Press, 1949), 56.

5 Tom Harris as quoted in Deborah J. Botti, "Seward's Shame: Why Florida Native William Seward Is Snubbed in Alaska," *Times Herald-Record*, December 18, 2005, updated December 17, 2010, www.recordonline.com/article/20051218/entertain/312189945.

6 Daniel Montieth, "Tongass, the Prolific Name, the Forgotten Tribe: An Ethnohistory of the Taantak̲wáan Tongass People," PhD diss., Michigan State University, 1998, 150.

7 The Taant'a kwáan (or Tongass) Tlingit were not allotted land under ANCSA, due to reasons that continue to be under investigation; they were also not chosen for subsistence priority under ANILCA, because the Federal Subsistence Board judged them to be "modern and urban in character." Quoted in Lee Gorsuch, Steve Colt, Charles W. Smythe, and Bart K Garber, *A Study of Five Southeast Communities* (Anchorage, AK: Institute of Social and Economic Research, 1994), vii. For more on the landless communities of ANCSA, and the impact of ANILCA on the Taant'a k̲wáan, see Gorsuch et al., *Study of Five Southeast Communities.*

8 James E. Young, "The German Counter-Monument: Memory against Itself in Germany Today," *Critical Inquiry* 18, no. 2 (Winter 1992): 267–96, 270.

9 Ernest N. Paolino, *The Foundations of American Empire: William Henry Seward and U.S. Foreign Policy* (Ithaca, NY: Cornell University Press, 1973), 36.

10 Ted C. Hinckley, *The Canoe Rocks: Alaska's Tlingit and the Euro-American Frontier* (Lanham, MD: University Press of America, 1996), 88.

11 Ramona Skinner, *Alaska Native Policy in the Twentieth Century* (New York: Routledge, 1997).

12 Stephen Haycox, public speech at the dedication of the Seward Monument, Juneau, Alaska, July 3, 2017, recorded by KTOO, the local TV/radio station in Juneau.

13 Rosita F. Worl, "Tlingit *At.oow:* Tangible and Intangible Property," PhD diss., Harvard University, 1998, 261. See also Hinckley, *Canoe Rocks*, 74.

14 Quoted in Hinckley, *Canoe Rocks*, 74.

15 Worl, "Tlingit *At.oow*," 261.

16 William Paul, "The True Story of the Lincoln Pole," *Alaska Journal* 1, no. 3 (Summer 1971): 2–16.

17 Montieth, "Tongass, the Prolific Name, the Forgotten Tribe," 147.

18 Daniel Lee Henry, *Across the Shaman's River: John Muir, the Tlingit Stronghold, and the Opening of the North* (Fairbanks: University of Alaska Press, 2017), 62.

19 Garfield and Forrest, *Wolf and the Raven*, 55–56.

20 William H. Seward and Frederick W. Seward, *William Henry Seward: An Autobiography from 1801–1834, with a Memoir of His Life and a Selection from His Letters* (New York: Derby and Miller, 1891), 433. In 2017 a naaxein robe (the Tlingit spelling for a style of weaving commonly known as "Chilkat" weaving) believed to have come from William Seward's personal collection was given to the Sheldon Jackson Museum in Sitka, Alaska. Unfortunately, any letters or other documents that would have recorded the exact origin of the robe were lost in a house fire (author's personal communication with Jacqueline F. Hamberg, curator of collections, Sheldon Jackson Museum, May 16, 2018).

21 Garfield and Forrest, *Wolf and the Raven*, 56; and Jackson Polys (Stephen Jackson), "First Friday Artist Talk: The Seward Pole," public lecture at Alaska State Library, Archives and MU.S.eum, Juneau, Alaska, September 1, 2017.

22 Although red markings on the ears of human figures are not necessarily indicative of shame, the red ears and white face of Seward has long been interpreted as such. See Garfield and Forrest, *Wolf and the Raven*, 56; see also the description of the Seward Pole in the *Saxman Pole Directory*, published by the City of Saxman, 2015, p. 13.

23 Montieth, "Tongass, the Prolific Name, the Forgotten Tribe," 175.

24 Emily L. Moore, *Proud Raven, Panting Wolf: Carving Alaska's New Deal Totem Parks* (Seattle: University of Washington Press, 2018), 116.

25 B. F. Heintzleman, US Forest Service Regional Forester, to C. M. Archbold, District Ranger, November 18, 1940. All quotes in this paragraph come from letters in Record Group 95, Records of the US Forest Service, Region 10 (Alaska), Correspondence Relating to Activities of the Civilian Conservation Corps (CCC), 1937–42, National Archives, Seattle.

26 Viola Garfield, anthropologist with the University of Washington, to C. M. Archbold, USFS District Ranger, December 30, 1940, Record Group 95, Records of the US Forest Service, Region 10 (Alaska), Correspondence Relating to Activities of the Civilian Conservation Corps (CCC), 1937–42, National Archives, Seattle.

27 As late as February 1941, when the CCC replica of the Seward Pole was being completed, the Forest Service did not know the pole ridiculed Seward ("Totem Pole Based on Odd History," *Ketchikan Chronicle*, February 22, 1941). It was not until 1948 that the full (if diplomatically stated) story was published in Garfield and Forrest, *Wolf and the Raven*, 56.

28 Moore, *Proud Raven, Panting Wolf*, 116.

29 Gorsuch et al., *Study of Five Southeast Communities*, 128.

30 Peter M. Metcalfe, *A Dangerous Idea: The Alaska Native Brotherhood and the Struggle for Indigenous Rights* (Fairbanks: University of Alaska Press, 2014).

31 Metcalfe, *Dangerous Idea*; and Donald Craig Mitchell, *Sold American: The Story of Alaska Natives and Their Land, 1867–1959* (Hanover, NH: University Press of New England, 1997).

32 Gorsuch et al., *Study of Five Southeast Communities*.

33 Polys, "First Friday Artist Talk."

34 Polys, "First Friday Artist Talk."

35 For an overview of Jackson's pathbreaking work, see Aldona Jonaitis, "A Generation of Innovators in Southeast Alaska: Nicholas Galanin, Stephen Jackson, Da-ka-xeen Mehner and Donald Varnell," *American Indian Art Magazine* 33, no. 4 (Autumn 2008): 58–62.

36 Author's personal communication with Jackson, September 30, 2017.

37 Mary L. Stephenson, "The Legacy of Saxman—Looking to the Future through Our Past," open letter to the City of Saxman, July–August 2015. A similar call for reconciliation, published on a local news site, appears in Mary L. Stephenson, "An Opportunity to Return Honor," *SitNews*, August 30, 2017, www.sitnews.us/0817Viewpoints/083017_mary_stephenson.html.

38 Polys, "First Friday Artist Talk."

39 Author's personal communication with Stephen Jackson, September 30, 2017.

40 Author's telephone interview with Willard Jackson, September 30, 2017.

41 Gorsuch et al., *Study of Five Southeast Communities*.

42 Dell Upton, "William H. Seward to Visit Seward," *Seward County (NE) Independent*, May 10, 2017, www.sewardindependent.com/news/william-h-seward-statue-to-visit-seward/article_54c9da88-3501-11e7-915b-8b193ea3bbb7.html.

43 David Rubin, a longtime resident of Ketchikan who raised a daughter who is Alaska Native, is actively involved in the debate on Seward's legacy. For more on the interesting history of the Rubins' bronze monument to Seward, see Liz Ruskin, "Schlepping Bronze: A Ketchikan Artist Retraces Seward's Route," *Alaska Public Media*, April 4, 2017, alaskapublic.org/2017/04/04/schlepping-bronze-a-ketchikan-artist-retraces-sewards-route.

44 James Brooks, "Preserving a Scar: Seward Statue Debate Exposes Differing Views on history," *JuneauEmpire.com*, September 27, 2016.

45 Panelist Ross Coen on a September 28, 2016, episode of *Forum@360*, "What Raising a Statue of William Seward Means to Alaskans 150 Years Later," recording available at www.360north.org/video/forum360-raising-statue-william-seward-means-alaskans-150-years-later-402/.

46 Rosita Worl in public commentary following Stephen Jackson's talk at the Alaska State Museum, September 1, 2017, recorded in "An Artist's Talk with Jackson Polys," *360North*, www.360north.org/video/artists-talk-jackson-polys/.

47 Coen, "What Raising a Statue of William Seward Means to Alaskans."

48 Polys, "First Friday Artist Talk."

49 Stephen Jackson, public speech at totem pole dedication, April 29, 2017, quoted in Scott Bowlen, "New Totem Pole Honors Seward Story's Complexity," *Ketchikan Daily News*, May 13, 2017, republished at www.ketchikandailynews.com/premium/scene-5-13.

CHAPTER 2

The Social Life of Stones

HAIDA HLG̲AS7AGAA/ARGILLITE AND THE MAKING OF INALIENABLE COMMODITIES

Kaitlin McCormick

Old Massett, 2017

"I love carving," says Haida argillite carver Myles Edgars with a smile. He sits at his carving desk on an overcast evening in Old Massett, early in July 2017. With each stroke of his carving tool—homemade from a carbon power saw—Edgars blows the fine, black argillite dust off the circular piece he carves. The airborne dust settles on the desk, walls, or floor of the small carving room attached to Edgars's home, which overlooks Massett Sound, at the north end of Haida Gwaii's Graham Island. He carves a pendant that represents an eagle, his clan crest, which he has superglued to an old tin of shoe polish. This method keeps the pendant stable and provides a wider working surface for his hands as he carves: "On a tin can, you can turn it around."

In Edgars's carving room, the late-afternoon sun and a small lamp on the corner of his desk shed light on his work; the walls, blackened with argillite dust from years of carving, are decorated with photographs of his extended family, his children, and his work. This is my second interview with Edgars since I first traveled to Haida Gwaii and Vancouver in the spring of 2014 to meet argillite carvers and learn about their work and the history of this unique and ongoing carving tradition. I ask Edgars what he thinks is the most important thing to know about argillite, a black carbonaceous shale obtained at a single quarry site on Haida Gwaii's Graham Island. "When the tourists come to see me, they ask me the same thing," he says. "Some of them say how happy they are that they finally got what they really wanted, [an argillite] carving from Queen Charlotte Islands, the only place in the world they can find it.[1] That's why they wanted to come here and buy it off me, so they can have something that can't be found anywhere else in the world."[2]

On Haida Gwaii and further afield, Edgars is known for his distinct and consistent style and subject matter. He mainly carves pendants, earrings, and the occasional miniature totem pole, which he sells to tourists and in galleries on Haida Gwaii and in Vancouver. Recurring figures in his repertoire include eagles, ravens, hummingbirds, half-moons, and salmon eggs as well as watchmen, characters from Haida oral histories, mythology, and everyday life. He decorates these with masterfully inlayed abalone or paua shell, tiny but brilliant circles of color that leap out from the flawless black argillite surfaces he polishes with an emery cloth.[3] Edgars loves carving argillite because he enjoys working with the material. "The best part is when you're almost finished, and it looks alive, you're putting life into it. Sometimes I make some so nice, I don't even want to sell it. But I know I could always make another one."[4]

Edgars, who makes his living carving argillite, values the recognition conferred upon his work from customers who seek out and wear his carvings. Haida artists have carved argillite for sale to outsiders since at least the 1820s, when the earliest documented carvings were collected by New England sea captains who exchanged Euro-American goods for sea otter pelts with Indigenous traders along the Northwest Coast of North America.[5] Collected across various regimes of value as souvenirs, curiosities, scientific specimens and art, argillite carving yielded wealth for Haidas throughout the nineteenth and twentieth centuries.[6] For twenty-first century carvers like Myles Edgars and others, it still does.

This chapter articulates the need for better safeguarding of argillite, both uncarved and carved, through frameworks of natural and cultural resource protections. Informed by the established social and art histories of argillite carving, this research positions argillite in light of a number of tensions and ambivalences regarding its material character—its physical and social properties—and constructions of value and utility.[7] On Haida Gwaii, argillite is a stable yet vulnerable economic and cultural resource of the Haida, which many carvers believe requires stronger protections than what is currently provided—or perhaps more accurately, respected—under Haida and Canadian law. The tensions surrounding this unique material have developed over argillite's two centuries of entanglement in Haida and Euro-Canadian affairs, as the Northwest Coast of North America was subjected to cycles of economic exploitation and social and cultural transformation. Grounded in Haida oral histories and knowledge, settler-colonial archival research, and material culture theory, this chapter illuminates these tensions and positions the argillite carving tradition as a compelling witness to the history and character of Haida and Euro-Canadian relations.

Haida hlg̱as7agaa/Argillite: Its Uses and Circulation

Argillite is a soft, black, carbonaceous shale. The material occurs in geological formations elsewhere in the world, but the deposit at Tllgaduu Creek, or Slatechuck—its common name—is distinctive.[8] The structure of this argillite deposit, located on a mountainside northwest of HlG̱aagilda (Skidegate), was formed through the heating and folding of a volcanic eruption. These geological events distinguished this material from other types of argillite and created Tllgaduu's "unique properties," which make it so responsive to the carver's tools.[9] To the Skidegate Haida band in whom control of this resource is vested, this material is known as hlg̱as7agaa, though many carvers and locals simply call it slate, or argillite, and the quarry site Slatechuck.[10] This essay uses the X̱aayda kil (Skidegate Haida dialect) and English names for hlg̱as7agaa (*argillite*) and Tllgaduu (Slatechuck) interchangeably.

This material and carving tradition is grounded in Haida peoples' relationship with their ancestral and unceded homeland of Haida Gwaii. Haida historian Captain Gold believes that argillite carving was discovered by Haidas long before the 1820s, the timeframe assigned to the earliest documented examples in New England and European museums.[11] Captain Gold explains that alongside daily life in their coastal villages and at sea, Haidas were also "in the forest quite often, gathering medicine plants and gathering red cedar, walking over land trails and so on . . . and that argillite deposit was in our memories for a long time before this so-called [1820s–1830s] beginning point."[12] Argillite carving, he explains, is part of the Haida's long history of illustrating their art with crest figures, which one would acquire the right to illustrate and wear by birth, through war, and in potlatches, where "vast forms of wealth" were expended to secure these rights. For contemporary Haida, crest figures "represent ancient ties to the old people and are worn [and represented] with pride."[13]

Where the history of carved argillite is the subject of considerable literature, this chapter focuses on argillite's material properties, an aspect that has not until recently been critically considered in the study of this body of work.[14] As anthropologist Tim Ingold has pointed out, studies of art and material culture have mainly focused on finished objects, and less on the processes by which objects' materials undergo transformation.[15] This is why, Ingold writes, it is common to describe materials as "raw" but not "cooked," since by the time materials are transformed into objects, materials have already disappeared from view, leaving the object as the focus of attention.[16] To be sure, scholars have not ignored the distinct qualities of Haida argillite.[17]

Until recently, however, the history and dynamics of "raw" (i.e., uncarved) argillite have not been critically addressed. The scholarly focus on finished argillite carvings, and not the material from which they are made, conceals important aspects of the carvings' stories and the social and physical world they illuminate.[18] This chapter argues that a material culture–oriented approach to argillite carving complements the art historical record by allowing us to better understand the significance and value of this material from Haida perspectives. Focusing on the historical and contemporary dynamics surrounding the use and circulation of raw argillite helps build a case for better protections for this cultural and natural resource. The need for protections is a concern to Haida people in the present and emerges from the history and ongoing conditions of settler-colonialism in Canada.

Transgressions to Tllgaduu/Slatechuck's Most Valuable Resource

Distinct from other forms of Haida cultural expression in its material properties, commercial purpose, and unbroken chain of production before, during, and after the potlatch ban (1885–1951), argillite has been, and still is, subjected to foreign transgressions. Many authors have documented Haida struggles—and successes—in protecting their range of natural and cultural resources.[19] While argillite has not been at the forefront of twentieth- and twenty-first-century conflicts over Haida Gwaii's more high-stakes resources, such as forestry and the fisheries, evidence of the Haida's centuries-old struggle to maintain sovereignty over argillite as an economic and cultural resource is traceable in the Euro-Canadian historical record and discernible in conversations with my interlocutors, who treat argillite as patrimony.

The Haida have resisted resource-hungry interlopers since at least the mid-nineteenth century.[20] When Haida Gwaii became part of Canada with British Columbia's 1871 confederation, Canadian federal agents tasked with assessing the archipelago's natural resources noted the Haida's use of argillite in their reports on Skidegate-area coal resources.[21] By 1889, New England journalist and tourist Emma Shaw Colcleugh observed that argillite appeared to be "central" to the economic operations at Skidegate.[22] The commercial mineral extraction activities near Slatechuck led amateur ethnographer and coal explorer James Deans to advocate for its protection in 1883. From Skidegate, Deans wrote a series of reports in which he recommended the formation of reserves to the superintendent of Indian Affairs in Victoria. Claiming to write on behalf of Haida people from the villages of Massett, Skidegate, Cumshewa, and Tasu, Deans advised the government to create reserves to protect the Haida's natural resources, including sea otter hunting places, black cod fisheries, salmon streams, and berry patches. These, Deans wrote, were places and resources that the Haida had long owned and used for subsistence and to acquire wealth but which risked being sold by the Crown to private commercial developers. In his report on the "Slate Quarries," Deans urged that Slatechuck be either reserved to the Haida or that the Haida be guaranteed the rights to work the quarry, given the material's apparent economic and cultural benefits.[23]

By the 1880s the colonial record reflected the tension between argillite's importance as a sustainable cottage industry and its vulnerability in the face of ongoing cycles of colonial resource extraction and land dispossession. Deans and federal geologist George Dawson each envisioned Haida Gwaii's eventual colonization and the difficulties thereof. Dawson concluded his 1880 report, for instance, by predicting that the "just" prosecution of settler-colonial industries on Haida Gwaii would necessitate the disposal of Indian title. This would be difficult since the Haida "hold their lands not in any loose general way, but have the whole of the islands divided and apportioned off as the property of certain families, with customs fully developed as to the inheritance and transfer of lands." Land claim negotiations, Dawson correctly predicted, would need to be carried out with skill and care, and at high cost to the settler.[24] Dawson's observations, and Deans's call for the protection of the argillite quarry, tie argillite into broader and ongoing political tensions around Haida land tenure and settler-colonial infringements on long-established systems of property. These historical documents introduce assertions of Haida resource sovereignty into the art historical record.

Action to secure the site as a federal Indian reserve followed a government survey commissioned in 1939 by the surveyor general of Canada. On May 7, 1941, a British Columbia Order-In-Council transferred forty-four acres, thenceforth called "Black Slate 11," to the federal government for "the use and benefit of the Skidegate Indians."[25] The argillite deposit was thus secured to the Haidas, a protection intended to end any other competition for this resource or other resources in its immediate vicinity. Still, despite its reservation status and remote location, Slatechuck still remains vulnerable to transgressions by non-Haida who seek to capitalize on this resource. Such transgressions violate the Haida's expression and protection of argillite as an inalienable commodity.

Strategies of Keeping and Giving: The Production and Protection of an Inalienable Commodity

"While *carved* argillite [is] . . . made for outside consumption and as such is alienable," anthropologist Solen Roth wrote, "the fact that *raw* argillite is sheltered from outsider access has helped maintain and reinforce its strong association—an exclusive one even—with the Haida, who treat it like an inalienable possession."[26] Roth explains that the Haida's treatment of raw argillite as patrimony renders the material, in theoretical terms, an inalienable commodity, while its finished artworks are freely circulated in the marketplace. Argillite, she observes, is a "quintessential [Haida] substance." With the "cultural value of being 'Indigenous' and the symbolic value of being 'local,'" argillite carvings gain added economic value on the art market.[27] Unlike other materials that are restricted by Indigenous or state laws for the use of distinct cultural groups, but that can still (sometimes problematically) be found circulating commercially (e.g., pipestone or baleen), the exclusivity and relative inaccessibility of the argillite quarried at Slatechuck makes it a "quite exceptional" material, "not only on the Northwest Coast, but arguably in the world as well."[28]

As Roth has pointed out, there are comparable materials with which Northwest Coast First Nations express their cultural and social identity, including cedar and abalone shell. Unlike cedar, abalone, pipestone, or baleen, however, argillite is unique because only it refers to a single Indigenous nation and is guarded—by Haida law and to an extent by Canadian law—for the use of Haidas only.[29] Still, despite being protected under Haida law and as a federal Indian Reserve, argillite has been subjected to two categories of foreign transgressions: the procurement and use of argillite by non-Haidas and commercial "art fakes." Both kinds of transgressions are attempts by unauthorized people or companies to profit from this distinct and culturally valuable Indigenous material. Whereas the former occurs on-island, and the latter from afar, each issue poses different challenges to, and possible pathways toward, maintaining Haida sovereignty over the use and circulation of argillite.

A reproduction argillite carving made of plastic, for instance, is displayed among Haida treasures at the Haida Gwaii Museum in Skidegate. "Artifakes," the museum label warns, may "look genuine on the surface however they lack the rich history and power that authentic Haida formline can evoke."[30] In recent decades there has been an "explosion" in the number of people and companies trying to emulate Haida products and formline art.[31] To counteract the harm that fakes pose to both consumers and artists, artists may register with the Council of the Haida Nation and be issued a Haida Art Authenticity Certificate. Artists receive a personal registration number to include on individual artwork tags, which confirm to galleries, collectors, and buyers that the artist is of Haida ancestry.[32] The artists I spoke with in 2014 and 2017 were strongly opposed to the idea of art ware companies reproducing their original works in particular and to the commercial art ware industry in general, which reproduces historical works: "There's too [many argillite] copies out there, from Japan, from Taiwan. . . . Get the real thing!"[33] Today imitation argillite carvings are available in prestigious Native art galleries and museum gift shops across Canada. Though these copies reference and render original Haida artworks affordable for the consumer, their manufacture is of no benefit to the Haida—the people who have worked hard through the generations to establish argillite's value and authenticity.

The issue of reproduction is not about the commercialization of Indigenous art but about reproduction and commercialization by non-Haida artists or companies. Haida artists have long made works of art for various contexts, and in recent years there has been a proliferation of commercial, mass-produced products made by Haida and other Northwest Coast artists for the tourist trade and household markets. As scholar Charlotte Townsend-Gault has suggested, crest designs made by Indigenous artists for reproduction onto oven mitts, tissue paper, and key chains, to name a few, may be a strategy of "keeping while giving."[34] Such "trivia," she argues, are deployed on the marketplace as a "line of defence against further encroachment," a way to maintain sovereignty over the sacred elements of crests that are inalienable and inaccessible to consumers.[35] In the case of argillite, however, neither the deployment of real (i.e., original) argillite carvings nor the proliferation of art fakes has defended against unauthorized encroachment to Slatechuck. According to interlocutors, such encroachment has actually increased in recent years. It appears that the argillite quarry warrants greater protections than what is currently afforded under Haida and Canadian law.

The literature suggests that Slatechuck's inaccessible location and Indigenous legal protections have led to a "commonly accepted understanding that 'the argillite of Haida Gwaii is reserved for the sole use of Haida artists.'"[36] However, my research—based on conversations with Haida and non-Haida people on Haida Gwaii and in Vancouver in 2014 and 2017—found that transgressions by white people reportedly occur with some frequency. One artist reported: "It seems like anybody goes up there, it was only the Haidas could go up there before, but now, everybody goes up there."[37] This artist had heard of unauthorized people quarrying argillite to sell to non-Haida artists in Vancouver. On Haida Gwaii in 2014, I heard of attempts by non-Haidas to carve and sell the material and present their work as authentic Haida art. For instance, a gift shop owner on Haida Gwaii recalled a white woman's attempt to sell a piece of argillite that she had procured from someone in the settler town of Masset. The woman had carved the argillite into a bear figure and tried to sell it to the gift shop owner, who emphatically refused, informing her that argillite was a restricted material. "She might have sold it to a tourist . . . she did a pretty good job, but there's no way I would have touched it, you know . . . she didn't get it."[38] Although anyone having obtained argillite could carve it—perhaps even to a convincing standard—the spurious character of that piece rendered it illegitimate, even untouchable. As the shop owner pointed out, the woman had no right to carve or sell the material, a restriction known in both Haida and settler communities on Haida Gwaii. She had no rights to this patrimony, no right to tell Haida stories; the work was thus counterfeit.

To be clear, the Haida assert sovereignty over Tllgaduu and the argillite that is quarried there. Traditionally and historically, control of Tllgaduu was vested in Chief Skidegate, who granted permission to northern Haida artists to freely quarry argillite. Massett artists' contributions to argillite carving have left a rich and impressive legacy of works in the world's museums and private collections.[39] Today, protected as a federal Indian Reserve, Tllgaduu is managed by the Skidegate Band Council, although title to these lands remains (from the Canadian legal perspective) vested in the Crown, whose claim is in conflict with the Haida Nation's claim to aboriginal title. The Haida Constitution asserts hereditary and aboriginal title and rights to Haida territories, including subsurface, and asserts the rights of every Haida citizen to access Haida Gwaii resources for cultural and commercial reasons, consistent with laws of the Haida Nation.[40] Haida sovereignty over Tllgaduu thus has historical precedent as the prerogative of Chief Skidegate, is asserted in contemporary Haida law and governance structures, and is articulated by carvers and citizens of the Haida Nation in various ways, including in the language of the sacred.

Several artists have described Tllgaduu as a sacred site. "I consider it a sacred place to Haida people," commented artist Walker Brown, "that's how I was brought up, thinking about it and knowing about it."[41] For Brown, Tllgaduu is sacred because it is the place that has provided "this unique stone . . . that our ancestors, up until the present, have been able to put our history and stories and crest figures into, at a time [when] a lot of that stuff might have been lost if that particular material didn't exist. [Without argillite] there would have been a gap in knowledge in the art style, the art form."[42] Credited for sustaining Haida art through the nineteenth and early twentieth centuries, artists speak about hlg̲as7agaa/argillite and Tllgaduu/Slatechuck with a reverence that confers sacred and spiritual importance to this material and place. One artist even likened the journey to Tllgaduu as a pilgrimage to a holy site.[43]

Despite the arduous and costly daylong journey, which takes place by car, boat, and on foot, many carvers prefer to quarry their own material, rather than pay others to source it for them. Artist Chris Russ of Old Massett explained that a piece of argillite has to be selected to suit a particular need. This selection is based on artists' cultural knowledge, training, and experience in that medium.[44] Russ is guided by personal ethics regarding the sourcing of argillite. "I use what I take," and "I don't need that much," he says. "For me, it's not right to sell . . . unless it's the finished product, I don't like selling pieces that are not finished."[45]

Another carver explained: "You gotta get it by yourself, the artists always have to get their own stuff, and know what they're looking for."[46] Carvers' knowledge and experience informs the integrity of their work. In 2014 and 2017 tensions around access were at the forefront of my interlocutors' concerns as they emphasized the need for better regulations to protect Tllgaduu for Haida artists. Expressing worry about non-Haidas' access to Tllgaduu, and the proliferation of fakes, Russ believes that "the way it's going, it's going to be worth nothing pretty soon. Just, like—an ordinary stone."[47] Protected in theory for the use of Haida citizens by Haida customary law and, to an extent, by Canadian federal law, can further measures be taken to guard Tllgaduu and hlg̲as7agaa from exploitation and cultural appropriation?

In 2015, when the Council of the Haida Nation directed all visitors to Tllgaduu to check in with the Skidegate Band Council, the question arose about the lack of a Watchmen Base Camp at Slatechuck Mountain. The Watchmen program, organized with the Skidegate Band Council and the Haida Nation in the early 1980s, has been successful in its primary aim to protect cultural heritage sites, educate visitors, and promote Haida contributions to world heritage.[48] Since the Watchmen provide protection for southern Haida village sites in the summer months, the program could provide a possible foundation for argillite protection at the Tllgaduu outlet area, which is currently unsupervised, during the spring through fall quarrying season when the days are longer and drier.

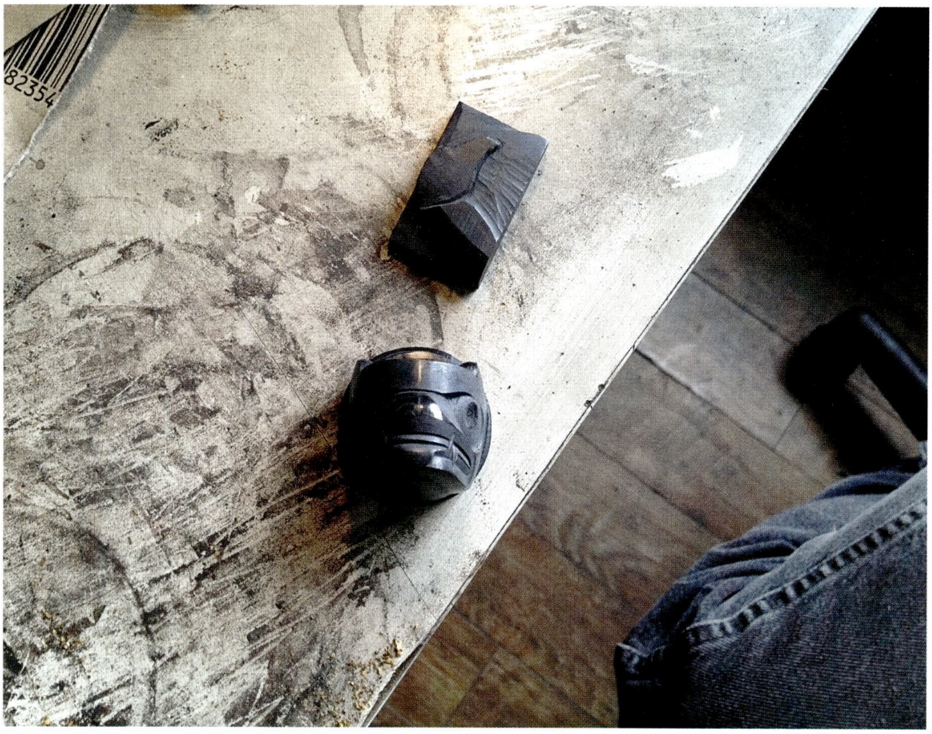

2.1. Argillite Bear pendant in the making, by Chris Russ, Old Massett, July 2017. Photograph by the author. Reproduced with permission of the artist.

Of course, it is up to the Haida to decide how to manage Tllgaduu and protect Haida art and artists. Strategies currently in place to protect Haida art in the marketplace, for instance, include the aforementioned Haida Art Authenticity Certificates. I have seen such labels on some artworks on Haida Gwaii, including baskets, but am unsure as to the breadth of their use among Haida artists on-island and off-island. More broadly, a range of approaches within and outside of Canadian legal frameworks seek to protect First Nations cultural heritage, including, but not limited to, supporting First Nations' own protection programs and respecting First Nations' diverse conceptions of cultural property, laws, and processes.[49] For instance, Haida strategies for land and natural resource protection could lead to argillite policies, including the *Haida Land Use Vision* (2005) and the *Haida Gwaii Strategic Land Use Agreement* between the Haida Nation and the Province of BC (2007). Each document outlines different pathways for the protection of Haida Gwaii lands and resources, with the former invoking the principle of yah'guudang (*respect*): bringing "land and resource use into balance to ensure the continuity of Haida culture and the economic well-being of the entire Island Community."[50]

International resolutions such as the United Nations Declaration on the Rights of Indigenous Peoples (UNDRIP), while not binding under international law, reflect member states' commitments to recognize the Indigenous rights this document asserts. In 2016, Canada's Liberal government officially removed its objector status to UNDRIP (established under the previous Conservative government), which recognizes that Indigenous people have "suffered from historic injustices as a result of... their colonization and dispossession of their lands, territories and resources," which has prevented them from exercising their right to develop and manage their resources as they see fit.[51] Under Article 31, UNDRIP recognizes the right of Indigenous people to "maintain, control, protect and develop their cultural heritage, traditional knowledge and traditional cultural expressions . . . designs . . . and . . . visual . . . arts [as well as] . . . the right to maintain, control, protect and develop their intellectual property over such cultural heritage." The declaration continues that States "shall take effective measures to recognize and protect the exercise of these rights."[52] As legal scholars Catherine Bell and Val Napoleon have point out, First Nations must have the power to restrict access to their sacred places.[53] It is the responsibility of visitors to Haida Gwaii, and of non-Haida who admire and profit from the sale of Haida art, to observe a standard of yah'guudang (respect) in their approach to the acquisition and circulation of Haida art.

Argillite carving provides a livelihood for artists whose works circulate locally, in the Haida Gwaii tourist trade, and off-island on the North American art market. Artists want better protections for this rare, unique, and intersecting natural and cultural Haida resource as well as a wider understanding and acceptance that unauthorized copying of Haida art is wrong and an infringement on their right to control the products they choose to circulate on the art market.

As archaeologist George Nicholas has pointed out, for Indigenous peoples, tangible and intangible heritage may be indivisible. The Haida's rights to use and control argillite as tangible and intangible heritage is grounded in their own laws, culture, and history, "based on social relations and responsibilities, and... [in this case, communal] ownership [and stewardship] . . .; and for whom infringement results in cultural, spiritual, and economic loss."[54] For many carvers, unauthorized reproductions and use of materials other than argillite devalue this art form, which they and their ancestors have cared for, for generations, and which has provided—and continues to provide—many artists with a livelihood in tough economic times. As artist Christian White has pointed out, on Haida Gwaii art production provides income in communities that have experienced sixty years of unemployment struggles.[55] The relations that White maintains with the galleries and collectors off-island who buy his work has enabled him to lead and support cultural production in his community of Old Massett. Enthusiasts and consumers of Haida art, for their part, must respect and recognize the Haida's sovereign relationship to Tllgaduu and hlg̱as7agaa, and avoid transgressing on this place and material.

This chapter has outlined the history of the Haida's affirmation of sovereignty over hlg̱as7agaa/argillite and Tllgaduu/Slatechuck since the mid-nineteenth century.

The recognition of Haida assertions of sovereignty over their lands and resources by non-Haida observers pepper the historical record from the inception of European encroachment onto Haida Gwaii to today.[56] As such, a history of argillite carving is incomplete without inquiry into the material itself, the place at which it is quarried, and the relations between hlg̱as7agaa and Tllgaduu, and the forces that lay claim to them. Haida sovereignty over Tllgaduu is apparent in the historical record, in contemporary Indigenous and Canadian law, and in how artists articulate their relationship with the place and material. While it is beyond the scope or authority of this chapter to argue particular pathways toward the guardianship of argillite, a precious and priceless material resource of the Haida, it seems that there is a stated need for stronger protections. At the very least, non-Haida must observe more respectfully the Haida's exclusive right to control argillite's use and circulation.

NOTES

Many people contributed their knowledge to this chapter. I would like to thank my interlocutors for their insights as well as the anonymous peer reviewers, Walker Brown, Kathryn Bunn-Marcuse, Captain Gold, Aldona Jonaitis, and Bob Preucel for their thoughtful feedback and comments. This research was undertaken with the support of the Social Sciences and Humanities Research Council of Canada and the Haffenreffer Museum of Anthropology at Brown University, in Providence, Rhode Island.

1 From 1787 to 2009 the archipelago was called the Queen Charlotte Islands. In 2009 it was renamed Haida Gwaii, popularly translated as "Islands of the People." In X̱aayda kil, the Skidegate Haida dialect, the Haida name for the islands is Xaaydlaa Gwaayaay, which translates as "taken out of concealment." See Mark Dowie, *The Haida Gwaii Lesson: A Strategic Playbook for Indigenous Sovereignty* (San Francisco: Inkshares, 2017).

2 Author, interview with Myles Edgars, Old Massett, 2017.

3 "Paua" is the Maori name for a species of gastropod mollusc found in New Zealand. Its scientific name is *Haliotis iris*.

4 Author, interview with Myles Edgars, Old Massett, 2017.

5 Robin K. Wright, "Haida Argillite Pipes," MA thesis, University of Washington, 1977; and Mary Malloy, *Souvenirs of the Fur Trade: Northwest Coast Indian Art and Artifacts Collected by American Fur Traders, 1788–1844* (Cambridge, MA: Peabody Museum Press, 2002).

6 Fred Myers, introduction in *The Empire of Things: Regimes of Value and Material Culture*, edited by Fred Myers, 3–61 (Santa Fe, NM: School of American Research Press, 2001).

7 Anthropologist Tim Ingold has described the properties of materials as stories that express how materials relate to their surroundings. For Ingold, the properties of materials are also the processes through which they undergo transformation. For more on this, see Tim Ingold, "Materials against Materiality," *Archaeological Dialogues* 14, no. 1 (2007): 1–16.

8 The suffix "-chuck" translates as "water" in Chinook jargon.

9 Peter McNair and Alan Hoover, *The Magic Leaves: A History of Argillite Carving* (Victoria: Royal British Columbia Museum, 2002), 11.

10 McNair and Hoover, *Magic Leaves*, 11.

11 Author, interview with Captain Gold, Skidegate, 2014. Also see Wright, "Haida Argillite Pipes"; Knut Fladmark, "The Richardson Ranch Site: A 19th Century Haida House," in *Historical Archaeology in Northwestern North America*, edited by Knut R. Fladmark and Ronald M. Getty, 53–93

(Calgary: University of Calgary, Archaeological Association, 1973); Malloy, *Souvenirs of the Fur Trade*; and McNair and Hoover, *Magic Leaves*.

12 Author, interview with Captain Gold, Skidegate, 2014. Captain Gold refers to the date that scholars have established for argillite's origins as a commercial carving tradition. See McNair and Hoover, *Magic Leaves*, 146–52, for a historiography of argillite carving.

13 Captain Gold, personal communication by e-mail, 2018.

14 On this considerable literature, see Robin K. Wright, *Northern Haida Master Carvers* (Seattle: University of Washington Press, 2001); Wright, "Haida Argillite Pipes"; and Leslie Drew and Douglas Wilson, *Argillite, Art of the Haida* (North Vancouver: Hancock House, 1980). For an exception, see Solen Roth, "Argillite, Faux-Argillite, and Black Plastic: The Political Economy of Simulating a Quintessential Haida Substance," *Journal of Material Culture* 20, no. 3 (2015): 299–312.

15 Ingold, "Materials against Materiality," 9.

16 Ingold, "Materials against Materiality," 9.

17 McNair and Hoover, *Magic Leaves*; and Drew and Wilson, *Argillite, Art of the Haida*.

18 Ingold, "Materials against Materiality."

19 See Ian Gill, *All That We Say Is Ours: Guujaaw and the Reawakening of the Haida Nation* (Vancouver: Douglas & McIntyre, 2009); Scott Steedman and Jisgang, eds., *That Which Makes Us Haida: The Haida Language* (Skidegate: Haida Gwaii Museum, 2011); and Dowie, *The Haida Gwaii Lesson*, 2017.

20 Wright, *Northern Haida Master Carvers*.

21 James Richardson, "On the Coal Fields of Vancouver Island and Queen Charlotte Islands," Report, Geological Survey of Canada, May 1873; George Dawson, "On the Haida Indians of the Queen Charlotte Islands," Report, Geological Survey of Canada, Dawson Brothers, Montreal, 1880; and Newton H. Chittenden, "Official Report of the Exploration of the Queen Charlotte Islands for the Government of British Columbia," Government of British Columbia, November 1884.

22 Emma S. Colcleugh, "Carved Totems: Not Idols, but Peculiar Picture Writings," *Boston Globe*, November 17, 1889, in Emma Shaw Colcleugh Collection, msESC, 90-678e, Haffenreffer Museum of Anthropology, Brown University.

23 James Deans, "The Slate Quarries. Report on Queen Charlotte Islands," 1883, British Columbia Provincial Archives, A/E/P87/D34.

24 Dawson, "On the Haida Indians of the Queen Charlotte Islands," 174B–175B.

25 Drew and Wilson, *Argillite, Art of the Haida*, 47–48.

26 Roth, "Argillite, Faux-Argillite and Black Plastic," 306.

27 Roth, "Argillite, Faux-Argillite and Black Plastic"; and Elizabeth E. Ferry, "Inalienable Commodities: The Production and Circulation of Silver and Patrimony in a Mexican Mining Cooperative," *Cultural Anthropology* 17, no. 3 (2002): 331–58.

28 Roth, "Argillite, Faux-Argillite and Black Plastic," 301. Baleen may be legally sold by Alaska Natives as "Traditional Native Handicraft" under the US Marine Mammal Protection Act and the Endangered Species Act. For baleen to qualify as handicraft, it must be cleaned and polished. Baleen handicraft may be taken out of Alaska but must not be transported outside of the United States. See National Oceanic and Atmospheric Administration, "Marine Mammal Parts and Products FAQs," https://alaskafisheries.noaa.gov/pr/buying-marine-mammal-products (accessed April 17, 2018). Under an Act of Congress of August 25, 1937, pipestone quarried at the Pipestone National Monument is reserved for the use of Indians of all tribes.

29 Roth, "Argillite, Faux-Argillite and Black Plastic," 301.

30 Haida Gwaii Museum panel text, 2017.

31 Haida Gwaii Museum panel text, 2017.

32 *Haida Laas: News from the Council of the Haida Nation,* March 2018.

33 Author, interview with Chris Russ, Old Massett, 2017. In 2014 one artist told me he refused a Canadian museum's request to reproduce one of his works: "If I want my pieces reproduced, I would do them myself" (author interview with anonymous interlocutor, 2014). Roth describes "art ware" companies as those that produce "wares adorned with artistic designs." Several such companies have been reproducing argillite carvings since the 1960s, sometimes under copyright arrangements, other times not. See Roth, "Argillite, Faux-Argillite and Black Plastic," 306–307 (on the dynamics of argillite reproductions) and 311 (on why art ware companies who reproduce argillite should—but are not legally compelled to—remunerate the Haida).

34 Charlotte Townsend-Gault, "Circulating Aboriginality," *Journal of Material Culture* 9, no. 2 (2004): 183–202.

35 Townsend-Gault, "Circulating Aboriginality," 183.

36 On the location, see Drew and Wilson, *Argillite, Art of the Haida.* On the legal protections, see McNair and Hoover, *Magic Leaves.* Roth, "Argillite, Faux-Argillite and Black Plastic," 305.

37 Author, interview with anonymous interlocutor, 2014.

38 Author, interview with anonymous interlocutor, 2014.

39 Wright, *Northern Haida Master Carvers.*

40 Constitution of the Haida Nation, 2014, A3–S1, A1–S1, A3–S3.

41 Author, interview with Walker Brown, Skidegate, 2017.

42 Author, interview with Walker Brown, 2017.

43 Author, interview with anonymous interlocutor, 2014.

44 Author, interview with Chris Russ, 2014.

45 Author, interview with Chris Russ, 2017.

46 Author, interview with anonymous interlocutor, 2014.

47 Author, interview with Chris Russ, 2017.

48 Catherine Bell and Val Napoleon, *First Nations Cultural Heritage and Law: Case Studies Voices and Perspectives* (Vancouver: University of British Columbia Press, 2008); and Eugene Thomlinson and Geoffrey Crouch, "Aboriginal Peoples, Parks Canada, and Protected Spaces: A Case Study in Co-Management at Gwaii Haanas National Park Reserve," *Annals of Leisure Research* 15, no. 1 (2012): 69–86.

49 Catherine Bell and Robert K. Paterson, *Protection of First Nations Cultural Heritage: Laws, Policy, and Reform* (Vancouver: University of British Columbia Press, 2009), 5–6.

50 Council of the Haida Nation, *Haida Land Use Vision,* available on the website of the Council of the Haida Nation, 2005, p. 18.

51 United Nations, *United Nations Declaration on the Rights of Indigenous People,* 2007, p. 2.

52 United Nations, *United Nations Declaration on the Rights of Indigenous People,* article 31, 1 and 2, 11–12.

53 Bell and Napoleon, *First Nations Cultural Heritage and Law,* 24.

54 George Nicholas, "Intellectual Property Issues," in *Oxford Companion to Archaeology,* second edition, edited by N. A. Silberman, vol. 2, 106–109 (New York: Oxford University Press, 2012).

55 Author, interview with Christian White, Old Massett, 2017.

56 See, for instance, *Haida Nation v. British Columbia (Minister of Forests),* (2004) 3 S.C.R. 511. In this case, Canada's Supreme Court ruled that the Crown has duty to consult Aboriginal groups before exploiting lands to which they may have claims. The Supreme Court also decided that the Haida have a strong prima facie claim for Aboriginal title and right.

CHAPTER 3

Morse Code for Creation

JIM SCHOPPERT'S PAINTERLY LANGUAGE FOR A POSTMODERN REVIVAL

Christopher Green

ART
If art has a master
Imagination cracks the whip.

If art is a celebration
the vernal equinox is its maiden.

Art is shorthand for expression.
Morse code for creation.

It causes us to move quantum leaps
in the blink of an eye
and fathom mysteries within blocked
by refuse of a generation left uncaring
and therefore uncared for.

Art speaks a language unique yet familiar.
It marks the way with signposts that
lead us still another step further into the
question—

WHAT IS ART?

—JIM SCHOPPERT

WHAT MEANS OF EXPRESSION WERE AVAILABLE TO NORTHWEST COAST ARTISTS immediately following the boom of the 1960s and 1970s revival? What aesthetic "shorthand" or visual "code," as Robert James (Jim) Schoppert (1947–1992) put it, could *be* art for the contemporary Native artist? At the height of his career,

Schoppert produced work that drew on the modernist practices of the European and American avant-garde in combination with Tlingit and other Indigenous visual forms. He took Euro-American art and its history of primitivist appropriations of Alaskan Indigenous art in particular head on to work beyond what he saw as the strict conventions of Northwest Coast art. During Schoppert's life, however, this approach troubled his critical reception, and very little consensus emerged as to what style his work followed, or even on how to describe his art.

Art critic Bill Berkson, writing about the Seattle art scene for *Art in America* in 1986, called Schoppert a "Northwest Neo-Expressionist painter."[1] In the catalog for the exhibition *New Directions Northwest: Contemporary Native American Art*, published a year later, the artist George Longfish wrote that he saw the influence of the neo-Dadaist Robert Rauschenberg in the hues and tones of paint washed across Schoppert's surfaces of carved wood and destroyed patterns.[2] Attempting to fit Schoppert into the context of modern and postmodern art, historian Gerhard Hoffman compared Schoppert to American sculptor Louise Nevelson but also connected his Eskimo-inspired sculptures to the surrealist tradition.[3] Writers and critics have likewise called him a neocubist, a minimalist, and an artist whose work evoked to one reviewer "the weathered look of ancient carvings" yet also "sang with contemporary geometries."[4]

A close look at *Blueberries* (1986), his best known of the painted panels he pioneered in the 1980s, demonstrates why various commentators had difficulty in categorizing Schoppert's work (Figure 3.1). Abstract lines and curves decorate the surface in which the knowing viewer can recognize the characteristic tapering and swelling lines of formline design and its vocabulary of geometric elements (sections of ovoids, U-forms, and trigons). Yet where one would typically expect a carefully composed or even symmetrical design that heeds the rules and principles of northern formline design, resulting in the representation of a figure like Raven or Bear, *Blueberries* is abstract and illegible. While hints of what might be an eye or claw can be made out, the elements of each panel are cut, rotated, and rearranged into a format that does not resolve into a figurative motif. The curves of the broken formline pattern end abruptly at the edge of each of the nine panels, organized into a 3 × 3 rectilinear grid that structures the carved abstract elements within the balanced horizontal and vertical divisions. The panels are painted but instead of the highly delineated zones of red, black, and blue pigments typical of traditional Northwest Coast paintwork, Schoppert makes free use of purple, red, orange, and blue applied across the panels in thick brush strokes, stains, and drips that follow the carved contours yet also transgress their edges and limits.

Schoppert's unique painterly treatment and abstracting operations complement his carving at times yet also contradict and obfuscate the expected vocabulary of Northwest Coast visual tradition. In this way *Blueberries* moves between the binary categories against which Indigenous artists are often defined, such as traditional

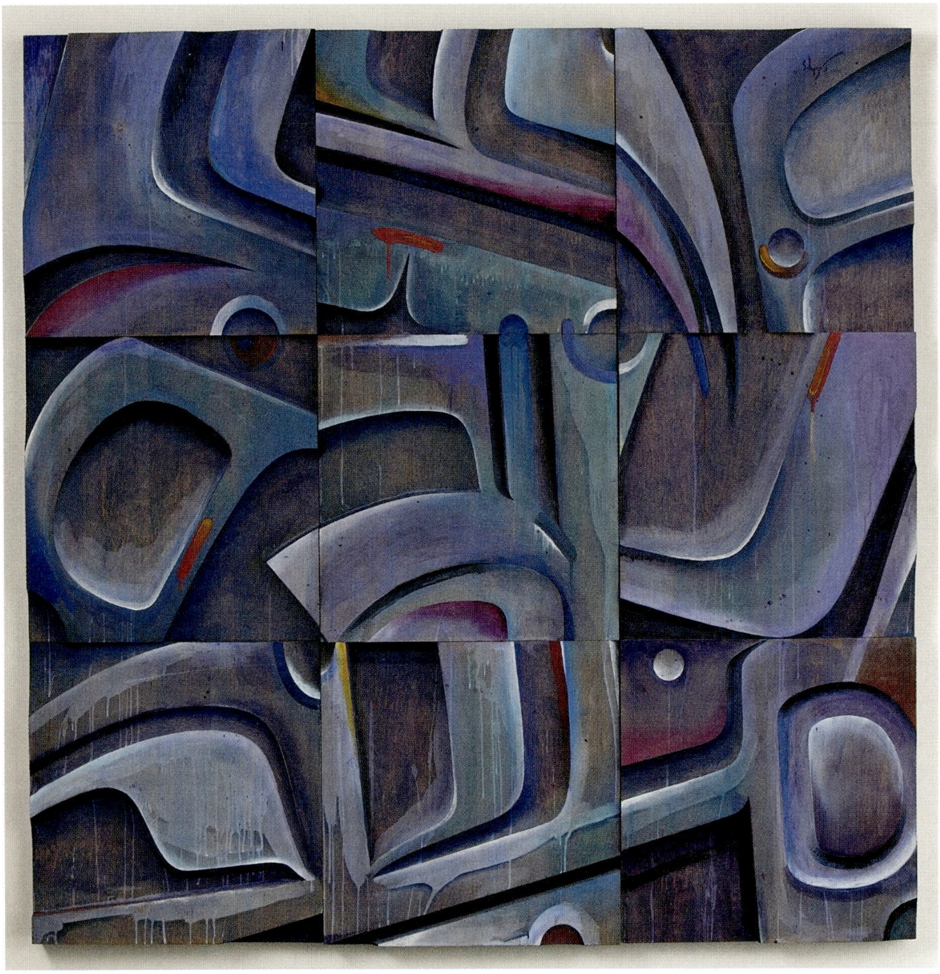

3.1. Jim Schoppert (Tlingit), *Blueberries*, 1986. Alder and paint, 71$\frac{15}{16}$ × 71$\frac{5}{8}$ × 3 inches. Anchorage Museum #1986.036.001AC. © Estate of Jim Schoppert. Photograph courtesy of the Anchorage Museum.

and innovative, or artist and carver or craftsperson, and likewise demonstrates how Schoppert could not easily be located by critics in reference to a particular modern Western art movement. The categorical confusion extended beyond style to what kind of "Native artist" Schoppert could be in the face of most restrictive and traditionalist definitions. The journalist Nancy Schmitt, sensing the changing possibilities for contemporary Native art, iterated as much when she asked in a 1981 article from the *Anchorage Times*, "Just who is the native artist? Is he the village carver who continues to carry on the tradition of his village?" In *Blueberries* Schoppert breaks the binding of cultural tradition in what Schmitt called a "very non-Tlingit way"; yet Schoppert considered this just one possibility of many for artistic creation that operated beyond such strictures.[5]

As an artist whose work is rooted in a multiplicity of traditions, sources, and visual languages, Schoppert used the legacy of Western modernism to respond to and work through the traditionalist status quo that came to define Northwest Coast art in the 1960s and 1970s. The modern renaissance, as it became known, was the revival and flourishing of forms and artistic practices based primarily on a nineteenth-century canon of objects and styles. The nineteenth century was held to be the ideal peak, a classical golden age, of Northwest Coast art, and the renaissance was a supposed rebirth of Indigenous culture following a twentieth-century decline. This myth has since been much critiqued for creating a false narrative of the death and rebirth of such artistic practices that in fact never ceased.[6]

Yet the myth encouraged a burgeoning market for Northwest Coast art in the 1960s and explorations of formline style and carving practices in relation to nineteenth-century formline principles and the emulation of past models. Schoppert used the vocabulary of Euro-American aesthetics to produce contemporary Tlingit art forms that drew on but were not limited by forms based on the past. Rather than merely adopt Western modes, materials, and techniques, he used them to inflect and translate the Indigenous visual language base of formline into a new aesthetic vocabulary for cultural expression. Through such a translation Schoppert sought to answer his repeatedly asked question: "What would have happened to Northwest Coast art if it hadn't been interrupted?"[7] Expressionist painting and geometric abstraction were tools alongside the adze and carving knife and, despite the response to his work by mystified journalists and historians, Schoppert did not see innovation as incompatible or opposed to tradition nor as "non-Tlingit."

Following art historian Aldona Jonaitis's suggestion to consider postwar Northwest Coast art not in terms of traditional and innovative but rather in terms of an "affinity with or distance from the canon of northern formline design," I propose that Schoppert's work can be understood as directly and intentionally disrupting the conventions of formline design in a way that is both Tlingit and contemporary, both innovative yet bound by concerns for the continuation of cultural tradition.[8] As opposed to recent studies of modern Northwest Coast artists such as Robert Davidson and Doug Cranmer that typically emphasizes their work as expanding beyond the limits of formline design, Schoppert makes its language illegible and abstract.[9] He does this while using and working through the legacy of twentieth-century modernist painting and Euro-American avant-garde practice to fold its painterly language onto and under the Tlingit language of form, whereby a new range of possibilities emerges from the drips, cuts, and curves of both. Schoppert's practice reflected his philosophy of art based on a universality of access and expression that extended to diverse sources in the histories of modernity and Indigenous forms, so long as one could speak their language or their code.

Schoppert, a Taku Tlingit Raven of the Ishkahittaan (Inland Frog) clan from his mother and half-German from his father, grew up in Douglas, Alaska. He began his art career at the age of twenty-five on February 26, 1973, when he bought a piece of soapstone and carved two birds out of it. He managed to sell one for $15 the next day, invested the money in more stone, made more carvings, sold those, and was soon hooked on the art-making cycle.[10] His early career consisted of carving and painting souvenirs goods and learning to create work in the classic Tlingit style through the study of art in museum collections, communities, and books, such as the archway he created for the entrance to the soapstone workshop and carving demonstration area of the Anchorage shop Cottage Crafts in 1973 (Figure 3.2).[11] The archway was copied from the reconstruction of the Chief Shakes xóots (*brown bear*) interior screen built in 1940 for the house front of the Chief Shakes Community House in Wrangell. Schoppert's study of the conventions of formline and other Native Alaskan arts was largely self-taught, and the art historian Steven Brown noted that Schoppert's "apprenticeship was with himself."[12]

In his travels across Alaska and interactions with other Native artists, Schoppert quickly became a proficient and talented carver in Tlingit form. A wooden Dukt'ootl panel (1974) in the Sealaska Corporation collection tells the story of Black Skin or Strong Man, a man who ripped a sea lion in half with his bare hands in an act of grizzly revenge. The panel is based on the house post form best known from the Klukwan Whale House and demonstrates Schoppert's adept carving skills and knowledge of the Tlingit style acquired in such a short period of time. While Schoppert hasn't filled every inch of the thin cedar panel, and the three figures (bear, sea lion, and Dukt'ootl himself) have somewhat more space between each other in their vertical arrangement than other examples of the design, Schoppert's deployment of ovoids, U-forms, and trigons throughout the figures demonstrate his early proficiency with the basic elements of Northwest Coast design.

Schoppert's formal Western-style education in fine art began with an associates of fine arts degree from Anchorage Community College in 1975, when he also spent five weeks studying bronze casting and lithography at the Instituto Allende in San Miguel de Allende, Mexico. He followed this with a BFA in sculpture and printmaking from the University of Alaska–Anchorage in 1978 and an MFA from the University of Washington in 1981. He trained in a diverse range of media and materials and studied Euro-American art history, which exposed him to new sculptural techniques and ideas that influenced his career going forward. Schoppert looked to figures from modern European sculpture such as Constantin Brancusi to make a leap into abstract geometric sculpture in the mid-1970s. His limestone sculpture *Six of One, Half Dozen of the Other* (1976) consists of two smooth white shapes: a rectangular prism standing vertically with a cylindrical quadrant resting its curved side

3.2. Jim Schoppert (Tlingit) with archway for Cottage Crafts, Anchorage, Alaska, 1973. © Estate of Jim Schoppert. Photograph courtesy of the Estate of Jim Schoppert.

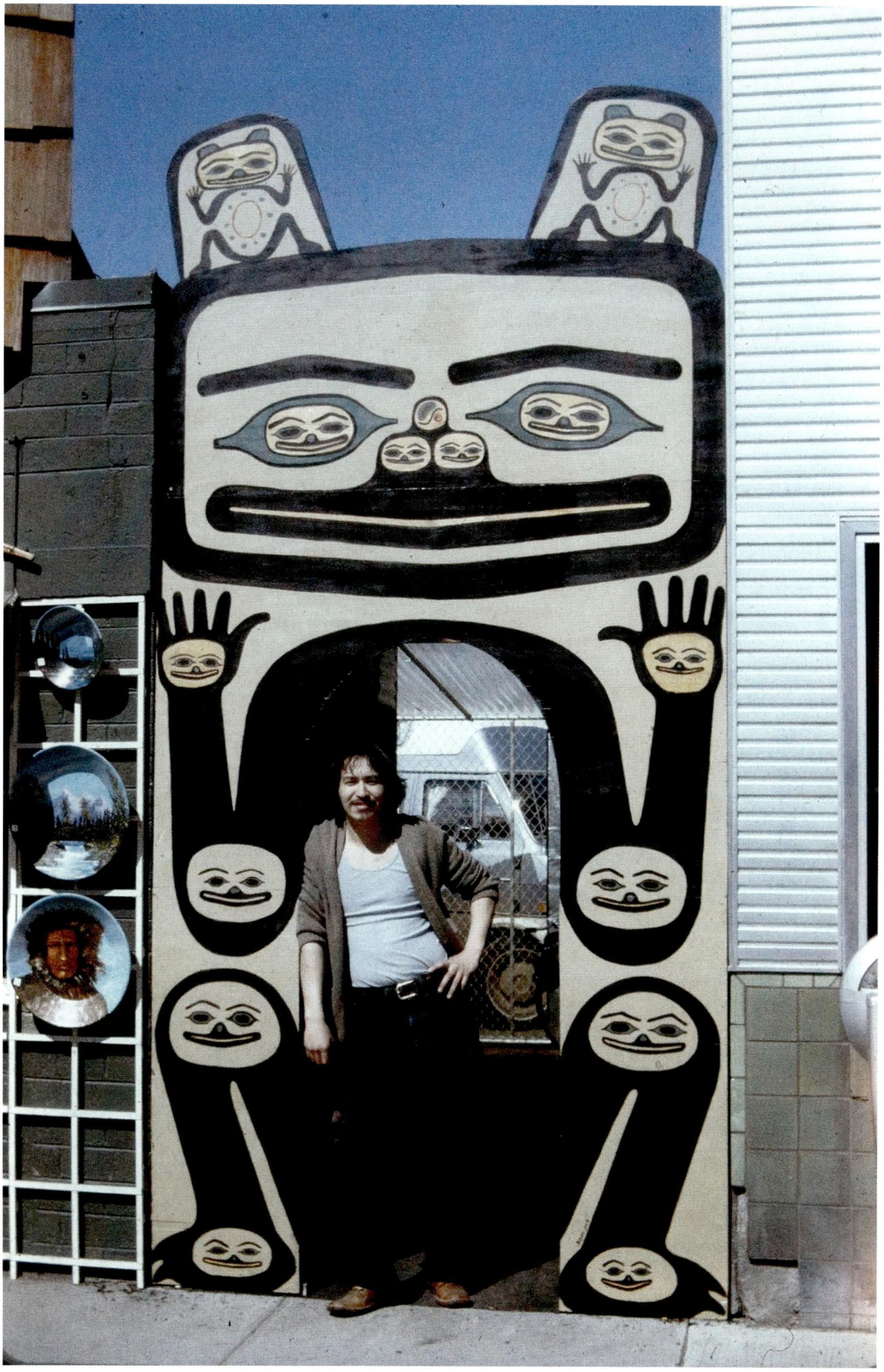

atop of the prism's upper face. Lacking any adornment, the sculpture consists simply of the relation between two counterpoised volumes, and with its lack of plinth and bare materiality the work evokes the geometric abstraction of Brancusi's early twentieth-century sculpture.

Thinking of the geometric forms that were a mainstay in minimalism, Patricia Carroll, writing for the *Alaska Journal* in 1979, dubbed Schoppert a "minimal sculptor" who was creating "minimal art in the traditional ivory of the Alaskan Native."[13] While Carroll improperly conflates minimalism with abstract sculpture in general, she notes that Schoppert cites Brancusi as his main influence. She quotes Schoppert as saying, his "minimalization comes from breaking the complex into the basic. For example, I break a bird form down to a very basic statement."[14] This is seen in the work *Two Birds* (1977), a pair of polished copper cylinders with angled faces that Schoppert described as depicting "the essence of bird forms and a depiction of the relationship of one object to another" (Figure 3.3).[15] *Two Birds* was inspired in part by the material and simple geometric "essence" of Brancusi's famed *Bird in Space*, and Schoppert frequently referenced Brancusi in his sketchbooks and notes. Schoppert valued Brancusi's graceful reductions of figurative forms to geometric essences and his truthfulness to the plastic nature of materials. Where Brancusi investigated form in marble and bronze, Schoppert emulated him in walrus ivory, soapstone, and wood. Schoppert's work *Meditation in Ivory* (1978), for example, is based on the smooth female heads of Brancusi—namely *Mademoiselle Pogany II* (ca. 1920), with a long graceful neck, oval head, and subtle arcs for eyes. Schoppert labeled a sketch of a similar work from January 1977 as "Brancusi figure," making his reverence for the modernist sculptor clear.[16]

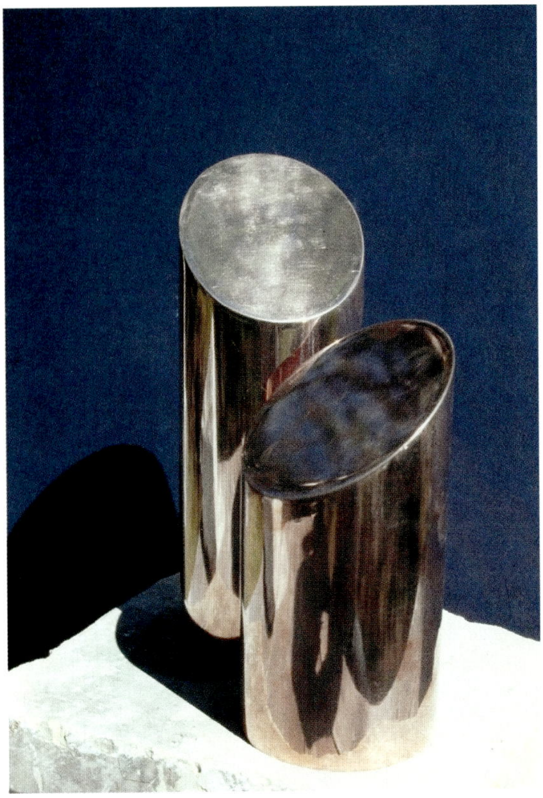

3.3. Jim Schoppert (Tlingit), *Two Birds*, 1977. Polished copper, height approx. 11 inches. Whereabouts unknown. © Estate of Jim Schoppert. Courtesy of the Estate of Jim Schoppert.

Schoppert won the $1,000 grand prize at the 1976 edition of *Earth, Fire, and Fiber*, the Anchorage Museum's biennial juried craft exhibition, with *Six of One, Half Dozen of the Other*. The abstract sculpture was his first winning entry despite having entered wooden masks and carvings in the competition for several years.[17] This positive reinforcement set him on the path of abstract sculptural production, the first mode he worked in outside typically Tlingit styles, and his experiments in sculpture informed the abstract operations of his painted panels several years later. Throughout his career Schoppert consistently made art in multiple styles and in response to numerous traditions, from seemingly traditional-style masks to ivory carvings to his abstract paintings and sculpture. He was never exclusively making modernist-inspired work and continued a diverse carving practice that reflected his ongoing interest in Tlingit and other Indigenous forms. This is demonstrated by the variety of works illustrated in Carroll's *Alaska Journal* article, which included not only the abstract sculptures *Two Birds* and *Six of One, Half Dozen of the Other* but also works such as *Totemic Tusk* (1976), a piece of walrus ivory carved all over with figures in the style of Haida argillite pipes. Such work affirms Schoppert's interest in historic Northwest Coast forms and Arctic materials. He claimed such works are representative of Native cultures in their materials, and the modern application of this material situated them at the point of what Schoppert called "the transition of Alaskan Natives from their cultures into Western civilization."[18]

To represent such a transition into "Western civilization," Schoppert deliberately invoked well-known modern artists of the European canon and experimented with their styles and techniques in his own practice. A wooden mask titled *Art Is a One-Eared Madman* (1986), for example, is formally based on a Chugach mask.[19] The mask, painted in bright blue and orange pigment, has the crooked smile and winking eye of the Chugach model but also a single oversized and bean-shaped ear on one side of its face. Its title is taken from Schoppert's three-line 1985 poem "Art," which reads "Art / is a one-eared / madman." Both mask and poem are references to Vincent van Gogh, the quintessential artist-as-tortured-genius whom Schoppert invoked not only as an inspiration and like-minded soul, but also to strategically signal his access to a non-Native artistic lineage. Likewise the titles of multiple acrylic paintings from the 1980s, such as *Miro and the Midnight Sun* (1985) and *Under Picasso Skies* (1989), make reference to Joan Miró and Pablo Picasso, the respective surrealist and cubist masters, to indicate Schoppert's fluency in the language of twentieth-century modernist styles and movements (Figure 3.4). These compositions place linear quasi-abstract figures in flat washed fields of color filled with shapes and symbols, influenced by the biomorphic forms and planar grids of Miró and Picasso respectively, although one should note the confluence of Piet Mondrian and Paul Klee, Inupiaq and Yup'ik pictographic forms, and Alaska Native basket patterns on which Schoppert draws.[20] The titles of these works evoke Alaskan landscapes, and Schoppert said of all his art that it has a "very strong mystical relationship with the land."[21]

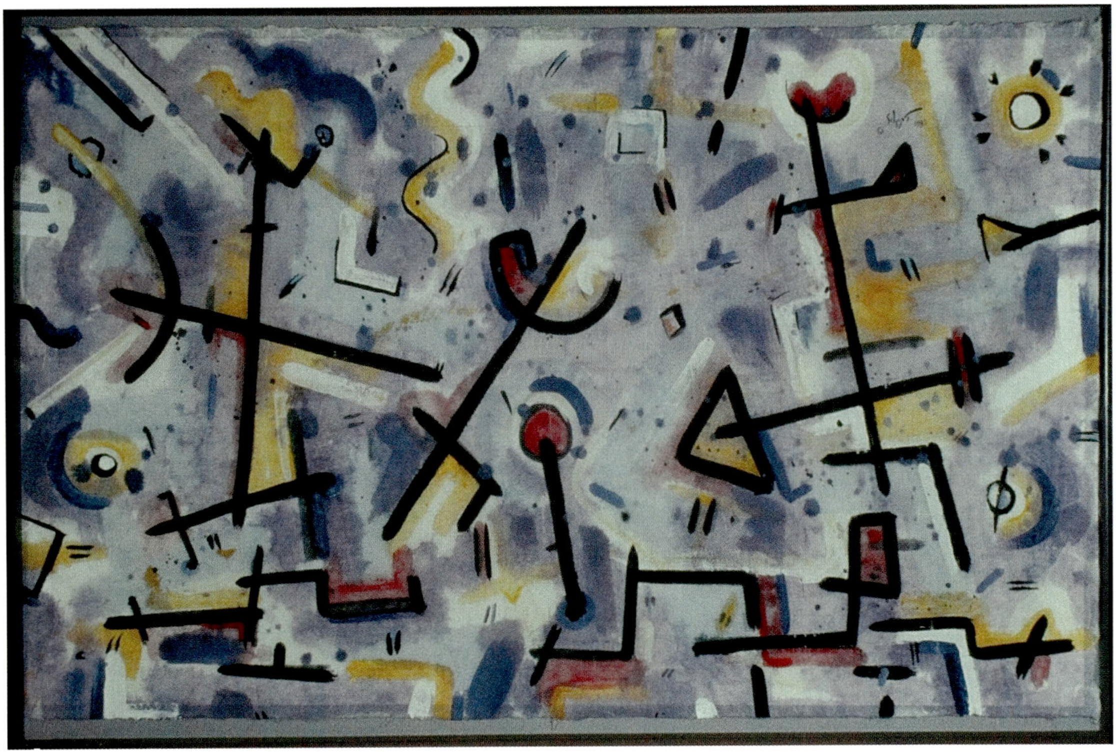

3.4. Jim Schoppert (Tlingit), *Miro and the Midnight Sun,* 1985. Acrylic on rice paper, 26 × 41 inches. Private Collection. © Estate of Jim Schoppert. Courtesy of the Estate of Jim Schoppert.

In *Miro and the Midnight Sun*, black lines scaffold the basic forms of two figures with triangular limbs and single curved lines for heads who dance against a dark purple ground with a bright white and yellow sun shining in the top right corner. The ebullient figures evoke this "mystical relationship" with the midnight landscape that flashes white and yellow around them, their linear forms ambiguously emerging from or connected to the lines defining the ground and the hovering atmospheric elements. Schoppert uses Western visual forms, in this case an abstract impulse that reduces the landscape painting and figures therein to rudimentary geometric elements, to express his own relationship to land, a fundamental component of Native art and identity. Schoppert described these figures as pictographic, and it is likely that he also had in mind the abstract forms of the petroglyphs that likewise inscribe a long Indigenous presence into the landscape of Alaska and the Pacific Northwest.[22]

In the title of *Miro and the Midnight Sun,* however, Schoppert suggests that the famed European artist is included in the visualization of this relationship to place. Schoppert was keenly aware of the Surrealists' own primitivist interest and their formal appropriations of Tlingit, Yup'ik, and Inupiaq forms, noting that he was likewise "inspired to take the pictographic and surrealistic imagery into a more modern context."[23] Did Schoppert depict Miró, whose paintings some scholars have suggested were inspired by Yup'ik masks, as one of the pictographic figures frolicking in the Alaskan landscape?[24] Alaska held an oversized position in the Surrealist Map of the World even though very few of the Europeans ever visited the region, and the "midnight sun" was a familiar motif to them.[25] As a well-known feature of the Alaskan summer, the midnight sun has long been used in tourist advertising to commercialize and exoticize the Arctic more generally. In a wryly ironic way Schoppert is fulfilling the Surrealists' desire to experience Alaska and the Indigenous Arctic by painting Miró's presence into the work, dancing beneath the midnight sun. But he also equates their desire with a major feature of the Alaskan commercial tourism industry. In addition, the titular reference to Miró can be read in terms of the incorporation of the European painter's abstract and biomorphic forms and style into Schoppert's depiction of the Alaskan landscape. In either sense, Schoppert turns the Surrealists' primitivist appropriations back around and becomes himself the appropriator. His emulations of Western artists and his stylistic borrowing were not mere indebtedness, but rather an incorporation of their legacy into his vision for contemporary Tlingit art.

Schoppert's painted abstract panels should thus be considered in the context of his avowed access to Western modernism, his staunch interest in modernist painting and abstract forms, and his proficiency with northern formline design. In 1987 he described his process for bringing these vocabularies together as a language for an uninterrupted Northwest Coast art: "Using the ideas of Northwest Coast art conventions, I divested it of cultural intent, social meaning, and accustomed appearances. In addition, I introduced freedom of color, fragmentation, abstraction and minimalization. Cultural solidarity once shattered is now seen to be rearranged in individual sections and soft, subdued and blended colors play into the composition accenting the relief and forces the eye to move about the piece. The colors used in this piece join the obvious fragmented sections, unifying the broken composition."[26]

In panels such as *Raven Opens Box of Stars* (1981), Schoppert arranged thin vertical sections of carved wood of varying length with fragmented formline elements that he rearranged in an offset manner so as to resemble the remnants of a panel put through an imagined paper shredder (Figure 3.5). While the title suggests a figurative scene, and one might catch glimpses of what appear to be fractions of claws or beaks, no singular form coalesces from this jigsaw. The Northwest Coast art conventions Schoppert speaks of are the formline designs, now fragmented, abstracted, and rearranged, united in composition not by line but by the color of the red, white, and pink acrylic paint he has applied all over the disjointed panels. It was through the introduction of the "freedom of color, fragmentation, abstraction and minimalization," Schoppert noted, that "the colors used [to] join the obvious fragmented sections, [unify] the broken composition."[27] In this case "color" refers not only to

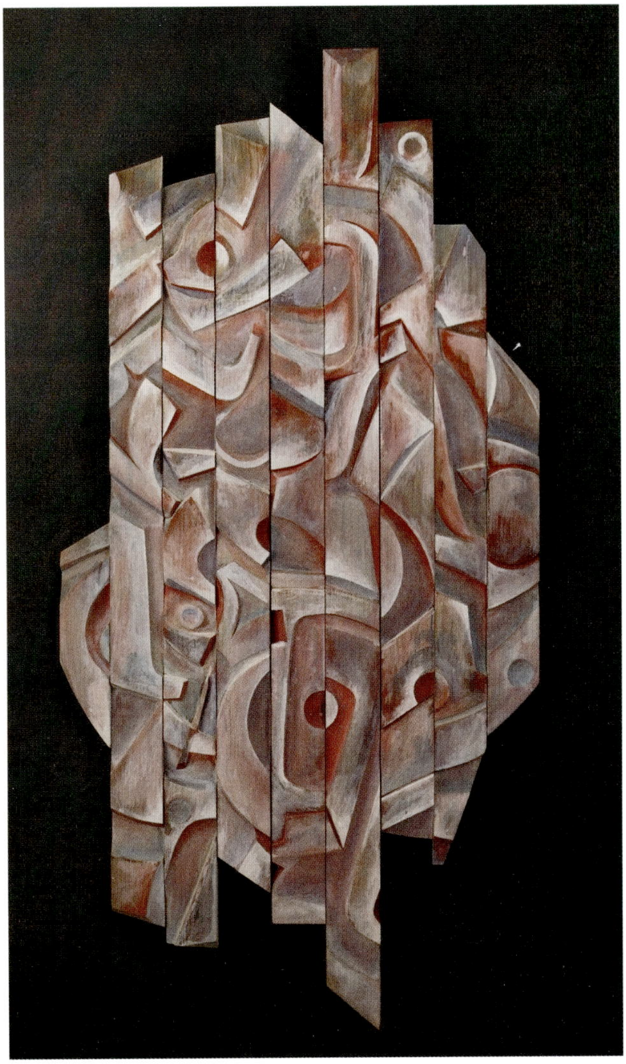

3.5. Jim Schoppert (Tlingit), *Raven Opens Box of Stars*, 1981. Red cedar and paint, 76⅜ × 39¾ inches. Anchorage Museum #1981.103.001. © Estate of James Schoppert. Courtesy of the Anchorage Museum.

the all-over color but also to the raw pigment, the brush stroke as an index, the trace of the line drawn by the hand, or the line of a drip of paint pulled across a panel by gravity, literally connecting the fragments together. As discussed in panels such as *Blueberries*, Schoppert repeatedly uses paint to connect the separate panels across their edges into whole compositions, as brushstrokes and drips span the otherwise sundered panels and curves.

The abstraction and breaking apart of the vestiges of formline reached its most extreme in works such as *Raven: In the Pink* (1984) (Figure 3.6). Also consisting of offset vertical carved wooden sections and painted in shades of purple, pink, and white, *Raven: In the Pink* is more dramatically cut and fractured. The curves and elements of formline that are disrupted but still recognizable in *Raven Opens Box of Stars* are barely visible here through the array of deep incisions and interrupted geometries.

Speaking of *Raven: In the Pink*, Schoppert said that "here all recognition of Northwest Coast imagery is destroyed. The formline is lightly referenced and is indicated with the slightest gesture of movement. . . . Although this work appears cubist-like it arrives at this conclusion from a different language base."[28] The panel is certainly cubist-like, with its linear curved cuts and gridded format, and a disruption of volume is achieved through the chiaroscuro-like shading of color that confuses depth in the carved wood with its painted surface. Recalling his explicit Picasso reference in the painting discussed earlier, *Raven: In the Pink* piles those elements of Western modernism onto the fragmented and abstracted formline to further disrupt it. However, as his working process shows, he arrived at this conclusion not from a cubist origin but rather initiated his abstract compositions from a starting point, or "language base," of cohesive Northwest Coast formline design.

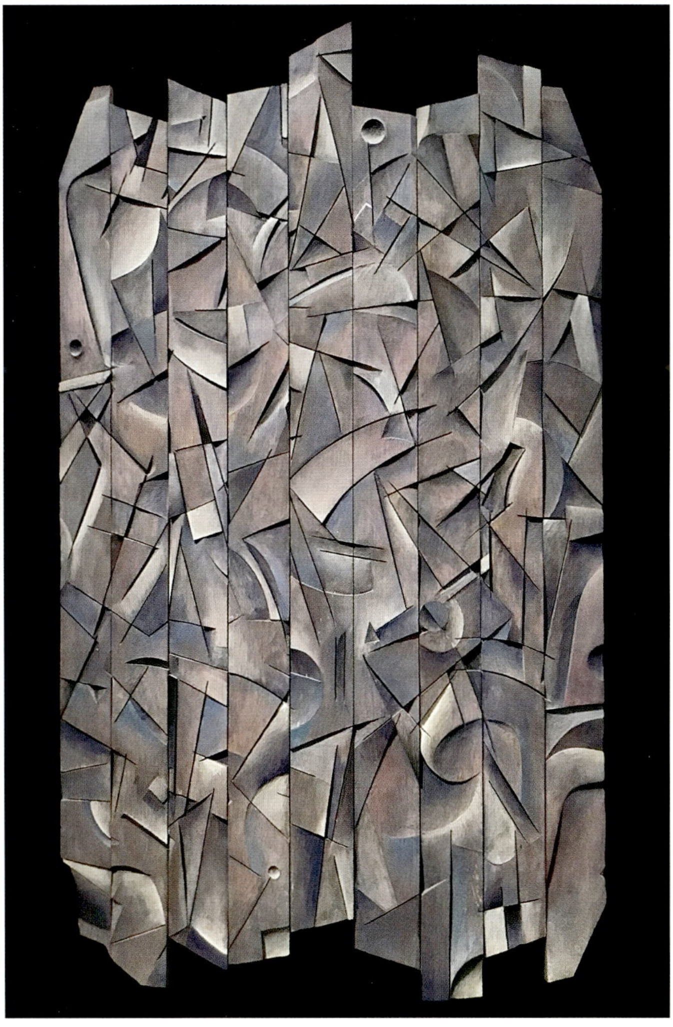

3.6. Jim Schoppert (Tlingit), *Raven: In the Pink*, 1984. Carved wood panel, paint, 65 × 40 × 4¼ inches. University of Alaska Museum of the North #UA1984-3-128. © Estate of James Schoppert. Photograph by Barry McWayne. Courtesy of UA Museum of the North.

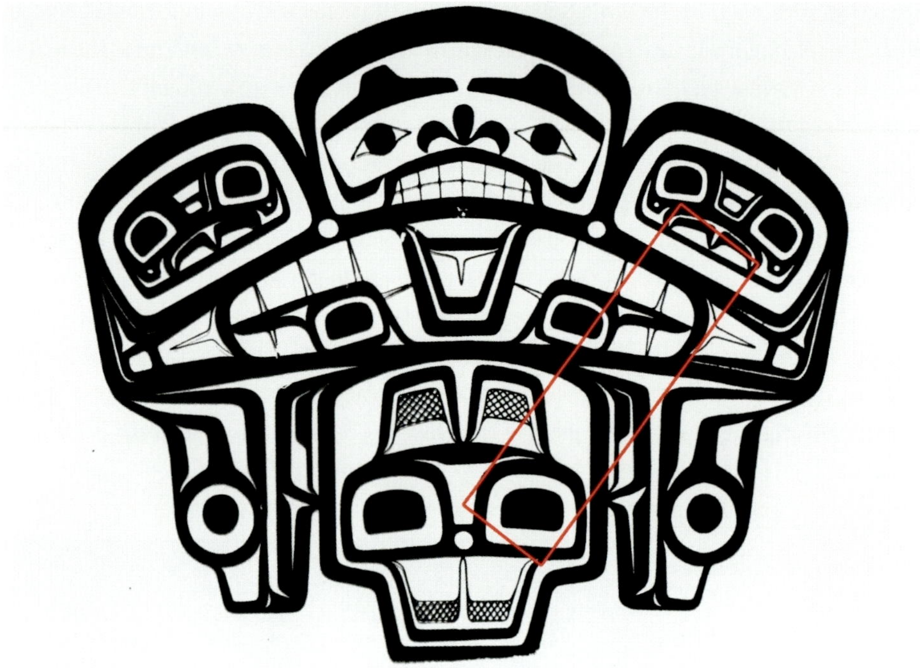

3.7. Design for *Bear Panel* (1979) by Jim Schoppert (Tlingit), with highlighted section showing the portion used in the design for *Big Sky Salmon*, 1984. © Estate of Jim Schoppert. Photograph and highlight by the author. Courtesy of the Estate of Jim Schoppert.

Schoppert initially achieved the abstraction of formline design through two operations: isolation and fragmentation, which through variations in size and arrangement allowed him a host of compositional possibilities, as his future panels demonstrate. Schoppert made this oeuvre-defining breakthrough during the course of the first year of his MFA from 1979 to 1980. This discovery provided him the means to investigate Northwest Coast formline while continuing to engage with the tenets of geometric abstraction and painting.[29] Schoppert's initial process consisted of laying a blank piece of paper with rectangular holes on top of a photocopy of a formline design to frame and isolate specific portions of the composition. In the earliest extant example he used the design for his *Bear Panel* (1979). Schoppert traced and extracted the portions of *Bear Panel* that were visible through the rectangular frames in the top sheet, set at an angle to the design itself (Figure 3.7). One portion from this example in particular spans the right-hand mouth, claw, and chest of the bear, but once removed from the overall design the isolated forms of the tracing appear as abstract forms rather than as parts of a figurative composition. Schoppert used this particular abstract extraction as the basis for a number of large-panel compositions, including his maquette for *Salmon, Halibut + Other Sealife* (1980) and the monumental thirty-two-foot long and seven-foot high carved and painted panel *Big Sky Salmon* (1984) installed at the Fort Richardson State Fish Hatchery outside of Anchorage (Figure 3.8).

With photocopies of another formline design, *Seabear Panel* (ca. 1979), Schoppert extended his isolation operation by fragmenting smaller sections of the design. Using scissors, Schoppert cut the composition into a variety of shapes: squares, rectangles, long thin strips, and ovoids. In several studies, one of which is titled *Fragments of the Seabear* (1980), Schoppert arranged these fragments into a linear series, in some cases in a straight horizontal configuration with space between the fragments, others at an offset or vertical (Figure 3.9). Larger fragments in such studies can be easily located within the original *Seabear* design, but smaller fragments are completely abstracted, legible only as elements of formline and not locatable in the larger composition from which they originated.

Once he had discovered the potential of the process of isolating and fragmenting formline compositions into abstract panels, Schoppert extended the operations into a variety of formats and sizes, including the square panel works such as *Blueberries* and the thin vertical panels of *Raven: In the Pink*. When Schoppert described this

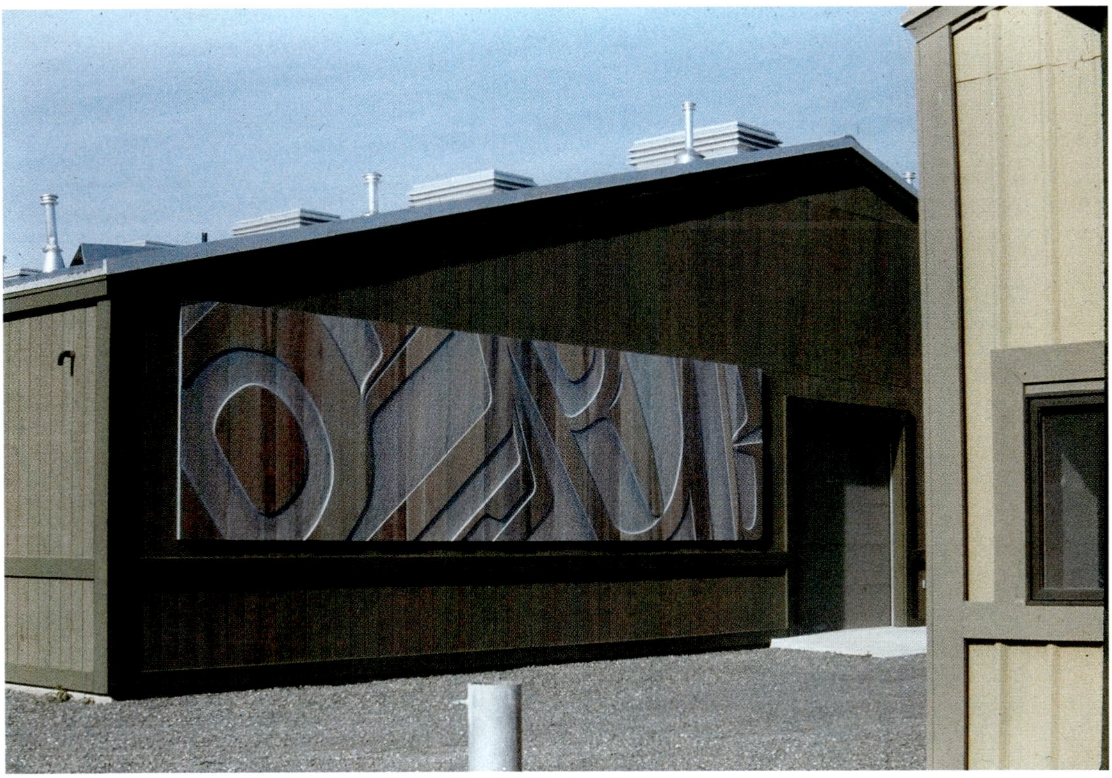

3.8. Jim Schoppert (Tlingit), *Big Sky Salmon*, 1984. Carved and painted red cedar, 96 × 384 × 2 inches. 1% for Art Commission, Fort Richardson Hatchery, Anchorage, Alaska. © Estate of Jim Schoppert. Courtesy of the Estate of Jim Schoppert.

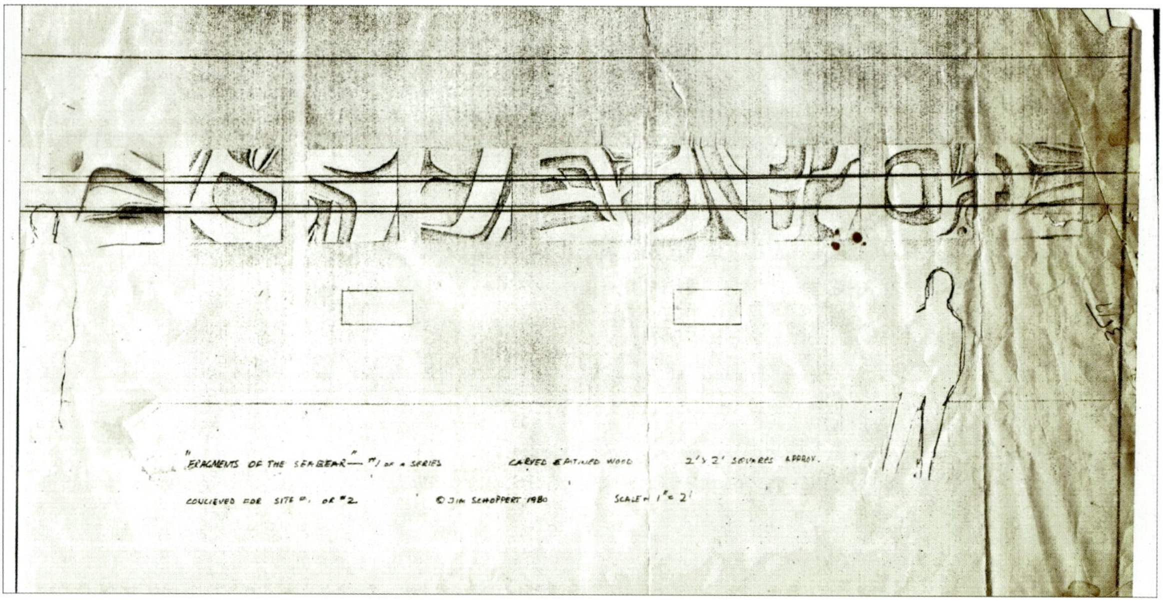

3.9. Jim Schoppert (Tlingit), *Fragments of the Seabear*, 1980. Pencil study on paper, 8½ × 14 inches. Private Collection. © Estate of Jim Schoppert. Photograph by the author. Courtesy of the Estate of Jim Schoppert.

process of abstracting formline design, he said he "got rid of the focused specific image," meaning crest figures, the signal of hereditary rights and associated intangible property.[30] Instead the panels become fragments of line, hints of ovoids, and isolated curves cropped from a larger image unknown to the viewer. How are crests and other Indigenous epistemologies and property relations read in these works that disrupt what Schoppert called the "cultural relevancy" of Northwest Coast art?[31] Is such cultural language part of Schoppert's code, or has his modernist operation disrupted the visual meaning of formline design beyond legibility?

Schoppert's interest in the disruption of formline was not a purely formal pursuit of abstraction, as in the case of his early geometric sculpture. Schoppert consistently made classical Tlingit works throughout his career alongside his abstractions, but the cutting and offset shifting of his panels suggest that he was pointedly investigating the disfiguring of formline and crest imagery. At this period in his career, scholars of Northwest Coast art such as Peter Macnair considered the "rebirth" of the formline tradition during the 1960s and 1970s to be a relearning of "the rules of the art [that were] virtually lost" and a demonstration of an understanding of those rules through the execution of "old forms of sculpture or two-dimensional design."[32] In 1983, George MacDonald recognized that the nineteenth-century system of crest imagery on Haida house fronts communicated information linking the household to the spiritual world and lineage history, and he later expanded on this to suggest that postwar Northwest Coast artists were primarily concerned with relearning formline's syntactical grammar to make that system of communicated information comprehensible again.[33]

Yet as Schoppert described earlier, by "[divesting] it of cultural intent," he intentionally made formline incomprehensible through abstraction and fragmentation at a moment in the early 1980s that the anthropologist Aaron Glass has also identified as a turning point in the renaissance discourse. The metaphor of a "rebirth" from some "ancient past" of Northwest Coast art, Glass notes, was coming under criticism from scholars favoring nuanced understandings of art emerging from a complicated network of values, institutions, and interests.[34] Schoppert came to his operations of illegibility slightly ahead of critiques of the renaissance discourse, but his art arrives at the same conclusion: by breaking what he called the "very rigid conventions established" in Northwest Coast art, he rejects the possibility of his art being read as an enclosed visual system based on a rebirth of the past and instead forces it into relation with the contemporary elements upon which he draws.[35]

Removing the cultural relevancy of the formline also involved removing the traditional use of black and red color for primary and secondary formline, precisely to unmoor and confuse the legibility of formline design. Schoppert began to think of painting as a language and means of further breaking from conventional thinking about Native art when he observed the interaction between what he considered nontraditional pigment and the carved wooden surface of his early masks. Describing how he made the mask *Of Wolves That Travel* (1983), Schoppert said:

> After I carved it out, I carefully painted it traditionally and took pictures of it and then something said, "You don't want to do this. You don't want to leave the mask looking just like that." So I applied freely, using nontraditional colors, using the whole palette of colors. . . . That was the big break from doing a mask that was locked into conventional thinking; that has to be hollowed out in back and has to fit the face and has to be painted in conventional colors to suit the culture that it's representing. By that time I think I had gotten to the point where those kinds of thoughts were intrusions on creativity and stifled free expression so they had to be done away with. I began looking at the thing I was making as modeled or textured surfaces to apply paint. They were like stretching canvas except I would carve them.[36]

Photographic documentation exists of the mask with its "traditional paint job" in black, blue, and red highlighting the helmet-like heavy lower rim and long split U-form ears. The final version of the mask departs from the standard Northwest Coast palette and is painted primarily in powder blue, orange, and brown, with red, white, and yellow highlights (Figure 3.10). These "nontraditional" colors, as Schoppert describes, allowed him to see his carvings as a surface for color with more

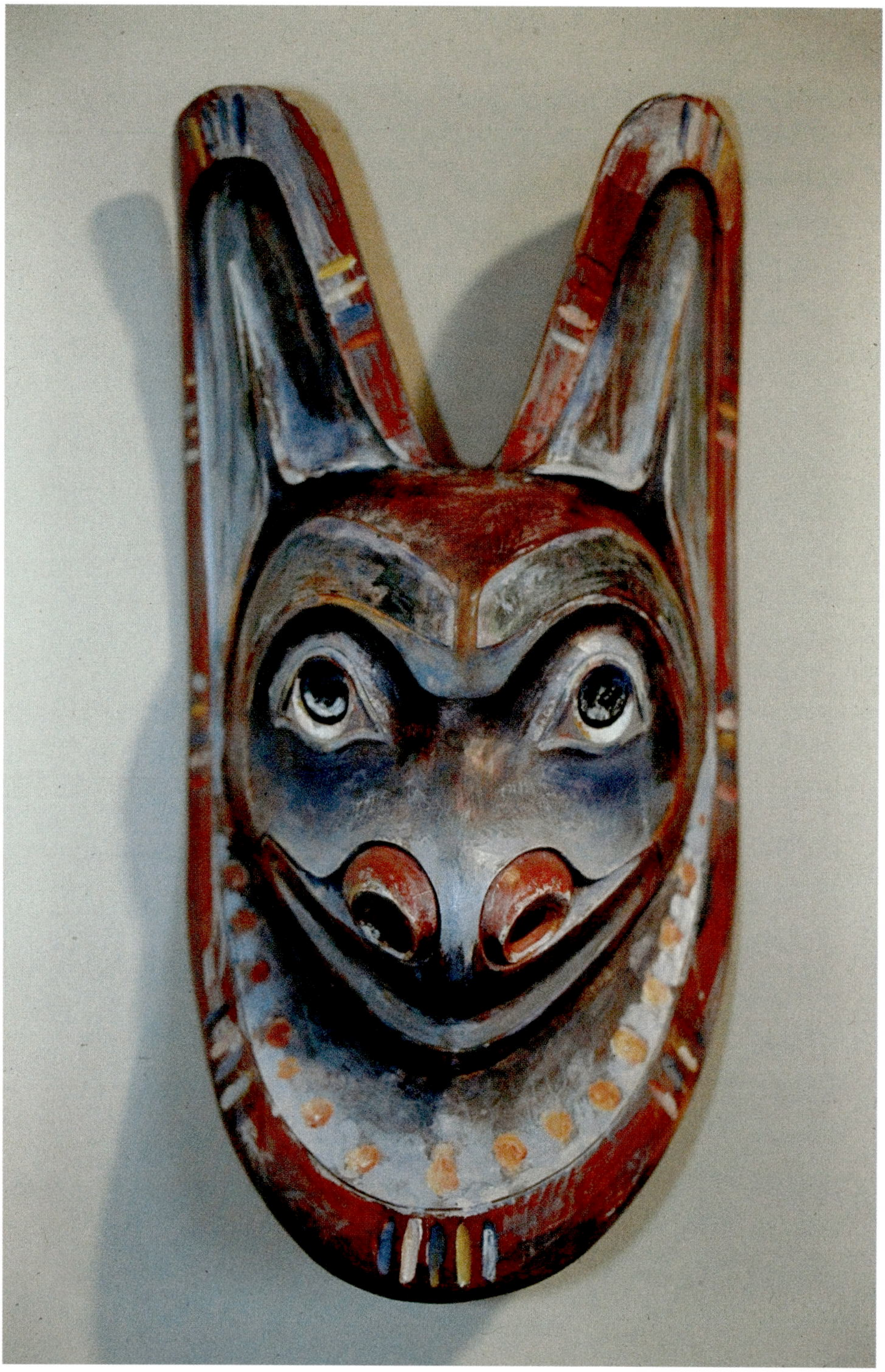

3.10. Jim Schoppert (Tlingit), *Of Wolves That Travel,* 1983. Alder, oil stain, and acrylic, 18 × 9 × 5 inches. 1% for Art Commission, Alaska State Troopers, current whereabouts unknown. © Estate of Jim Schoppert. Photograph courtesy of the Estate of Jim Schoppert.

"freedom" than the typical black, red, and copper blue of the Tlingit palette.[37] He used pigment to break from not just color traditions but also the convention of using color to codify primary, secondary, and tertiary formline and thus the traditional relationship between color and carved line in Northwest Coast design. As his panels reflect, the all-over pigmentation breaks the hierarchy of formline; no line or curve is distinguished as primary or secondary. Schoppert said he came "to the realization that what I was doing was painting. Instead of painting on canvas I was applying paint to a formed surface."[38] Painting was not only a site to engage Western modernism but also a point at which he could depart from the conventions of classical Tlingit form without resorting to strictly geometric abstraction.

A 1984 photograph of Schoppert in front of his monumental work *Raven's Descent* (1984) demonstrates the play of paint across his panels' surfaces in relation to their ambitious scale (Figure 3.11). In the photo Schoppert rests his hand against the wood, physically connecting his body to the mark-making gestures of his brushstrokes, splashes, and drips that he painted while the piece was alternately lying horizontally on the ground and standing upright. One large brushstroke follows the peak of the curving formline's swell at the top of the panel second from left, while drips streak into the recessed space below it. The horizontal mode of production and drips and splatters recall Jackson Pollock, and Schoppert's mural-sized composition is directly evoking with the monumental scale Pollock's best-known works. The photograph of Schoppert echoes the famous portrait of Pollock in front of his *Mural* (1943) painted for Peggy Guggenheim. Art historian Jackson Rushing has shown how the modern New York school movements such as abstract expressionism were founded on primitivist principles with forms appropriated from Indigenous art, particularly from the Northwest Coast.[39]

Here, Schoppert meets Pollock head on as he did with the Surrealists, using the forms and scale of the primitivist to create new contemporary possibilities for the once so-called primitive art. He uses the drips and splatters of Pollock to claim a place in relation to the legacy of modernism. Despite the insistence of the critics of his time, Schoppert's art is not about "making the traditional modern." He is responding to the modern and using it as a tool to break apart formline, rearrange it, and make a new visual language out of the remains. Layered over and under the abstracted ovoids and U-forms is the gestural application of abstract color, the painterly expression of abstract expressionism. Both Tlingit and modernist forms cohabit his art as a third zone in which multiple visual sovereignties are nested and operative throughout these painted panels.[40]

Today, Schoppert's panels are often discussed as visual metaphors for the breaking-up of Tlingit culture by colonization and cohesive wholeness of a culture that remains strong and unified, if different from what it was in the past.[41] The unifying force in Schoppert's work is abstraction, color, and brushstrokes, sourced in Western modernism and inspired by Alaskan Native forms. An uninterrupted

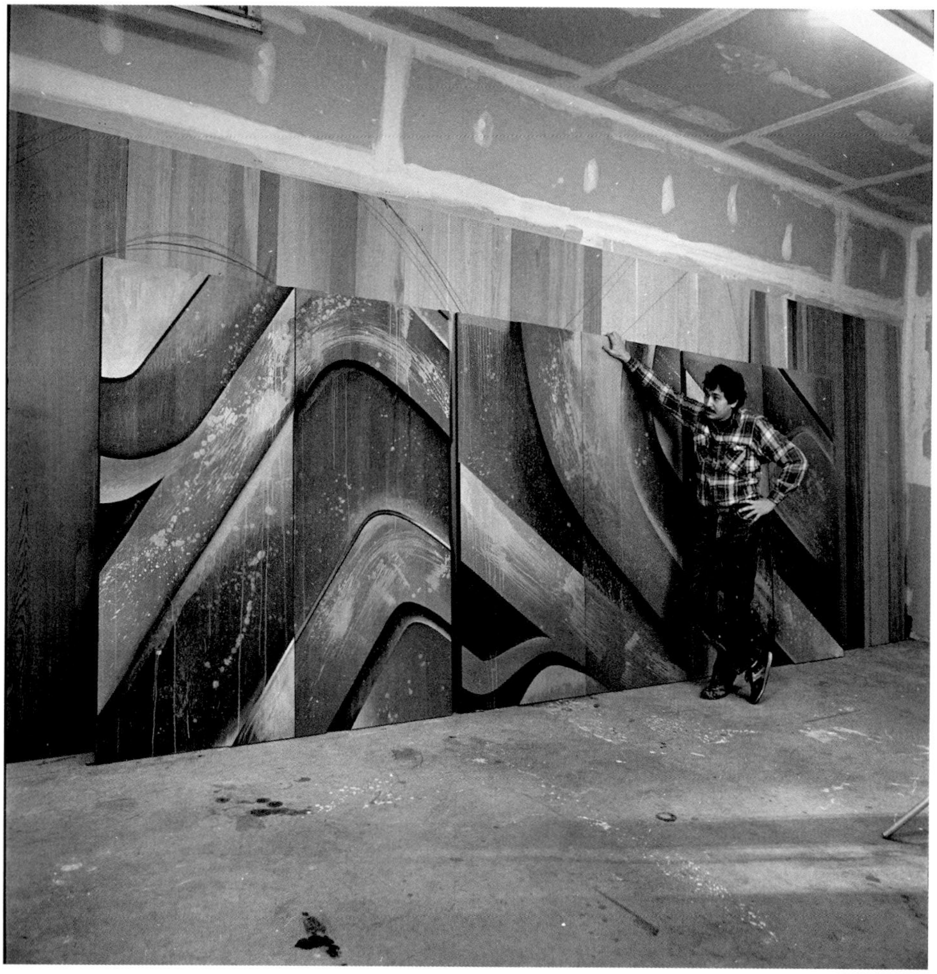

3.11. Mary Randlett, *James Schoppert, Tlingit Artist, January 1984*, 1984. Black-and-white photograph. Courtesy of University of Washington Libraries, Special Collections, UW26560.

Northwest Coast art, in that case, seems to be synonymous with one that is dynamic in what it adapts and adopts from Euro-American tradition to suit its own needs. Schoppert both worked through and responded to Western modernism as much as the forms of Tlingit tradition, and in doing so he found new possibilities for the future of Tlingit forms and expanded the conception of what both the traditional and modern could be in their meeting.

NOTES

This chapter is dedicated to the memory of Sidiya Schoppert, without whom this research would not have been possible. I am grateful for her generosity and the care she dedicated to her father's legacy, alongside the support of Shevea Schoppert and the extended Schoppert family. I thank Aldona Jonaitis and Kathryn Bunn-Marcuse for their close reading and insightful comments on this chapter and particularly thank Kathryn Bunn-Marcuse for opening her space to allow essential archival research to be conducted.

Epigraph: Robert James Schoppert, "Of Clouds and Sacred Cows: A Personal Interpretation of Alaskan Native Cultural Art," Alaska Anthropological Association Annual Meeting, Anchorage, March 13–14, 1987.

1 Bill Berkson, "Seattle Sites," *Art in America*, July 1986, 79.

2 George C. Longfish and Joan Randall, "Runners in the Tribe," in *New Directions Northwest: Contemporary Native American Art* (Olympia, WA: Evergreen State College, 1987), 17.

3 Gerhard Hoffman, "Native American Artists in the Context of Modern and Postmodern Art," in *The Arts of the North American Indian: Native Traditions in Evolution*, edited by Edwin L. Wade, 257–82 (New York: Hudson Hills Press, 1986), 272.

4 Jan Ingram, "Sculptor Shows New playfulness, Wit," *Anchorage Daily News*, May 15, 1983, D-4; Deborah Everett, "Jim Schoppert," in *Encyclopedia of Native American Artists*, edited by Deborah Everett and Elayne Zorn, 187–90 (Westport, CT: Greenwood Press, 2008); Patricia Carroll, "Jim Schoppert: Minimal Sculptor," *Alaska Journal* 9, no. 2 (Spring 1979): 88–91; and Deloris T. Ament, "Old Visions, New Forms," *Seattle Times*, April 3, 1989, F1 and F4.

5 Nancy Schmitt, "Artists: A Blend of Culture, Contemporary Style," *Anchorage Times*, February 8, 1981, I-2.

6 Aaron Glass, "Was Bill Reid the Fixer of a Broken Culture or a Culture Broker?" in *Bill Reid and Beyond: Expanding on Modern Native Art*, edited by Karen Duffek and Charlotte Townsend-Gault, 190–206 (Vancouver: Douglas and McIntyre, 2004); Aldona Jonaitis, *Art of the Northwest Coast* (Vancouver: Douglas & McIntyre, 2006); and Aaron Glass, "History and Critique of the 'Renaissance' Discourse," in *Native Art of the Northwest Coast: A History of Changing Ideas*, edited by Charlotte Townsend-Gault, Jennifer Kramer, and Ki-Ke-In, ,487–517 (Vancouver: University of British Columbia Press, 2013).

7 Jan Steinbright, "Interview: Jim Schoppert," *Journal of Alaska Native Arts* (March–April 1987); and Schoppert, "Of Clouds and Sacred Cows."

8 Aldona Jonaitis, "Contemporary Northwest Coast Art: The Canon and Beyond," in *Northwest Coast Representations: New Perspectives on History, Art, and Encounters*, edited by Andreas Etges, Viola König, Rainer Hatoum, and Tina Brüderlin, 169–88 (Berlin: Dietrich Reimer Verlag, 2014).

9 Karen Duffek, ed., *Robert Davidson: The Abstract Edge* (Vancouver: University of British Columbia Museum of Anthropology, 2004); Barbara Brotherton, Sheila Farr, and John Haworth, *Robert Davidson: Abstract Impulse* (Seattle: Seattle Art Museum, 2013); and Jennifer Kramer, *K'esu': The Art and Life of Doug Cranmer* (Vancouver: Douglas & McIntyre, 2012).

10 Schoppert, "Of Clouds and Sacred Cows."

11 Reproduced in "Tlingit Design Decorates Doorway of Local Shop," *Anchorage Daily Times*, May 24, 1973. In the article Schoppert goes by the name "Dom-Yetz" to emphasize his Indigenous identity during this early period in which he primarily carves traditionalist work.

12 Steven C. Brown, "Of Eyes and Teeth and Sacred Clouds: Jim Schoppert—Releasing the Individual," in *Instrument of Change: James Schoppert Retrospective*, edited by Dave Nicholls, 17–27 (Anchorage: Anchorage Museum of History and Art, 1997), 17.

13 Carroll, "Jim Schoppert," 89.

14 Carroll, "Jim Schoppert," 89.

15 Carroll, "Jim Schoppert," 89.

16 This sketch is followed by a lengthy entry in his sketchbook dated February 28, 1977, and titled "Brancusi's Beginning of the World/Schoppert's Bird Egg," in which Schoppert compares the genesis of his artistic practice to Brancusi's *Beginning of the World* (ca. 1920),

including a sketch of the Brancusi sculpture. Robert James Schoppert personal archives, Box #5 "Jim's Sketchbook," private collection.

17 The work is reproduced on the exhibition catalog's cover, though it is labeled as "Untitled" within. Schoppert submitted his *Snowy Owl* mask (1973) to the third annual *Earth, Fire, and Fibre Show* in 1973, a white mask with feathered hoops loosely based on Yup'ik forms, which only placed second in the wood division. *Earth, Fire and Fibre VII*, exhibition catalog, Anchorage Historical and Fine Arts Museum, November 7–December 5, 1976.

18 Carroll, "Jim Schoppert," 88.

19 Steve Henrikson, "Art Is a One-Eared Mad Man: The Art of Jim Schoppert," in *Instrument of Change: James Schoppert Retrospective*, edited by Dave Nicholls, 4–15 (Anchorage, AK: Anchorage Museum of History and Art, 1997), 8.

20 While Miró, Picasso, and Eskimo pictographic traditions are most often cited in reference to such paintings, the kernel of the dashes and stick figure–like compositions can be found in a sketch intended as a study for an ivory sculpture and labeled as "reminiscent of Mondrian's trees" (though more accurately reminiscent of Mondrian's first forays into the abstraction of building facades, piers, and oceans). Schoppert listed alongside the sketch a number of material constraints but evidently resolved the constraints on the sculptural form by translating his idea to painting.

21 Steinbright, "Interview: Jim Schoppert."

22 Schoppert described his paintings as works "which include pictographic representation, mask images, abstraction, and anything else I can think of to record." Schoppert, "Of Clouds and Sacred Cows." Thank you to Kathryn Bunn-Marcuse for suggesting the resonance with petroglyphs as a line of further research.

23 Schoppert, "Of Clouds and Sacred Cows," n.p.

24 The influence of Yup'ik and other Alaskan Indigenous art on Joan Miró is contested, but in this case Miró operates a stand-in for surrealism's primitivist interests more generally. See Elizabeth Cowling, "The Eskimos, the American Indians, and the Surrealists," *Art History* 1, no. 4 (1978): 484–500; Aldona Jonaitis, "Creations of Mystics and Philosophers: The White Man's Perceptions of Northwest Coast Indian Art from the 1930s to the Present," *American Indian Culture and Research Journal* 5, no. 1 (1981): 8–17; Evan Maurer, "Dada and Surrealism," in *Primitivism in 20th Century Art: Affinity of the Tribal and the Modern*, edited by William Rubin, 541–81 (New York: Museum of Modern Art 1984); James Clifford, "On Ethnographic Surrealism," in *The Predicament of Culture: Twentieth Century Ethnography, Literature and Art* (Cambridge, MA: MIT Press, 1988), 117–51; and Marie Mauzé, "Surrealists and the New York Avant-Garde, 1920–60," in *Native Art of the Northwest Coast*, edited by Townsend-Gault, Kramer, and Ki-Ke-In, 270–303.

25 The Surrealists were interested in the contradictory nature of the midnight sun and its ability to, like the eclipse, cast ambiguous and nonindexical shadows. In André Breton's *Manifestos of Surrealism* (Ann Arbor: University of Michigan Press, 1969), 86, the artist referred to himself as tanning only "in the midnight sun." Tristan Tzara, responding to a questionnaire by Breton published in the May 1933 issue of *Le surréalisme au service de la révolution*, described the time of day in Giorgio de Chirico's painting *The Enigma of a Day* (1914) as "Midnight sun." Mary Ann Caws, in *The Surrealist Look: An Erotics of Encounter* (Cambridge, MA: MIT Press, 1997), 214, notes that for the Surrealists a "sudden revelation like the sun at midnight" or "a baroque-surrealist lightning flash" fulfills the conditions of unimpeded invention through chance. Also see Denis Hollier, "Surrealist Precipitates: Shadows Don't Cast Shadows," translated by Rosalind Krauss, *October* 69 (1994): 111–32.

26 Schoppert, "Of Clouds and Sacred Cows," n.p.

27 Schoppert, "Of Clouds and Sacred Cows," n.p.

28 Schoppert, "Of Clouds and Sacred Cows," n.p.

29 Material evidence of this experimental breakthrough is present in Robert James Schoppert personal archives, Box #5 "Jim's Sketchbook," private collection. See Christopher Green, "Masked Moderns: Northwest Coast Native Art Beyond Revival," PhD diss. (in progress), The Graduate Center, CUNY.

30 Robert Breunig and Erin Younger, "The Second Biennial Native American Fine Arts Invitational," *American Indian Art* 11, no. 2 (Spring 1986): 60–65, 65.

31 Breunig and Younger, "Second Biennial," 65.

32 Peter Macnair, Alan L. Hoover, and Kevin Neary, *The Legacy: Continuing Traditions of Canadian Northwest Coast Indian Art* (Victoria: British Columbia Provincial Museum, 1980).

33 George MacDonald's insistence on the scholarly contribution to this revival is evident when he wrote that through the "interplay between anthropologists, art historians, and the new generation of artists, this grammar has been revived and extended." George MacDonald, *Haida Art* (Seattle: University of Washington Press, 1996), 225.

34 Glass, "History and Critique of the 'Renaissance' Discourse," 490.

35 Steinbright, "Interview: Jim Schoppert."

36 Jim Schoppert quoted in Alvin Amason, "Jim Schoppert," *Journal of Alaska Native Arts* (July–August–September 1992): 4–5.

37 Schoppert, "Of Clouds and Sacred Cows."

38 Schoppert, "Of Clouds and Sacred Cows," n.p.

39 Jackson Rushing W. III, *Native American Art and the New York Avant Garde: A History of Cultural Primitivism* (Austin: University of Texas Press, 1995), 169–90.

40 Audra Simpson suggests that an Indigenous sovereign political order can exist nested within a sovereign state, and I suggest that visual sovereignty, after Jolene Rickard's conception, can likewise exist nested within and beside a settler aesthetic. See Audra Simpson, *Mohawk Interruptus: Political Life across the Borders of Settler States* (Durham, NC: Duke University Press, 2014); and Jolene Rickard, "Visualizing Sovereignty in the Time of Biometric Sensors," *South Atlantic Quarterly* 110, no. 2 (Spring 2011): 465–86.

41 Jonaitis, *Art of the Northwest Coast*, 273–74.

CHAPTER 4

From "Artifakes" to "Surrogates"

THE REPLICATION OF NORTHWEST COAST CARVING BY NON-NATIVES

Janet Catherine Berlo and Aldona Jonaitis

REPLICATION HAS LONG BEEN A VITAL PART OF ARTISTIC PRACTICE ON THE Northwest Coast. Carvers have remade masks and poles that had worn out or been lost. They were given—or paid for—the rights to carve imagery that belonged to a particular individual or family, both locally and across geographic regions. But since the mid-twentieth century, carvers lacking blood ties to Tlingit, Kwakwa̱ka̱'wakw, Haida, and other communities have played diverse roles in the transmission of these artistic traditions. For example, some have carved simply for the market; others have earned varying degrees of acceptance within certain families and communities, acceptance that has evolved with the passage of time and the rise of a new generation of artists and culture brokers. While a short chapter cannot cover this topic exhaustively, we seek to examine some key moments concerning the replication of Northwest Coast imagery, from useful objects that some non-Native makers have unabashedly called "artifakes," to objects made both for sale in the marketplace and for use within Native communities, to objects made in Indonesia as outright fakes, to a new twenty-first-century version of replication carried out as a cross-cultural scientific experiment.[1]

Should non-Natives make Native-style art? Today, many people would unequivocally say no to that question. Sometimes, however, it is not that simple. Some non-Native carvers have been validated as kin in ceremony, in part because of their knowledge of and respect for these artistic traditions. Others made work before protocols were as strict as they are now about cross-cultural "appropriation." While technical knowledge can be acquired without regard to ethnic affiliation, it must be asked, what are the consequences to Native people of market competition from non-Natives artists? Does the work of non-Natives in the marketplace for Northwest Coast carving simply continue the unauthorized appropriation of Native culture by outsiders that is the legacy of nineteenth-century colonialism? What about Northwest Coast–style work made by Native artists not from that region? Or artists who used to be considered Native but whose identities are now open to question? Finally, what about work made by machine in a high-tech cross-cultural collaboration?

These are not simply academic queries; they are essential to the management of political relations between Indigenous and settler societies. Regardless of their connection to culture, it can be argued that most white artists who engage in and sell Northwest Coast–style carving are economically benefiting from Native heritage and, in doing so, earning income that should go to Native carvers. But an informed marketplace might well take care of this problem. Many discerning consumers prefer that artists have authentic knowledge about and experience participating in Native ceremonies to validate their work. The art market—often influenced by Native pressure—has responded with practical solutions, including careful listing of Native artists' tribal affiliations or narratives of their cultural experiences and knowledge, or amending "Northwest Coast *style*" to the work of non-Native artists.[2] These tactics help manage—but do not solve—the political or ethical problems involved in this particular appropriative dynamic. Regardless of their knowledge about the cultures, or their skill in producing stylistically accurate objects, the connection through inheritance to a long-standing artistic tradition distinguishes Native from non-Native artists.

"Artifakes": Carvings by Non-Native Artists

We open this chapter with a carving that exemplifies the intercultural complexity of our topic. In 1976, in honor of the United States bicentennial, the Sitka National Historical Park sponsored a design competition for a pole to be raised there. A committee chaired by Ellen Lang (Tlingit), who was both the superintendent of the park and chair of the Sitka Native Cultural Center Board of Directors, chose non-Native carver Duane Pasco for the commission.[3] The pole (Figure 4.1) is a linear visual narrative that reads from bottom to top. At the base is a precontact Native man holding both a halibut hook and a rattle as emblems of sustenance and ceremony. Above, Raven and Eagle appear, representing the two moieties of the Tlingit. Higher up, a white man with a gun, a document, and a cross represents the three main strategies of colonial interference. At the top a contemporary Native figure holds two staffs, one richly carved in honor of the complexity of Indigenous cultural history, the other unfinished, suggesting an open-ended future. Pasco has written that he intended to represent "a pan-coastal Native history."[4] Today, this pole stands directly in front of the Sitka National Historic Park's visitor center, with a plaque explaining its imagery but not mentioning the non-Native status of its carver.

Were such a competition held today, more than forty years later, it is unthinkable that the commission would be given to a non-Native artist. But in 1976, Pasco (b. 1932) had been making Northwest Coast–style art for many years and had taught in 1969 at the Gitanmaax School of Northwest Coast Indian Art (also known as 'Ksan)

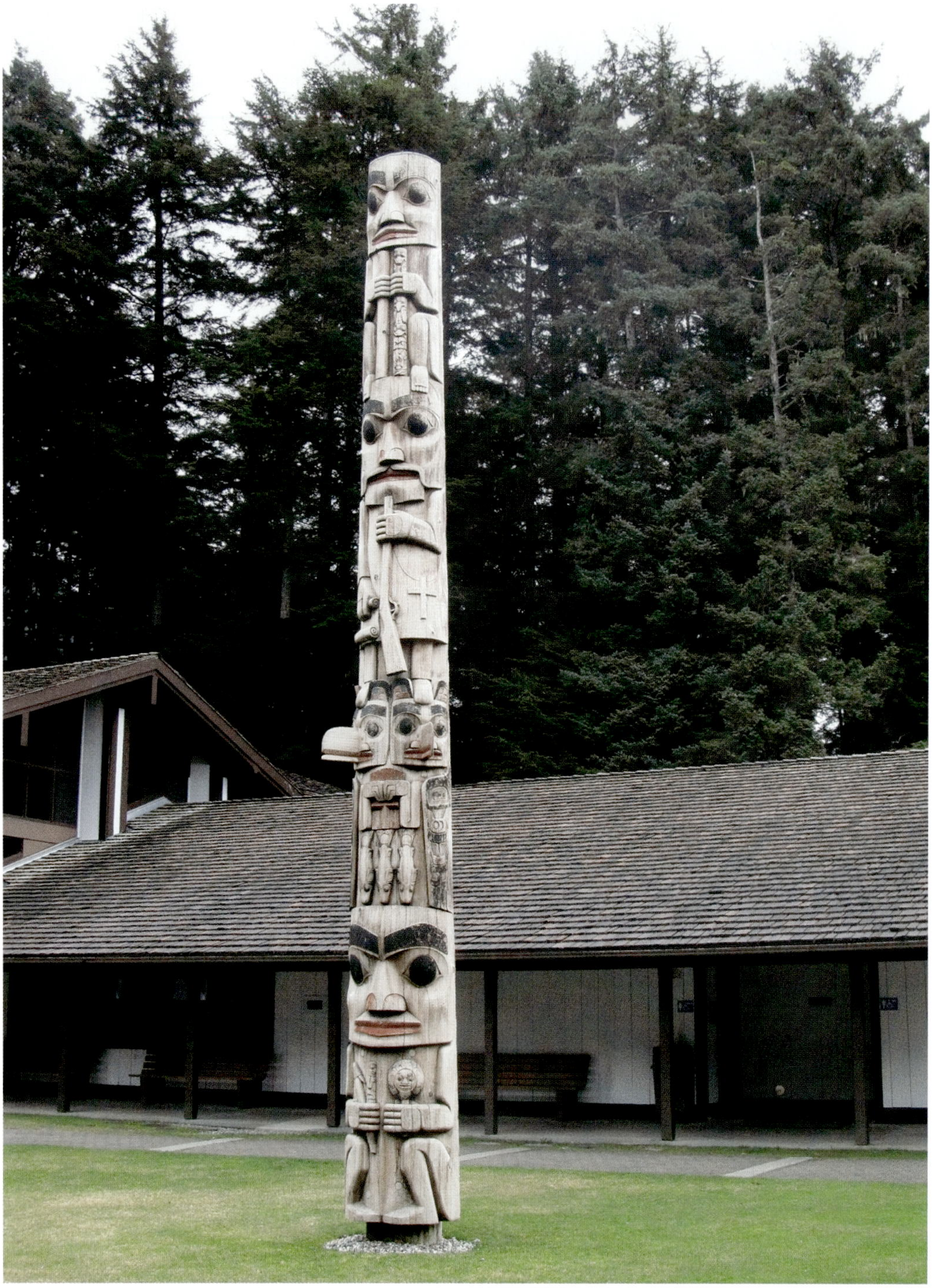

4.1. Duane Pasco, *Bicentennial Totem Pole*, 1976. Western red cedar, height 27 feet. Sitka National Historical Park, Alaska. Photograph by Denny Rofkar.

in Hazelton, British Columbia, where the Gitksan people honored him with a Naxnox (or *spirit being*) name. Pasco was one of many carvers, both Native and non-Native, who helped educate the next generation of Native carvers about formline style.[5] By the 1970s, Pasco earned his living through carving, so his work exemplifies precisely what some Native artists and commentators object to: a non-Native carver economically benefiting from Native heritage. According to their reasoning, such income should go only to those artists who are direct cultural heirs to a particular tradition. Pasco, in writing about his career, is generally unapologetic about working in Northwest Coast style: "I am an artist . . . I don't need papers to prove who I am, what I am, or what I do," though he does say that he stopped making Hamatsa masks in 1985 because "the characters they represent are the prerogatives of members of the Kwakwa̱ka̱'wakw people, and as such I don't feel comfortable in their manufacture for the marketplace."[6]

Pasco became a skilled Native-style artist during the so-called Northwest Coast Renaissance. By the end of the nineteenth century, the precise, elegant formline style that characterized northern Northwest Coast art had been gradually replaced by less complex paintings and carvings made both for ceremonial use and the souvenir market. Artist and art historian Bill Holm (Swedish American, b. 1925) wanted to understand how artists had created the kinds of eighteenth- and nineteenth-century works of art found in museums. In the 1950s he began deciphering the formal rules of historical arts, making objects that conformed to those rules, and published his findings in the brilliant exegesis *Northwest Coast Indian Art: An Analysis of Form*.[7] This publication provided the vocabulary for articulating the aesthetic rules for understanding (and re-creating) historic Northern formline style.[8] Both Native and non-Native artists studied this book and worked with Holm to learn how to make art that adhered more closely to these prototypes. An explosion of artistic creativity followed.

It is important to emphasize that Holm's work in this area was educational rather than commercial; indeed he almost never sold artworks and only did so when he was starting out. A firm believer that making something provides the best way of understanding it, he embarked on crafting Northwest Coast–style objects to comprehend them more fully. Holm is a self-effacing man and has often spoken of his carvings as "artifakes," for he has never wanted them confused with objects made by Indigenous carvers with inherited rights.[9] While many of us repeatedly heard him use this word, it is hard to find in print, for Holm seldom wrote about his own work.[10] Holm's use of the term "artifakes" casually denigrates the importance of his work and distinguishes it from the towering artistic achievements of the past. We have never heard any other non-Native carvers refer to their work in this humble fashion.

Belying the self-deprecating term "artifakes" is the fact that Holm's carvings are masterful, well-researched copies that have proved useful for understanding the history of Northwest Coast art. In 1970, Holm made a replica of a Dzunuk'wa figure that had originally stood in the village of Gwa'yasdams on Gilford Island and was known only in photographs and a painting (Figure 4.2). This copy provides an excellent example of an otherwise lost artwork that serves to enhance our understanding of Kwakwa̱ka̱'wakw art. Holm's carvings provided his students and others with the experience of touching and even using works to better understand their formal and material characteristics.[11]

Holm spent a great deal of time in Kwakwa̱ka̱'wakw territory and was highly regarded by numerous Native people there. His relationship with Kwakwa̱ka̱'wakw carver Mungo Martin (1879–1962) began in 1953, and in 1957, Mungo bestowed upon Holm the first of his many Kwakwa̱ka̱'wakw names and a Hamatsa position.[12] As an invited participant in potlatches and Hamatsa dances, Holm has always worn the objects he made. While it is becoming increasingly common for a younger, more politicized generation to decry the participation of outsiders in ceremony and in the making of regalia, it is important to know that this is not the only view. When asked about Holm's place today, seated among the chiefs at potlatches, Chief Calvin Hunt of Fort Rupert replied: "During my childhood, even before my teens, I knew of Bill and admired his work. It was only later I found out he was adopted by Peter Smith, who is my Grandmother Abaya's brother. There were very few non-Native artists around at the time. Our Elders embraced his commitment to our culture, and he still has the passion to learn. He is always willing to share his knowledge, which is the same teachings of our Elders and Ancestors."[13] Holm has honored Native culture by researching and analyzing their arts deeply and with respect, and he has been honored in return numerous times by the Kwakwa̱ka̱'wakw and other Native peoples for studying and participating in their cultural practices in a respectful way, and for unstintingly sharing his research with community members.[14]

A small number of non-Native artists who make contemporary Northwest Coast–style art have been accepted by many (although not all) Indigenous groups. John Livingston (b. 1951) grew up with the Kwakwa̱ka̱'wakw Hunt family and learned to carve from the distinguished master Henry Hunt. Steve Brown (b. 1950) has had a long career carving canoes, replicating works, and teaching formline style to Native artists and others.[15] It is noteworthy that many contemporary Native artists have expressed considerable debt to the non-Native artists who helped train or inspire them. Distinguished carver Nathan Jackson (Tlingit, b. 1938) credits Bill Holm's influence and has chosen Steve Brown to assist on numerous projects. Moreover, Jackson is agreeable to non-Natives making Northwest Coast art, if they are respectful of the culture. "The problem happens when White people don't care about the culture," Jackson says. "People who do Northwest Coast art but don't understand its meaning—that's not right."[16] But some non-Native carvers do not practice reciprocity with the Native communities whose traditions underpin their artistic practice. And some Native people understandably have resented them for selling and

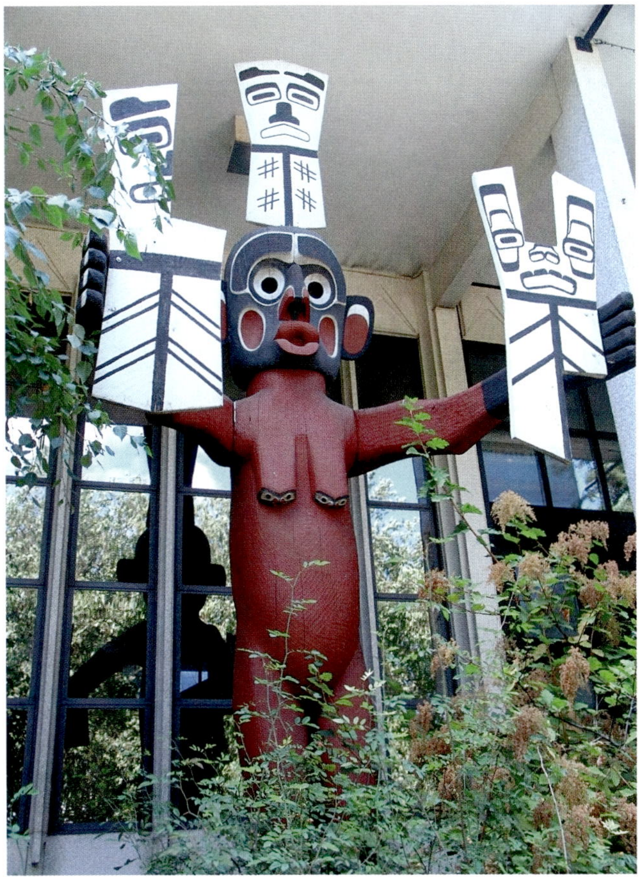

4.2. Bill Holm, Dzunuk'wa figure holding coppers (replica), 1970. Red cedar, height 23 feet. Burke Museum, University of Washington # R-200.

profiting from Northwest Coast–style work while giving back nothing. Other Native people, especially younger ones, strongly believe that no one lacking Northwest Coast heritage should be working in this style—that it is simply cultural theft. Tony Hunt (Kwakwa̱ka̱'wakw, 1942–2017) forcefully asserted that non-Natives should not make Native-style art, a belief that has grown more widespread in recent decades, especially on social media.[17] At a carving workshop coinciding with Celebration in Juneau in 2006, several individuals objected to the presence of non-Natives among the participants.

This raises the question of the locus of authenticity in the Northwest Coast art object: is it the ethnic identity of the artist or rather the formal qualities of the object that determines its status as "Native art"? Artist Da-ka-xeen Mehner (Tlingit, b. 1970) asserts that skill in formline design does not make a Native artwork; for that the artist must have the requisite cultural background. He asks if "anybody that picked up the stylistic form suddenly became a Native artist? . . . [there is] an assumption that all Native art was all about form and anyone could pick up [that] . . . form and become a Native artist, which is not true."[18]

As more people take seriously the need to respect cultural sovereignty, and to understand that appropriation of art forms can be interpreted as a continuation of colonialist practices, these issues become ever more urgent. In his analysis of contemporary Australian Aboriginal art, anthropologist Nicholas Thomas identified two hierarchies of value: the primitivist's archaizing preference for tradition, and the contemporary critic's deconstruction of the essentialism underlying that primitivism. The former idealizes the "primitive" in his supposedly unacculturated, pristine culture, while the latter challenges the romance of the past and the insistence that accommodation to the contemporary world renders culture inauthentic. Many Northwest Coast artworks of the late twentieth century represent interesting articulations of what might be termed the "authentically primitive" within the commoditized, contemporary art world. While some consumers may fantasize that their contemporary masks by Native artists are genuinely "traditional," in fact, these artworks are the products of more than two centuries of intercultural exchange. Nonetheless, many greet such works with, in the words of anthropologist Nicholas Thomas, a "fetishization of an unacculturated authenticity."[19]

"Cherokee/Kwakwa̱ka̱'wakw"? Blurred and Uncertain Identities

The non-Natives discussed so far have never claimed to be Native. This is not the case with carver Don Smith (1933–1996), however. A generation ago, most of us in Native art history were familiar with the work of this man, who generally went by the name "Lelooska" or "Chief Lelooska" and produced many works of art in Northwest Coast style. His work not only lingers in some public collections of Native American art but, surprisingly to us, has been accessioned into museums even within the past few years.

In 2007 the Montclair Art Museum in New Jersey accepted into its collection a mask made by Smith in 1984 and included it in the reinstallation of their Native American galleries in 2014 (Figure 4.3). This is a transformation mask, of a type that has long been a hallmark of Kwakwa̱ka̱'wakw stagecraft: the wearer controls hidden cords that open one carved face to reveal another within. Cords also control a pleated muslin cloth behind the head that unfurls into a corona. The carved face is that of K'umugwe, chief of the Undersea Kingdom. It copies a mask made by master carver Bob Harris (Kwakwa̱ka̱'wakw, ca. 1870–ca.1935) around 1890. According to community standards, in order to wear such things, one must have inherited the rights to particular images and stories; it is an extreme breach of protocol for carvers who do not have such rights to appropriate crests for their own personal or commercial use. But there are other ways, in addition to descent, that individuals gain these privileges, such as having rights bestowed as a gift in formal, public ceremony.

The label on this work calls the artist "Cherokee/Kwakwa̱ka̱'wakw." Those unfamiliar with Smith's history might surmise that the artist perhaps has a parent or

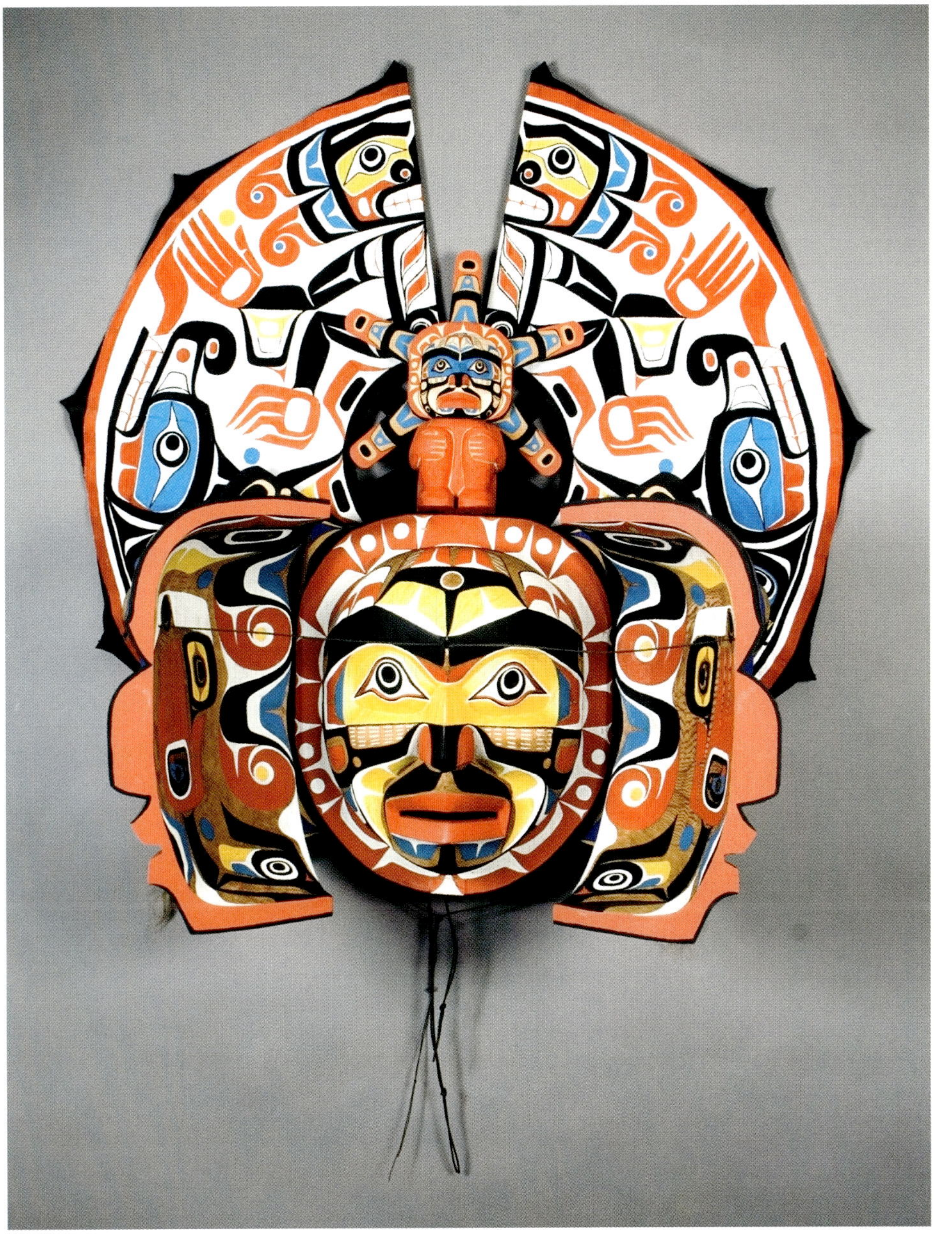

4.3. Don Smith, Kwakwa̱ka̱'wakw-style *Transformation Mask*, 1984. Cedar, pigment, and muslin. 40 × 40 × 13½ inches. Gift of Marilyn and Stephen Greene. Montclair Art Museum, Montclair, New Jersey, # 2006.19.

grandparent of each ethnicity (though of course Native heritage is often far more complex than that). If a museum label identifies Smith simply as a Cherokee artist, as some do, the viewer might ponder the legitimacy of a Cherokee carving a Kwakwa̱ka̱'wakw–style mask. But is he, in fact, Cherokee? Lelooska's life has been well-chronicled but presented without critical analysis.[20] It is a troubling story for anyone favoring a simple essentialist story of Native identity. Smith was born in 1933 in California to a woman whose mother (said to be Cherokee) had been adopted by a white family. His father was not Native. His parents had a shop near Salem, Oregon, where his mother's curios and baskets were sold. Smith dropped out of school in ninth grade, and making art became his full-time job. He began to experiment with Northwest Coast–style carving in the 1950s, when collector, hobbyist, and museum curator Norman Feder (1930–1995) commissioned Northwest Coast replicas for his hobbyist demonstrations.[21] In the early 1960s the Indian Arts and Crafts Board sent Smith to Neah Bay, ostensibly to "teach" Northwest Coast–style carving to the Makah people; the board subsequently bought everything he had made in the demonstrations.[22] Smith carved a totem pole for the 1959 Oregon Centennial, and he carved poles for his then-home city of Kalama, Washington, as well as for many other cities and institutions. He got enough attention for this that he was included in the pivotal exhibition *Arts of the Raven* in 1967.[23]

For Smith, the most important event of the 1960s, was meeting Kwakwa̱ka̱'wakw chief Jimmie Sewid (1913–1988). In 1965 the artist accompanied Bill Holm and anthropologist Edward Malin to potlatches in Alert Bay. In the summer of 1967, Sewid commissioned Smith to make a mask for his upcoming potlatch. That December, Smith's younger brother danced the Undersea Eagle mask that Smith had carved during the potlatch festivities.[24] This was the first of several public acknowledgments that Chief Sewid was giving the Smith family the right to make masks and to dance them. Smith's case puts into conflict the individual and family rights that are the cornerstone of Northwest Coast cultural protocols and the collective rights of an Indigenous nation seeking to control its heritage in the modern world. Individual chiefs, when revitalizing the potlatch in the mid-twentieth century, granted privileges to outsiders. Such decisions, as anthropologist Aaron Glass has observed, "were made at particular historical conjunctures and for specific personal reasons having to do with preserving Kwakwa̱ka̱'wakw art and culture as well as negotiating productive social and intercultural relations."[25]

Given that it is an important arbiter of protocol, it is noteworthy that the National Museum of the American Indian (NMAI) acquired several dozen items by Smith when the Indian Arts and Crafts Board transferred their entire art collection to NMAI in 2000. Smith is simply listed as Cherokee in NMAI's online data base, though in fact there is no known documentation of his Cherokee heritage. Smith's work lives on in the public eye, not only at NMAI and the Montclair Art Museum but also in other institutions. Some museums either believe that he is a legitimate Native maker of Northwest Coast objects, or they are (understandably) unacquainted with the complexities of his avowed identity, or do not feel it is their place to adjudicate complex identifications of heritage. Moreover, it is important to remember that the Indian Arts and Crafts Act of 1990 applies to the sale of objects; it does not legislate what can be exhibited in a museum. We suggest that works made by this artist on display in museums should be framed to tell the narrative of intercultural appropriation and/or the adoption of rights and privileges that make up the cultural biography of such objects. Art history and museology in the twenty-first century must offer the public no less than these complicated and messy stories.

Actual Fakes: Made in Indonesia

A far simpler story concerns forgeries of contemporary Northwest Coast sculpture. Around 2001, a Santa Fe couple with an important collection of Northwest Coast contemporary art were at a popular local flea market and spotted a contemporary Northwest Coast mask in excellent condition, on sale for very little money (Figure 4.4). As soon as they held it they knew it was not right, for it was too lightweight to be cedar or alder. They bought it for $50 to serve as an educational example of the modern world's propensity for knock-offs, fakes, and copies.[26]

The mask, which combines human and bird-like features, has medium-length strands of hair inserted into holes at the top. The skin area is unpainted, revealing the grain of the wood. The lips, nostrils, and eyebrows are red, and formline designs are painted in red and black on the cheeks, eyebrows, and forehead. After some scrutiny it is clear that the artist was not adept at the elegant tapering of formlines that a skilled Northwest Coast painter will do nearly automatically. The black designs in the eyebrows, for example, do not have the calligraphic grace of real formline designs.

Since at least 1990, Northwest Coast–style masks (and other objects, including rattles and model totem poles) have been made in workshops in Indonesia and imported to North America. Many are sold as outright forgeries of the work of well-known artists. Before the widespread use of Google images, and the advent of online sales at eBay (established in 1995), these were not easy to track. But Stephen Lazarus, who has sold authentic contemporary First Nations art in Montreal since 1990, has documented

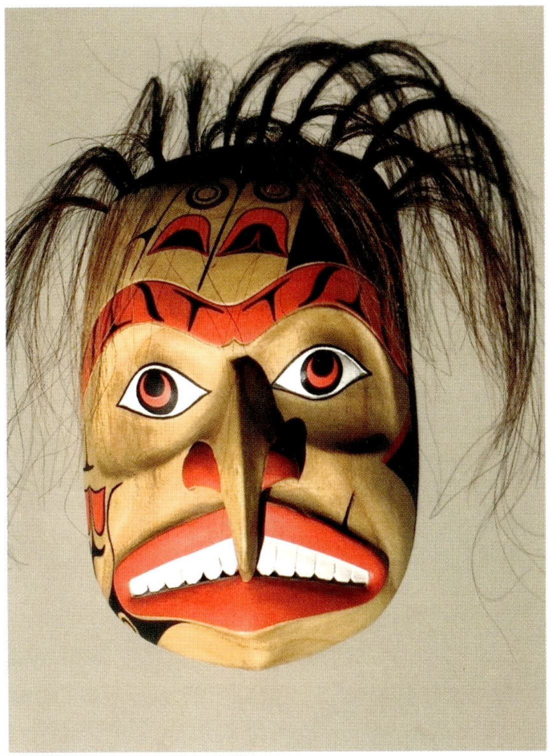

4.4. Fake Northwest Coast mask from Indonesia, post-1994. Albesia wood. Collection of Richard and Joan Chodosh, Santa Fe, New Mexico.

the flood of these fakes since the early 1990s.[27] He recognized this mask immediately as a knock-off of a mask by Don Yeomans (Haida, b. 1958) published in Gary Wyatt's book *Spirit Faces*.[28] Clearly the book was taken to Indonesia to serve as a handbook for deliberate forgery.

When pictures of Yeomans's mask and its fake are compared, the deficiencies of the Indonesian mask are all too apparent. The painted designs on Yeomans's *Thunderbird Spirit* mask (1993) are masterful. Moreover, his mask has inset operculum shell teeth, which would not have been clear to a carver copying from a book; the teeth on the Indonesian mask are delineated by shallow cuts in the wood. The hair on the fake is shorter and sparser than the long, lustrous horsehair in Yeomans's mask.[29] While most authentic Northwest Coast masks are made of red cedar or alder, Indonesian forgeries are usually made of albizia, a fast-growing tropical wood.

When queried about this theft of his work, Yeomans remarked that his *Thunderbird Spirit* mask sold for $7,500 in 1993 and would be worth more than twice that today. He said: "The truth is most people interested in our art cannot afford to buy the real thing. Sweatshop products from wherever do not threaten the value of the real object. In every art form, not just Northwest Coast art, there is a very small core of original artists; everything else is derivative. If your business is being original, dwelling on what anyone else is doing tends to stop the creative process."[30]

The Surrogate: Cross-Cultural Collaborations in the Digital Age

Some copies have the complete support of Indigenous people. The twenty-first century has produced a new category of replica in Northwest Coast carving: the 3-D digital surrogate made by machine.[31] In 2005 a Tlingit Killer Whale clan hat was repatriated to the Dakl'aweidi clan of Angoon from the Smithsonian's National Museum of Natural History (NMNH); it was carried back to the Smithsonian in 2010 so that a surrogate could be made to show museum-goers the meaning of repatriation of culturally significant objects (Figure 4.5). The original hat was flown to Sitka and placed on the head of Mark Jacobs Sr., its legitimate caretaker, just days before he died.[32]

After Jacobs's death a new clan leader, Edwell John Jr., became the caretaker of the clan hat. Interestingly enough, John is a computer specialist who believed that if the clan hat were replicated, there would be great potential for education about the repatriation process; he liked the idea of a surrogate being placed in the museum to illustrate the story of the clan hat's journey home. He worked out a protocol with Smithsonian staff that the surrogate would be used only for educational purposes and always accompanied by labels describing it as a replica of an important clan-owned crest object. Not only did John authorize the project, but he also worked closely with the Smithsonian staff and participated in the publication documenting this historic collaboration.[33]

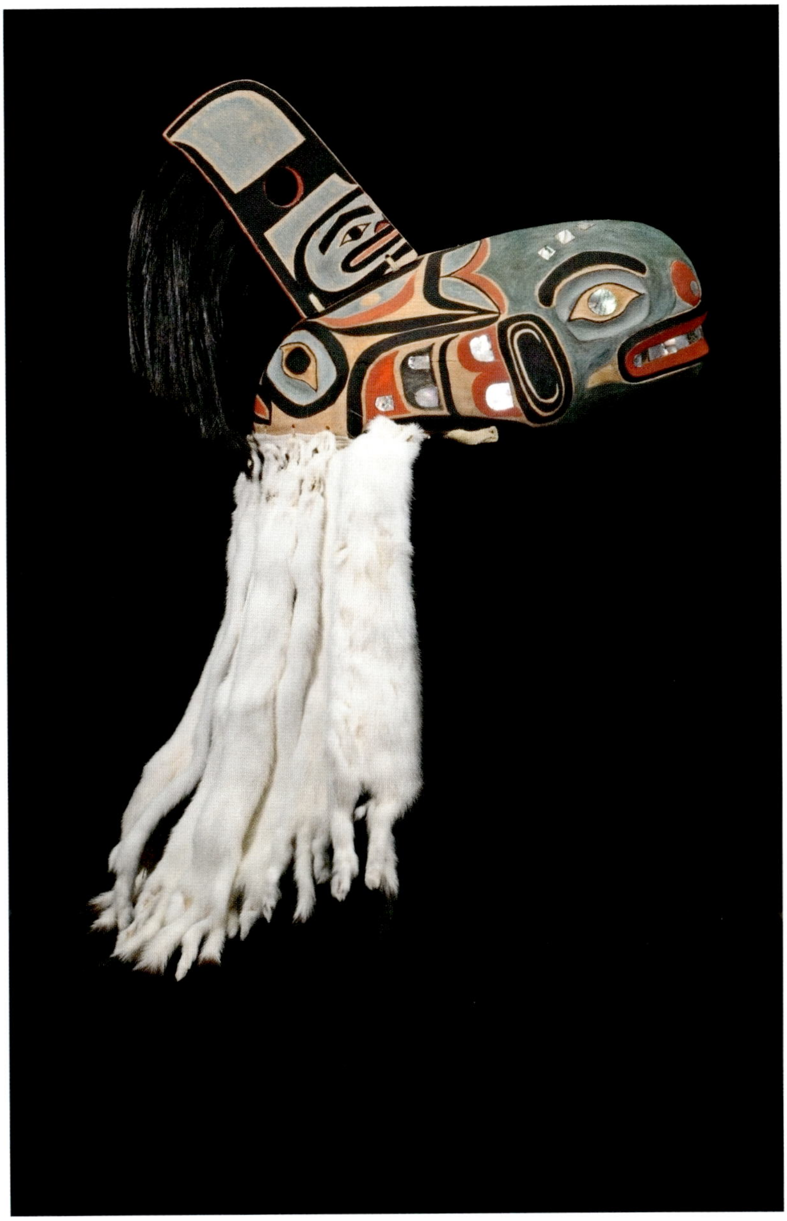

4.5. Digital replica of Kéet S'aaxw (Tlingit Killer Whale clan crest hat), 2011. Alder, abalone shell, commercial pigments, ermine skins. Catalog number E433020, Smithsonian Institution, National Museum of Natural History, Department of Anthropology. Photograph by James DiLoreto.

The replication process (described in great detail in the publication) involves 3-D laser scanning in conjunction with photogrammetry to accurately measure the object. A Computer Numerical Control milling machine shaped the surrogate, using alder, as in the original. Abalone and human hair were donated to the project, and commercial paint painstakingly matched to the colors of historical Tlingit objects in the museum. Notably, the surrogate reveals aspects of the ceremonial splendor of the original no longer extant: while the original hat has holes at the back for the attachment of ermine skins, no skins were attached when it came to the Smithsonian in 1904. Ten ermine skins were sent from Hoonah, Alaska, and affixed to the surrogate. While John was adamant that the surrogate was not at.óow (i.e., a precious object that had been instilled with power and status), it *was* danced along with real clan hats at a Tlingit Clan Conference in Sitka in 2012 and at NMNH in 2013.[34]

Customarily a clan leader pays an artist for a commission; clan leader Herman Davis was concerned about the surrogate, asking "How do I pay a machine?"[35] By this he meant, how can technology be integrated into traditional protocols?[36] Both the dancing of the surrogate and Davis's query suggest that this new technology adds complexity to standard notions of originals and replicas, provoking some tension as this idea is incorporated into Tlingit and museum cultures alike. Smithsonian anthropologist Gwyneira Isaac has pointed out that 3-D digital replicas "are about the power to replicate something but also about the potential to transform it and, therefore, to transform the current social order." She notes that in the surrogate's accession records "the specific expertise was listed both for the original and the replica."[37]

Some Tlingit leaders believe that participating in digital scanning and replication may have value for their communities. As the authors of the report on this project wrote: "Clans that have their objects digitally scanned and archived can call upon the digital files for whatever purposes they deem appropriate. . . . Some may be interested in displaying their 3D digital images of their crest objects on a web site to teach clan members about the history of their crests and crest objects. Others may wish to have replicas made for educational purposes. At the very least the digital files serve as a back-up should anything happen to the originals."[38]

Conclusion

This discussion of copies of Northwest Coast carvings demonstrates the complexity of judging non-Natives making Native-style art. The examples covered here have positions on a sliding scale of acceptability that is complicated by the fact that what is acceptable necessarily changes over time and differs according to the standards of different communities. At one end—unacceptable and unethical—are foreign-made fakes appealing to consumers who want masks but are unwilling to pay for the real thing. Then come objects by well-trained artists without ties to Native communities; these conflict directly in the market place with Native-made pieces. The next category, works by individuals with close ties to Indigenous groups and deep understanding of the cultural significance of art, are accepted by many Native people but criticized by others. Most acceptable seem to be recent digital replicas made with the full participation of Indigenous collaborators for use in Native communities or as educational props in museums. It is perhaps appropriate that the most acceptable form of copy in the twenty-first century is one dependent on computers, three-dimensional printers, and other contemporary technological advances.

As historians of Native American art, each of whom has been involved in this field for decades (Berlo outside the subfield of the Northwest Coast and Jonaitis within it), we hope that the examples in this chapter have illustrated how complicated judgments about intention, ethnicity, and ethics can be, especially when viewed over time. Historical circumstances have changed, and younger generations of artists have grown up in communities where successful cultural revitalization has taken place. They are understandably impatient with stories in which non-Native people seem to "save" or "instruct" Native ones. Every year, there are fewer of us who remember how different—and sometimes how pessimistic—people felt fifty or sixty years ago. While younger artists and scholars may disparage or dismiss events and actions that took place in the past, it would be irresponsible not to examine the specific historical circumstances that gave rise to particular actions.

It is incumbent upon us to analyze these stories, actions, and objects in light of their particular and varying historical trajectories and imperatives. Otherwise, the past becomes simply a one-dimensional backdrop for events of the present, and the work of all of our ancestors recedes into an undifferentiated mass. There are multiple histories of art history, multiple histories of museums, and multiple histories of Indigenous communities. All of these need to be examined and analyzed, and their stories told in many different ways in order that the complexities of the past be allowed to rival the complexities of the present.

NOTES

The authors thank Bruce Bernstein, Steve Brown, Kathryn Bunn-Marcuse, Richard and Joan Chodosh, Chip Colwell, Aaron Glass, Trevor Isaac, Da-ka-xeen Mehner, Shgen George, Eric Hollinger, Ishmael Hope, and Steven Lazarus for their help with this research. We are particularly grateful for Kathryn Bunn-Marcuse's close reading of this chapter; the changes she suggested have improved our work.

1 This chapter grew from a paper presented by Aldona Jonaitis titled "Authenticity and Ethnicity: Non-Native Carvers of Northwest Coast Art" in a panel chaired by Janet Catherine Berlo on "Not Native American Art: Falsification and Misattribution" at the 2008 College Art Association Conference. Sections on Lelooska and Filipino forgeries form part of Berlo's book-in-progress, "Not Native American Art: Replication, Misrepresentation, and Other Vexed Identities."

2 Lloyd Averill and Daphne Morris, *Northwest Coast Native and Native-Style Art: A Guidebook for Western Washington* (Seattle: University of Washington Press, 1995).

3 Ellen Lang was later Ellen Hope Hays. Duane Pasco and Barbara Winther, *Life as Art: Duane Pasco* (Poulsbo, WA: Jayhawk Press, 2012), 164–67.

4 Pasco and Winther, *Life as Art*, 166.

5 Pasco was commissioned to make four masks for a potlatch held in the early 1980s by Haida artist Robert Davidson. Karen Duffek, "'Authenticity' and the Contemporary Northwest Coast Indian Art Market," *BC Studies* 57 (Spring 1983): 103–22; both Joe David (Nuu-chah-nulth, b. 1946) and Marvin Oliver (Salish, b. 1946) worked with Pasco and were influenced by his stylistic innovations.

6 Pasco and Winther, *Life as Art*, 40, 69.

7 Bill Holm, *Northwest Coast Indian Art: An Analysis of Form* (Seattle: University of Washington Press, 1965).

8 Although Holm is rightfully acknowledged for his codification of the formline style, Canadian anthropologist Wilson Duff (1925–1976) and Haida artist Bill Reid (1920–1998) also studied museum collections to understand these rules. See Wilson Duff, Jane Wallen, and Joe Clark, "Totem Pole Survey of Southeastern Alaska: Report on Field Work and Follow-up Activities, June-October 1969," manuscript, Alaska State Museum, Juneau.

9 Holm always clearly signed or even burned his name into his carvings so that they could not be misattributed. Kathryn Bunn-Marcuse, personal communication with the authors, May 2018.

10 Janet Catherine Berlo and Aldona Jonaitis, personal communication with Robin K. Wright, April 2018.

11 The Burke Museum at the University of Washington holds twenty-five totem poles, masks, bracelets, and other objects made by Holm in its collection. The database lists these as "replicas" and their maker is named and listed as a "Euro-American artist."

12 Lloyd Averill, *A Man from Roundup: The Life and Times of Bill Holm* (Seattle: Burke Museum, Bill Holm Center, University of Washington), 23–29, www.burkemuseum.org/sites/default/files/man-from-roundup-biography-averill.pdf (accessed 2018).

13 Chief Calvin Hunt, personal communication with Kathryn Bunn-Marcuse, January 2019. Tommy Hunt of Fort Rupert, BC, had the following comment about Holm: "When [Bill Holm] is called on by his Kwakwala name and offered a seat of honour in the ceremonial space and house of the host Chief, Homiskanis is himself validated as a man of the People and acknowledged as an initiated member of a secret society. Bill was chosen by the old people to take a place in Kwakiutl society and he is Hamatsa" (Tommy Hunt, personal communication with Kathryn Bunn-Marcuse, April 2018).

14 This fact is not always recognized by contemporary writers. Indeed, in a recent exhibition catalog, contemporary curator Candace Hopkins (Carcross/Tagish First Nation) completely misrepresented Holm, writing that he collapsed "the distance between himself and those who were the objects of his study, by not only taking part in their ceremonies, but by mimicking their cultural production as well. Not only did he 'turn Indian,' he also claimed that he was better at it than Native people themselves." See Candace Hopkins, "On the Commodification of Native Culture," in *Without Boundaries: Visual Conversations*, edited by Sonya Kelliher-Combs, 32–40 (Anchorage, AK: Anchorage Museum, 2016), 35. No one who knows Holm well has ever heard him claim this, nor would such a humble man ever do so.

15 Brown was hired by the Makah tribe to lead the work of five young Makah carvers to create the four traditional cedar canoes in the museum in Neah Bay (1975–79). He lived for many years in Wrangell, Alaska, where he was hired by the Stikine tribe to lead a carving project (including Tlingit artists Wayne Price and Will Burkhart) replicating the eighteenth-century house posts of the Nanya'aayi clan. He has continued working with Native communities on art projects for which the Kiksadi Tlingit gave him the name of the original artist, Kadjis-du'axtc. Brown and Price also replicated four nineteenth-century totem poles that were greatly deteriorated, and Brown later led the group that was hired to re-create the nineteenth-century Brown Bear screen for the Chief Shakes house.

16 Nathan Jackson, personal communication with Aldona Jonaitis, 2003.

17 Tony Hunt, personal communication with Aldona Jonaitis, 1990.

18 Da-ka-xeen Mehner, personal communication with Jonaitis, April 2018. While numerous contemporary First Nations artists embrace the traditions of their ancestors, others have pursued different, more innovative cultural expressions.

19 Nicholas Thomas, *Colonialism's Culture: Anthropology, Travel, and Government* (Princeton, NJ: Princeton University Press, 1994). Today, many Northwest Coast artists themselves are challenging the essentializing of tradition, often in the context of innovative work, some of which directly seeks a younger, hipper audience.

20 Chris Friday, *Lelooska: The Life of a Northwest Coast Artist* (Seattle: University of Washington Press, 2004). Friday makes it clear that he has close ties to the Lelooska family, and that his book is "largely the story that Lelooska chose to tell" (viii).

21 Friday, *Lelooska*, 124.

22 Friday, *Lelooska*, 130–46.

23 Wilson Duff, Bill Holm, and Bill Reid, *Arts of the Raven: Masterworks by the Northwest Coast Indian* (Vancouver: Vancouver Art Gallery, 1967).

24 Edward Malin, *Masks and Totems: A Northwest Coast Odyssey* (privately printed, 2012), 199–207 and plates 86, 87, 106–108.

25 Aaron Glass, "Conspicuous Consumption: An intercultural History of the Kwakwaka'wakw Hamat'sa," PhD diss., Department of Anthropology, New York University, 2006, 839.

26 Richard and Joan Chodosh, personal communication with Janet Catherine Berlo, Santa Fe, New Mexico, May 2017.

27 Lazarus owned the well-respected Red Cedar Gallery in Montreal from 1990 through 2002. He notes that Indonesian carvers seem to keep up with at least some of the books, for the mask types that were prevalent in the 1990s have been "retired" in favor of newer masks.

28 Gary Wyatt, *Spirit Faces: Contemporary Art of the Northwest Coast* (Seattle: University of Washington Press, 1994), 45.

29 The fake also lacks the feathers that rise from the top of the original, presumably because it is illegal in the United States to transport migratory bird parts.

30 Don Yeomans, personal communication with Janet Catherine Berlo, May 1, 2017.

31 A surrogate is a proxy or a replacement—someone or something that stands in for another. The term has been used before in discussions of the digitalization of historical objects. See Fiona Cameron, "Beyond the Cult of the Replicant: Museums and Historical Digital Objects—Traditional Concerns, New Discourses," in *Theorizing Digital Cultural Heritage: A Critical Discourse*, edited by Fiona Cameron and Sarah Kenderdine, 49–75 (Cambridge, MA: MIT Press, 2007).

32 Eric R. Hollinger, Edwell John Jr., Harold Jacobs, Lora Moran-Collins, Carolyn Thome, Jonathan Zastrow, Adam Metallo, Gunter Waibel, and Vince Rossi, "Tlingit-Smithsonian Collaborations with 3D Digitization of Cultural Objects," *Museum Anthropology Review* 7, no. 1–2 (2013): 201–53.

33 Hollinger et al., "Tlingit-Smithsonian Collaborations with 3D Digitization of Cultural Objects," 203–204.

34 Nora M. Dauenhauer, "Tlingit *At.óow*: Traditions and Concepts," in *The Spirit Within: Northwest Coast Native Art from the John H. Hauberg Collection*, edited by Steven C. Brown, 21–29 (Seattle: University of Washington Press, 1995); and Hollinger et al., "Tlingit-Smithsonian Collaborations with 3D Digitization of Cultural Objects," 212.

35 Hollinger et al., "Tlingit-Smithsonian Collaborations with 3D Digitization of Cultural Objects," 215.

36 E. Hollinger, personal communication with Janet Catherine Berlo, July 2019.

37 Gwyneira Isaac, "Perclusive Alliances: Digital 3D, Museums, and the Reconciling of Culturally-Diverse Knowledges," *Current Anthropology* 56, Supplement 12 (December 2015): S288, S292.

38 Hollinger et al., "Tlingit-Smithsonian Collaborations with 3D Digitization of Cultural Objects," 216.

ONE SQUARE INCH

Lily Hope

Three Hours of my life
Traded for finger-twined,
braided shapes
Mimicking our formline art

One Square Inch
Fourteen miles up the mountain
Mountain goat and cedar bark
Hunted, harvested, thanked
Skinned, stripped, spun
Animal and plant become one

One Square Inch
Four pounds of wool
Hand dyed
With hemlock bark, wolf moss
Copper shards, and human urine
Saved for many days

One Square Inch
Hundreds of years
Woven documents of histories
Our clan stories
Recognition
These Chilkat robes
Bestowing honor

One Square Inch
Weaving four generations
Honoring our teacher's oral
traditions
Her dreams, her insistence
Practicing gratitude for this gift
Fasting from breakfast
Abstaining from men

One Square Inch
Kilos of Cultural Pressure
Heavy taboos
No five fingered hands
Sparing use of red
These Chilkat inches
We lead our
daughters to weave
Weaving
One Square Inch
Opportunity cost minutes
Weighed between joy for weaving
Frustration from having to
Care for self
Attend the husband
Play with kids
Clean the house
These minutes I could be weaving
But seeking balance in all

One Square Inch
Unity of Women
Dropping into meditation
Seeking weaver camaraderie
Training apprentices
To take our places
Learning these inches until

One square inch
Embodied every day
Chaos Organized
Universe aligned
Twine by twine
Braid by braid

These inches in the
Life giving robes of
our Tlingit lives.

PART II

Women's Work

STORIES, ART, AND POWER

CHAPTER 5

Stl'inll ~ Those with Clever Hands

PRESENTING FEMALE INDIGENOUS ART AND SCHOLARSHIP

Jisgang Nika Collison

Hlk'yak'ii ~ To Start a Fire

This chapter discusses the presentation of female Indigenous "art" and scholarship from the perspective of a female Indigenous (Haida) curator. The first part provides an introduction to the foundational strength and roles of women in Haida society and explores the marginalization of their artistic creations, wisdom, and general existence by Yaatsx̱aaydaG̱a (Iron People) postcontact.[1] The second part looks at the respect our Haida Nation has maintained for women despite this colonial past, demonstrated through the strong history of exhibiting female Haida artists at the Haida Gwaii Museum (a practice in juxtaposition to most venues focused on the arts of the Northwest Coast).

Nang Jaadas G̱iisda Ga Sdaaga ~ Born from the Woman

> Almost every household would have artists. There would be specialists in different things. . . . It was a form of writing, the artwork, to retain the oral histories. That's why it became a higher-ranked activity. . . . The chief's daughters became weavers of spruce root and mountain goat wool.
>
> CHRISTIAN WHITE[2]

In Haida society women and men are equal. There is reverence for women and the vital contributions we make to our complex society, including the passing down of lineage, property, and status and the recognition of, and respect for, artistic achievement, scholarship, and wise leadership. Just as a high-ranking man plays a significant role within Haida society, so does a k̲'uuljaad (*woman of high esteem*, literally, *boss lady*). Of these ladies, those who become matriarchs give balance to the chief. Among other responsibilities, a matriarch holds knowledge, ensures a clan's affairs are kept in order, and advises the chief on important matters. GwaaG̱anad (Diane

Brown) of the K̲aay'ahl Laanas X̲aaydaG̲a (née Ts'aahl clan) reminds us that "to be a matriarch is the most powerful position a woman can have. A matriarch plays a very major role within one's clan and our Nation. You don't get there until you're old, and you won't get there unless you're respected. So, there isn't much pressure to stay young."[3]

Under certain circumstances women can hold chieftainships, though these positions are customarily held by men. Regardless of a chief's gender, a head chief—the highest of chiefly positions—is referred to as 'Laana AwG̲a (Town Mother). This way of understanding and respecting women was complicated by patriarchal circumstance upon contact with the Yaatsx̲aaydaG̲a (Iron People), with ship captains refusing or reluctant to bargain with our women. It is said that Haida negotiation tactics changed, with the women stepping back so the men could do business. This did not minimize female influence over commercial activities, however, as noted in the journal of Captain Joseph Ingraham during his 1791 excursion to Haida Gwaii: "Here in direct opposition to most other parts of the world, the women maintain a precedency to the men in every point insomuch as a man dares not trade without the concurrence of his wife. Nay, I have often been witness to men being abused by their wives for parting with skins before their approbation was obtained."[4] While this excerpt makes me chuckle, I am of the opinion that the woman is not berating the man for getting a bad deal; she is reminding him of her equality.

Colonial attempts to erase women in Haida society, first through acts of refusal and later by acts of violence, were fortified by turning our matrilineal society upside down using the force of church paternalism, which attempted to undermine the maternal descent of the clan system in the late nineteenth century.[5] Extreme disenfranchisement of women in Haida society soon followed through Canada's Indian Act.[6] Section 12(1)(b) of the act saw women lose their "status" if they married a non-status man (Indigenous or not), effectively removing these women and their children (who were also denied status) from their societal roles, responsibilities, and rights, estranging them from family and community.[7] In 1884 the Indian Act was amended to outlaw the potlatch, which interfered with the female transmission of lineage, property, and rights.[8] Another colonial mechanism impacting the roles and contributions of women in Haida society was the residential school system.[9]

The suppression of important female roles, and the erasure of their existence, is evident in other, more nuanced ways. There are more than twelve thousand cultural treasures attributed as Haida held in global museums and universities.[10] When looking at what was "collected," the patriarchy of colonialism becomes even more clear. The amount of art made by women held in collections versus those of men is unbalanced. Art historians Kathryn Bunn-Marcuse and Megan Smetzer have discussed this phenomenon in their essay "Working to Change the Tide": "While totem poles and similar works are integral to crest display and ancient histories of Indigenous identity proclamation, they also resonated with two core precepts of

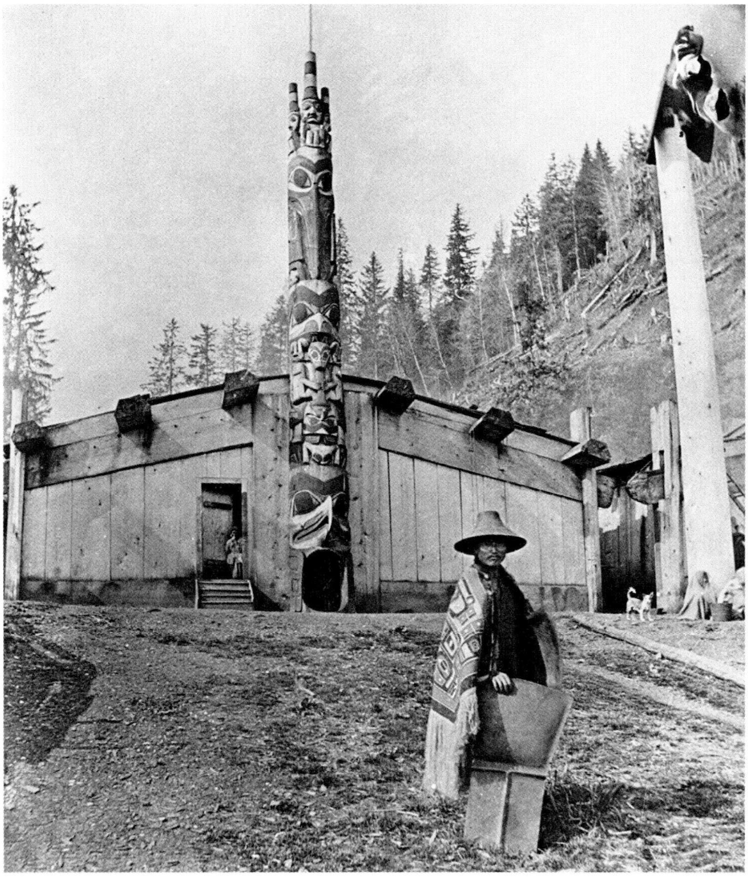

5.1. Chief NEnkaidsuglas stands in front of House Where People Always Want to Go in the village of Xaayna, ca. 1888. Photograph by Richard Maynard. Courtesy of Field Museum 6BAAB2.

nineteenth-century male-centric European art history: the concept of 'great art'—painting, sculpture, and architecture—and 'great artists' (more specifically, the autonomous 'genius' revered by the Western canon). Seen in that context, the carved and painted arts were identified as solely men's creations and were thus propelled into the forefront of collecting, exhibiting, and art historical analysis."[11]

I imagine that these "new world" men, who would have come by their authoritarian ways naturally (given the society they were raised in) were rattled by Haida social structure. I wonder if the authority contained within and emanating from the treasures made by women in Haida society might have been too omnipotent for the comfort level of those who seem to have been wired to see women as "less than," or to not see them at all. The virile view dominates certain circles even today.

Even the photographic and written records document this invisibility or marginalization of women. In these resources Haida women are rarely present, or identified, in comparison to Haida men. However, if one reads between the lines, with an understanding of Haida dynamics, the roles of women in Haida society *were* documented—some of it consciously, some of it not. Figure 5.1 is a photo taken in the village of Xaayna in 1888. Chief NEnkaidsuglas (The Highest Peak of a Mountain Range), known in English as David McKay, stands with great prominence as the hereditary leader of the Yaku Gitinai, adorned in his chiefly regalia and holding his coppers.[12] In the background two elderly women and a dog sit on the right-hand side, wrapped in blankets. On the left a younger woman—presumably NEnkaidsuglas's wife Skiljadai, whose English name is believed to be Lucy McKay—is barely noticeable as she stands in the doorway of the House Where People Always Want to Go.[13] Given the era in which the photograph was taken, it is not surprising the composition would be so male-dominated.[14] We can only presume she is his wife, as none of the women's identities seems to have been recorded at the time this photograph was taken.

Just as one cannot properly "read" Haida art without knowing the story behind it, one cannot properly read this photograph without understanding the underpinnings of Haida society. Although the image focuses on NEnkaidsuglas, the women—no matter how pushed out of the way—maintain a forceful presence. Given Haida reverence for the wisdom of female Elders, we can assume the two elderly women are well-respected. It's not certain that Skiljadai is the woman pictured in the image, but she was a forceful presence in the historical record. While conducting research on the house frontal pole in this photograph, British immigrant and ethnologist Charles F. Newcombe documented the names and lineages of both the wife and husband who owned House Where People Always Want to Go. NEnkaidsuglas's wife was named Skiljadai, a high name that translates into Property Woman. She belonged to the esteemed Skoa'ladas clan.[15] Both facts attest to her standing in the world. The prominent placement of one of her high crests at the base of the house frontal pole, the Thunderbird, further solidifies the esteem in which she was held.[16] Contrary to popular belief, the bottom figure of a pole is more often than not the most significant of positions in its composition. Knowing NEnkaidsuglas is Skiljadai's husband speaks to her rank and status, just as Skiljadai being married to NEnkaidsuglas gives credit to *his* standing.

A traditional colonial approach to demonstrating a man's power through imagery is to present him as one of individual authority, but the truest visual of a hereditary leader's stature can be witnessed in a potlatch.[17] When hosting a potlatch, a hereditary leader's matriarch, maternal uncles, and/or siblings, among others, often stand with him as he addresses his guests. If they are not standing, they have surely been introduced to the guests, their presence known. His greater clan is also present and known. These are the people who have put their trust in, and have respect for, his ability to represent them all in a good way. The presence of invited guests is necessary to affirm the clan's support. In asserting this, I am not suggesting singular portraiture is negative. There are many beautiful portraits of chiefs, matriarchs, and others of high rank. But in deconstructing an image manufactured by and during the height of colonial regimes, it is important to give substance to one's ability to be recognized as a "chief." To be a hereditary leader is not a right, it is not a dictatorship. It is a position of responsibility, acquired and managed through female lines.

The regalia worn by NEnkaidsuglas is an additional testament to the critical involvement of women in Haida society. His Naaxiin (Chilkat) robe and spruce root hat—extraordinary works that would have been brought to life by the mind, spirit, and hands of women—are essential to communicating his high rank. Works such as these also document the reciprocal creative relationship between men and women, as Naaxiin motifs were (and most often still are) designed by men before being transformed into royal-wear by weavers. Likewise, spruce root hats often have painted designs, classically executed by men. The transformative power of female hands, mind, and spirit, whether in human or supernatural realms, occurs in many of our narratives maintained over millennia. In the ancient story of Tc!aawu'nk![A], a nanaay (*grandmother*) sees sG̱aaga (*medicinal and spiritual practitioner*) qualities in her grandson. The boy is not accepted in this role by others, so his nanaay fashions him a dancing skirt from a woven mat, trimming it with puffin beaks. She works a bone into a healing implement, and to further strengthen his position, sings for him. In the dancing skirt, he performs like a sG̱aaga and thus becomes recognized as one.[18] That it took the potent ability of an elderly woman to propel the young man's talents into public acceptance is grand testament to the power of women's creations.

Publications written by non-Indigenous scholars acknowledging the power of Northwest Coast women through their creations are rare. On this topic the 1986 exhibition and publication *Robes of Power: Totem Poles on Cloth* stands out. The exhibition was initiated and curated by Gitsxan artist Doreen Jensen; the book was brought together by Jensen and researcher Polly Sargent. UBC Museum of Anthropology director Michael M. Ames noted in the book's foreword that it was the first full-length study of this important ceremonial art form, the button blanket (Figure 5.2).[19] The text of *Robes of Power* draws the reader in first by celebrating the power of the robe in its physical, aesthetic form. Secondary is the celebration of the makers. This is not a criticism. By putting the regalia forward as "art" first, the text grounds the creations *as art* before introducing the female artists. This avoids the trap of considering women's work as "craft"—a designation that has often devalued women's work and repelled those interested in high "art." This can be likened to the strategy used in the Athlii Gwaii movement of 1985, where the Haida Nation took a stand to stop unsustainable logging occurring in the lower region of Haida Gwaii, known as Gwaii Haanas. Our leaders' strategy was first to protect the area, then to have other governments recognize the authority of our Nation over our territory.[20] It was a successful approach; see the power, see the beauty, see the importance; then see who holds the responsibility to keep Gwaii Haanas as such.

The book was rightfully focused on an art form whose celebration was well overdue in the greater world. I was pleased that in addition to calling out the creative

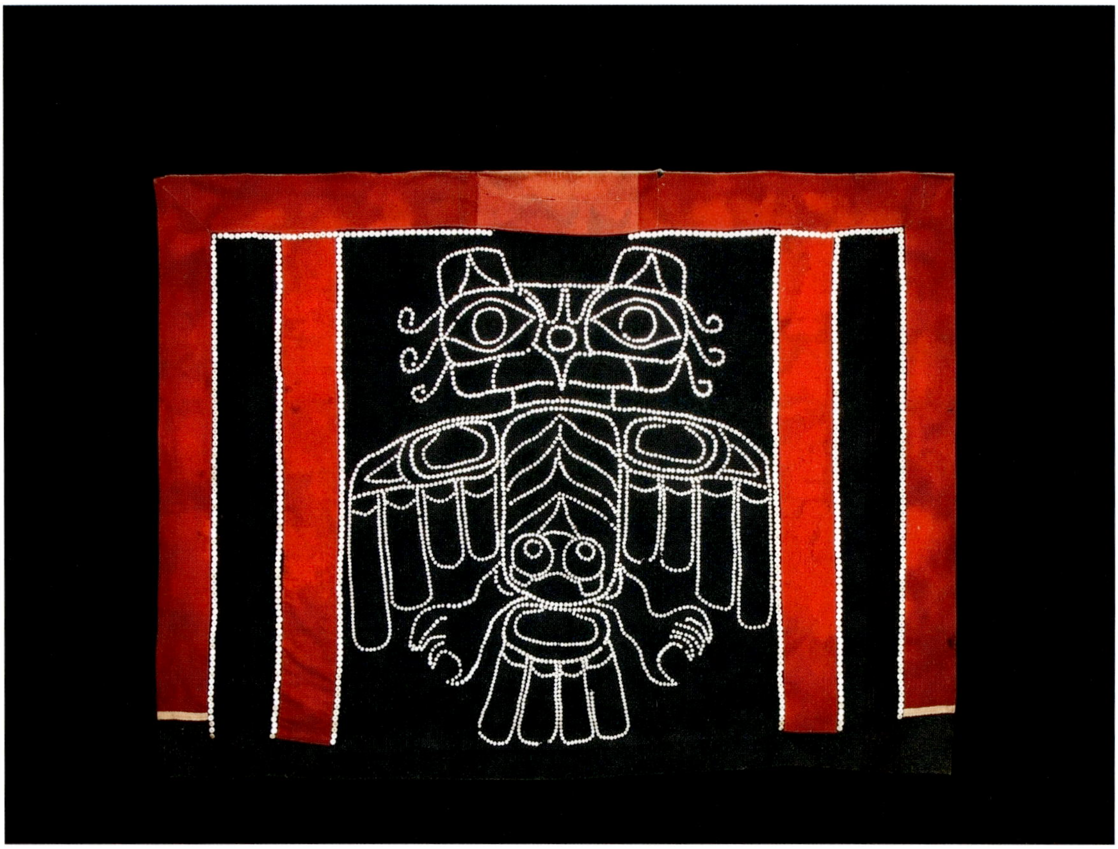

5.2. Chief Son-i-hat's gung.alang.uu gyàa.ad (*button blanket*), ancestral, ca. 1880s. Hudson's Bay wool blanket, cloth, shell buttons. Gwaii Haanas Collection, Haida Gwaii Museum KX.79.4.1A. Photograph by Jack Litrell, 2014. Courtesy of the Haida Gwaii Museum.

power of the female button blanket makers, the book did not erase the existence, importance, and force of the men who customarily play a role in these creations (similar to their role in Naaxiin weavings, or in their contributions to spruce root weavings). Historically, and oftentimes today, men design motifs representing supernatural and natural beings, crests-rights, lineages, and histories that women bring into existence. An exception to these collaborations is the complex geometric weavings of Ravenstail and unpainted spruce root hats, where meaning is embedded solely through a feminine language. Both are designed and created by the weaver alone, both forms stand on their own as high art serving high society.

While gender expectations and roles existed in Northwest Coast communities, they did not become rigidly codified until the patriarchal laws and institutions of settler colonialism affected the customary status of women and devalued their tangible cultural expressions.[21] In the story of Tc!aawu'nk![A], for example, the grandmother not only creates a doctor's apron and sings persuasively to empower her grandson's calling in life, she also fashions a healing implement made from bone, a material characteristically employed by men.[22] There are more instances where a female creates what is archetypally a male art practice. Another ancient Haida narrative tells of a chief's daughter who creates a set of bow and arrows from copper so the young boy she had raised could hunt birds. Creating something so commanding, from a most precious material, provided the boy the spiritual faculty to move himself forward to become one of the most highly regarded and powerful Supernaturals.[23] Instances such as these are not stuck in supernatural times. Their continuum is evidenced by other Northwest Coast female artists working now or in past generations in male-gendered art forms.[24] One example dates back as early as 1799, where Haida women were witnessed creating wooden pipes in the village of Dadens.[25]

Oral history attests to the origins of weaving over time with a variety of different materials for various uses; cedar bark is said to be one of the earliest weaving materials used on Haida Gwaii. Swiftly-sliding-Woman, a daughter of Jiila K̲uns, is recorded as sitting up and weaving a yellow cedar blanket on which she put two coppers; she is credited with teaching others how to do this.[26] Although working in cedar bark is deemed a woman's domain, it is not without male participation. In another ancient story a four-faced being turns itself into Redhead, a medium-sized diving duck (identified by the storyteller, Tom Stevens, as Aythya Americana). Redhead told a man to pull bark and weave mats, and to twist it into ropes for fishing.[27]

Wool weaving was also introduced in the times of the Supernaturals. In one story, while a woman is working on a Naaxiin blanket, the being/design on the robe lamented about the length of time the blanket was taking to be finished, stating: "To-morrow, too, one of my eyes [will still be] unfinished, unfinished."[28] Of all of our Ancestors' creations held in museums, Naaxiin and Ravenstail weaving are the most underrepresented and ignored by many collectors. Wool weaving was replaced in part with the introduction of Yaatsx̱aaydaG̱a trade cloth (which led to the art of the button robe and other forms of sought-after regalia). Later, it was almost silenced through the impacts of cultural genocide.[29]

Nang Kilsdlas, more commonly known as Raven, the cultural hero of the North Coast, is also said to have introduced weaving to our people. Raven can present as either feminine or masculine, depending on the scenario at hand. This opens the need for consideration of the *gendered spirit* in addition to one's physical being, both in life and in art. William White is a celebrated Tsimshian weaver of wool. His feminine spirit surely deepens both his connection to his art and his commitment to passing it down to others. He does not lose sight of the art's feminine nature. As White himself has described it: "It's a gift from the women of the Northwest Coast, and a privilege for me to be accepted into their circle. I am honoured to have the opportunity to teach women an art form that was developed and continues to be practiced by First Nations women who have the right and responsibility to carry this forth for future generations, like the women before them."[30]

When Haida artist Frances Williams first saw Chilkat blankets, he interpreted them as works of "art." As he learned their role in coastal societies, he "became aware of what the dance robes were .. . . I was overwhelmed by the power of the robes, and I couldn't find the words to express myself. There was something about this that was so important. There was so much power in them, an important message that was trying to come through." He reflects that not everyone realized this, but for Williams "these ceremonial robes. . . are used to display your lineage and display it proudly. They are worn like a king wears his robe."[31] The understanding of female art became not only that of aesthetic achievement but of the significant importance these works play in defining who we are as individuals and as a people. From a colonial viewpoint, it seems the importance is often put solely on the status of the wearer, especially if they are male.

Colonialism often dictated what women and men should be and what they should do. But flexibility in the gendered expectations of art-making increased from the mid-twentieth century on. By the time *Robes of Power* was published, some button robes were being created by individual artists, both female and male. Female Haida artists working in two- and three-dimensional design reemerged, and continued to grow in the latter half of the 1900s, including Marjorie (Bubby) Pearson and Joan Hart as well as Freda Diesing, who is recognized as one of those to birth the revitalization of the arts of the Northwest Coast. Diesing has an art school named after her, the Freda Diesing School of Northwest Coast Art. It continues today with such artists as Faye Russ, Cori Savard, Kwiaahwah Jones, Raven Pearson, and Shoshannah Greene.

Naa K'uuing'as ~ House Dressed Up to Show Off

The public presentation of female-gendered Indigenous art and scholarship does not begin or end in a gallery.[32] It regularly occurs in Haida society through the Potlatch and other formal events where people don their regalia, largely comprised of weaving and textile art, to show who they are. Feminine arts are also presented regularly outside of ceremony. Day-to-day fashion includes cedar bark hats woven in contemporary forms such as top hats, poor boy caps, and fedoras. Woven jewelry suspends from ears, embraces wrists, and graces necks. These practices are now a part of the western high-fashion world as well: Award-winning haute-couture designer Dorothy Grant (Haida) is credited with forging the pathway of Indigenous runway fashion via "feast wear" for all. More recently, in 2018 the highly regarded wool-weaver Meghann O'Brien (Haida and Kwakwa̱ka̱'wakw) paired her hand-sewn mainstream clothing with her exceptionally fine and intricate Naaxiin (Chilkat) weavings for Indigenous Fashion Week Toronto.

As it presents Indigenous female art and scholarship in museums and galleries, the Haida Gwaii Museum operates quite differently. The creation of Saahlinda Naay (Saving Things House), the name given to the museum by our Elders, is one of the oldest examples of reconciliation in the museum world in that it was brought into being through the vision and cooperation of both Haida and Canadian citizens living on Haida Gwaii. The Museum's society formed in 1971 with the museum opening in 1976. Given that the majority of the Haida Nation's treasures left our territories during the height of colonial regimes, we have been active in repatriation since the museum's inception. The treasures we keep safe have come through generous gifts from Haida families as well as the ethical and sensible actions of both local settlers and our growing group of allies in the greater world.

In 2000 the museum partnered with the Skidegate Band Council and the Gwaii Haanas/Parks Canada organization to create the Haida Heritage Centre at K̲ay Llnagaay. Reminiscent of an ancient village, the Haida Heritage Centre, from which our museum operates, is situated where land and ocean intersect, itself a juncture of ancient and modern society. It took seven years to build and is as alive as our people. As females are integral to a healthy Haida society, featuring female art and scholarship was natural for the museum to do before the Haida Heritage Centre, during its development, and after its opening. It's not often we have to incorporate deliberate strategy to hold up our women since it is a part of an everyday way of being. However, during the creation of the Centre a purposeful approach was taken to highlight women's artwork, based on observation of how female Indigenous art is often viewed in mainstream museums, galleries, the art market, and the greater public.

Because men's work was favored while collecting our Ancestor's material culture, the collection at K̲ay Llnagaay is also dominated by the creations of men. These are beautiful, stunning works but in need of balance. Therefore, to properly "dress up" our house, we commissioned several female-made pieces to give better prominence to the work of women, ensuring feminine art is present throughout each gallery. Despite our best efforts, however, a limited budget meant the imbalance remained. It was important to present weaving "first" in the gallery. While stunning monumental poles catch the viewers' eye as they tower at the far end of the gallery, our guests walk through displays of fine weaving to get to them. Visitors cannot help but be drawn to the elegance and integrity these works radiate (Figure 5.3).

Except for this purposeful act, and the need to balance the collection, I had not thought too much about the ubiquitous presence of female art and scholarship in the museum's exhibits and publications, for that was a natural outgrowth of our Nation's societal structure. When I was invited to participate on a conference panel exploring the presentation of female Indigenous art and scholarship in 2017, I was

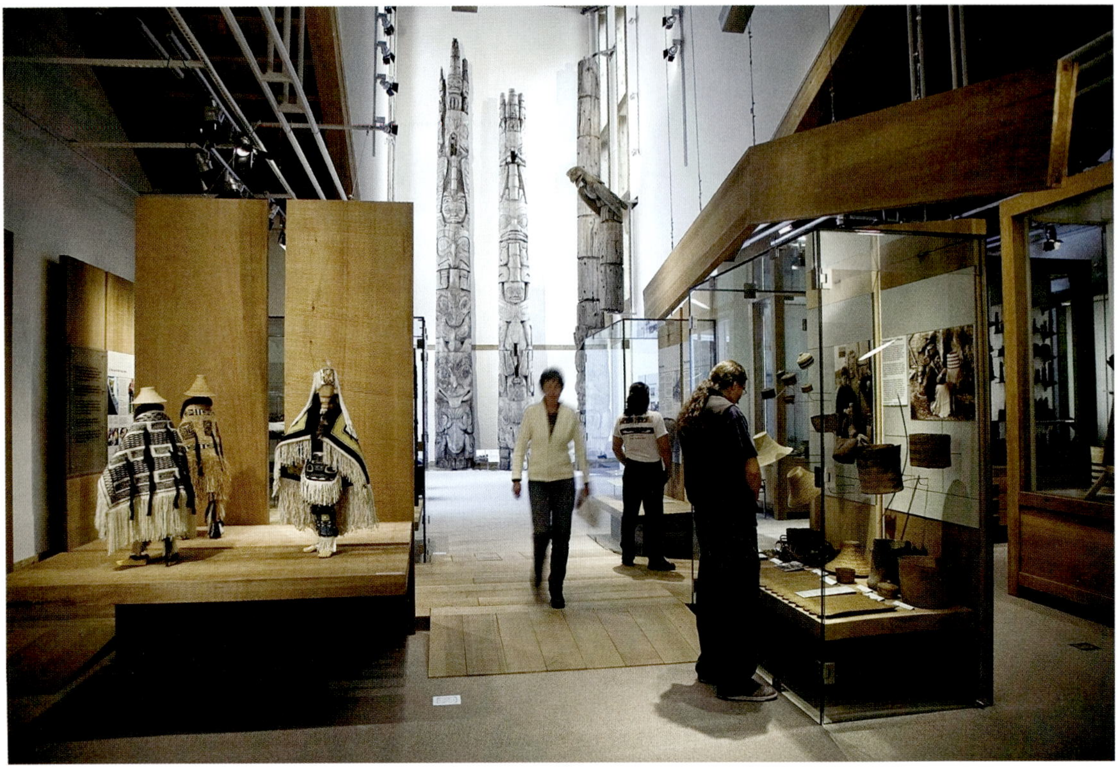

5.3. The Haida Gwaii Museum's *Keeping Our Way of Life* gallery. Courtesy of photographer Rolf Bettner, 2008.

fascinated by the exercise of envisioning how our exhibition history of women's artwork would seem from an outside viewpoint.[33] Whether envisioned or curated by women or men, the Haida Gwaii Museum has an expansive record of female-led arts exhibits and scholarship over decades. The remainder of this chapter details some of the museum's more recent exhibitions.

FROM A FEW WEAVERS, 2009

Exhibition curated by Kwiaawah Jones (Haida) and Nathalie Macfarlane (Canadian)

Out of a desire to honor the weavers, Haida artist Robert Davidson lent his extensive collection of basketry and wool weavings to the museum for exhibit. The exhibition *From a Few Weavers* featured historic and contemporary baskets, hats, and textiles of the finest quality, paying homage to the unbroken line of artists that have kept, and keep, this high art form alive (Figure 5.4). In art museums, weaving is often marginalized as "craft" or as a decorative art, but for the museum, weavings are central to both function and artistry. Having access to so many works was an exciting opportunity for weavers, the Haida Nation, and the greater public to learn

5.4. *From a Few Weavers,* 2009 exhibition poster featuring a spruce root basket woven by Isabel Rorick (1983) with *Raven Fin Killer Whale* design by Robert Davidson (2001). Courtesy of the Haida Gwaii Museum.

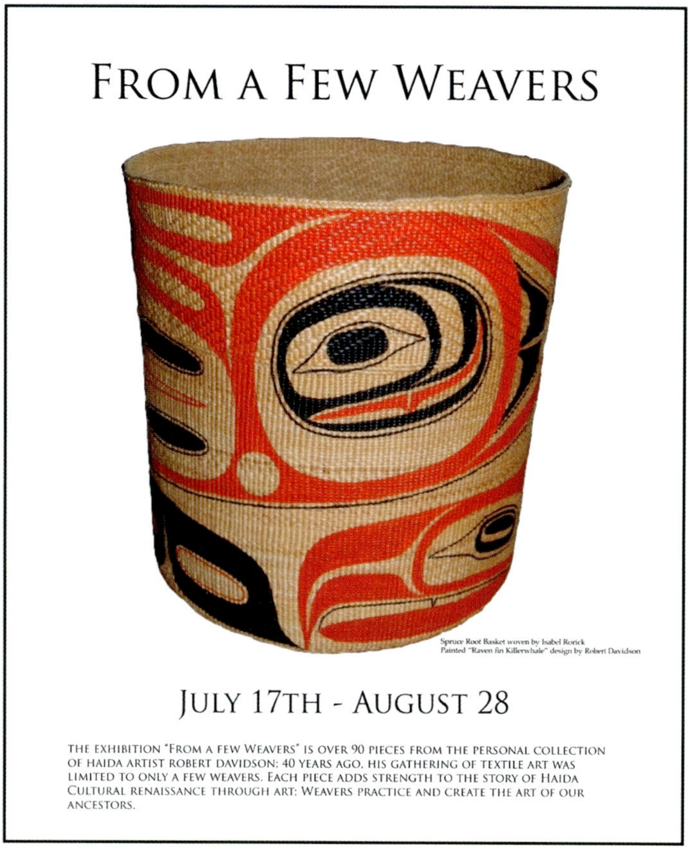

about, examine, and appreciate the breadth of artistic skill and the environmental and cultural knowledge required to attain the standards of the works shown. The scholarship of weaving begins with a deep knowing of the spiritual and physical characteristics of the lands, waters, airways, and seasons in order to harvest high-quality materials. Once gathered, artists spend hours and days preparing their materials, an expertise that takes years to master. Then there is the knowledge of the function the weaving will serve, necessary so that the works will serve properly and proudly. Finally, there is the demanding skill of weaving itself.

The mind-set and techniques involved in weaving are a science unto themselves, as Davidson noted in the exhibition text for *From a Few Weavers*: "You can't fake weaving. You need to really understand weaving to make it look good, or for people to appreciate. For carving it seems like you just polish or paint and it looks okay for sale, but [with] weaving you have to put a lot more thought into it. So, the short of it is, there is a higher percentage of good weavers than there are good carvers... and I will stand by it."[34] 'Wiiguux̱aay (*weaving*) is a formidable art form. With a feminine spirit and expertise at the very core of its being, how can weaving be seen otherwise?

THAT WHICH MAKES US HAIDA: THE HAIDA LANGUAGE, 2011

Exhibition curated by Jasḵwaan Amanda Bedard (Haida) and Jisgang Nika Collison (Haida)

That Which Makes Us Haida holds up the art of X̱aayda kil, the Haida language and all it contains, the incredible scholarship of our Elders, and the lives they've lived.[35] Almost all Elders featured in the exhibition and book had attended residential school or had parents who did, which silenced their tongues for decades, but did not vanish the language from their minds or spirit. Although it was not an exhibit about women specifically, more than half of the celebrated knowledge holders featured were women, testifying to the critical role that females play in the preservation and continuing use of X̱aayda kil and the philosophies, poetries, and knowledges contained within it. The exhibit and book featured evocative portraits of Haida Elders by Iraqi Canadian photographer Farah Nosh (Figure 5.5).

Focused on language, *That Which Makes Us Haida* makes the critical argument that language is central to all forms of Haida expression, art, and storytelling included; the push to keep the language is essential for this generation.[36] In the book's epilogue, I reflected on this historical moment: "Like art, language can both portray and dictate the progress of a culture.. . . I hope (that one day) my daughters marvel, in X̱aayda kil, at the thrill of growing up during the revival of their language, the same way I marvel at my luck of having grown up during the revival of our artistic and cultural practices."[37]

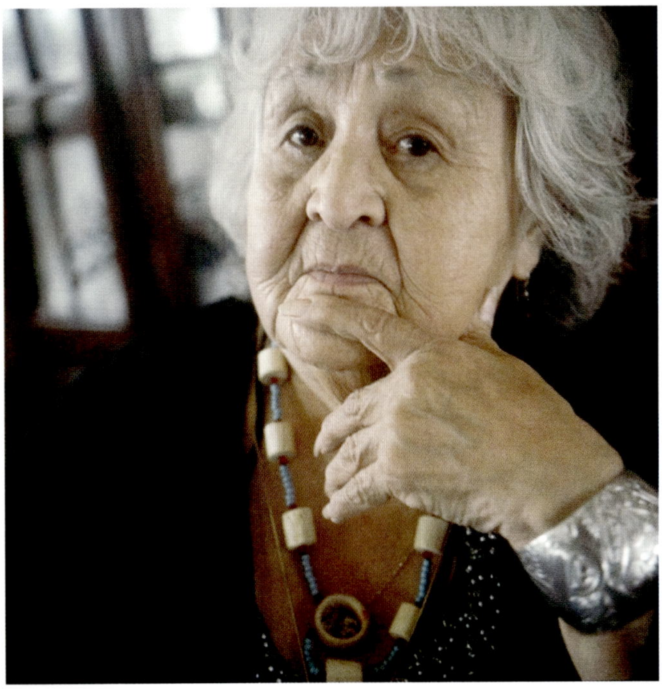

5.5. Gaada Mary Swanson, fluent speaker and teacher of the Haida language, featured in the exhibition and book *That Which Makes Us Haida: The Haida Language*. Photograph by Farah Nosh, ca. 2010. Courtesy of the Haida Gwaii Museum.

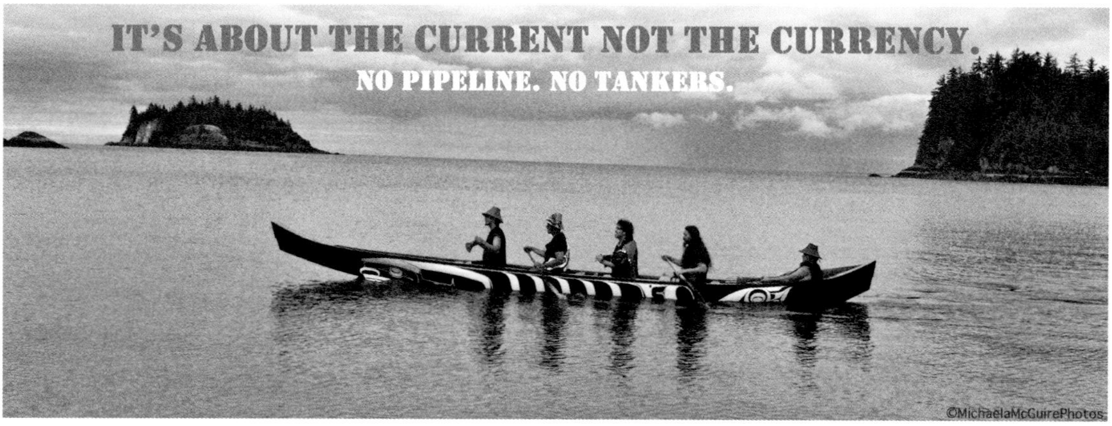

5.6. Members of the Skidegate Saints basketball team paddle *The Spirit of Rediscovery* for an anti-Enbridge campaign. Courtesy of the photographer, Michaela McGuire, 2012.

THANKS, BUT NO TANKS, 2013

Curated by Jisgang Nika Collison (Haida) and Taawla Jaad Kelsey Pelton (Haida)

Thanks, but No Tanks was a critical inquiry into how human relationships with their environment change when under perceived threat or perceived opportunity, using the proposed Enbridge Northern Gateway Pipeline (NGP) as catalyst.[38] *Thanks* featured nineteen artists from Haida Gwaii, British Columbia, and Alberta. The impetus for the show was the work of Michaela McGuire (Haida), who was twenty-four at the time of the exhibition. Two years prior, in a fiery response to the NGP, McGuire embarked on an anti-Enbridge campaign. Working with Haida citizens to create strong political imagery and messaging, her work spread like wildfire on social media, building on the empowerment of local testimony given at the 2012 Joint Review Panel Hearings and catching the eye of the Haida Gwaii Museum.[39] One key image was a collaboration between McGuire and members of the Skidegate Saints basketball team, who are known both on and off the court for their stance against oil and gas development on the coast (Figure 5.6). The exhibition's co-curator was Kelsey Pelton, who was nineteen years old at the time; her research, insight, and contributions to the forming of this show were integral to its success.

Thanks, but No Tanks was one of our museum's most successful exhibitions, inspiring intense critical thought, dialogue, and debate. It did not matter that McGuire was twenty-four, or an amateur photographer, or that she was studying criminology instead of arts and heritage. It did not matter that the exhibition's co-curator was a nineteen-year-old summer student who'd just begun her journey into postsecondary education. Women in our Nation—no matter their age—are seen and heard; our contributions to our Nation valued and expected.

GINA SUUDA TL'L X̱ASII ~ CAME TO TELL SOMETHING: ART & ARTIST IN HAIDA SOCIETY, 2014

Curated by Jisgang Nika Collison (Haida)

The exhibition *Gina Suuda Tl'l X̱asii ~ Came to Tell Something* explored the roles and responsibilities of art and artists in Haida society. It was the largest survey of classical Haida art—both ancestral and contemporary—in the museum's history, featuring eighty works (which packed the small gallery beyond its limits).[40] Pieces spanned weavings in cedar bark, spruce root, and wool, including the art of male weaver Albert Hans, along with fabric arts. Of course, there were also works in wood, ivory, baleen, argillite, and precious metals, including the art of female carver, Cori Savard. The exhibition featured the art and power of song and dance—breaking down the YaatsX̱aaydaG̱a categorization of visual arts as separated from the intangible contexts of song and ceremony (Figure 5.7).

The power of female song and dance was noted in ancient times and is still treasured today. The origin of song is said to have come from sisters of an Eagle lineage living on the West Coast just north of Kaisun. As they went into the woods for cedar bark, a great fog separated them from one sister's husband, who became a Supernatural being. Once the fog lifted, the sisters went up into the clouds and became Supernatural Beings known as The-Singers, the older named One-out-of-who-Mouth-Songs-hang; the younger named The-One-who-dances-about. In the

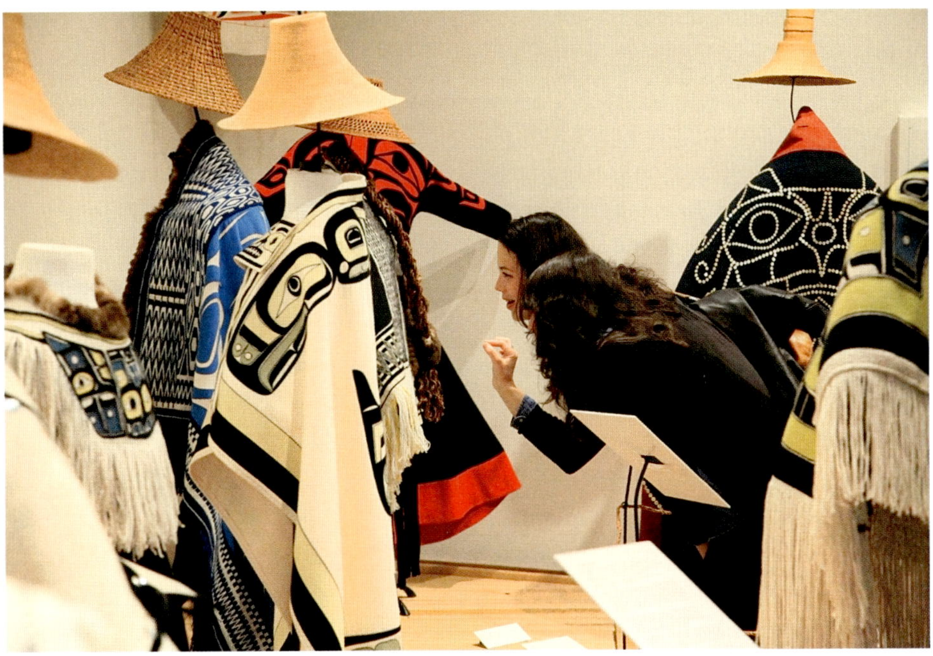

5.7. Visitors taking in the fine weaving and textiles featured in the exhibition *Gina Suuda Tl'l X̱asii ~ Came to Tell Something: Art & Artist in Haida Society*. Courtesy of photographer Rolf Bettner, 2014.

spring the sisters dance on top of Plain-Place mountain. When winter returns, they go back into the sky. It is said these women learned the songs from birds.[41] The Singers are mentioned several times throughout Haida history, providing songs and/or dancing for potlatches, to manage bad weather, to heal the dead or in other circumstances, aiding in grief.[42] Song and dance, like regalia, are critical parts of Haida life, interwoven in their roles of expressing proper respect to and enacting the work of day-to-day life and ceremonial occasions.

Looking back, 60 percent of the artworks in the *Gina Suuda Tl'l X̱asii* exhibition were by women. Almost 60 percent of the contributors to the book were women, with half of the works featured in the publication having been born from female hands.[43] I am told these percentages are remarkable in comparison to other exhibitions and books focused on the general arts of the Northwest Coast, but they are not remarkable to me. Drawing on the knowledge and skills of Haida women is part of my everyday life, which heavily informs my professional practice. Male artists such as Bill Reid, Robert Davidson, and James Hart are rightfully celebrated for their roles in the revitalization of Haida art and culture; Freda Diesing has received less public acclaim despite her critical role in the movement. When people write of Northwest Coast artistic and cultural revitalization, it is often centered on male-dominated art forms—carving and painting. Western society's recognition of female-gendered arts, and the artists themselves, are rarely spoken or thought of when celebrating Indigenous cultural and artistic revolutions. And yet they've been there all along.

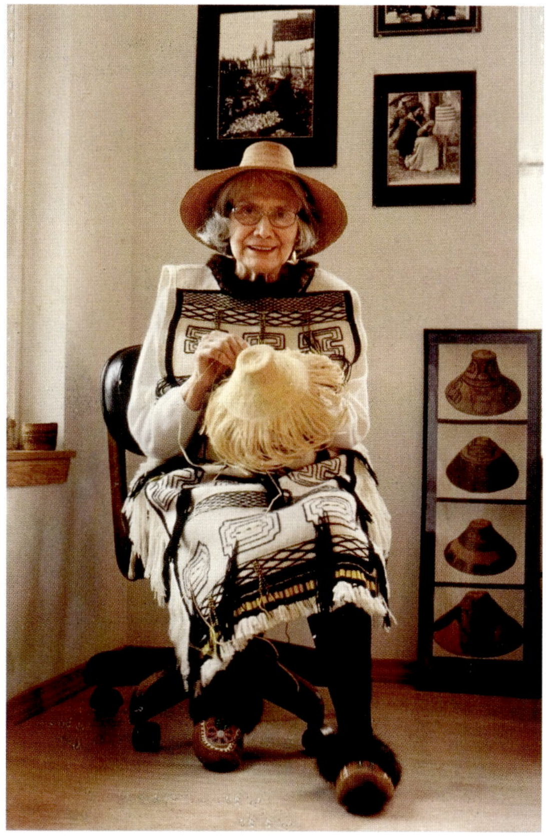

5.8. Ilskyalas Delores Churchill weaving *Long Ago Man's Hat*, replicated from a 300- to 550-year-old hat found with Kwäday Dän Ts'inchi, discovered in a melting glacier in northern British Columbia in 1999. Photograph by Hulleh Tsinunahjinnie, ca. 2012. Courtesy of the Haida Gwaii Museum.

One of the esteemed female artists in the *Gina Suuda Tl'l X̱asii* exhibition was weaver Delores Churchill (Figure 5.8), who was at the helm of revitalizing arts of the Northwest Coast. Learning from a long line of family weavers, Churchill has learned from the works of her Ancestors, spending more than forty years researching Haida (and other North Coast weavings) held in institutions around the globe. The volume of knowledge she has gained and shared is stupendous, as are the gathering and weaving techniques themselves. Churchill has taught people of various backgrounds about Haida weaving—not to encourage appropriation but to further the appreciation of our weavers, ancestral and living. In this, she educates her students on the individuality of northern weaving cultures, along with cultural rights and privileges. By receiving an introduction to this high art form, and the knowledge, skill, and time it takes to gather, prepare, and weave, views of women's "work" change. To know even a tiny bit about Haida weaving is to know that these works are of great, great value both intrinsically and economically.

I was fortunate to participate in one of Churchill's weaving classes in 2018. As we labored over our roots, Churchill spoke passionately about weaving, mentioning a notion that had been shared with her—weaving might be considered an invention more important than the wheel. Certainly, in the environment of Haida Gwaii, where canoes were our main mode of transportation, baskets and nets were integral to food gathering, and weaving kept us clothed, the wheel is not the yardstick for a great invention.

Perhaps the most important of Churchill's legacies is that she has passed her expertise and passion for Haida weaving on to her daughters, keeping the knowledge flowing through matrilineal lines. The art of cedar bark and spruce roots are predominantly held by Holly and April Churchill; wool by Evelyn Vanderhoop. Churchill has not only gifted her daughters with the ability to weave, she's also gifted them with the spiritual, environmental, and historical scholarship required to weave *properly.* Most important of all, she's passed on the understanding and responsibility that comes with carrying this expansive knowledge.

OUT OF CONCEALMENT: FEMALE SUPERNATURAL BEINGS OF HAIDA GWAII, 2017

Curated by Jisgang Nika Collison (Haida)

Most recently the museum presented the solo exhibition *Out of Concealment: Female Supernatural Beings of Haida Gwaii* by Haida lawyer, writer, singer, and visual artist Terri-Lynn Williams-Davidson. In the accompanying publication, Williams-Davidson writes of her lifelong fascination with Supernatural Beings, noting her observations from an early age that these Beings were well represented in sculpture and flat design, along with narration and song. Williams-Davidson began her personal exploration of the Supernatural by writing songs about them but found she could not escape her desire to visualize them.[44] In honoring this desire, Williams-Davidsons chose to represent the Supernaturals in her own image through photographic composition (Figure 5.9). She provides a new envisioning of Supernatural Beings, presented from a female world view.[45] While focused on the feminine, she brings gender balance through incorporating subtle imagery of her husband Robert

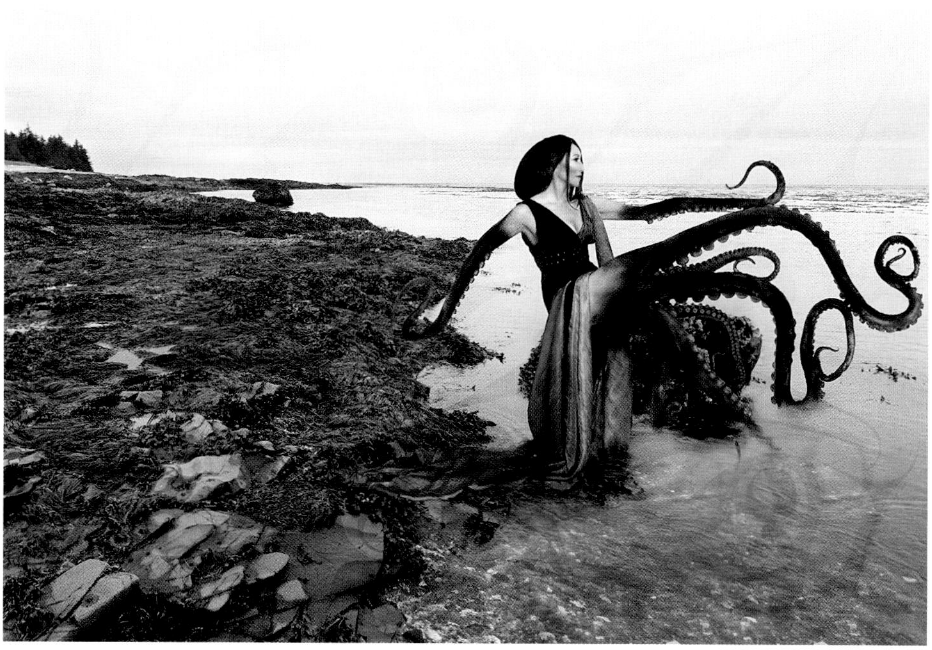

5.9. Terri-Lynn Williams-Davidson, *Naaw Jaad | Octopus Woman*, 2017. Courtesy of Raven Calling Productions. For a full list of artistic credits, see the exhibition publication *Out of Concealment: Female Supernatural Beings of Haida Gwaii* (Vancouver, BC: Heritage House Publishing, 2017).

Davidson's two- and three-dimensional art in each of her images. This provides the viewer another "bridge to the Beings and how they might be represented in two-dimensional or abstract art."[46]

In her endeavors to bring a contemporary existence to these Supernatural Beings, Williams-Davidson dressed in Indigenous fashion. She explains: "Traditionally, the power of Supernatural Beings is contained in dress and adornment. Dress in Indigenous cultures is integral to dramatizing and bringing to life Supernatural Beings and Crest Figures."[47] Interestingly, but not surprisingly, given the role of women in the arts of clothing and adornment in Haida society, all but one of the fashion designers were women. In the case of jewelry, the precious metals Williams-Davidson wore were created by men, while materials strung or woven together were made by women. Most important, *Out of Concealment* investigates not only the power of female Supernatural Beings, but also the power of female *human beings*, both in relation to the Earth and humanity:

> Many narratives, and especially narratives about female Supernatural Beings, are inherently sensual and sexual. In traditional Haida culture, and in many Indigenous cultures, female power is intrinsic to healthy sexuality. Christianity suppressed Indigenous feminine power and sexuality, and that suppression

> throughout colonial history is related to violence against women. Violence against women is further related to the wanton destruction of the land and sea. Stated positively, our respect for the land and sea is intimately tied to our respect for women. I dearly hope that sharing these Supernatural Beings will contribute to both the continued growth of women who own and radiate their power in respectful balance with masculine power, and of men who respect women, thereby reducing violence against women.[48]

Ultimately, the photographs featured in *Out of Concealment* illustrate the holistic nature of women's roles in Haida society, from the creative capacities of the female Supernaturals to the symbolic and operative powers of body adornment; from the rightful potency of women's sexuality to their role as protector and visionary.

Guudsdll ~ Ending

Indigenous peoples have faced violent and degrading colonial assaults that deeply injured the people, their cultures, belief systems, lands, and waters, with a particularly vehement approach to the silencing and persecution of women. While such colonial assaults are often thought of today as happening "over there"—in places such as the Middle East or Africa—they are still prevalent "over here." Nation-states such as Canada demonstrate continued acts of violence toward the lands and waters (and airways) by way of relentless promotion of the oil and gas industry. Other examples include the long-standing lack of action against the missing and murdered Indigenous women of Canada as well as its slow recognition of the power of female Indigenous art and scholarship.

Just as Haida artists hold a responsibility far greater than the ability to create physical artworks, museums and galleries hold a responsibility far greater than the care-taking of objects and the dissemination of knowledge associated with them. Museums and galleries can be agents of change. Nation-state museums hold the physical evidence of the Canada's genocide against Indigenous Nations (in this they carry the legacy of patriarchy), but they've also played an incredibly important role in the revitalization of Haida art forms and cultural practices as our Nation's scholars work with these museums (see chapter 10 by Kathryn Bunn-Marcuse in this volume). This new role of museums, and the softening of their colonial identity, continues to grow with these types of relationships, initially forged in the latter half of the 1900s by Indigenous artists such as Bill Reid and later through grassroots movements such as repatriation.

The foundation of Haida society is yahguudang (*respect*). My aunty GwaaGanad (Diane Brown) taught me we must have respect for all things; only then can we be worthy of respect ourselves. Women are no greater than men. Men are no greater than women. Human beings are not supreme in their existence. From this understanding comes the privilege of responsibility. Somewhere along the line, Haida Gwaii and the Supernatural Beings decided to believe in us. That is why we are here. They taught us how to live with Haida Gwaii and entrusted us with the stewardship of our home and of each other. This is the highest honor—to not only exist but to exist with the gift of consciousness, conscience, and a quest for knowledge. We are *privileged* to exist, and our relationship to the Earth and each other can only be one of reciprocity. The feminine powers surrounding us, and the feminine powers that exist in all of us, must be respected and embraced. It is all of our responsibility. Strong girls, strong world, as the saying goes.

NOTES

The author extends a huge haawa (*thank you*) to Kathryn Bunn-Marcuse for her guidance, assistance, and patience in all aspects of this chapter—as well as that of Aldona Jonaitis; Walker Brown for his research contributions and insights; the scholars/artists for their permissions as well as contributions to the Haida Nation and greater society; Elders of the HlG̱aagilda X̱aayda Kil Naay (Skidegate Haida Immersion Program) for Haida language assistance; Diane Brown for her ongoing cultural mentorship and scholarship; Evelyn Vanderhoop and Terri-Lynn Williams-Davidson for their review of some texts. Haawa to id Kuuniisii (*our Ancestors*). Haawa to Haida Gwaii—her lands, waters, and airways—and the Supernatural: that which makes us Haida.

1 YaatsX̱aaydaG̱a (Iron People) is the general term used by the Haida when referencing “white” people (historically this predominantly referred to European, Euro-American, and British men; foreign women were referred to as ‘Waasdan jiinas [Washington women]). The name arose from the plentiful amounts of iron these sailors brought in trade, which was highly valued by our Ancestors.

2 Christian White, quoted in Nika Collison, “Creating for Culture: Edenshaw’s Haida Roots and Cultural Transformations,” in *Charles Edenshaw*, edited by Robin Wright and Daina Augaitis, 21–27 (London: Black Dog Publishing, 2013), 22.

3 Nika Collison, “Ḵ’uuljaad Lady of High Esteem,” in *Gina Suuda Tl’l X̱asii ~ Came to Tell Something: Art & Artist in Haida Society*, edited by Nika Collison (Skidegate, Haida Gwaii: Haida Gwaii Museum Press, 2014), 5.

4 Captain Joseph Ingraham as cited in Margaret Blackman, “The Changing Status of Haida Woman: An Ethnohistorical and Life History Approach,” in *The World Is as Sharp as a Knife: An Anthology in Honour of Wilson Duff*, edited by Donald N. Victoria, 65–78 (Victoria: British Columbia Provincial Museum 1981), 69.

5 Missionaries arrived on Haida Gwaii following the devastating effects of the 1862 smallpox epidemic, which was purposefully introduced to our people with vaccines withheld; see *Haida Laas – Journal of the Haida Nation*, March 2009, www.haidanation.ca/wp-content/uploads/2017/03/jl_mar.09.pdf (accessed on July 16, 2018); Greg Lange, “Smallpox Epidemic of 1862 among Northwest Coast and Puget Sound Indians,” *HistoryLink.org*, April 2, 2003, www.historylink.org/File/5171 (accessed on August 1, 2018); and Joshua Ostroff, “How a Smallpox Epidemic Forged Modern British Columbia,” *Maclean’s*, August 1, 2017, www.macleans.ca/news/canada/how-a-smallpox-epidemic-forged-modern-british-columbia/ (accessed on

August 1, 2018). Like ship merchants, the missionaries did not care for the position of women in Haida society. It was not long before the church imposed Anglicized names upon our people along with its patrilineal system, whereby identity, lineage, rank, and property are inherited from men instead of women.

6 With the Indian Act of 1876, the Canadian government imposed a system on Indigenous Peoples that put them in a generic category of "Indians" and made them wards of the state. The goal was assimilation, which would erase Indigenous Nationhood, culture, and connection to territories, rights, and privileges. For more on the Indian Act, see "The Indian Act," *Indigenous Foundations*, https://indigenousfoundations.arts.ubc.ca/the_indian_act/ (accessed on September 9, 2018).

7 Section 12(1)(b) of the Indian Act provided a "legal" mechanism for the disenfranchisement of Indigenous women from their homes and communities. For more, see "The Indian Act," *Indigenous Foundations*, https://indigenousfoundations.arts.ubc.ca/the_indian_act/ under the heading "Bill C-31 and gender discrimination" (accessed on September 9, 2018).

8 The potlatch is our legal system and integral to the health and function of Indigenous social, political, and economic systems up and down the Northwest Coast. For information on the potlatch ban, see "The Indian Act," *Indigenous Foundations*, https://indigenousfoundations.arts.ubc.ca/the_indian_act/ under the heading "The 'Potlatch Law' & Section 141" (accessed on September 9, 2018).

9 The residential school system took young children away from their families and homes into institutions meant to destroy their connection to Nation, culture, and language. Most women did not have their children to raise and nurture, and children in residential school were devoid of family or safe upbringings—most subject to horrible abuses. This affected many survivors' abilities to reconnect with their communities, speak their languages, or develop the skills needed to raise a family. For more on the residential school system, see National Centre for Truth and Reconciliation, https://nctr.ca/map.php (accessed on November 14, 2019).

10 This count is based on Haida Gwaii Museum records of Haida collections held in 134 global institutions. There are many more inventories to be gathered and attributions to be sorted out.

11 Kathryn Bunn-Marcuse and Megan Smetzer, "Working to Change the Tide: Women Artists on the Northwest Coast," in *Hearts of Our People: Native American Women Artists*, edited by Jill Yohe, 258–72 (Minneapolis: Minneapolis Institute of Art, 2019), 272.

12 Charles F. Newcombe Files V.36-F.1., Haida Gwaii Museum. Haida orthographies have varied over the years, depending on the source. Names gleaned from historic records throughout this chapter are spelled as documented. Spellings of contemporary personal names have been provided by the name holders. All other Haida words are written in our own Haida orthography, developed and standardized by our Elders. A big haawa (*thank you*) to Walker Brown for bringing together the names, lineages, crests, and so on related to Figure 5.1.

13 On Skiljadai, see Charles F. Newcombe Files, V.38-F1 and V.55. On Lucy McKay, see the 1891 Skidegate census report and 1892 Skidegate baptism records, Haida Gwaii Museum.

14 Although the photographer in Figure 5.1 is attributed as Richard Maynard, evidence suggests the photo may have composed if not taken entirely by his wife, Hannah Maynard, who emigrated from England to Ontario, Canada, where she trained to be a professional photographer. Just as Indigenous women were pressed to be invisible, so were wives of the Yaats X̱aaydaG̱a (Iron Men), the legacy of colonialism being the erasure of female contributions to history in general. Robin K. Wright, "Skidegate Haida House Models in the White City: 'Laana Gaada guu.u HlGaagilda X̱aaydaG̱a naa gii niijing.a k'ad.dala kwaan" (working title), Bill Holm Center for the Study of Northwest Native Art, University of Washington Press (forthcoming).

15 Charles F. Newcombe Files V.38-F1.

16 Charles F. Newcombe Files V.55.

17 Giida Kuujuus (Walker Brown), personal communication with the author, 2018.

18 Jimmy Sterling, "Tc!aawu'nk![A]," in *Haida Texts and Myths: Skidegate Dialect*, Smithsonian Institution Bureau of American Ethnology 29, recorded by John R. Swanton and edited by W. H. Holmes, 58-69 (Washington, DC: Government Printing Office, 1905).

19 Doreen Jensen and Polly Sargent, *Robes of Power: Totem Poles on Cloth* (Vancouver: University of British Columbia Press, 1986).

20 Miles Richardson Jr., "Upholding Haida Law," in *Athlii Gwaii: Upholding Haida Law at Lyell*, edited by Jisgang Nika Collison, 13–28 (Haida Gwaii: Council of the Haida Nation Press, 2018), 16.

21 Bunn-Marcuse and Smetzer, "Working to Change the Tide."

22 It is important to note that female sG̱aaga were not uncommon in Haida history. There are sure to be plenty of instances where women hold the scholarship necessary to turn a piece of bone or other material into a potent instrument of healing.

23 Walter McGregor, "How Shining-Heavens Himself To Be Born," in *Haida Texts and Myths: Skidegate Dialect*, 26–31.

24 Bunn-Marcuse and Smetzer, "Working To Change the Tide."

25 Robin K. Wright, *Northern Haida Master Carvers* (Seattle: University of Washington Press, 2001).

26 John R. Swanton, "Contributions to the Ethnology of the Haida," in *The Jesup North Pacific Expedition, Memoir of the American Museum of Natural History*, volume 5, part 1, recorded by John R. Swanton and edited by Franz Boas (Leiden: E. J. Brill Ltd., 1905), 92. Jiila K̲un is spelled as Djila'qons in "Contributions of the Ethnology of the Haida."

27 Tom Stevens, "Story of the House-Point Families," in *Haida Texts and Myths*: *Skidegate Dialect*, 318–21.

28 Evelyn Vanderhoop, "From One Realm to Another: The Naaxiin Robe," in *Gina Suuda Tl'l X̲asii ~ Came to Tell Something: Art & Artist in Haida Society*, edited by Nika Collison, 7–11 (Skidegate, Haida Gwaii: Haida Gwaii Museum Press, 2014), 10.

29 Cultural genocide refers to implementation of the Indian Act, the residential school system, and the extreme social and economic marginalization of Indigenous communities by colonizers.

30 William White, personal communication with the author, 2017.

31 Francis Williams, as quoted in Jensen and Sargent, *Robes of Power*, 27.

32 This title is borrowed from the name of the Haida Gwaii Watchmen longhouse at G̱andll K'in (Hotsprings Island) located in Gwaii Haanas, the lower southern region of Haida Gwaii.

33 Native American and Indigenous Studies Association, Vancouver, BC, session on "Women's Work—Native American and First Nations Women Artists in Exhibits and Scholarship," organized by Kathryn Bunn-Marcuse.

34 Robert Davidson, From a Few Weavers, quoted in exhibition text (in a label in the show), 2009.

35 Scott Steedman and Jisgang Nika Collison, eds., *That Which Makes Us Haida: The Haida Language* (Skidegate, Haida Gwaii: Haida Gwaii Museum Press, 2011). There are three main regional dialects of the Haida language: Skidegate, Old Massett, and Alaskan. X̲aayda kil means *Haida language* in Skidegate dialect; in Old Massett and Alaskan dialect, it is X̲aad kil.

36 The Haida language is an endangered linguistic isolate with fewer than twenty fluent speakers alive today. However, there are almost fifty active learners, most of them women, dedicated to saving this precious art form.

37 Jisgang Nika Collison, "Just My Luck," in *That Which Makes Us Haida: The Haida Language*, 238.

38 The Enbridge Northern Gateway Pipeline (NGP) would have transported bitumen from Alberta to the coast of BC through a pipeline, then through Haida waters to other countries via oil tankers.

39 The Joint Review Panel (JRP) was an independent body mandated by the Canadian government and the National Energy Board to assess the environmental effects of Enbridge's proposed NGP. They heard from interveners across British Columbia and Alberta, testifying for or against the NGP. When the JRP came to Haida Gwaii in 2012, testimony spanned several days with more than two hundred locals participating, ranging in age from as young as five to Elders. Not one was in favor of the pipeline. The JRP gave the green light for the NGP, but in 2016 the Canadian Courts overturned the JRP's approval of the project.

40 *Gina Suuda Tl'l X̱asii ~ Came to Tell Something: Art & Artist in Haida Society,* edited by Nika Collison (Skidegate, Haida Gwaii: Haida Gwaii Museum Press, 2014). In using the term "classical," the author refers to the traditional art forms and techniques the Haida developed and have maintained over thousands of years.

41 Swanton, *Contributions to the Ethnology of the Haida,* 30–31.

42 Swanton, *Contributions to the Ethnology of the Haida,* 30–31, 36–37, 64, and 170.

43 The number of female-made works dropped to 50 percent due to augmenting the book with additional artworks.

44 Terri-Lynn Williams-Davidson, Artist Statement, "The Hope of the Supernatural Beings," in *Out of Concealment: Female Supernatural Beings of Haida Gwaii,* edited by Lara Kordic, xiv–xvi (Vancouver, BC: Heritage House Publishing Company, 2017).

45 Author's note: Male-gendered arts (carving and two-dimensional design) generally depict the likeness of a Supernatural Being as individuals within a greater story. Female-gendered arts (weaving and geometric design) typically bring the Supernatural to life through visual representations of the greater narrative in which the Being exists.

46 Terri-Lynn Williams-Davidson, personal communication with the author, 2018.

47 Williams-Davidson, "Hope of the Supernatural Beings," xv.

48 Williams-Davidson, "Hope of the Supernatural Beings," xvi.

CHAPTER 6

Copper Seaweed and Woven Octopus Bags

SHGEN GEORGE AND THE ART OF RESILIENCE

Megan A. Smetzer

THE BEADED, APPLIQUÉD, AND WOVEN WORKS OF TLINGIT ARTIST SHGEN DOO Tan George are evocative of the long history of Indigenous women's resilience in maintaining important cultural knowledge through the passing on of aesthetic and technical abilities from one generation to the next. Resilience has become an increasingly powerful and expansive concept in relation to the cultural expressions of Indigenous women. Mohawk curator Lee Ann Martin has argued that resilience is more than just recovering from difficult circumstances, rather, it should be viewed "as being embodied by endurance, adaptability and sovereignty in relation to historical practices and contemporary identities."[1] George's series of woven and appliquéd octopus bags is a potent example of this perspective as it unsettles the history of settler colonialism and its repercussions, particularly in Southeast Alaska. Not only do these bags embody the ways in which early encounters, the imposition of religion, and the impact of salvage ethnography contribute to the complexities of the present day, but they also reinforce those aspects of Tlingit ways of knowing that have survived or been revived due to the efforts of women.

More broadly, scholars Maile Arvin, Eve Tuck, and Angie Morrill's essay on decolonizing feminism contends that rather than being at the margins in terms of their lived experiences and intellectual contributions over the past five hundred years, Indigenous women "have been an invisible presence in the center, hidden by the gendered logics of settler colonialism."[2] This perspective is particularly relevant to the Northwest Coast as the categories defining Indigenous cultural expressions that developed from the patriarchal and paternalistic institutions of settler colonialism beginning in the nineteenth century created hierarchies of value: gender (male over female); materiality (locally acquired over trade goods); and use (community based over made for sale). The monumental and public artworks carved and painted by men fit neatly into Western hierarchies of artistic value, overshadowing the woven, sewn, and beaded works created by women, and colored the ways in which women's cultural expressions have been received outside of their communities of origin throughout most of the twentieth century.

Despite the imposition of these external categories of value, Tlingit women have continued to pass along cultural knowledge through the making of woven and appliquéd robes, baskets, and beadwork that engage with the complex realities of the era within which they have been created. Though the richness and complexity of this ongoing cultural production has only begun to be acknowledged in the art historical literature, many community members have continued to value women's cultural expressions and their role in maintaining cultural practices. As Arvin, Tuck, and Morrill state, Indigenous women do not need to be "saved" from settler colonialism; rather it must be recognized that "they are already, and have long been, working toward decolonization within and beyond their own communities' boundaries."[3] Through her octopus bags, George approaches this history in a subtle manner, using weaving, appliqué, and the materiality of copper to acknowledge Tlingit women's resilience throughout the past two centuries. Due to their origins and uses, octopus bags are a particularly powerful expression of this intercultural history.

A Brief History of the Tlingit Náak̲w gwéil (*Octopus Bag*)

Made from cotton and woolen cloth and embellished with seed beads in floral and seaweed designs, octopus bags acquired their name in Southeast Alaska from the four pairs of "tabs" or "legs" hanging below a large pouch. They were (and continue to be) worn as ceremonial regalia, hung from a beaded strap or braided cord across the chest. These bags were brought into Tlingit territory during the last quarter of the nineteenth century via Indigenous trade routes along the major rivers and over mountain passes from the interior. As I have argued elsewhere, octopus bags became widespread throughout Southeast Alaska for a variety of reasons, including resonance with Russian Orthodox Church banners, which also feature richly embellished cloth and dangling tabs; the significance of the numbers four and eight within Tlingit cultural practices; as well as the acknowledgment of octopuses as powerful creatures.[4]

Initially, the scarcity of octopus bags in Tlingit territory likely signified exclusive rights to important trade routes to the interior as there would have been no other way to acquire them. This is illustrated by the appearance of the earliest known bag in Southeast Alaska displayed among other significant clan belongings in an 1878 photograph of Kaawishté (Chief Shakes V), the head of the Naanya.aayí clan, lying in state near present-day Wrangell. By the 1890s octopus bags had become a popular item of ceremonial regalia worn by women and men throughout the region, appearing in photographs of koo.éex' (*memorial feasts*) and other significant

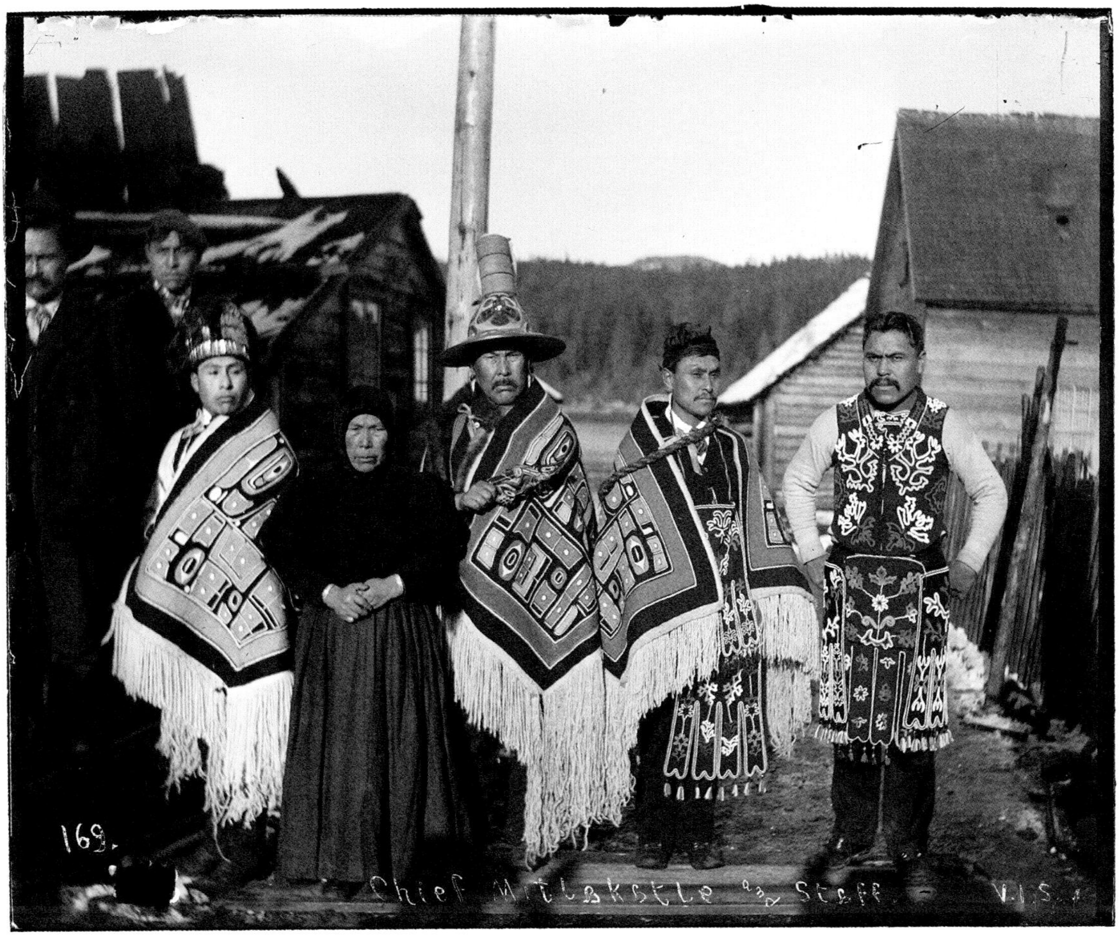

6.1. Incorrectly captioned “Chief Mitlakatle and Staff,” this photograph depicts a Basket Bay headman and his relatives. The two men at the right of the photograph, identified as Billy Jones (L’aangooshú, Nahóowu) and Peter Dick (Kaatéenaa), wear multiple octopus bags embellished with seaweed designs. Alaska State Library, Vincent Soboleff Photograph Collection, ca. 1896–1920, photograph by Vincent I. Soboleff, P1-018.

gatherings from Wrangell to Yakutat, such as this image depicting a headman from Basket Bay and his relatives (Figure 6.1).[5]

Early bags, either traded into Southeast Alaska or made locally, were embellished with a wide range of designs inspired by interior Athapaskan floral beading practices and Victorian decorative scroll motifs found on china and other imported goods. Within a few years of the octopus bag’s arrival in Southeast Alaska, Tlingit women developed an original pattern that more accurately represented the local environment and cultural concerns identified as “seaweed” or “kelp.” These designs are still in use today on octopus bags and other regalia; historically, they were used in souvenir form on moccasins and wall pockets. The latter usage distracted from the important role beadwork had on ceremonial regalia acting as a diversion from the continuation of important cultural practices despite the attempts to suppress them. Because beaded souvenirs used introduced materials and were made for sale to tourists, they were perceived as articles reflecting assimilation rather than resistance to missionaries and government officials. Settler perspectives such as these blinded them to the ways in which beadwork could signal resistance, which may explain the explosion of beading on regalia during the era of extensive ethnographic collecting for museums. Beaded regalia from the Northwest Coast was rarely acquired prior to the early twentieth century, and even then only by special access collectors as beadwork was perceived as inauthentic because of its "contamination from European wares."[6]

Seaweed

Beaded seaweed designs are well-known within Tlingit communities. Though color and shape may vary, seaweed designs consist of two to four rows of beads creating an outline of a scroll-like shape. Colors tend to be segmented and switch at curves or "contour changes."[7] The prevalence of these designs on Tlingit regalia and other items indicate the importance of all types of seaweed to the health and well-being of Tlingit people in terms of sustenance, medicine, and other social and spiritual attachments to place. Despite this cultural significance, works exhibiting beaded seaweed designs have rarely appeared in academic scholarship.

In 1904 anthropologist John R. Swanton recorded an origin story called Géesh Daax̱ woogoodi Yéil (Raven Who Went Down along the Bull Kelp), told in Sitka by Dekina'k![u], an elder from the Ḵóok Hít (Box House). This story explains how Raven created the tides (which had been previously controlled by an old woman), allowing all Tlingit people access to the rich resources of the intertidal zone, including different kinds of seaweed.[8] This origin story is beautifully embodied when multiple seaweed motifs are sewn onto a bag or garment, each pattern connected one to the other by a single row of beads. In 1938 an unrecorded Tlingit individual told Axel Rasmussen, the superintendent of schools at Skagway, that "a meander line of beaded work on a shirt was said to represent the pattern left on the sandy beach by the water of the receding tide."[9]

Some seaweed, such as géesh (*kelp*), was used as fishing line or was known as a good place to gather herring eggs; other types were dried and eaten for food or medicine; or traded or sold within the cash economy that emerged after contact. More recently, the importance of seaweed as a significant dietary staple has been recognized in public events. At Celebration—a four-day biannual event featuring dance, song, oration, and an art exhibition—a laaḵ'ásk (*black seaweed*) contest acknowledges its value. Prizes are awarded based on the taste and texture of the locally processed vitamin-rich food.[10] As well as being an important food source, kelp and other seaweed have additional cultural meanings. Nineteenth-century ethnographer George Thornton Emmons noted a Raven moiety seaweed crest, though he did not state its specific clan association.[11] Kelp is also embodied in the ceremonial practices of specific clans, such as the Ravens from Angoon, who have a kelp dance that emulates the movement of seaweed as the tide changes.[12] In these ways and others, seaweed is implicated in everything from physical survival to cultural revival.

Copper

In George's *Géesh* octopus bag (Figure 6.2) the seaweed design takes on additional layers of meaning, becoming a metaphor of women's wealth through its rendering in copper—a material of affluence along the entire coast, often formed into valuable shield-shaped objects known in Tlingit territory as tina.a. George has affixed three curvilinear copper seaweed shapes to the center of the bag, which is woven in red, black, and white wool using geometric Ravenstail patterns. Intriguingly, the transformation of the seaweed design from beads to copper and its addition to an octopus bag brings together two related stories from the Raven cycle that indicate the powerful nature of the devilfish (octopus) and the value of copper, linked through the marriages of a high-ranked Tlingit woman.

Shared with Swanton in 1904 by Katishan, chief of the Wrangell Kasq!aque'di, the first story tells of the young woman's marriage to a devilfish, which ends in an interspecies war and the death of the devilfish husband at the hands of her family.[13] In the second story, without permission from her parents, the same young woman marries the seemingly poor young man who helped defeat the devilfish. When her mother goes to retrieve her, she finds her daughter living in a home entirely made from copper. After the new husband gifts the mother eight copper plates, her family approves of the marriage through the gifting of eight slaves in return.[14]

Though copper seems rigid and inflexible, it is in fact one of the softest and most workable metals, even softer than the wood used by men for carving. As such, there is a natural affinity between copper and the malleable materials typically used by women, thus becoming an appropriate medium to represent women and their multiple connections to wealth. One version of the origin story of L!ê'naxxi'daq (Property Woman), for example, describes her carrying her child on her back and two coppers under her cloak. In one encounter she scratches a man with her copper fingernails when he takes her child. To get her child back, Property Woman gives him the two coppers and explains that the scabs from her scratches will bring great wealth to his family.[15]

Women's wealth includes the skills and knowledge passed down from generation to generation—the seasonal gathering, processing, and management of seaweed and other food stores to feed family and community (a task that most often

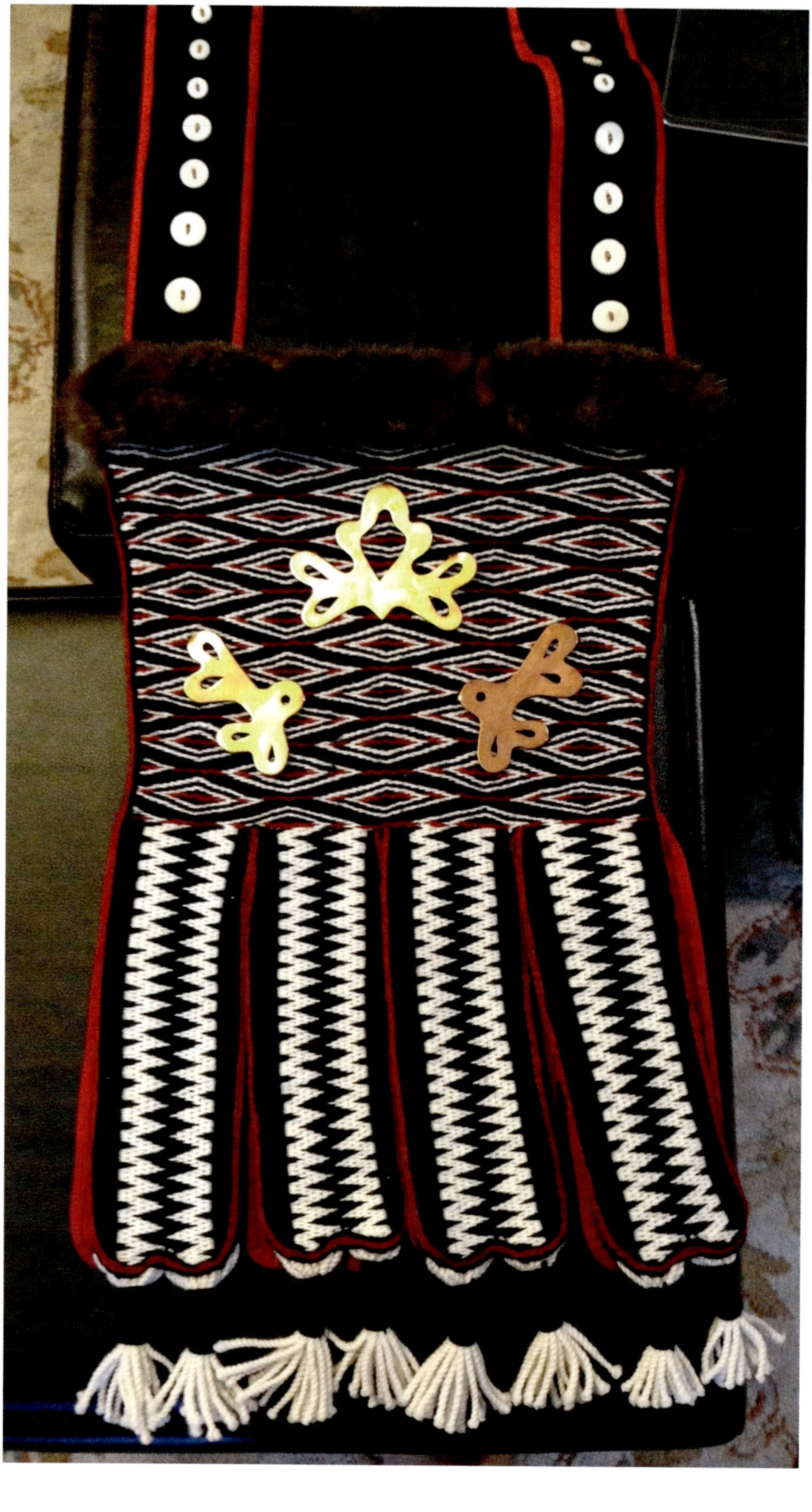

falls to women). More broadly, it also includes the weaving, sewing, and beading practices used to communicate personal and clan membership as well as specific knowledge of and relationships to the land developed over thousands of years. The transformation of the kelp design from beadwork into copper on George's *Géesh* bag is a powerful acknowledgment of women's ways of knowing and resilience in the face of the enormous pressures brought to bear on Tlingit people and their cultural expressions by settler colonialism.

Chilkat Weaving

While seaweed designs rendered in copper might represent the tangible outcomes of women's wealth, George's woven octopus bags suggest the intangible wealth of clan histories, family connections, and the acquisition of artistic abilities. The diversity of George's artistic education enables her to weave the wefts of Tlingit ways of knowing through the warps of settler colonialism, thus evoking the complexities of contemporary Tlingit identity in her octopus bags. George credits the cultural knowledge and oratory of her community as well as the practice of her mother, non-Indigenous wildlife artist JoAnn George, for influencing her own artistic path. As a girl, George learned how to bead from her paternal grandmother, the late Lydia George, an intergenerational teaching practice experienced by many Tlingit women. She supplemented her community-based knowledge with a fine arts degree from the University of Puget Sound, where she first experimented with copper seaweed designs.[16]

Upon returning to Alaska to become an elementary school teacher, George expanded her artistic knowledge by apprenticing with Clarissa Rizal to learn Chilkat weaving and with Cheryl Samuel to learn Ravenstail. George's artistic path—from community, to university, and back again—illuminates the power of her work as she effectively combines intercultural histories and disparate inspirations into each compelling and complex piece. *Keet Oox̱ú*, the title of George's bag, woven primarily with the Chilkat braided-twining technique (Figure 6.3), directly references her Dak̲l'aweidí clan house, Keet Oox̱ú Hít (Killer Whale Tooth House), in Angoon. Though George's bag depicts a complete crest design, it resonates with the nineteenth-century potlatch practice of tearing and distributing Chilkat robes to pay high-ranked witnesses. Combining Chilkat weaving techniques in the body of the bag, which depicts a killer whale dorsal fin with a hole, above a side view of a toothy killer whale face, and Ravenstail weaving techniques at the end of each leg, the bag emulates those pieces of distributed robes that were subsequently transformed into

6.2. Shgen Doo Tan George, *Géesh*, 2011. Copper, wool, sea otter fur, abalone buttons. Photograph courtesy of the artist.

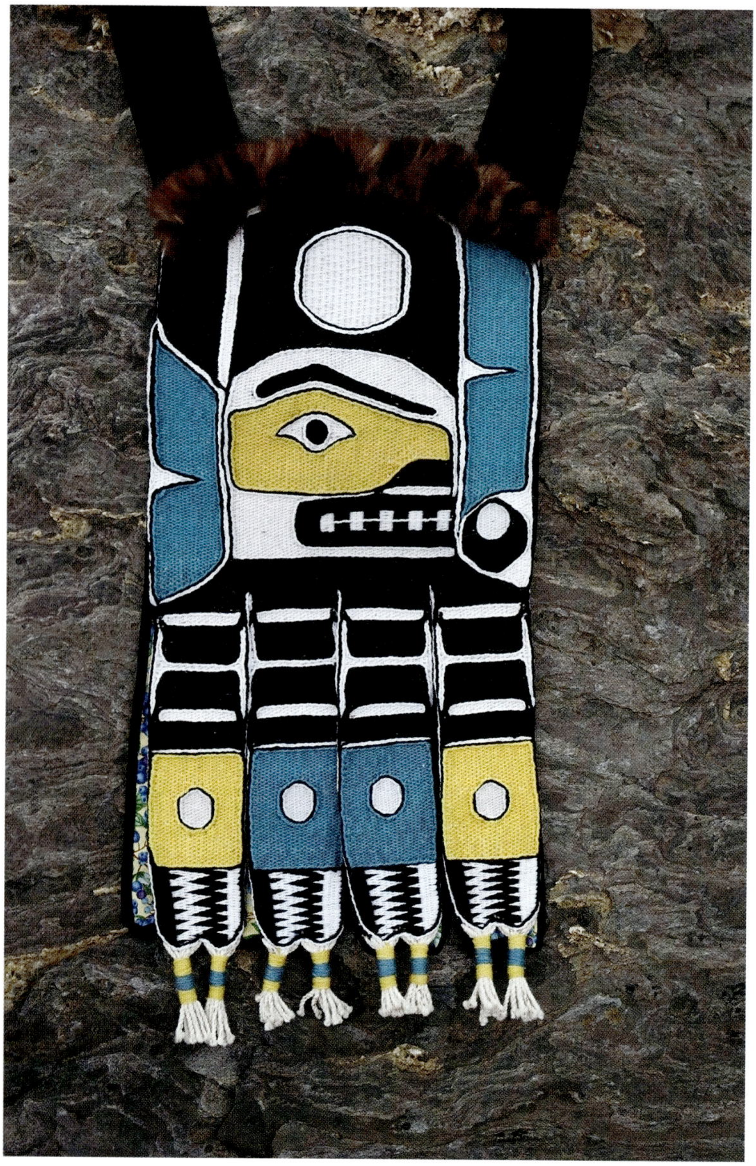

6.3. Shgen Doo Tan George, *Keet Oox̱ú (Killer Whale Tooth)*, 2014. Wool, sea otter fur. Photograph courtesy of the artist.

new items of regalia, such as leggings, hats, and bags.[17] As each robe fragment was imbued with great status and meaning, the new regalia enabled the recipient to visually reinforce their own rank and gain additional prestige at subsequent ceremonial occasions.[18]

In a subtle way, similar to rendering seaweed from copper, the seemingly fragmented Chilkat design in the shape of an octopus bag links women's aesthetic abilities to the customary roles of Tlingit women in trading relationships that contributed to the acquisition of clan wealth prior to and through the early years of settler colonialism. Marriage was perhaps the most significant means to consolidate relationships as women brought wealth and strengthened clan connections. In addition, high-ranked, older Tlingit women were expert negotiators and controlled trade—talents often remarked upon with various levels of frustration by early visitors. Major C. E. S. Wood, who traveled to Alaska in 1877, noted: "Their [women's] authority in all matters is unquestioned. No bargain is made, no expedition set on foot, without first consulting the women. Their veto is never disregarded."[19] Although both marriage and trade contributed to a clan's wealth, women's central roles in facilitating its acquisition were generally not recognized outside of Tlingit communities. Through the combination of a customary weaving practice with a form acquired through trade, this bag serves as a reassertion of those significant aspects of Tlingit women's lives that were devalued by the processes of settler colonialism.

Ravenstail Weaving

In addition, the Ravenstail designs on the tabs of the *Keet Ooxú* bag and that which comprise the whole of the *Géesh* bag embody the ways in which women, both Indigenous and settler, have worked to revive and pass on this previously dormant technique. Unlike the customary practices of Chilkat weaving in which men provide the curvilinear formline design and women weave the materials, Tlingit women both design and execute Ravenstail. The geometric designs themselves directly relate to patterns found on spruce root baskets, some of the names of which highlight women's connections to the natural and spiritual world. For example, the zigzag "lightening" pattern is also known as the "tongue of the thunderbird." Another pattern known as "garter"—a series of long and short dashes—refers to split quillwork patterns used to adorn leggings made by interior Athapaskan-speaking women and acquired by Tlingit people through trade and intermarriage. Other patterns such as "the cross" indicate the development of a new design after the arrival of the Russian Orthodox Church.[20] These connections underline the deep and relatively unexplored history of designs attributed specifically to women and their adaptability in terms of developing designs that embody current realities and incorporating diverse materials and forms.

Corresponding to the development of new basketry patterns, the supplanting of Ravenstail by Chilkat weaving at some point in the eighteenth-century points to the desire for innovation and experimentation by Tlingit women in the past. No doubt the challenge of creating curvilinear instead of geometric forms was appealing in terms of the ability to create more complex designs. The capacity to represent clan crests in ways similar to male carvers likely increased the prestige of the weaver. Taking inspiration from these female ancestors, contemporary Tlingit artists have embraced innovation and experimentation in terms of materials and designs, both as beaders and weavers but also as jewelers, painters, carvers, and installation artists. Too often, the recognition of this long-standing practice of embracing the new has been stifled by those patriarchal categories of value imposed by external institutions, whether museums, art markets, or other places that have historically evaluated cultural expressions executed by men as more significant than those made by women. By recentering women and their practices in terms of an ongoing engagement with new ideas and materials, the vitality of women's work becomes increasingly apparent.

Appliqué

Like the woven *Keet Ooxú* bag, the innovative bag called *Keet* (Figure 6.4) also illustrates George's clan crest. Incorporating a crest is highly unusual in an octopus bag, though it is done quite subtly here as the bag is cut from a black felt formline design of a killer whale appliquéd on a dark-blue ground. The flowing design of the blue and white beads affixed to the bag's surface represent the water vapor exhaled from a whale's blowhole. By adding a crest to a type of regalia made by women and that typically does not incorporate those designs, George brings attention to the customary matrilineal acquisition of clan identity. As scholars Richard and Nora Dauenhauer have pointed out, however, this aspect of Tlingit cultural practice has been undermined due to the nineteenth-century imposition of patrilineal laws of inheritance and has contributed to a "reorientation" of Tlingit social organization from one of "traditional" ethnicity to "civic" ethnicity.[21]

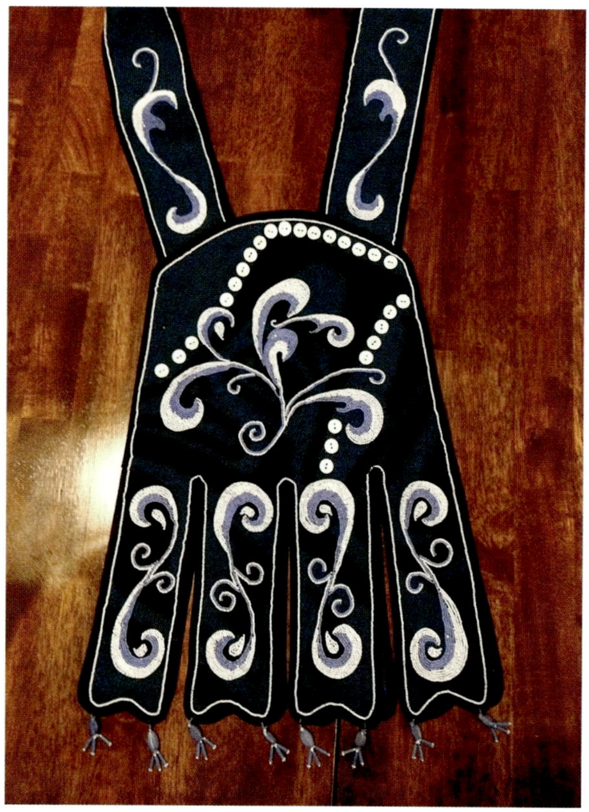

6.4. Shgen Doo Tan George, *Keet,* 2013, front view. Felt and cotton cloth, beads, abalone buttons. Photograph courtesy of the artist.

The Dauenhauers suggest that many individuals have come to identify themselves more broadly as culturally Tlingit rather than specifically as being from a certain clan and house. In part, this is due to the need to organize at a community level to gain rights within settler institutions throughout the first half of the twentieth century. In more recent decades, community members have undertaken the important work of researching and reasserting the rights and privileges of specific clans and houses, including those obtained matrilineally. George's purposeful transformation of curving Victorian floral motifs into a killer whale spout, like the transformation of beaded seaweed designs into copper, suggests the reclamation of the power of Tlingit women, acknowledging the reemergence of Indigenous ways of knowing through the weight of settler history. The layering of multiple motifs and meanings through beadwork and appliqué acknowledges the intercultural realities of the present but also engages with concerns around the access to and translation of cultural knowledge.

Access to Indigenous Knowledge

In a 2014 artist statement, George noted: "Each of my bags has its own secret. I have always been drawn to art that is more than its first impression."[22] Her comment reveals how the nuanced use of material has meanings that are not accessible on first view or to everyone. The secrets alluded to tend to be aesthetic in nature. For example, the decorative fabric used to line the appliquéd octopus bag renders killer whales from patterns loosely based on formline design. Moreover, our conversations over

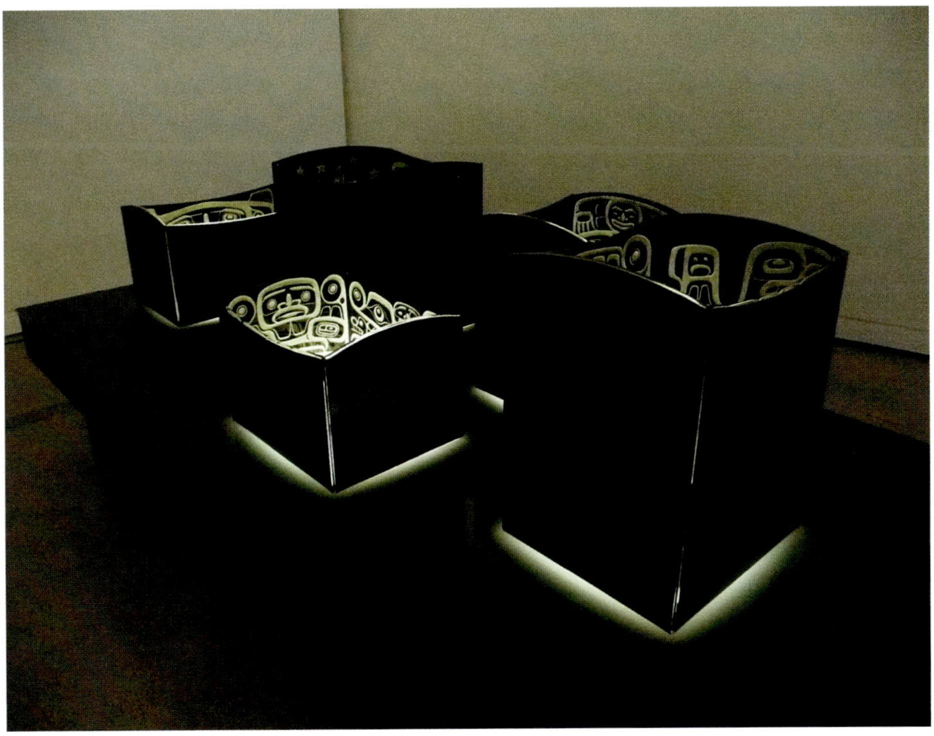

6.5. Marianne Nicolson, *Wanx'id: to hide, to be hidden*, 2010, exterior view. Glass, light, photographic prints. Photograph by Karen Duffek. Courtesy of Marianne Nicolson and UBC Museum of Anthropology (2826).

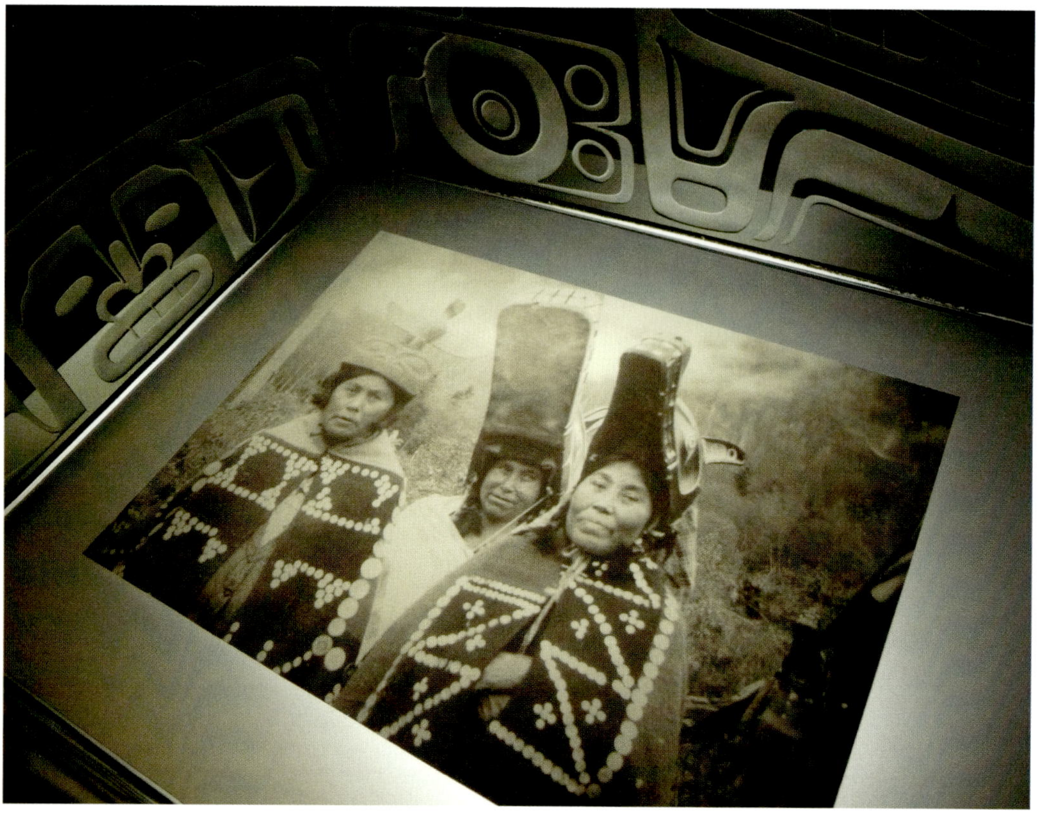

6.6. Marianne Nicolson, *Wanx'id: to hide, to be hidden*, 2010, interior view. Glass, light, photograph prints. 33 cm × 51.4 cm × 41.5 cm. Photograph by Karen Duffek. Courtesy of Marianne Nicolson and UBC Museum of Anthropology (2826/3).

several years have touched on the subject of who has access to or the right to share certain kinds of knowledge. This has become an increasingly important dialogue that has grown as public displays of crests and regalia have flourished in community-based ceremonies as well as in public events such as Celebration.

Many Indigenous artists along the Northwest Coast share George's interest, as the needed discourse around Indigenous sovereignty and rights gain increasing public attention. Particularly relevant to the consideration of George's octopus bags is Dzawada̱'enux̱w (Kwakwa̱ka̱'wakw) artist Marianne Nicolson's 2010 sculptural work *Wanx'id: to hide, to be hidden* (Figure 6.5). When viewed from a distance, the seven forbidding black forms in the shape of bentwood boxes suggest an impenetrable wall regulating access to knowledge and enforcing cultural boundaries. Glimpses of glowing figures composed from ovoids and other formline designs compel the viewer to draw near and peer inside. Illuminated from below, a photograph of regalia-clad matriarchs become visible at the bottom of one box, embraced by the powerful figures embellishing the interior spaces (Figure 6.6). Nicolson's

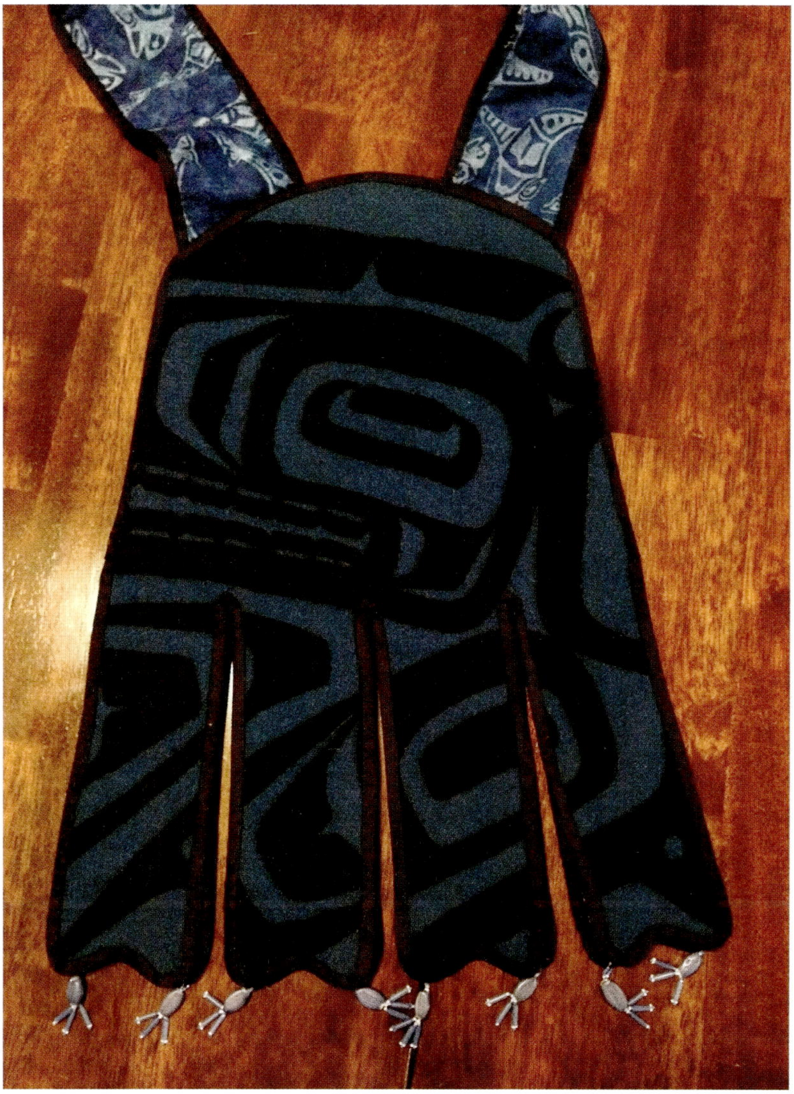

6.7. Shgen Doo Tan George, *Keet*, 2013, back view. Felt and cotton cloth, beads, abalone buttons. Photograph courtesy of the artist.

work positions Indigenous women and their wealth of knowledge as central to the process of decolonization, even as it has not been recognized in this way until recently, substantiating the perspective of Arvin, Tuck, and Morrill.[23]

Though more subtly than Nicolson, George's *Keet* bag resonates with these concepts by using small white buttons on the front of the bag to emphasize the dorsal fin—the most frequently observed and easily recognized characteristic of a killer whale above the water's surface. The part of the design concealed on the back (Figure 6.7) includes the eye, mouth, and pectoral flipper, suggesting that some types of knowledge are only visible to and communicable by specific individuals. The layering of each material and design element in this bag—beads, buttons, wool appliqué, and cotton lining—acts as a metaphor for the reclamation of women's power and knowledge and the care with which it should be transmitted. As George herself notes, the beadwork is the first thing you notice, but as you take more time to look, other layers become apparent. The whole process of its creation embodies the history of intercultural relations on the Northwest Coast—from early contact, through the imposition of the institutions of settler colonialism, to the hard work being done today within communities to decolonize. The crest, initially created from whole cloth, is nearly destroyed as it is cut into a new form, yet when it is recombined and embellished, it becomes something more than it was, suggesting a way forward, a renewed strength, and a reclamation of the power to determine the boundaries around cultural knowledge.

Women at the Center

In his 1921 discussion of spruce root basketry, Tlingit ethnographer Louis Shotridge noted the importance of women to the continuation of cultural practices despite the pressures of settler colonialism. "An invader might satisfy himself in saying that the native customs and habits have about disappeared," Shotridge wrote, "but could the lid of the true woman's mind be thrown wide open there would be seen the mystic veneration of her art still alive and active."[24] He eloquently points out that as the more overt cultural practices of Tlingit people were being suppressed and outsiders were committing salvage ethnography, women were maintaining Tlingit ways of knowing in quiet yet powerful ways.

Nonetheless, despite the recognition of women's abilities in this history, the legacies of settler colonialism have contributed to the alteration and devaluation of their customary roles and cultural expressions. Fortunately, this reality is shifting as women today are being acknowledged as central to the current processes of decolonization. Shgen Doo Tan George's woven and appliquéd octopus bags embody the cultural continuity noted by Shotridge in terms of the execution of her complex designs and her unique combination of materials and methods. She subtly acknowledges the multiple layers of meaning accreted to the seaweed design specifically, and octopus bags more generally. In this way George affirms the customary status of the materials, motifs, and techniques she uses. She also acknowledges that their recombination and subsequent transformation embodies the ongoing resilience of Tlingit women and suggests some of the ways in which she and other Indigenous artists from the region are unsettling the past to create a more equitable future.

NOTES

I am deeply appreciative to Shgen George for her generosity in sharing her considerable knowledge and beautiful work with me over the years—gunalchéesh! I would also like to thank Kathryn Bunn-Marcuse, Mique'l Dangeli, and Aldona Jonaitis for their insightful comments on various drafts as this work transitioned from symposium paper to fully fledged chapter.

1 Lee Ann Martin as quoted in Jen Zoratti, "Showing Resilience: MAWA Exhibits Works from Indigenous Women from Coast to Coast," *Winnipeg Free Press*, March 3, 2018, www.winnipegfreepress.com/arts-and-life/entertainment/arts/showing-resilience-476821553.html.

2 Maile Arvin, Eve Tuck, and Angie Morrill, "Decolonizing Feminism: Challenging the Connections between Settler Colonialism and Heteropatriarchy" *Feminist Formations* 25, no. 1 (Spring 2013): 8–34, 14.

3 Arvin, Tuck, and Morrill, "Decolonizing Feminism," 15.

4 Megan A. Smetzer, "Tlingit Dance Collars and Octopus Bags: Embodying Power and Resistance," *American Indian Art Magazine* 34, no. 1 (Winter 2008): 64–73.

5 The individuals in this photograph are identified in Sergei Kan, *A Russian American Photographer in Tlingit Country: Vincent Soboleff in Alaska* (Norman: University of Oklahoma Press, 2013), 70.

6 Franz Boas, *Primitive Art* (New York: Dover Publications, 1955).

7 Kate Duncan, *Northern Athapaskan Art: A Beadwork Tradition* (Seattle: University of Washington Press, 1989), 176–79.

8 John R. Swanton, *Tlingit Myths and Texts,* Bureau of American Ethnology 39 (Washington, DC: US Government Printing Office, 1909), 9–10.

9 Letter from Axel Rasmussen (superintendent of the Skagway Public Schools) to Frederi H. Douglas (at the time, curator of Indian Art at the Denver Art Museum), March 10, 1938.

10 Other types of seaweed include k̲'áach' (*ribbon seaweed*), tayeidí (*yellow seaweed*), sú (*bull kelp*), hairy grass on which herring spawn né (*seaweed*), and daaw (*kelp on which herring spawn*). Kerry Edwards, *Dictionary of Tlingit* (Juneau: Sealaska Heritage Institute, 2009), 451.

11 George T. Emmons and Frederica de Laguna, eds., *The Tlingit Indians* (Seattle: University of Washington Press, 1991), 441.

12 Author, personal communication with Shgen George, 2001.

13 In this story the devilfish dies but, more generally, devilfish are seen as creatures with enormous often supernatural power. They are associated with shamans and have the ability to wipe entire villages off of the face of the earth. Moreover, the eight legs of the devilfish parallel the significance of the number eight within Tlingit cultural practices. For a more thorough examination of devilfish, see Aldona Jonaitis, "The Devilfish in Tlingit Sacred Art," *American Indian Art Magazine* (Summer 1980): 42–47, 77.

14 Swanton, *Tlingit Myths and Texts*, 130–33.

15 Swanton, *Tlingit Myths and Texts*, 174–75.

16 Author, personal communication with Shgen George, 2014.

17 Emmons and de Laguna, *Tlingit Indians*, 228.

18 Smetzer, "Tlingit Dance Collars and Octopus Bags," 65.

19 Major C. E. S. Wood, "Among the Thlinkits in Alaska," *Century Magazine* 24, no. 3 (1882): 323–39.

20 Frances Paul, *Spruce Root Basketry of the Alaska Tlingit* (Sitka, AK: Sheldon Jackson Museum, 1991), 49, 55, 61.

21 Richard Dauenhauer and Nora M. Dauenhauer, "Evolving Concepts of Tlingit Identity and Clan," in *Coming to Shore: Northwest Coast Ethnology, Traditions, and Visions*, edited by Marie Mauzé, Michael Harkin, and Sergei Kan, 253–78 (Lincoln: University of Nebraska Press, 2004), 254.

22 Artist's statement for the exhibition *Tlingit Octopus Bags* at the Juneau Arts and Culture Center, August 2014.

23 Gerald Taiaiake Alfred, "Our Art Is Our Life: The Power of Marianne Nicolson's Work," *UBC Museum of Anthropology*, November 14, 2014, http://moa.ubc.ca/borderzones/features_nicolson.html.

24 Louis Shotridge, "Tlingit Woman's Root Basket," *Museum Journal, University of Pennsylvania* 12, no. 3 (September 1921): 160–78, 163.

CHAPTER 7

Ellen Neel and Carving on the Coast

THREE DECADES OF CHANGE AND RENEWAL

Lou-ann Ika'wega Neel

"GIRLS AREN'T SUPPOSED TO CARVE," HE MUTTERED AS HE WALKED PAST ME. It was 1977, I was fourteen years old, busy working on my first carving, a red cedar Thunderbird plaque. I did not know how (or whether) to respond to his remark, so I kept carving.

On my way home from school, I wondered if it was true that girls are not supposed to carve. I did not personally know of any women carvers, but I did not think that mattered. Despite the fact that our Native art teachers welcomed all students, girls and boys from all cultures, a seed of doubt had been planted, and I wondered whether I was really "allowed" to carve. I completed my Thunderbird plaque and decided to stop carving for a while so I could refocus my energy on textiles, since I was anxious to learn how to make button blankets. As I worked on my textile projects, I thought about carving; I saw the appliqué design as a carved plaque or mask or rattle. Later that school year, I asked George Hunt Jr., one of our Native art teachers, whether he knew of any women carvers. I thought that if there were a woman carver I could learn about, reference, and maybe even meet in person, I could free myself of those doubts about carving and take it up again, knowing for certain that it was okay for me to do so. George said that he only knew of one, her name was Ellen Neel (1916–1966). She was widely regarded as one of the only woman carvers of her era; he recalled hearing that she was very active in the tourist industry in Vancouver through the 1950s and 1960s.[1]

I was anxious to learn more about Ellen Neel, so I searched the library for any books, audio recordings, film, or photos of her artworks. Early in my search I found none and constantly asked family and friends to check with others that might be able to help. Before long, I discovered that Ellen Neel was my grandmother! Now I was even *more* inspired and motivated to learn about Ellen Neel, the carver, and to learn about this side of my family tree. Over the next four decades I continued my family research, visiting with my aunts, uncles, and other family members as often as I could, to hear memories of my grandmother—memories that became stories, and stories that became part of our oral tradition, our family histories.

From my aunts and uncles, I quickly learned that it was it okay for me to carve. In fact, it was encouraged, as our family had an unbroken line of artistic tradition in carving. Uncle Bob once said to me: "The idea that women didn't carve is a haywire colonial fantasy; Mum even wrote it down that her grandfather, Charlie James, was taught to carve by one of his aunties."[2] I also learned (and continue to learn) more about the diversity of artistic works and art products my grandmother created, the advocacy work she carried out as an artist, and the role model she became as an entrepreneur and independent business owner. Of all the stories told by family members, one especially significant in shaping the history of Northwest Coast art in the twentieth century is the keynote address my grandmother delivered for the 1948 Conference on Indian Affairs, held at the University of British Columbia. In her keynote my grandmother shifted her audience's perceptions about Native art by taking the idea of "artifacts" and "objects" and transforming it to that of a living, breathing contemporary culture of fine art and artistic practice.[3] The address was particularly important because it envisioned Native art as being an exciting new sector in the Canadian economy, an idea my grandmother had already begun to test in the mid-1940s with new commercial products for the tourism and gift markets.

Throughout this chapter I reflect on that 1948 address and share my best recollections of conversations with my aunts and uncles, and many other relatives, about the ideas, concepts, and visions my grandmother shared in the keynote. On more than one occasion relatives pointed out the way my grandmother always maintained her connections to her family, her culture, and her people, somehow able to balance the ancient artistic and cultural traditions and practices of our people while taking on a leadership role in the contemporary world of postwar Canada and raising her children. As my Aunt Vera Newman says, "She was country before country was cool." Many other relatives put it this way: "She was way ahead of her time."

My grandmother, Kakasolas (Ellen May Newman), was born on November 17, 1916, in Alert Bay, BC, fifty years after confederation (1867) during the era of the Potlatch Ban (1867–1951) and World War I (1914–1918). She was the eldest of three daughters, born to parents 'Nulis (Charlie Newman) of the 'Namgis, Kwagiulth, and Heiltsuk; and Lalaxsa (Lucy Newman nee James) of the Kwagiulth, 'Namgis, and Kwickwasutaineuk. In addition to two younger sisters (Margaret and Louisa), my grandmother had two older brothers (Carey and Herbert); they would be called half-brothers in today's terms, but among our people, the Kwakwa̱ka̱'wakw, there is no such thing as a half-sibling. Ellen's dad had two older sons from his previous marriage to Harriet Kemano from the Heiltsuk; both Carey and Herbert would have been in their teenage years when their sisters, were born.

Ellen's mum, Lalaxsa (Lucy James), was the daughter of Yakuglas (Charlie James) (1867–1938) from the Kwagiulth and Kwickwasutaineuk; and Nega̱ga̱ (Sara Nina Findlay) from the Kwagiulth. Sara had three sons—Spruce, Herbert, and Mungo—from her first marriage to Yax̱'nukwa'las (Martin). Spruce, Herbert, and Mungo were young adults when their sister Lucy was born, and they were in their late thirties when their niece Ellen was born. When Charlie James married Sara Nina in 1897, he was already an established carver. He became an arts mentor to his son (stepson), Mungo Martin, who would have been about eighteen years old. The two of them worked together on various carving projects over the course of twenty-five years before Ellen began to practice basic design and painting in 1925 at age nine. By the time Ellen was twelve, she was ready to begin her apprenticeship as a carver.

As part of her apprenticeship, Ellen would have learned each of the family legends and the crests that she was entitled to use as an artist as well as the designs to which she had the right to use through her Kwagiulth, 'Namgis, Mumtagila, Tlowitsis, and Kwickwasutaineuk lineage. This was important, as it is a foundational teaching of the Kwakwa̱ka̱'wakw that an artist only creates from their "box of treasures"—that is, having the rights, privileges, and prerogatives to share legends and crests from their family's history. The only exception to this rule is when an artist is commissioned by another family to create a work with their crest. In this instance the artist can create the work, but they do not acquire ownership rights or the rights to continue making works with the crest.[4] In a 1958 letter to Perry Culp Jr., my grandmother described these rights by providing an artist biography that spoke to her lineage. Culp worked for Cole & Weber, an ad agency that was preparing promotions for an upcoming totem pole carving demonstration and a trade show in Seattle.[5]

From Apprenticeship to Practicing Professional

My grandmother's first language was Kwakwala. She learned to read, write, and converse in English during her years at Saint Michael's Residential School. According to my aunts and uncles, my grandmother excelled in her schoolwork, receiving top grades for her work. By eighteen, she had graduated from Saint Michael's Residential School and was working part time at the local hospital while also apprenticing with her grandfather, carving model totem poles she would sell to tourists and other visitors that passed through Alert Bay. Because she was fluent in both Kwakwala and English, she was able to speak to the meanings behind the figures on the model totem poles. According to several family members, she became very well versed in managing sales. My aunts and uncles shared similar memories about always seeing Grandmother working on something—carving, sanding, finishing, or painting. I found their memories to be incredibly inspirational as I learned more about our artistic traditions, and this instilled the practice of lifelong learning as part of my own artistic journey.

My grandmother continued her apprenticeship until age nineteen, when she met my grandfather, Edward Lyle Neel (Ted), a tradesman who had set up a sheet metal operation in Alert Bay. Within a year, they married and had their first son, David Lyle Neel. Not long after David's birth, they moved to Vancouver. My aunts believe the move was because their mum lost her Indian status when she married their father, a non-Native. At that time, only registered, status Indians were permitted to live on reserve-lands. Uncle Bob agreed that the loss of status was probably one of the reasons for moving to Vancouver, but "it all worked out because there were already quite a few Kwagiulth people living in town [Vancouver]; and they already had good connections for selling artwork as several shops in Vancouver had been ordering pieces from the old man [Charlie James] for years, and Mum used to handle the orders."[6]

Over the next seven years, between 1938 and 1945, through her working relationships with the Museum of Anthropology as well as several retail shops and galleries, she was commissioned to carve totem poles of various sizes—from small eighteen-inch-high model poles to full-size poles, measuring eighteen to twenty-four feet). Her artistic practice became her professional career, and a means for steady income. In 1946, after my grandfather Ted Sr. suffered several strokes, my grandmother became the primary provider for the family, which had grown to seven children ranging in age from infant to nine. Eventually, Ellen's three older children—David (nine), John (eight), and Bob (seven)—learned basic designing and carving and were able to assist in the production of various smaller carvings for commercial sale in tourist and curio shops. Ellen's daughters—Cora (six), Theo (five), and Theresa (three)—were not old enough to help, but within a couple of years they became part of "the family assembly line" as they called it, and helped out with painting and packaging finished pieces.[7] Uncle Bob told me: "We all pitched in to create the little tourist poles—they were our bread-and-butter pieces, but Mum's new products and commissions for full-sized poles meant that sometimes we could feast."[8]

Between 1946 and 1951, with access to new tools, materials, technologies, and a wider audience, Ellen began experimenting with fresh ideas and methods. She set about developing some of her first commercial products to be created with Kwakwa̱ka̱'wakw designs. "Mum was a really sharp business woman," Uncle Bob said. "She saw our designs everywhere—on the smallest thing, like a pen; to the entire side of a building. And she volunteered for lots of different causes, especially things that would benefit our artists and our people; and I guess all of that caught the attention of the government people who were organizing the 1948 conference at the University of British Columbia, so they asked her to come and talk about our Native art."[9]

I finally got to see the full transcription of the speech while visiting with Uncle Bob in the summer of 1982. Phil Nuytten, a longtime friend of the family, was working on a book titled *The Totem Carvers,* telling the stories of Charlie James, Ellen Neel, and Mungo Martin as carvers. Phil had sent copies of the manuscript to my aunts and uncle for review, so I got to peruse it during my visit. I was so excited when I saw that early in her speech, my grandmother talked about Native arts and cultures being alive, with many more creative possibilities waiting to be discovered. The first point she made was about outdated and ill-informed ideas around Native art being categorized and viewed as the art of a dead or dying culture: "If our art is dead, then it is fit only to be mummified . . . packed into mortuary boxes, and tucked away in museums."[10]

In the speech she spoke passionately about the importance of recognizing that Native artists are the descendants of a living art and culture that utilize the materials, tools, techniques, and technologies of the modern world to give expression to the world around them. She said:

> Our art continues to live, for not only is it part and parcel of us, but can be a powerful factor in combining the best part of Indian culture into the fabric of a truly Canadian art form.
>
> When the white man came, he brought with him saws, axes, hatchets, steel chisels and knives—paints in brilliant white, red, green and yellow. There was no involved question of propriety—as to whether the new tools should be used . . . rather, they were seized on, avidly, and with startling results!
>
> . . . New techniques were adopted, new materials incorporated, new ideas were welcomed and used. I can find no instance where an idea, a material, or a tool was not used simply because it had not been used before.[11]

Taking these ideas a step further, Ellen spoke of the potential for Native art to be applied to modern, everyday items. "As far as applying this art to everyday living . . . ," she said, "I believe it can be used to stunning effect on tapestry, textiles, sportswear and in jewelry. Many pieces of furniture lend themselves admirably to Indian designs. Public buildings, large restaurants and halls have already begun to utilize some of this art."[12]

To further demonstrate her belief in the living art and culture of our people, she put her ideas to action—continuing to create carvings of all sizes and types. In 1949 she collaborated with Royal Albert Bone China to develop a new collectable set of Bone China titled Totemware. In keeping with her practice of creating artworks that reflected her family history, each of the products in the collection—teacups, saucers, platters, teapots, and more—shows an image of three totem poles from our family lineage. The central Totemland Pole shows a Thunderbird, perched on a globe featuring the coastline of British Columbia, which rests on the shoulders of the First Man. This pole was created by my grandmother for the Totemland Society, a group that sought to promote Vancouver and British Columbia as the "land of the

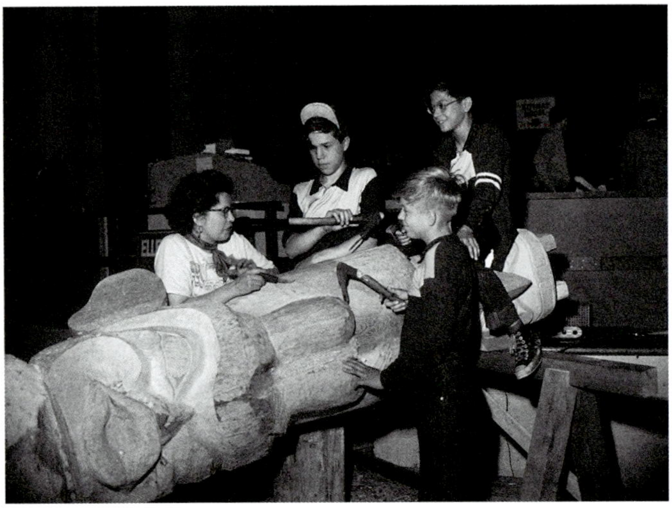

7.1. Ellen, Ted Jr., Dave, and Bob Neel, 1952. City of Vancouver Archives. Pacific National Exhibition. Reference Code: AM281-S8-: CVA 180-1802.

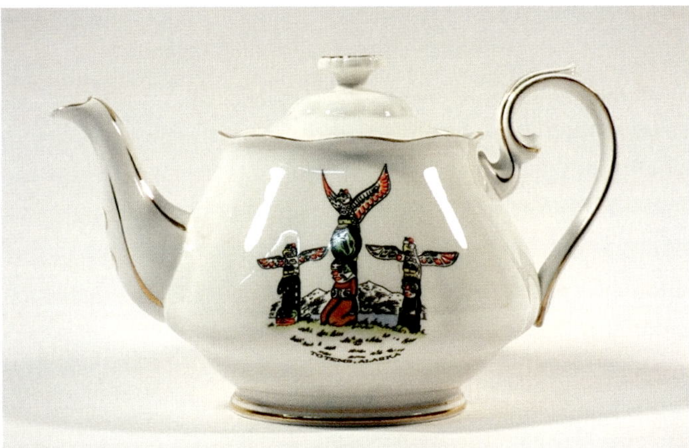

7.2. Ellen Neel, Bone China Totemware Teapot by Royal Albert, 1941. Image courtesy of University of Victoria Legacy Art Galleries. Private Collection. Photograph by Holly Cecil.

totems." On either side of the Totemland Pole are the Thunderbird/Killerwhale Pole and the Thunderbird/Man Pole.

This is significant in terms of my grandmother's interest in employing new materials, tools, techniques, and technologies. It is also important in terms of her personal commitment to the standards of the traditional practice, ensuring that only designs from her family's lineage would be used in her works. The Thunderbird, Killerwhale, and First Man emblems are derived from our Kwagiulth, 'Namgis, and Kwickwasutaineuk lineages. She shared these teachings and histories with her children, and they in turn have shared this teaching with my generation. It is now my responsibility to ensure our next generation of grandchildren receives these teachings and the histories of their family lineage.

The Totemware series was a precedent-setting collaboration as it demonstrated the applicability of Native art to everyday items and created a new standard and

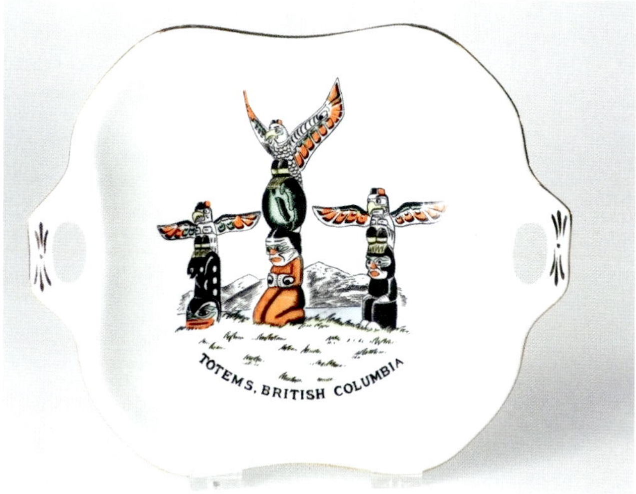

7.3. Ellen Neel, Bone China Totemware Serving Dish by Royal Albert, ca. 1950. Image courtesy of University of Victoria Legacy Art Galleries. Gift of Gary White and John Veillette. Photograph by Holly Cecil.

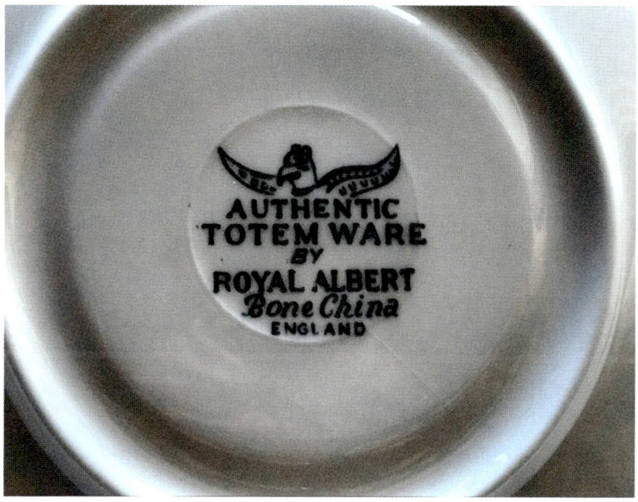

7.4. Totemware Authenticity Mark, ca. 1950s and 1960s. Lou-Ann Neel personal collection. Photograph by Lou-ann Neel.

level of production that over the next fifty years transformed into a global Indigenous gift market involving Indigenous artists from hundreds of nations. More locally, it meant that Indigenous artists could build a career in the arts that enabled them to continue creating one-of-a-kind commissioned works while also creating works for which they could negotiate royalties. This was important to many remote and semiremote communities, as this growing market became a means of livelihood for many artists in subsequent generations.[13]

In Ellen's hometown of Alert Bay, for example, carvers, jewelers, textile artists, painters, and weavers are able to harvest traditionally used materials locally while employing tools and technologies such as chainsaws, power-engravers, sewing machines, and paints of every color to create works for ceremony and community. These works are also for sale on commercial markets around the world.

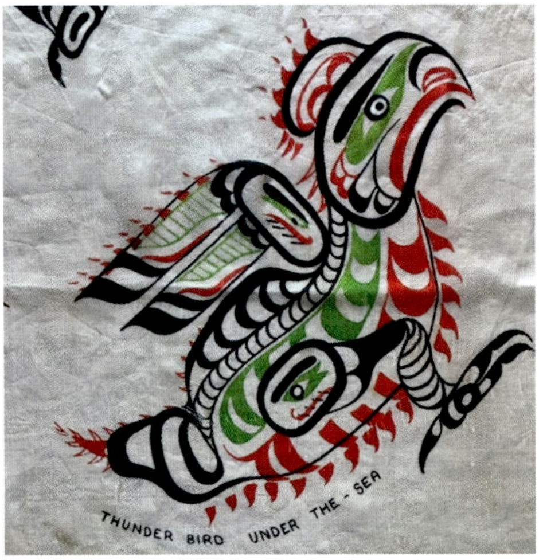

7.5. Thunderbird Under the Sea, by Ellen Neel, scarf detail. Lou-ann Neel personal collection. Photograph by Lou-ann Neel.

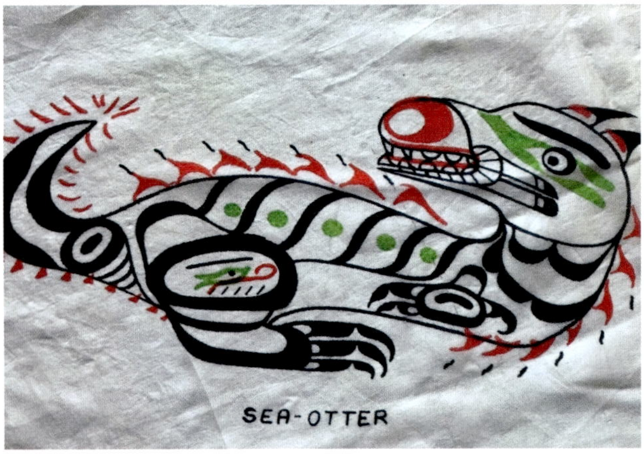

7.6. Ellen Neel, Sea Otter, scarf detail, 1952. Lou-ann Neel personal collection. Photograph by Lou-ann Neel.

Another important perspective on the creation of these new types of work relates to a goal that I believe my grandmother had in mind regarding her partnership with Royal Albert Bone China. When I talked with some of my aunts, they mentioned how their mothers and aunties loved to receive the Totemware pieces at feasts and potlatches. They talked about how important it is in our potlatch system to select special gifts that will be gifted to the noble women, and how these gifts should always be unique and of the highest quality. I believe that it was my grandmother's intent to show how these everyday items could be created in a way that features the work of our artists, maintains the integrity (and ownership) of the designs, and are heirloom collector-quality gifts. The same intent may have been at work when my grandmother began screenprinting designs from our family's crests on silk scarves. My Auntie Gootsa once said, "Everyone really liked those scarves your grandmother made; no one had ever done anything like those before, so they were popular and everyone wanted one."[14]

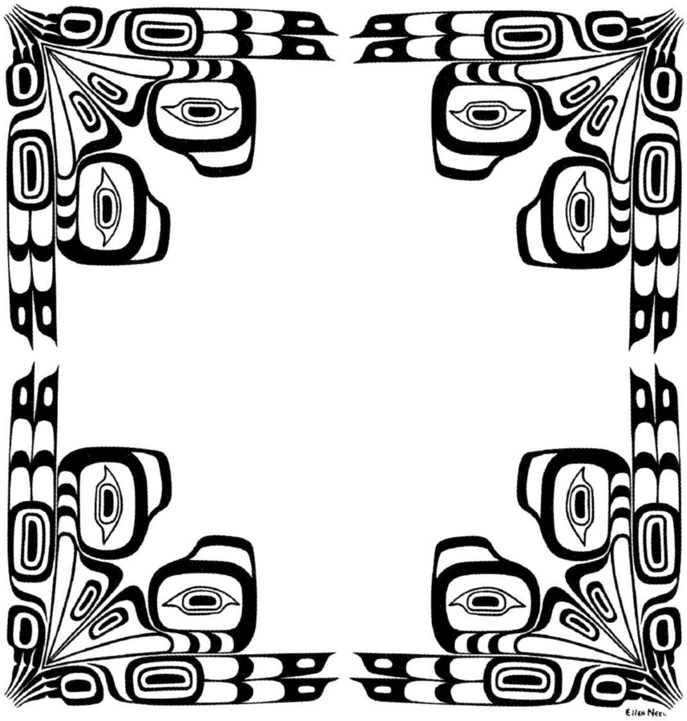

7.7. Ellen Neel, Raven Scarf, 1956. Lou-ann Neel personal collection. Photograph by Lou-ann Neel.

As with the image on the Totemware collection, these silk scarves carry the same family designs of the Thunderbird, Totemland Pole, and Killerwhale, and also show family stories associated with the Old Man Under the Sea, Thunderbird Under the Sea, Kingfisher-Man Mask, Cannibal Bird Mask, Sea Otter, and Grouse Mask. In all her works my grandmother created from her family's lineage, and in doing so, maintained the integrity of the crests, the designs, the traditions, and the practice. In addition to the scarves with the family's crest symbols, two of her designs, the Raven Scarf and the Thunderbird Scarf, reflect an important transition in my grandmother's personal artistic design style—from traditional styles to contemporary motifs. When I compare the artistic, technical, and practical considerations and design choices that are made when carving a totem pole, with the considerations and choices for designing a silk scarf, the scarf offers entirely new surface, material, and shape with seemingly endless design possibilities. The two designs show how my grandmother was able to skillfully tailor the formline design—a Raven or a Thunderbird—to fit the shape of the scarf.

All of these new works—the Totemware Collection and screen-printed scarves and other everyday garments—became popular gift items and souvenirs that my grandmother sold wholesale to curios and gift shops throughout the Vancouver area. These new products are some of the earliest known examples of mass production of Native giftware by a Native artist, in what has become a flourishing Indigenous gift market industry throughout British Columbia, Canada, and around the world.[15]

While my grandmother promoted the use of new materials and technologies in the practice of Native art, she was consistently vocal about the theft and appropriation of Native art designs as well as the creation of cheap, low-quality imitations of Native art by local and offshore companies. By the late 1940s and early 1950s, she was becoming well-known for her advocacy work to promote Native art and artists by encouraging collectors and consumers to purchase *authentic* works (i.e., those created by Native artists) and to stop the appropriation of Native art. This excerpt from the April 1948 speech shows my grandmother's efforts:

> Curio dealers have so cheapened the art in their efforts to profit, that I doubt if one could find a single household where the authenticity of the art is important to them. I have strived, in all my work, to retain the authentic, but I find it difficult to obtain even a portion of the price necessary to do a really fine piece of work.
>
> We need only to have some sort of an organization to which architects, builders and manufacturers could go to guarantee authentic products. Both my husband and myself stand ready to contribute . . . we have plans and are willing to share.[16]

The BC Indian Arts and Welfare Society (formerly the Society for the Furtherance of BC Indian Arts and Crafts, 1940–50) eventually became the BC Indian Arts and Crafts Society. In the late 1970s the organization developed a series of authenticity trademarks, logos, and stamps that member artists could use with their artworks. Unfortunately the society dissolved in 1986, taking the authenticity-labeling program with it. Over the past thirty-odd years, there have been many community-based local and regional Indigenous arts organizations formed around the province, but there has not been a province-wide Indigenous arts organization since 1986.

Questions around authenticity and appropriation continue and are a big part of my own artistic practice (see chapter 4 by Janet Catherine Berlo and Aldona Jonaitis). National and international copyright laws (e.g., the Canadian Copyright Act and the Berne Convention of 1886) still have a way to go before they specifically address the unique artistic traditions, practices, and laws of Indigenous nations. Cheap imitations and fraudulent copies of original artworks erase Indigenous artists from their own economies. The continued appropriation of Indigenous shapes, forms, and symbols for use in advertising campaigns and products that harm the integrity of the work is a direct breach of the United Nations Declaration on the Rights of Indigenous Peoples, of which Canada is a signatory. At the same time, our family believes it is important to show communities, organizations, and governments an example of how things can be done more respectfully to recognize and protect Indigenous art histories, traditions, and practices. We continue to work closely with organizations and other First Nations communities to strengthen and expand on the gifts Grandmother provided.

Education and Sport Logos

Another example of important work my grandmother did was to show support for Native students. Between 1948 and 1958 she created designs for two well-known schools in the BC Lower Mainland—the University of British Columbia Thunderbirds and Aldergrove High School's Totems. My grandmother set out to ensure Native students felt welcomed while they were attending schools so far away from their homes; at the same time, she added to their sense of community and identity by bestowing names on their respective sports teams.

THE UBC POLE

The pole she carved for the University of British Columbia's Student Association was much more than a totem pole. It involved a name, a symbol of welcome, and an important family legend.

The bestowal of the name Thunderbirds was precedent-setting, as it was one of the first instances of a Native name, symbol, and legend having been formally or officially shared with a postsecondary institution. In the ceremony that took place on October 23, 1948, Chief William Scow (Ellen's uncle) proclaimed:

> On behalf of Ellen and Edward Neel, and with the full consent and approval of our tribal council and our people, I present this Totem to the Alma Mater Society of this University. I give to you also the right to use the name Thunderbird

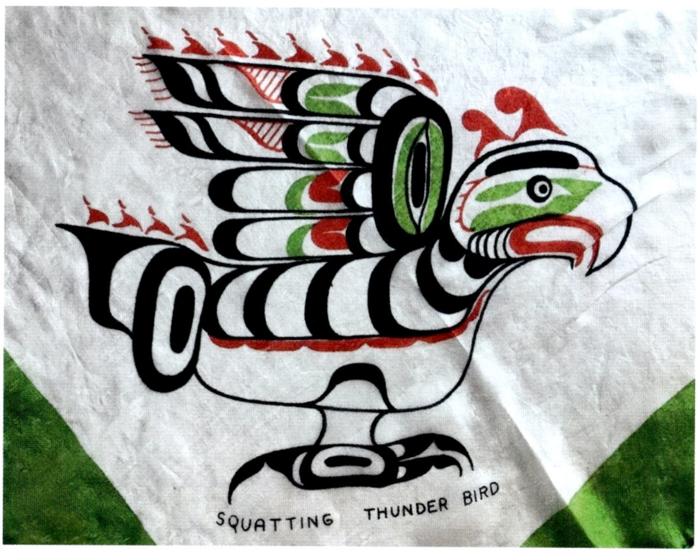

7.8. Ellen Neel, Squatting Thunderbird, scarf detail. Lou-Ann Neel personal collection. Photograph by Lou-ann Neel.

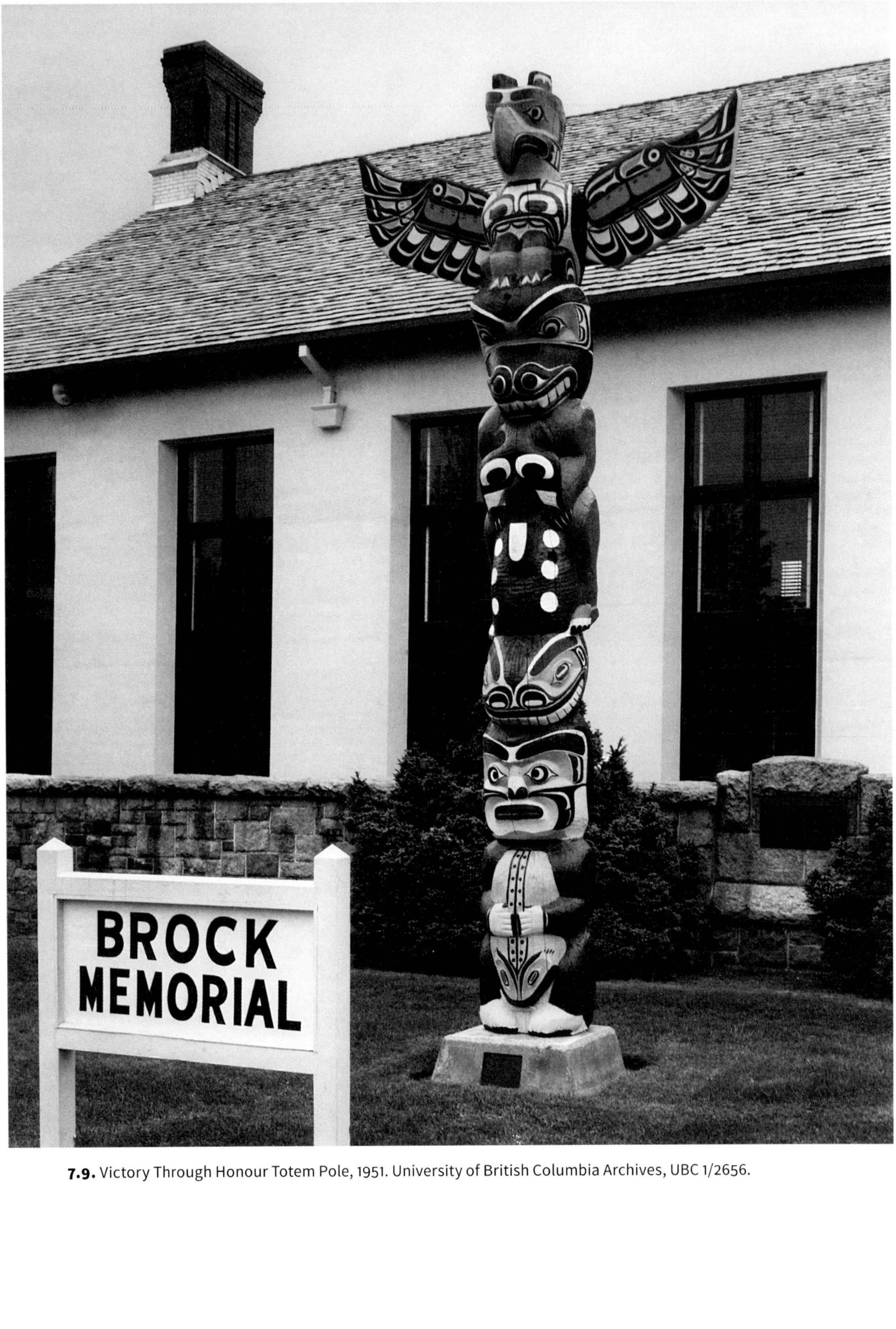

7.9. Victory Through Honour Totem Pole, 1951. University of British Columbia Archives, UBC 1/2656.

for your teams. This is according to the laws of my people, and is hereby legal for the first time. The totem has been carved for you by our two best tribal carvers. It has a long and an honorable history: a totem of which your teams have every right to be proud. It is yours now, and if you follow the precepts accepted with it, you cannot fail.[17]

Alma Mater Society president Dave Brousson said: "It is my hope that when this totem has been erected in a place of honor in front of our own Brock Hall, that it will be a constant reminder to every person of native decent at the University, that this institution is peculiarly his. I hope also that it will be a constant reminder to this and future Student Councils to make native students especially welcome on our campus. We shall welcome the opportunity to help."[18]

Also present at the ceremony, Ellen Neel stated: "To the Native people of the whole province we can give our assurance that your children will be accepted at this school by the Staff and Student Council, eager to smooth their paths with kindness and understanding. We need now only students to take advantage of the opportunity, so that some day our doctors, lawyers, social workers and departmental workers will be fully trained University graduates of our own race."[19]

Auntie Theo often talked about how many of the articles and papers written about the Thunderbird Pole focused on the connection to the sports teams, but it was also meant to be a sort of touchstone for Native students who were far away from their homes. The pole would be a reminder that their ancestors are with them during this important journey at university. "Mum was a really big advocate for education," Theo said, "she wanted native students to feel at home, even if it was just one totem pole on the entire campus, they'd have a reminder of home."[20] As part of the gift of the Thunderbird name and totem pole, my grandmother transcribed "The Four Tests of Tsi-kumi" legend as told to her by Charlie James. She provided a copy of the transcription with the pole to ensure that the university community would understand and appreciate the meaning of each figure on the totem pole. In 1951 she registered her transcription of the legend with the Canadian Copyright office and was issued a copyright certificate for "The Four Tests of Tsi-kumi."

This was another important precedent, as it is the only known instance of a Kwakwa̱ka̱'wakw legend being registered and acknowledged as an original literary work. I asked my Auntie Theo if she knew about the copyright on "The Four Tests of Tsi-kumi." She said, "Mum was a real activist long before that word became popular; she was always speaking out against the theft of our peoples' designs and stories, because in our traditional ways, these things belong to specific families and villages. I didn't know she had done this, but it doesn't surprise me as she knew that putting that legend out there into the world meant that it was going to need some protection."[21]

Uncle Bob shared several recollections about the pole and the legend. During one of our visits he spoke about the time he restored the pole.

> I restored the pole at UBC in the 80s, and quite a few people from the museum [the Museum of Anthropology] and university professors stopped by to watch. Most of them had never even heard the legend and some never even knew the history of the pole; maybe they filed the written version away and forgot to share it! So I talked to them about its meaning and shared the legend as best as I could remember it. People were amazed by the legend, but even more amazed that a woman carved the pole—so I had to set them straight about that fact that there were women carvers all throughout our history, but I guess because of their beliefs they still found it hard to believe.[22]

Since students, staff, and faculty have naturally changed over the years, by 1999 there were very few people at UBC who remembered that there was a legend for the pole. When the pole began to rot after having been outdoors for over fifty years, it had to be taken down and placed in storage. Soon after the pole was stored, the university assembled a Totem Pole Committee to discuss plans for the creation of a replica. The committee was comprised of representatives from the Neel family, from Musqueam First Nation, and UBC officials.

In preparation for the replica of the pole to be made, family members carried out research on the history of the pole and were able to find a transcript of the legend

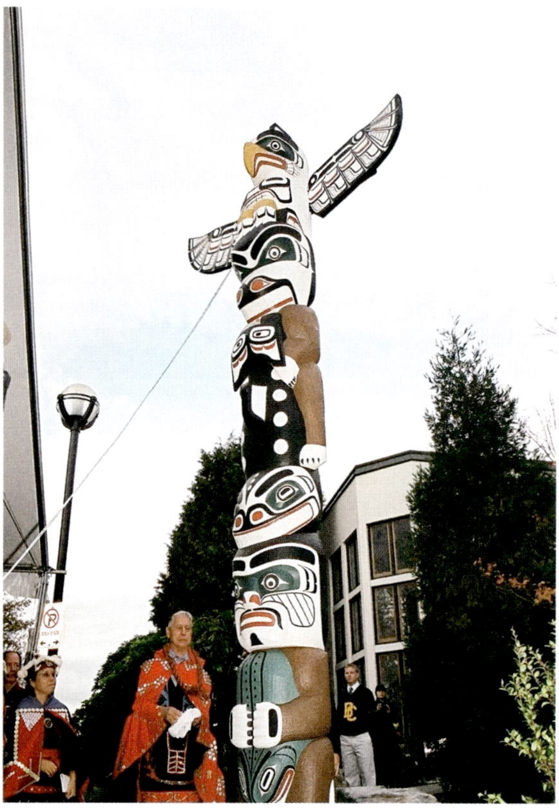

7.10. Replica of Victory Through Honour Totem Pole, 2003. University of British Columbia Archives, UBC 125.1/025.

along with photos of the pole being repaired and repainted on several occasions. In the spring of 2003 the committee hired Calvin Hunt and his team to create a replica; in October 2003 a ceremony was held to unveil and rededicate the pole. The pole was placed near its original location, next to Brock Hall and the Student Welcome Centre. During the rededication ceremony the late Chief Frank Nelson shared the legend once again to remind guests that the pole has a rich history to which they are connected. My uncle, Chief Edwin Newman, spoke to the dream Ellen (his auntie) had for Native students at the university. Judge Alfred Scow, who stood with my grandmother and his father, Chief William Scow, during the 1948 ceremony, spoke to the significance of Kwakwa̱ka̱'wakw laws being recognized alongside Canadian laws. Musqueam Elder Larry Grant spoke to the long-standing relationship the Neel family has with each of the local First Nations people and acknowledged the pole as having been placed with the blessings of the Musqueam people.

THE ALDERGROVE POLE

The second team emblem my grandmother gifted was to (then) Aldergrove High School. As with the UBC pole, the Aldergrove Pole is comprised of figures or characters from our family's lineage—Thunderbird, Bear, Eagle, and Frog, with a Sturgeon as a symbol of local First Nations' histories. The pole similarly connects our family and the Kwakwa̱ka̱'wakw to the school and local community.

My grandmother's gifts to both UBC and Aldergrove Community Secondary School created an opportunity for many people to see how this type of partnership could be achieved in a positive, honorable, and proactive manner. In the fifty years since her passing, however, there are still very few examples of this precedent being followed, as evidenced by the recent examples of professional and collegiate sports teams whose Indigenous names or logos are being called into question. I have been researching and studying my grandmother's work for over thirty-five years. In addition to her incredible range of artworks, I have come to appreciate the significance of her advocacy work for artists and First Nations communities.

Through my journey to find out if girls were allowed to carve, I learned so much more than I could have dreamed possible. First and foremost, I learned that I was most certainly "allowed" to carve and was strongly encouraged to do so by family and other carvers from my community. I stopped asking whether I was "allowed" to carve and instead affirmed, validated, and acclaimed my right, responsibility, and obligation to carve, as a descendent of artists in a family with an unbroken line of artistic history. From my renewed perspective, I was able to see that as a result of my grandmother's work, our family's teachings and traditions in arts and culture had been successfully transferred from all previous generations of grandparents to our current generation, who now mentor the next generation—our children and grandchildren. In this way our living culture continues.

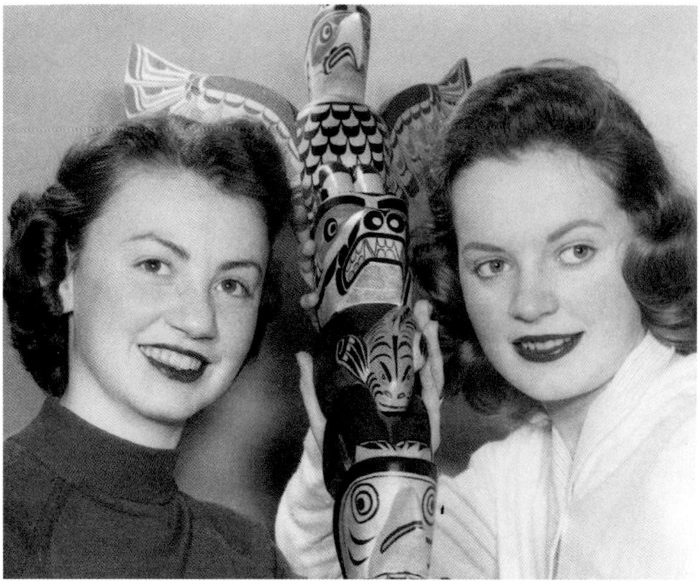

7.11. Ellen Neel, Aldergrove Totem, 2018. Image courtesy of Aldergrove Community School.

Alongside other Native artists and arts advocates of her era, my grandmother Ellen Neel helped to establish some of the early building blocks of a movement that set in motion a shift in perceptions of Native art—from "object and artifact" to fine art and a living culture. Her connections with secondary and postsecondary educational institutions through the creation of team and school emblems was groundbreaking work in its time, establishing some of the first instances of Native art—visual art and storytelling—being formally bestowed and gifted versus infringing, taking, or appropriating. Although it has taken more than fifty years for many of her innovative ideas to take shape and become part of the contemporary Canadian arts world and gift market industry, Indigenous artists now have access to both traditional and modern materials, tools, techniques, and technologies as well as the ability to self-publish their own art products and gift items any time of the day, any day of the week. My grandmother's entrepreneurial spirit and her vision for the contemporary application of Native designs in modern, everyday items provided tangible examples of new commercial products that, over the course of the past sixty years, have become a thriving gift market and souvenir industry.[23]

There are still some that believe the use of modern materials, tools, techniques, and technologies is inauthentic, I've even heard people say that the use of anything modern is "cheating," but I know that my grandmother would disagree and would continue to uphold Indigenous arts practices as living cultures. In my own practice I have picked up where she left off—continuing to learn from all the works she created, which now serve as my study pieces and help me to imagine what it would have been like to learn from her directly. I continue the work she started in advocating for an Indigenous arts organization that will provide the kinds of supports Indigenous artists need to keep our arts and cultural ways alive and "to which architects, builders and manufacturers could go to guarantee authentic products." I have begun the process of mentoring my nieces and nephews, so they can continue our family's unbroken line of artistic tradition.[24]

Ellen Neel's legacy and contributions as a Kwagiulth artist, arts advocate, entrepreneur, and business owner are important to the history of Northwest Coast art in the twentieth century. While some of this has been documented in academic papers and in Nuytten's book, *The Totem Carvers*, there are still many more stories to be shared about her contributions. She was (and continues to be) an important role model to girls and women who are interested in carving but may be reluctant to pursue apprenticeships in this practice.

NOTES

1 Throughout this chapter, I share my best recollections of the conversations I have had with my family and mentors, as this forms an important part of my own artistic and cultural learning (and practice), following our Kwakwa̱ka̱'wakw tradition of transferring knowledge from one generation to the next.

2 Author, personal communication with Bob Neel, 1982.

3 Phil Nuytten, *The Totem Carvers* (Vancouver, BC: Panorama Publications, 1982), 50.

4 This is a teaching that I received during my first year (1977) in my Native art class at SJ Willis Jr. Secondary School in Victoria, BC. The Native art class was one of three Native studies courses (including Native social studies and Native languages—Kwakwala, Nuu-chah-nulth, and Hal'qumi'num) offered by School District 61 (Victoria). It was a new curriculum, delivered with the help of Elders, fluent speakers, historians, and artists. Guest artists that year included Henry Hunt Sr., Oscar Matilpi, and Floyd Joseph.

5 Letter to Perry Culp Jr., Neel Family Files, personal correspondence, 1958.

6 Author, personal communication with Bob Neel, 1983.

7 Neel Family Files, personal communication, 1982–present.

8 Author, personal communication with Bob Neel, 1983.

9 Author, personal communication with Bob Neel, 1983.

10 Ellen Neel's 1948 keynote speech, as cited in Nuytten, *The Totem Carvers,* 50.

11 Ellen Neel's speech, as cited in Nuytten, *The Totem Carvers,* 50.

12 Ellen Neel's speech, as cited in Nuytten, *The Totem Carvers,* 50.

13 Aboriginal Artists Project Steering Committee, *Aboriginal Artists Project Report*, (Victoria: BC Ministry of Small Business, Tourism and Culture, 1994), 1–28.

14 Author, personal communication with Auntie Gootsa, 1993.

15 Aboriginal Artists Project, *Project Report,* 1–28.

16 Ellen Neel's speech, as cited in Nuytten, *The Totem Carvers,* 50.

17 Chief William Scow, as quoted in Native Brotherhood of British Columbia, *The Native Voice* 2, no. 11 (November).

18 Dave Brousson, as quoted in *The Native Voice* 2, no. 11 (November).

19 Ellen Neel, as quoted in *The Native Voice* 2, no. 11 (November).

20 Author, personal communication with Auntie Theo, 1984.

21 Author, personal communication with Auntie Theo, 2004.

22 Author, personal communication with Bob Neel, 1995.

23 Aboriginal Artists Project, *Project Report*, 1–28.

24 Lou-ann Neel, 1982–2018, personal communication with family and mentors.

LET INDIGENOUS REIGN

Ishmael Hope

Always with Spielberg kids on bikes
knifing dark paths, violet gravel clusters
crunching under rubber tires. Wrinkled brown
alien fingers point to the moon.
With pigtailed Drew Barrymore, little as me,
who I meet later as an Inuit paddler in her whale movie.

With Elder who speaks at Sitka ANB Hall Camp I,
same strange language that made my mother cry
when I sang to her Vida Davis' *Itsy Bitsy Spider*
translation. Silver bracelets lining
her wrists jangle as she hugs me, silver animals
with sad eyes that peer from under Sitka harbors.

With silver bracelets etched by John Cross
jangling on Sophie Gladstone Reid's elegant
arms, speaking Haida to her friends in her city home.
With screech owl mother inviting herring
to leave spawn and milt at the rock
paid for by every generation of my grandfathers
with blood, with Hudson's Bay blankets, hammered copper.
With Frog mouth chiseled on clan hats
that keeps speaking, that keeps singing
songs that float under a couple's canoe in heavy fog,
that stands in the middle of the path down
our mountain that outlasted the Flood,
with eyes that scan the opening mouth of daylight,
with spotted back that scurries under young women's feet
who are drawn into his village behind ferns.

With blood, with blood, with blood,
with land, with stewards, with land.

PART III

Changing Museums

CHAPTER 8

In the Spirit of Reconciliation

RETHINKING COLLECTIONS AND THE ACT OF ENGAGEMENT AT THE MUSEUM OF VANCOUVER

Sharon Fortney

IN THE AFTERMATH OF THE TRUTH AND RECONCILIATION COMMISSION IN CANADA, many museums are entering new dialogues about social justice, as they reflect upon past curatorial practices and publicly recognize the social inequalities that were established during the eras in which many of their collections were formed.[1] Museums, as institutions of public education, often see themselves as ideal vehicles for educating their audiences about Canada's repressed memories relating to residential schools and other forms of colonial subjugation. This cannot be accomplished effectively without recognition of the role museums played in colonist agendas—often receiving confiscated belongings and ancestral remains from Indian Agents and missionary collectors. At the Museum of Vancouver (MOV) the response has been to adopt reconciliation as a guiding principal for museum practice, in activities ranging from collecting, repatriation, exhibit curation, and audience engagement to governance. This chapter examines the MOV's redefined curatorial practice of reconciliation through the lens of the City of Vancouver's "Coast Salish" collections.

For many institutions the work of reconciliation builds upon previous conversations reflecting a need to be more engaged with First Nations, and other source communities, to democratize museum practice in Canada.[2] For many Canadian museums the decolonization process began after the release of the 1992 "Task Force Report on Museums and First Peoples." The report outlined strategies for establishing equal partnerships by adopting new policies for interpretation, access, repatriation, training, and implementation. However, some institutions have changed more quickly than others. For example, changes are more noticeable in institutions with large collections of First Nations belongings rather than those focused upon documenting municipal histories. The current reconciliation movement in Canada has a broader mandate as it calls for widespread societal changes and has been adopted by many municipal governments and their cultural institutions.

Within the city of Vancouver "the term reconciliation is now commonly used to describe the many efforts to work together, and to form relations of 'mutual respect and understanding with local First Nations and the Urban Indigenous Community.'"[3] What distinguishes the reconciliation movement from past approaches to postcolonialism is the focus on "redress."[4] This requires the implementation of new practices that move beyond recognition of past wrongs, to substantive changes that enable Indigenous agency through the relinquishing of power and authority by people in positions that continue to perpetuate imbalances. Those actively engaged in "redress" work seek to correct silences and representational imbalances whether they are being created through funding strategies, staffing policies, or other processes.

The Museum of Vancouver, like many other institutions in the Vancouver area, publicly recognizes that the city is located within the unceded traditional territories of the hən̓q̓əmin̓əm̓-and Sḵwx̱wú7mesh-speaking peoples: the Musqueam, Sḵwx̱wú7mesh, and Tsleil-Waututh Nations. The museum strives to recognize all three of these "Coast Salish" communities equally, as it sits within the center of their shared (and overlapping) unceded traditional territories.[5] However, MOV staff are being taught not to use imposed and generic terminology like "Coast Salish," but rather to identify local peoples as they choose to be recognized in their own languages. Since we are dealing with two distinct languages, MOV staff have been asked to use hən̓q̓əmin̓əm̓- *and* Sḵwx̱wú7mesh-speaking peoples (as opposed to Coast Salish) when referring to these three nations as a group and do so accordingly.

The museum is in the unique position of being situated directly atop of an ancestral village site. For this reason there is an immediate need for site-specific acknowledgment. The village is known as Sen̓áḵw in Sḵwx̱wú7mesh (Squamish) language and sən̓aʔqʷ in the hən̓q̓əmin̓əm̓ language spoken by the Musqueam and Tsleil-Waututh peoples. Families in each of these communities have members that recognize genealogical connections to this place. Sen̓áḵw (sən̓aʔqʷ) was set aside as part of Kitsilano Indian Reserve #6 in 1869 and specifically designated a Sḵwx̱wú7mesh reserve by colonial officials in 1880.[6] Over the next few decades the reserve underwent several reductions, as the city annexed lands for development, until the remaining residents were forcibly relocated in 1913. A small parcel of the original reserve, taken for the railway in 1901, was reclaimed by the Sḵwx̱wú7mesh community in 2000 after several decades of legal action.[7]

Adjacent to this reacquired parcel is Vanier Park, the site of MOV, the HR MacMillan Space Centre, the City of Vancouver Archives, and the city's Maritime Museum. An archival image from the collections of the city's first archivist, Major Matthews, shows a portion of the village, located at the foot of Chestnut Street, where the museum now stands. Many Vancouver residents are unaware of this painful story of colonization and removal. MOV recently worked with the Sḵwx̱wú7mesh Nation on a display to recognize the village and the coercive annexing

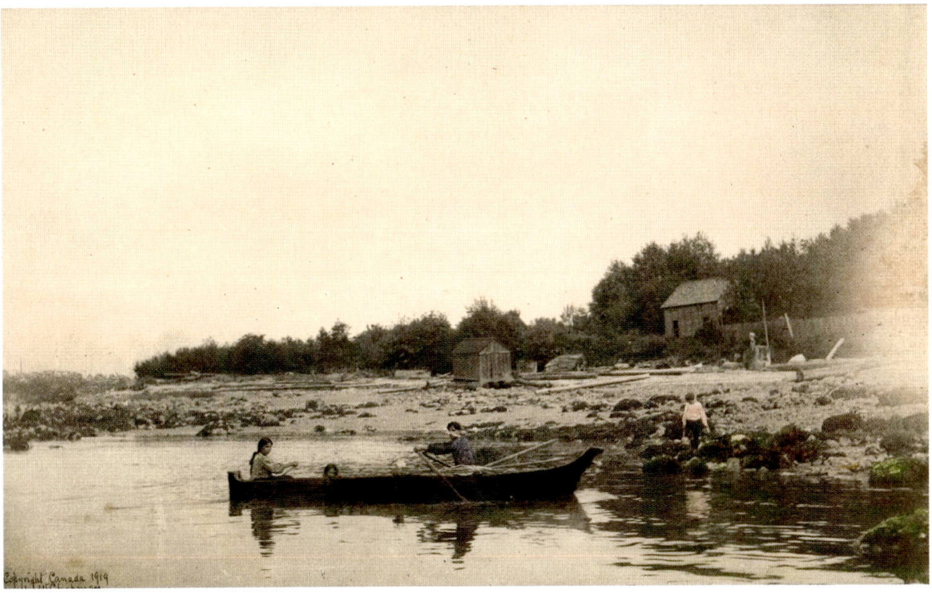

8.1. August Jack Khatsahlano and his family in a canoe at Seṅáḵw. Stepfather Jericho Charlie's home at the base of Chestnut Street in background. Seṅáḵw house post faintly visible to the right of the house. City of Vancouver Archives 1376-203.

of these lands for city building. It was installed at the entrance to the museum's galleries in early 2018. This is an example of a smaller initiative to enact reconciliation through truth-telling and public acknowledgment of Indigenous place-names, positioned where both paid museum visitors and casual passersby might see them.[8]

Museum objects, by their very physicality, have power to affect those who look at them. A carved human figure, which once stood outside the home of Sḵwx̱wú7mesh síýáṁ Shenáwtsut (Jericho Charlie), can be faintly seen in the background of a photograph used in the "Sḵwx̱wú7mesh History at Seṅáḵw" display. This figure continues to mark the site today, although it now resides inside MOV's collections storage due to its fragile condition. Instead, a 27.5-foot canoe that once belonged to Shenáwtsut anchors this display.

At the Museum of Vancouver reconciliation is being implemented on many fronts: from board membership for host nation representatives and changes in staffing, to increased community access to collections (both digitally and physically), to complimentary admission for First Nations people, to proactive repatriation of ancestral remains, burial goods, and culturally sensitive items, and through efforts to ensure the three host nations have an active and contemporary presence in MOV's exhibits and programming, regardless of theme.[9] Accomplishing these goals requires a change in museum culture that will likely require several more years to implement effectively. I am hopeful that we will continue to move forward, accomplishing meaningful acts of redress. Education initiatives that target noncuratorial staff and elected board members have been identified as a key element of the process. A three-year plan is being developed to deliver reconciliation training.

This is not to say that MOV has not previously worked with the host nations, but rather that it is intensifying its efforts and striving for greater accessibility and accountability in all departments, not just curatorial. Significant institutional changes were triggered by the consultation process for the 2015 exhibit, *c̓əsnaʔəm, the city before the city.*[10] Musqueam community members challenged museum staff to consider the idea that they were not dealing with "archaeological collections" or "objects" but ancestral belongings. Conceptually, this meant that specific items were no longer anonymous or detached from descendants in source communities but anchored to their ancestors who created and used them for daily life and ceremony. This is just one example of a new framework for MOV's curatorial practice.

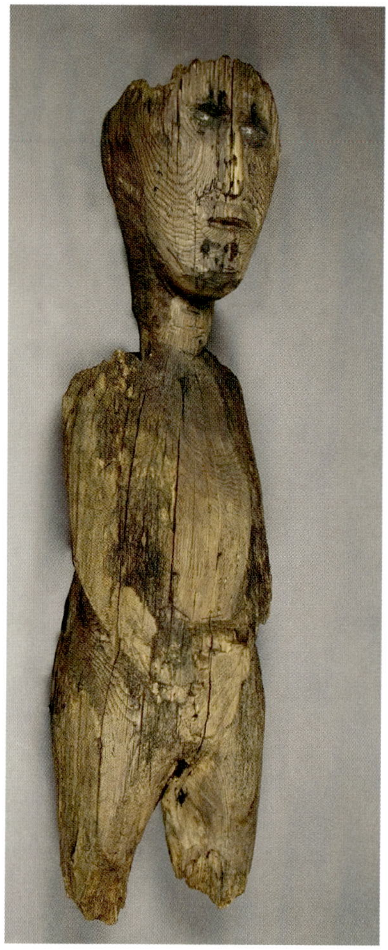

8.2. Seṅáḵw house post. Museum of Vancouver, MOV Collection AA 2270.

This novel lens of understanding, combined with a commitment to increased accessibility for community members, facilitates the rekindling of meaningful relationships between communities and their ancestral belongings. Through such visits, the collections team are becoming more familiar with local protocols and practices necessary for respectful care. In addition to the changes already discussed, MOV staff are working toward establishing lasting partnerships with the Musqueam, Sḵwx̱wú7mesh, and Tsleil-Waututh Nations. Staff has worked to change the institution's engagement strategy. Several Coast Salish collections demonstrate how these updated, stronger relationships foster an active presence by community in the museum and the development of exhibits that challenge colonial narratives still present within Canadian society.

Creating a First Nations Steering Committee

Several years after the Canadian Museum Association and the Assembly of First Nations released their Task Force Report on Museums and First Peoples, MOV began work to strengthen its relationship with the hən̓q̓əmin̓əm̓- and Sḵwx̱wú7mesh-speaking peoples of Vancouver.[11] A meeting was held on November 25, 1999, to discuss working together. According to the guiding principles, "the purpose of the meeting was two-fold: first, for representatives of the Vancouver Museum to relate plans for the new and expanded galleries depicting the story of Vancouver, and secondly, to discuss the role that each of the aforementioned First Nations might play in the development of the new Vancouver Stories galleries."[12]

At this time there was no space in the museum dedicated to telling First Nations history. The plan that evolved, through the consultation process, was to develop the *Vancouver Stories* exhibits—in which Vancouver history was told sequentially through a series of connected galleries, to include First Nations voices as an unbroken thread from the beginning to end. This would contrast with the approach taken for immigrant minorities, whose stories would focus on the specific decades when certain immigrations peaked, and collections were best able to represent their respective communities. MOV curatorial staff began to implement practices that recognized that Vancouver history did not exist apart from First Nations history.[13]

The consultation process conveyed that oral history should be paramount to any efforts to share local First Nations perspectives and stories. Community representatives identified their youth as a target for such efforts. A First Nations Steering Committee was established to oversee process and content development. In 2001 work began on several projects—an expansion to the museum known as the Joyce Walley Learning Centre, which included an education gallery, a new history gallery about the 1950s, and an archaeology discovery space. I was hired as a First Nations program developer, through a screening process involving both the steering committee and museum staff, to assist with exhibit development for these spaces that opened in 2002. Three guest curators, one from each of the three host nations, had already been hired to research and curate a temporary exhibit on Coast Salish basketry.

Honouring the Basketmakers, 2002–2004

A first step in the process of building better relationships was to develop exhibit projects that promoted the shared values and teachings of the Musqueam, Sḵwx̱wú7mesh, and Tsleil-Waututh communities. The exhibit *Honouring the Basketmakers* (2002–2004) realized this goal. Elder and educator N. Rose Point (1934–2012) was hired on contract in 2001 to represent the Musqueam community as a guest curator. She had a long-standing connection to the museum, as she (along with fellow community member Della Kew) had been a volunteer in the 1970s.[14] For *Honouring the Basketmakers* she partnered with two other guest curators, Chief Janice George of the Sḵwx̱wú7mesh Nation and Carleen Thomas from the Tsleil-Waututh Nation.

Today, both George and Thomas remain engaged with exhibits and programming at the Museum of Vancouver.

The curatorial process for *Honouring the Basketmakers* included bringing Elders and weavers into collections storage to view the Salish basketry and archival photograph collections. As a result of these visits, artist attributions were given for several previously anonymous baskets. The entrance to the exhibit presented personal stories of three local basketmakers—Rose Sparrow of Musqueam, Annie George of Tsleil-Waututh, and Mary Anne John of Sḵwx̱wú7mesh. In addition, each community spoke of the importance of basketry to their community. The Tsleil-Waututh introduction noted:

> In honouring our basket makers, the Tsleil-Waututh Nation is proud to acknowledge our women and their families, and to share some knowledge and history of our people. This exhibit weaves together stories of the basket makers of the Musqueam, Squamish, and Tsleil-Waututh Nations. In doing so, it posits a little known history of Vancouver and the First Nations who have lived here since time immemorial.
>
> The art of cedar weaving transcends time and reflects change. In recent times, many people have taken up this fine art, and so continue this cultural aspect of our contemporary lives. Although basketry is now used for different purposes than in the past, it visibly illustrates our aptitude for adapting and responding to the times.
>
> As these women wove cedar, they also wove together families and communities. We learn that they moved between two worlds—the deep, quiet solitude

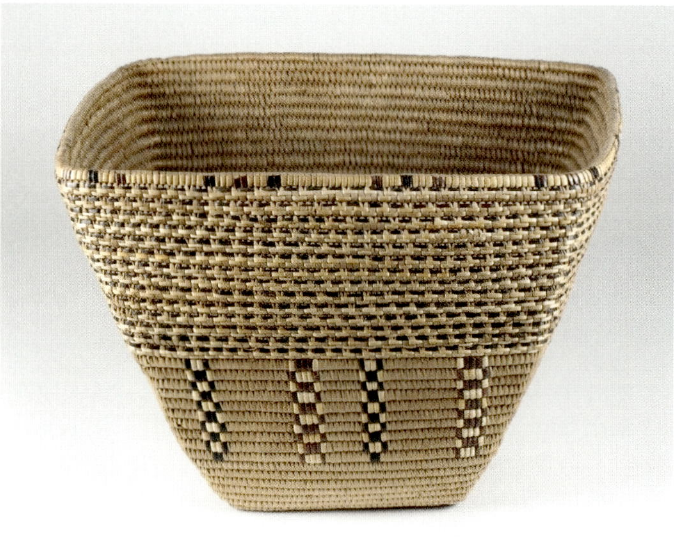

8.3. Berry basket from the Lipsett Collection, attributed to Mary Grant during the *Honouring the Basketmakers* exhibit. Museum of Vancouver, MOV Collection AA 1907.

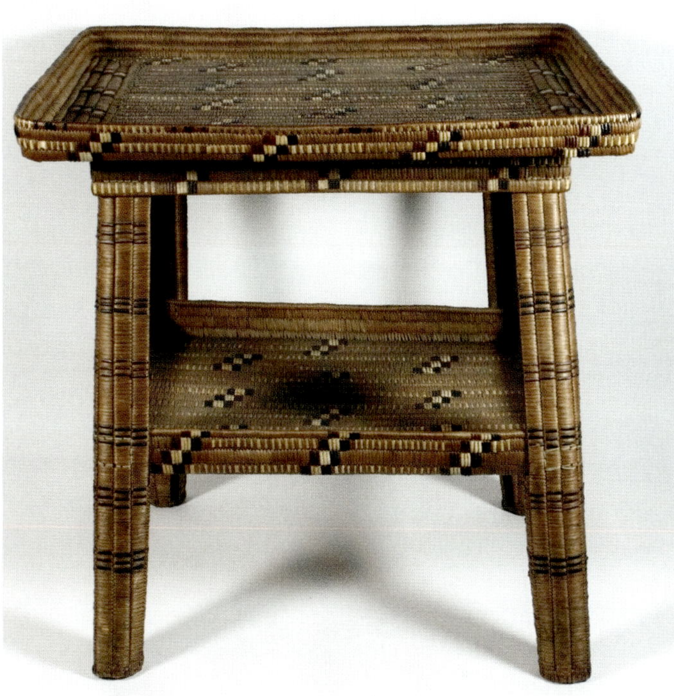

8.4. Coiled cedar root table featured in the "Uses of Basketry" section, of the *Honouring the Basketmakers* exhibit, Museum of Vancouver, MOV Collection AA 2127.

> of the forests, and the economy of the fledgling city of Vancouver. We have learned much from these women, their histories, and their specific knowledge. It is with great respect that we hold up our women and their legacies. We invite you to do the same.[15]

The exhibit featured community loans, new commissions, along with baskets and many other items from the MOV collection. The project resulted in several baskets in the MOV collection being attributed to specific Musqueam and Sḵwx̱wú7mesh makers, including Mary Grant, Mary Anne John, Margaret Lewis, Sophie Moody, Mary Anne Jack, and Margaret Baker. The exhibit showcased many privately owned heritage baskets from the Tsleil-Waututh community. A diversity of weaving tools, unique basketry items, and other forms of weaving practiced locally were highlighted using examples from the MOV collection. This collaboration, which predated the 2010 Olympic games by eight years, was possibly the first exhibition in the city of Vancouver that involved the three host nations working together to tell a shared history. It was unique in that it employed community curators from each of the host nations rather than one specialist to engage with all three.

Developing long-term partnerships with First Nations and other source communities can be a complex process, as museums have to overcome their colonial roots while contending with larger societal issues that foster social inequalities. Working with multiple host nations adds another level of complexity, as each community has its own unique interests and needs. The Museum of Vancouver had some difficulty maintaining an active relationship with the three host nations after *Honouring the Basketmakers* was completed. School programming for the exhibit was offered until 2004, but participation in exhibit work fluctuated.

That same year the exhibit *You Say You Want a Revolut*ion—MOV's 1960s and 1970s gallery—opened. This project did not involve in-depth consultation; instead the curator selected a poster depicting Chief Dan George's 1967 speech "A Lament for Confederation" to represent First Nations history in the space. By 2011 it appeared that relationships with the three host nations had completely derailed when all of them withdrew from the exhibit project "The Unnatural History of Stanley Park." The difficulty arose over how to tell a common history for this contested place. After a hiatus of almost a decade, the museum tried again—with a new curator at the helm, and this time working with a single community.

c̓əsnaʔəm, the city before the city, 2015

First Nations voice would once again become prominent at MOV with *c̓əsnaʔəm, the city before the city*. This exhibit opened January 22, 2015, in the museum's permanent galleries wing. *c̓əsnaʔəm* was developed in partnership with the community of Musqueam, the UBC Museum of Anthropology, and Dr. Susan Roy from the University of Waterloo and author of the book *These Mysterious People*.[16] The exhibit involved a three-year curatorial process, which resulted in the production of a trio of exhibits, each at a different venue, about the ongoing relationship between the Musqueam community and the Vancouver neighbourhood of Marpole, the site of a massive archaeological midden associated with the ancestral village of c̓əsnaʔəm.[17]

MOV curator Viviane Gosselin and Musqueam guest curator Jordan Wilson worked closely with a Musqueam advisory committee to create the MOV exhibit. Each of the c̓əsnaʔəm exhibits offered a different perspective and in some cases targeted different audiences. The MOV exhibit explores the ongoing cultural significance of *c̓əsnaʔəm* to the Musqueam community. The exhibit is described as follows on the MOV website:

> The curatorial premise of this project is simple: the bone, stone, and shell objects from c̓əsnaʔəm, which have survived thousands of years, are great catalysts for conversations about the relationship between Indigenous and settler societies in Vancouver. They are reminders of the connections between the history of colonialism, and the continuum of Musqueam culture. During the 1920s and 1930s, the Art, Historical and Scientific Association of Vancouver (MOV's predecessor) undertook excavations at the Marpole Midden and removed over 1,500 "artefacts" for the museum's displays, discarding others. The presence of these objects or "belongings" as this exhibition calls them

since they were, in fact, personal possessions and ancestral remains in the museum's collections point to an unsettling history. The museum constructed a story about Vancouver's past that distanced and excluded the Musqueam, viewing the village as an ancient forerunner to Vancouver instead of as a place of ongoing significance to Musqueam. This exhibition re-examines the historical collection and display practices of the museum itself within this context of colonialism.[18]

Whereas the exhibits at the UBC Museum of Anthropology and MOV targeted general audiences, serving to educate them about Musqueam world view and ongoing interests and actions to protect lands in Vancouver, an exhibit created for the Musqueam Cultural Centre specifically targets the Nations' youth, showing the complexity of Musqueam culture past and present. The exhibit is thus intended for cultural renewal rather than public education.[19]

This project introduced MOV staff to new ways of thinking about archaeological collections. The Art, Historical and Scientific Association of Vancouver had actively "investigated" the midden created by c̓əsnaʔəm (DhRs1) between 1928 and 1932 and treated ancestral remains and belongings as scientific specimens. The *c̓əsnaʔəm* project led museum staff to give deeper consideration to the ethics of archaeological collecting. As a result, they willingly discussed repatriation with community members as part of the research process for this exhibit. The Museum of Vancouver will respond promptly when the community feels ready to initiate a request.

Indigenous Voices and the Telling of Vancouver Stories

In 2017 staff at MOV identified four pillars to guide future exhibition and collecting strategies: reconciliation, immigration, natural history, and social history and contemporary issues within the province of British Columbia. The first of these pillars signals a shift in curatorial focus and a return to public exhibits of the city's much forgotten collection of Indigenous belongings. According to a 2017 MOV document, "integrating the theme of Reconciliation in all areas of the organization is a focus for 2018 and beyond with a focus on the history and contemporary issues around Indigenous communities. This involves hiring of Indigenous curators, collaborators and scholars, the display of the first nations' collection and the recall of all monumental objects currently on loan. Associated programming will focus on the delivery of the TRC's calls to action."[20]

These are not new strategies for the institution but rather a renewed effort. This year, more than 450 items from the Haida collection were brought into the light again with *Haida Now*, an exhibition project developed in partnership with the Haida Gwaii Museum. Haida guest curator Kwi Jones was integral in bringing a diverse group of Haida community members, both urban and rurally based, into collections storage for this project. Effort was made to include all three host nations, who played a prominent role in welcoming the Haida to their shared unceded territories at the opening of the exhibition.[21]

Only one of the host nations, Musqueam, is currently featured in a long-term installation. The exhibition *c̓əsnaʔəm, the city before the city*, which opened in 2015, introduces the permanent Vancouver Stories galleries at the museum. This exhibit was placed at the beginning of a series of galleries that tell Vancouver history, decade by decade. Plans are under way to develop two new "permanent" exhibitions that feature all three host nations more prominently, beginning with *That Which Sustains Us*, an exhibit that will explore the convergence of different knowledge traditions in the Vancouver area by examining peoples interactions with forests, past and present.[22] *That Which Sustains Us* is scheduled to open in 2020, and once it is complete *c̓əsnaʔəm* will close and a new exhibit will be developed featuring all three host nations in equal proportions.

The Origins of a "Collection"

The belongings housed at the Museum of Vancouver—the largest civic museum in Canada—are diverse in scope and origin.[23] In its entirety, the MOV collection exceeds seventy thousand pieces, encompassing the disciplines of archaeology, Asian studies, ethnography, history, natural history, and the city of Vancouver's 2010 Olympic Legacy collection. Indigenous belongings comprise over twenty-two thousand (or 32 percent) and can be found in several categories.

While the belongings that form the museum's archaeology and ethnographic collections originate from source communities from around the world, almost 8,879 items are identified as "Coast Salish," many from archaeological sites in the Greater Vancouver area. The proportionally small number of ethnographic items in the museum may be due to the unwillingness of many "Coast Salish" people to part with personal belongings considered to be imbued with spiritual power.[24] It is not uncommon to hear stories of people breathing or singing life into carved objects or weaving prayers into blankets. Anthropologist Michael Kew once noted that "Central Coast Salish art was probably always less abundant than art among northern coastal tribes, for it was closely associated with private religious expression and used less in secular display."[25] However, as MOV is located within the center of the Coast Salish world, ancestral belongings from "Salish" communities are generally well represented.

Systematic collecting for the museum began in the 1890s with the formation of the Art, Historical and Scientific Association of Vancouver. Salvaging First Nations heritage objects was a prime motivation for many of the association's founding members, including Amy and Ronald Campbell-Johnston, whose collections were among the first to be gifted to the Museum of Vancouver. The Campbell-Johnstons also collected several totem poles for a proposed "educational village" in Stanley Park. Ironically, this preservation work was undertaken in the same period when "Coast Salish," Native Hawaiian, and mixed heritage settlers were being evicted from the park at the beginning of the twentieth century.[26]

Many local amateur ethnologists and First Nations art enthusiasts, some association members, have added to the collections over the years.[27] The MOV collection contains many hidden treasures as a result. I refer to them as "hidden treasures," because the practice of exhibiting ethnographic and archaeological materials waned in the late 1980s. In the following decades, curatorial staff shied away from long-term exhibits that would highlight these collections as they struggled with appropriate ways to undertake this work. Since the 1990s, staff have explored different ways of developing collaborative relationships with Vancouver's host nations—Musqueam, Sḵwx̱wú7mesh, and Tsleil-Waututh—and the other BC First Nations whose cultural belongings are in the collection.

Belongings in the Collection That Tell Stories of Displacement

Individuals from the three host nations have engaged with the museum at various times, together and separately, since the museum was established in 1894. Accession files for the Campbell-Johnson collection make direct reference to items collected from Sḵwx̱wú7mesh community members.[28] Other members of the Art, Historic and Scientific Association of Vancouver undertook excavations of c̓əsnaʔəm in the 1920s and 1930s, removing fifteen hundred belongings from the midden for the museum's collection while discarding others. Sḵwx̱wú7mesh síýáḿ (August Jack Khatsahlano, 1877–1971) features prominently in the writings of Major Matthews, a member of the association and the city's first archivist, and belongings featured in interviews conducted in the 1930s through the 1950s are now found in the MOV collection.[29]

Items made by, or collected from, August Jack and other Sḵwx̱wú7mesh community members tell a story of changing land use and occupancy. In particular, a carving referred to as the Seńáḵw house post documents the forced removal of Sḵwx̱wú7mesh families from their residences at Seńáḵw. In 1913 the provincial government ordered Sḵwx̱wú7mesh families to be moved by barge from Seńáḵw to reserves across the inlet. Subsequently, a West Vancouver couple salvaged the house post from the remains of the village and used the figure whom they called "Kitsilano Man" as a garden ornament for several decades, before it was donated to MOV in 1969. Stylistically, this house post has traits common to mortuary figures and may have once served such a purpose. However, a 1907 photograph shows it displayed on the beach in front of Jericho Charlie's house at Seńáḵw. An early study of Salish sculpture notes that human figures were used both for house posts and to mark individual graves or mortuary houses—the former often holding an animal that alluded to the owner's spirit power, the latter being a portrait of the deceased person.[30] Decay makes it difficult to determine if the Seńák̲w figure is holding something in its hands, but arrangement of the arms suggest it once did.

It is possible that the Seńák̲w house post was repurposed or moved from another site. In 1913, when the Royal Commission on Indian Affairs visited the province of British Columbia, Musqueam leadership prepared for the visit by decorating the entrance of their catechism house—the community's meeting space—with house posts taken from homes on the reserve. This was done to "transform it into a place considered appropriate for giving testimony."[31] This was a significant act because house posts function to "remind visitors of social status and common history."[32] The display of the Seńák̲w figure in front of Jericho Charlie's home arguably invokes the same traditions, linking high status to knowing one's own history.

Other evidence to support that the Seńák̲w figure served a marker of identity, or architectural element, can be found in a letter that accompanied the donation, which notes that it was one of a male-female pair as is common with house posts. The collector's son wrote: "My parents were attracted to the area, I understand, and found workmen demolishing the former native residences and their remaining contents. From the debris they retrieved two carved cedar statues, one of a man, the other of a woman—each approximately five feet tall. They could only carry one, so they hid the other in a ditch to be picked up later. Unfortunately the second one, the woman, had disappeared when they returned the next day."[33] The fate of the second figure remains a mystery.

The male Seńák̲w figure may have inspired two other human figures now in the MOV collection. In the 1920s, Jericho Charlie's stepson, August Jack Khahtsahlano (1877–1971), carved a similar style human figure named Wáxayus. This "Salmon Chief" was placed on the Squamish River at the community of Poquiosin. Wáxayus, although smaller in scale, bears several stylistic similarities to the older Seńák̲w figure.[34] Both are three-dimensional sculptures depicted in a realistic manner, each with hands placed in front of the body. Wáxayus clearly grasps a salmon in his hands, while decay makes it unclear whether the Seńák̲w figure likewise once held an object or animal in its hands; its arms are arranged in a similar manner. The Wáxayus figure carved by August Jack may have been commissioned to replace an earlier figure at this Squamish River site. The story of this salmon chief was recounted by Charles Hill Tout, an amateur ethnologist and archaeologist, in *Museum and Art Notes* published in June 1929.[35] At the time of publication Hill Tout noted that his story was over thirty years old, predating the new carving by August Jack by several decades.

In 1989, Wáxayus served as inspiration for a larger-scale salmon chief figure carved by *Stó:lō* and Semiahmoo artist Stan Greene. This one was adorned with cedar bark regalia and red paint. Each of these three figures was carved in a distinctive manner, for different spaces on the landscape, but together they illustrate a wider conversation about cultural continuity. In the first instance of replication,

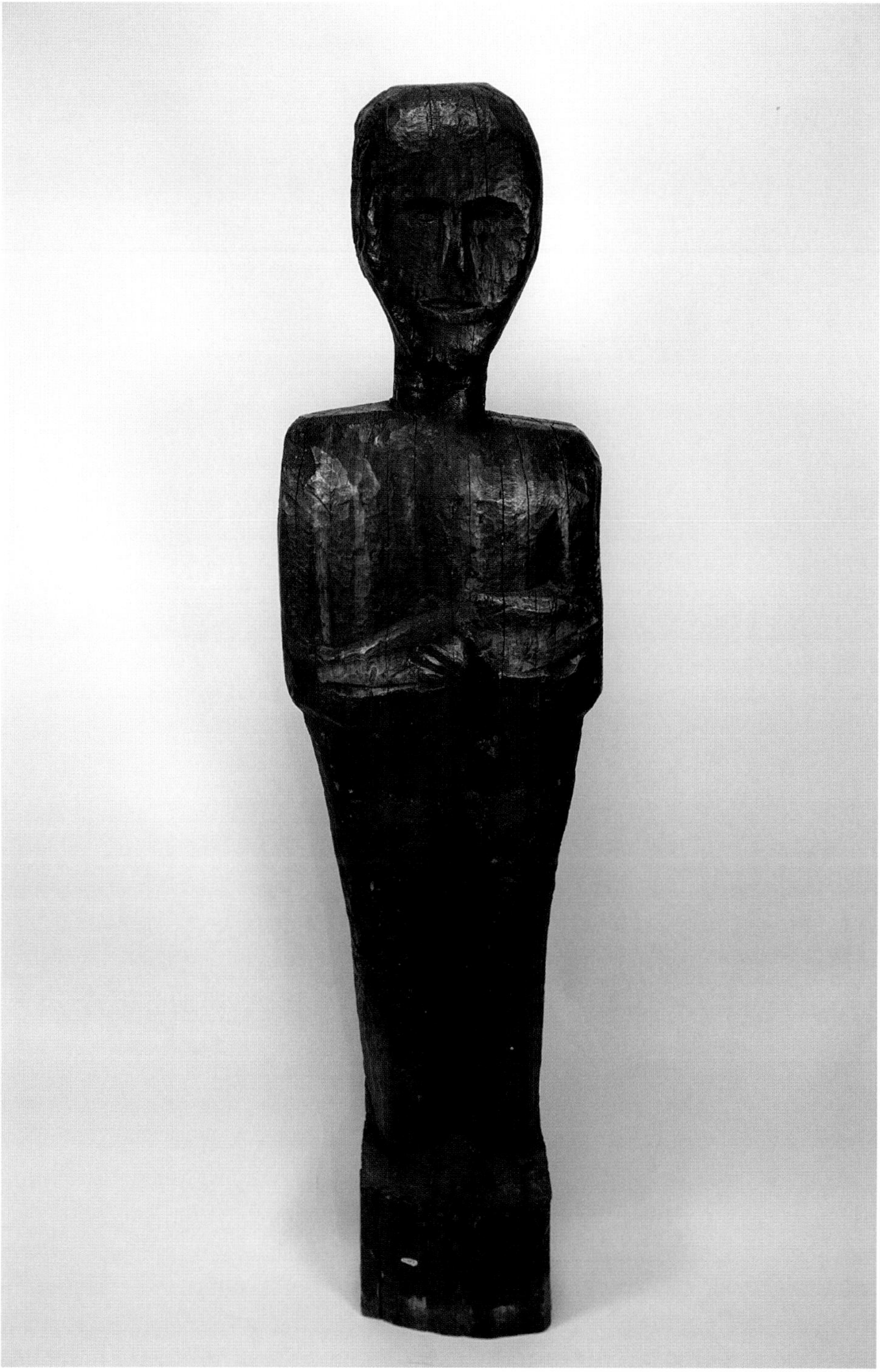

8.5. Wáxayus, a Salmon Chief figure, was acquired from Indian Agent Charles C. Perry in 1929. Carved by August Jack Khatsahlano. Museum of Vancouver, MOV Collection AA 687.

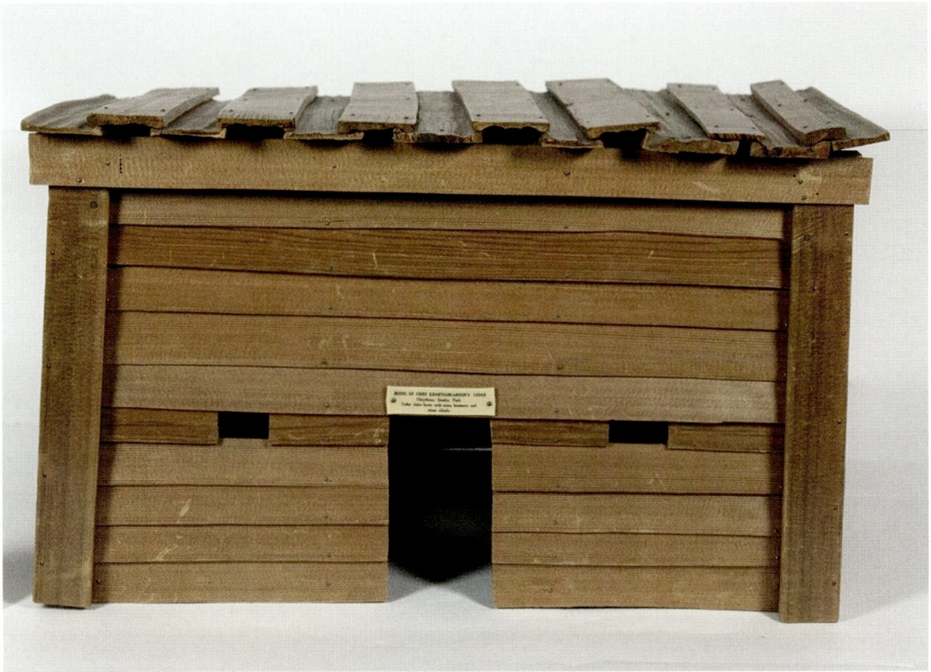

8.6. Model of Chief Khatsahlano's house at Claythoos (Prospect Point) in Stanley Park. Chief Khatsahlano was a canoe builder and the father of Supple Jack and the grandfather of attributed maker August Jack Khatsahlano. Major J. S. Matthews Collection. Museum of Vancouver, MOV Collection AA 2598.

the breadth of traditional territory and kinship networks is demonstrated when specific imagery is transported across the landscape to be realized in a new location within the same traditional territory. In the second instance, we see how older belongings can inspire contemporary artists from a broader Coast Salish world to express widely shared cultural beliefs—such as the teachings about respect that are enacted each spring with the First Salmon Ceremony.

These monumental carvings serve to mark a connection between people and places. As such, their subsequent removal by newcomers can be read as an act of violence—the symbolic severing of Indigenous histories in specific places. This is an agenda that has also been accomplished through mapping and the renaming of landscapes in honor of settlers and colonial officials. Colonialism frequently employs the doctrine of terra nullius (empty land) to justify resettlement, while simultaneously requiring the physical removal of people and their belongings to legitimize city building.[36] Other items in the collection that speak to displacement include two mortuary figures found in a duck pond near the former zoo in Stanley Park; a model of Chief Khahtsahalano's house at Chaythoos (Prospect Point) made by his grandson August Jack; a replica duck hunting spear of the type once used in Coal Harbour made by August Jack's brother Willie; and a black cod lure of the type once used at Brockton Point.[37] These are but a few examples from the collection that speak to the loss of access to specific places and their resources, which directly correlates to the damaging consequences of city building.

From the Forests and Sea to the Mountains

In the MOV collections, baskets, wood carvings, and fishing gear speak to the presence of hən̓q̓əmin̓əm̓- and Sḵwx̱wú7mesh-speaking peoples in the forests and waters of what is now Greater Vancouver, while other items remind us of connections to the local mountains that surround us. Items made of mountain goat hair and horn convey that traditional territories were diverse, not just for access to different types of resources but for spiritual matters as well. Salish weavings speak to both these concepts, as the wool is gathered high in the mountains while the blankets are woven with protection and prayers, to be worn for ceremonies, both public and private.

The significance of Salish blankets is conveyed by Chepximiya Siyam' (Chief Janice George) and her husband, Skwetsimeltx̱w (Willard "Buddy" Joseph), as follows:

> The Salish worldview understands that robes and blankets already exist in the spirit world and it is the weaver who brings them into the human realm. She is directed by an Ancestral Spirit that the weaver has called on for guidance. Many people have spoken of feeling their grandmothers or great grandmothers near them and having their hands guided during the creation of the work. The robes themselves are considered to be objects of power and are talked about as being alive with a heartbeat of their own. The touch, sweat, breath, and voice of the maker become woven into the textile, animating it, shaping it, and giving it memory.[38]

A small woven mat in the collection made by Buddy Joseph's grandmother, Harriet Johnnie, and donated to the Museum of Vancouver as part of the Lipsett Collection has been a source of inspiration for their contemporary work.[39] The collection contains six wool blankets—two known to be sheep's wool from Vancouver Island made by Mrs. Walter Joseph of Songhees, and four with mountain goat hair fibers. One of the mountain goat hair blankets was purchased in 1948 at conference of the BC Arts and Welfare Society, but the accompanying documentation does not reveal the community of origin. A wool sample studied under advanced microscopy revealed the presence of dog hair, suggesting it may date to the mid-nineteenth century, when hair from the Salish wool dog was still in use.[40] Source communities for the three remaining mountain goat hair blankets is undocumented, but current research suggest two are of Sḵwx̱wú7mesh origin.[41]

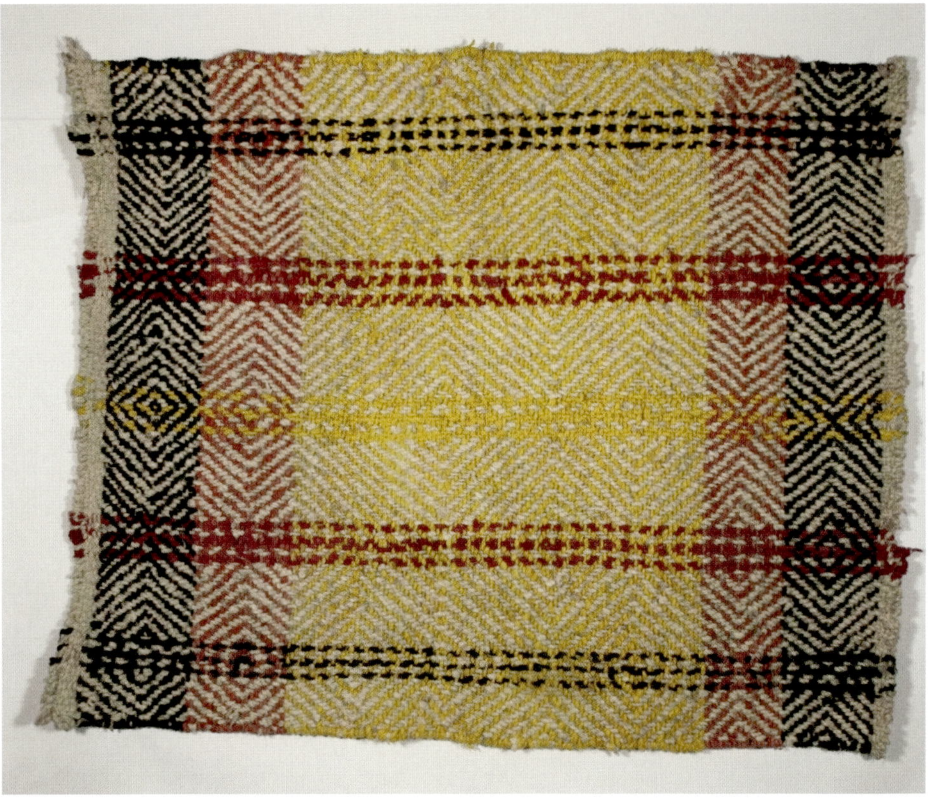

8.7. A swéwkw'elh blanket made from mountain goat hair (and possibly Salish wool dog hair). Museum of Vancouver, MOV Collection AA 1268.

MOV's collecting strategy is now centered on ethical practice, requiring a shift away from historic pieces to contemporary items that showcase resilience and the creativity of surviving traditions. To create a collection that properly documents the history and revival of Salish weaving in British Columbia will require the addition of contemporary works that demonstrate local revivals. The first local revival occurred in the Fraser Valley, with the Salish Weavers Guild in the 1960s, and inspired a revival downriver at Musqueam in the 1980s. A third was led by Chief Janice George and Willard "Buddy" Joseph of the Sḵwx̱wú7mesh Nation in the early 2000s, inspired by their personal studies with master weavers Susan Pavel and Subiyay (Bruce Miller) in Washington State.

The first of these local revivals was documented by transferring a Salish Weavers Guild blanket from the MOV teaching collection to the main collection at the end of 2018. A review of ethnographic items in the teaching collection revealed the presence of four Salish Weavers Guild weavings, one of which was woven by Martha James of the Skwah Reserve (near Chilliwack) and bears the Guild's tag. It was selected for the main collection as it had the best provenance. In May of 2018 the

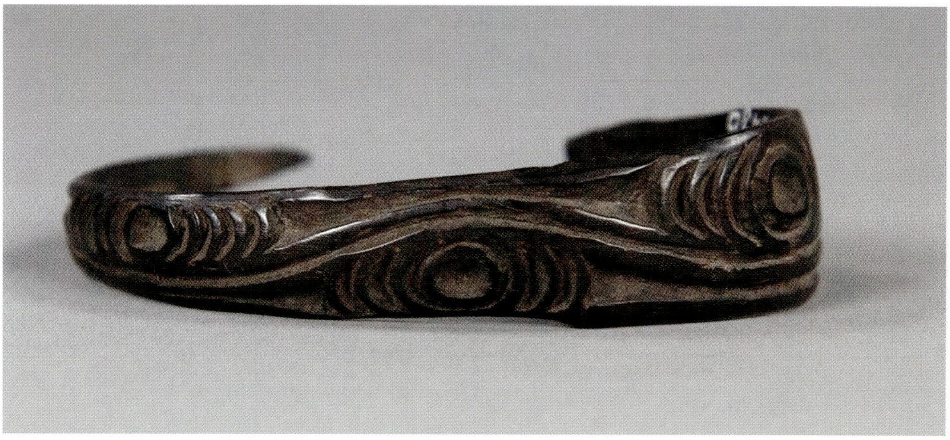

8.8. Eighteenth-century mountain goat horn bracelet purchased in 1983 for the exhibit *Captain George Vancouver: A Voyage of Discovery*. Museum of Vancouver, MOV Collection AA 2430.

museum acquired two new weavings, representing the Sḵwx̱wú7mesh weaving revival, by bidding in a fundraising auction at a gala for *Kwi Awt Stelmexw*—a nonprofit working toward Sḵwx̱wú7mesh language revitalization. Weavings by both Skwetsimeltxw (Buddy Joseph) and Chepximiya Siyam' (Chief Janice George), cofounders of the *L'hen Awtxw Weaving House*, were acquired at this event organized by their nephew, Khelsilem. Weavings that represent contemporary practice at Musqueam and Tsleil-Waututh are a top priority for future collecting.

Although exact provenance for many of the older belongings housed at MOV remains unknown, these items remain a vital element in creating opportunities for new generations to relearn lost knowledge, practice endangered languages, and to feel spiritually connected with ancestors through their belongings. Weavers and traditional technologists are more frequently accessing the MOV collections to study raw materials, manufacturing techniques, and use of designs. For example, the museum has the distinction of housing the only example of a mountain goat horn bracelet remaining in a Canada museum collection.[42] This beautiful piece features distinctive Coast Salish engraved designs—circles, crescents, and trigons, arranged in an hourglass formation—and has inspired several contemporary versions in silver, including one in my personal collection by Tawx'sin Yexwulla / Poolx̱tun (Aaron Nelson Moody).

Moving Forward

Coast Salish art traditions are once again thriving.[43] Although the Museum of Vancouver does not actively collect "art," it does collect items that support the sharing of contemporary stories and experiences in the city of Vancouver. Collecting practices are moving away from accepting older items that may have been acquired through coercion or theft.[44] Instead, MOV seeks to document revitalization of local First Nations cultures, including those that represent the diverse urban First Nations community in Vancouver, by collecting contemporary pieces made for sale.

In the *Vancouver Stories* galleries the host nations are depicted as complex and vibrant, actively entwined with the history of Vancouver—a continuous thread. A conscious effort is being made to include the perspectives of the host nations in temporary exhibits on a wide array of topics from natural history to social activism to immigration. This requires an understanding of their respective capacities, as they are being actively engaged on numerous projects daily. At present these communities are prioritizing long-term projects over short-term ones; MOV is trying to be mindful of the number of requests and is fundraising to assist with staffing in each community.

The museum's goal is to build healthy relationships with the host nations and members of the urban Indigenous community, while redressing past wrongs through exhibits and programming that sheds light on difficult subjects. The traveling exhibition *There Is Truth Here: Creativity and Resilience in Children's Art from Indian Residential and Day Schools*, which opened April 5, 2019, is one such effort. MOV strives to provide engagement opportunities for the general public and corporate sponsors, to increase public awareness of the difficult and hidden elements of Canadian history. The collection is viewed as secondary to the process of strengthening these relationships. Repatriation will likely play a prominent role in future redress initiatives, but MOV leadership is committed to moving forward on timelines determined by source communities rather than internal policy decisions.

NOTES

1 The Truth and Reconciliation Commission was an important element of the Indian Residential Schools Settlement Agreement. It documented the testimony of six thousand Indian residential school survivors from across Canada and presented it in an executive report published in 2015. The report culminates in identifying calls to action to bring about reconciliation in Canada and mandates policy changes in all areas of Canadian society—social justice, child welfare, education, health care, business, and cultural policy, to name a few.

2 Canadian museum professionals having been writing about adopting new ways of working with First Nations since the 1980s. See Duncan F. Cameron, "Museums and Public Access: The Glenbow Approach," *International Journal of Museum Management and Curatorship* 1 (1982): 177–96; Julia Harrison, "Completing a Circle: The Spirit Sings," in *Anthropology, Public Policy, and Native Peoples in Canada*, edited by Noel Dyck and James B. Waldram, 334–58 (Montreal: McGill-Queen's University Press, 1995); Margaret Holm and David Pokotylo, "From Policy to Practice: A Case Study in Collaborative Exhibits with First Nations," *Canadian Journal of Archaeology* 21, no. 1 (1997): 33–44; Michael Ames, "How To Decorate a House: The Re-negotiation of Cultural Representations at the University of British Columbia Museum

of Anthropology," *Museum Anthropology* 22, no. 3 (1999): 41–51; Stephanie Bolton, "The Task Force on Museums and First Peoples, a Decade Later: A Case Study of the McCord Museum of Canadian History," paper presented at the Centre of Canadian Studies conference, University of Edinburgh, 2005; Ruth Phillips, *Museum Pieces: Toward the Indigenization of Canadian Museums* (Montreal: McGill-Queen's University Press, 2011); and Charlotte Townsend-Gault, Jennifer Kramer, and Ki-ke-in, eds., *Native Art of the Northwest Coast: A History of Changing Ideas* (Vancouver: UBC Press, 2013).

3 Kamala Todd, "Truth Telling: Indigenous Perspectives on with Municipal Governments," Vancouver Park Board Report, 2017, 11.

4 "Redress" was situated as a more active reconciliation process at "Reconciliation and the Arts in Vancouver," held on October 26, 2018. At this event arts institutions from the Greater Vancouver area were challenged to move beyond "tokenism and brief marquee appearances. Reconciliation shouldn't be a funding opportunity—it should be genuine and society-wide" (Irwin Oostindie, www.allianceforarts.com/blog/2017/10/25/upcoming-event-redressing-settler-cultural-policy-in-the-era-of-reconciliation [accessed 2018]).

5 Most of the province of British Columbia is considered "unceded" as Aboriginal rights and title were not extinguished through the signing of treaties. Many nations are today engaged in a new treaty process that involves negotiating agreements with both the provincial and federal governments.

6 For this reason I use only Sḵwx̱wú7mesh sníchim (*language*) when referring to the twentieth-century village for the remainder of this chapter.

7 Squamish Indian Band v. Canadian Pacific, 2002. Specific Claim.

8 I use "place-names" plural, as the entrance to the exhibit *c̓əsnaʔəm, the city before the city* is visible from the same vantage point.

9 A third of the MOV Board of Directors is now comprised of First Nations representatives: Leona Sparrow (Musqueam), Chief Janice George (Sḵwx̱wú7mesh), Karen Rose Thomas (Tsleil-Waututh), and Kory Wilson (Kwakwa̱ka̱'wakw). This is a first in British Columbia and possibly Canadian museums. In the *Wild Things* exhibition that opened June 2018, representatives of the three host nations participated in meetings that shaped the themes of this natural history–based exhibition and contributed content that is featured throughout. The *Haida Now* exhibit, which opened in March 2018, directly acknowledges that one-fifth of the Haida community lives in Vancouver, the unceded lands of the Musqueam, Sḵwx̱wú7mesh, and Tsleil-Waututh Nations.

10 *c̓əsnaʔəm* is the hən̓q̓əmin̓əm̓ name for the xʷməθkʷəy̓əm (Musqueam) village site known today as the Marpole midden.

11 Trudy Nicks and Tom Hill, *Turning the Page: Forging New Partnerships between Museums and First Peoples Task Force Report* (Ottawa: Assembly of First Nations and Canadian Museums Association, 1992).

12 Lynn Maranda, First Nations Exhibit Files, Guiding Principles document, 1999.

13 Joan Seidl was curator of history, and Lynn Maranda was curator of ethnology.

14 At that time, Rose processed new acquisitions, wrote descriptions of objects on file cards, and helped to train education docents (Sharon Fortney, "Forging New Partnerships: Coast Salish Communities and Museums," PhD diss., UBC–Vancouver, 2009, 178). After finishing university, Rose managed education and cultural programming at Musqueam for several decades and started the first Native preschool in Canada at Musqueam in the 1960s (Cheryl Rossi, "Norma Rose Point School a Fitting Tribute: West Side School Represents First Nations," *Vancouver Courier*, October 21, 2014; and Anderson, "An Indian Woman's Triumph, Rose Point Starts School, Becomes a Teacher," *Vancouver Sun*, April 22, 1971, 43).

15 Tsleil-Waututh Nation introduction label in *Honouring the Basketmakers* exhibition, 2002.

16 Susan Roy, *These Mysterious People: Shaping History and Archaeology in a Northwest Coast Community* (Montreal: McGill-Queen's University Press, 2010).

17 All three exhibits opened in 2015 and were called *c̓əsnaʔəm, the city before the city*. The exhibit at the UBC Museum of Anthropology closed after one year; the other two exhibits are still open at their respective host institutions.

18 Museum of Vancouver, "Current Exhibitions: c̓əsnaʔəm," March 2018, https://museumofvancouver.ca/csnam-the-city-before-the-city.

19 The Musqueam Community Centre resides within the former Four Host Nations pavilion from the 2010 Winter Olympic Games. It is both a gathering place for community members and a museum gallery open to the public.

20 Museum of Vancouver, "Four Pillars" internal document, 2017.

21 All three were invited to participate in the exhibition, but only the Sḵwx̱wú7mesh Nation had the ability to participate at the time. There is an open invitation to add a story to the first gallery at any time while *Haida Now* remains on display.

22 In 2019 this project was retitled from "Vancouver Transformation" as consultation with the host nations shifted the focus of the project.

23 Robert D. Watt, *Cabinets of Curiosities: Collections of the Vancouver Museum 1894–1981* (Vancouver: Vancouver Museum and Planetarium Association, 1988).

24 Brian Thom, "Harlan I. Smith's Jesup Fieldwork on the Northwest Coast," in *Gateways: Exploring the Legacy of the Jesup North Pacific Expedition*, edited by I. Krupnik and W. Fitzhugh, 139–80 (Washington, DC: Arctic Studies Center, National Museum of Natural History, Smithsonian Institution Press, 2001), 149.

25 J. E. Michael Kew, "Sculpture and Engraving of the Central Coast Salish Indians," *UBC Museum of Anthropology Museum Note*, no. 9 (1980): 1.

26 Kanaka or Kanaka maoli is a historical term on the Northwest Coast used to refer to Native Hawaiians and other Pacific Islanders who settled in British Columbia. A Kanaka Ranch was once present in what is now Stanley Park, on Burrard Inlet. Jean Barman, *Stanley Park's Secret: The Forgotten Families of Whoi Whoi, Kanaka Ranch and Brockton Point* (Madeira Park, BC: Harbour Publishing, 2005), 207.

27 Donors include archaeologist Charles Hill-Tout, artist Mildred Valley Thornton, city archivist Major James S. Matthews, Methodist missionary George Raley, scenery shop founder William Webber, and most notably Edward and Mary Lipsett, whose major collection transferred to the museum in the 1970s after a new facility was opened at Vanier Park.

28 Sharon M. Fortney, "Entwined Histories: The Creation of the Maisie Hurley Collection of Native Art," *BC Studies*, no. 167 (Autumn 2010): 71–95.

29 Matthews's writings on early Vancouver date between 1931 and 1956. See Major J. S. Matthews, "Conversations with Khatsahlano 1932–1954," Vancouver City Archivist, 1955.

30 Paul S. Wingert, *American Indian Sculpture: A Study of the Northwest Coast* (New York: J.J. Augustin Publisher, 1949), 12, 13.

31 Susan Roy, "Making History Visible: Culture and Politics in the Presentation of Musqueam History," MA thesis, Simon Fraser University, 22.

32 Roy, "Making History Visible," 23.

33 Donor letter to Lynn Maranda, Curator of Anthropology, April 23, 2004.

34 Wáxayus measures 147 centimeters tall, while the Seńáḵw figure measures 113 centimeters. However, the latter is incomplete—missing its lower legs.

35 Charles Hill Tout, "Myth of Salmon Coming to Squamish Waters," Vancouver Art, Historical and Scientific Association *Museum and Art Notes* 4, no. 2 (June 1929): 62–64.

36 Elizabeth A. Povinelli, *The Cunning of Recognition: Indigenous Alterities and the Making of Australian Multiculturalism* (Durham, NC: Duke University Press, 2002), 39.

37 All three host nations have histories that connect to the lands that are now Stanley Park, but published histories tend to focus on Sḵwx̱wú7mesh history of use.

38 Leslie Tepper, Janice George, and Willard Joseph, *Salish Blankets: Robes of Protecting and Transformation, Symbols of Wealth* (Lincoln: University of Nebraska Press, 2017), 3–4.

39 The couple re-created Harriet Johnnie's design in a new blanket that was showcased at the Portland Art Museum, Center for Contemporary Native Art Gallery exhibit, *Restoring the Breath—Sacred Relationship*, in 2016.

40 Author's personal communication with Elaine Humphrey, UVIC Advanced Microscopy Facility, September 17, 2018.

41 Meeting minutes of the Vancouver Art, Historical and Scientific Association revealed that Amy Campbell-Johnston purchased a Sḵwx̱wú7mesh blanket for the museum in 1917, and accession records identified Mildred Valley Thornton as the donor of a second Sḵwx̱wú7-mesh blanket.

42 Robert D. Leece, "Coast Salish Mountain Horn Bracelets: Evidence of Change and Continuity in Coast Salish Art Production and Use during the Early Contact Period on the Northwest Coast of America," MA thesis, University of Victoria, 1995.

43 See Rebecca Blanchard and Nancy Davenport, eds., *Contemporary Coast Salish Art*, (Seattle: University of Washington Press, 2005); Andrea Walsh, *Out of the Frame: Salish Printmaking* (Victoria, BC: Legacy Gallery, University of Victoria, 2016); Vancouver Art Gallery, *Susan Point, Spindle Whor* (Vancouver, BC: Black Dog Publishing, 2017); Sharon M. Fortney, *Intangible: Memory and Innovation in Coast Salish Art* (Vancouver, BC: Bill Reid Gallery, 2017); Tepper, George, and Joseph, *Salish Blankets*; and Ed Carriere and Dale Croes, "Re-Awakening Ancient Salish Sea Basketry: Fifty Years of Basketry Studies in Culture and Science," *Journal of Northwest Anthropology Memoir 15*, 2018).

44 When source community is known, potential donors are redirected to representatives from those First Nations.

CHAPTER 9

The Museum Disappeared

NORTHWEST COAST ART AND THE OBJECT OF DISPLAY

Karen Duffek, Peter Morin, and Karen Benbassat Ali

> If there were a Tahltan museum, it wouldn't be a building. It would be a place for potential learning in the landscape. I could travel to this place to gather knowledge and bring that learning back to our community.
>
> —PETER MORIN

FOR ABOUT TEN WEEKS IN 2011, WHEN YOU WOULD STEP OFF THE ELEVATOR TO visit Vancouver's downtown Satellite Gallery, you would enter the unexpected. The experimental exhibition space had been transformed into *Peter Morin's Museum*, an installation conceived by the eponymous artist to be a place where Indigenous knowledge specific to his community, and the result of thousands of years of culture and experience, was practiced. Some of the structures that carry that knowledge—the Tahltan language, family photographs, handmade baskets and snowshoes, tents, new songs and songs from a time before time, and a kitchen table—were displayed there, although they would appear or disappear over the run of the show.[1]

By the final week, all of the contents of *Peter Morin's Museum* had been evacuated by the artist. The vitrines stood empty, the tent was removed from its frame, the displays dismantled. Only a metaphorical river remained, comprised of hundreds of bright red prints of spawning salmon tacked to the gallery's walls as though swimming upstream. Several visitors came to view the exhibition in its closing days. One woman returned for a second time with a friend to share what she had witnessed a few weeks earlier. On surveying the room, she was almost in tears. "Where has the museum gone?" she asked in astonishment. Gallery staff reminded her that the exhibition was intended to continually shift and change—that the artist would alter it through a series of performances. But this explanation did little to assuage her sense of loss.

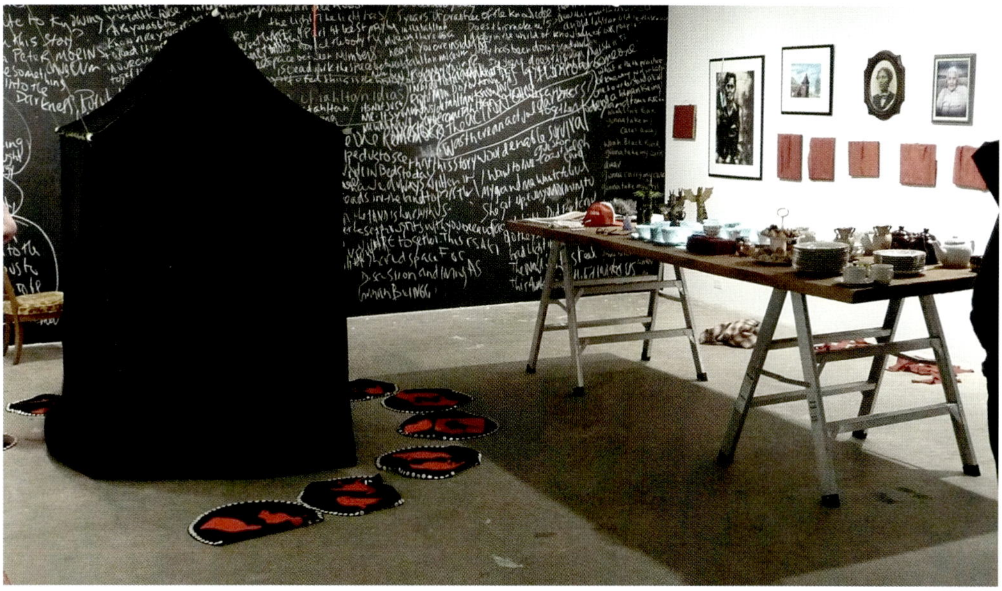

9.1. *Peter Morin's Museum*, partial installation view, 2011. Satellite Gallery, Vancouver, British Columbia. Photograph courtesy of UBC Museum of Anthropology (MOA)/Satellite Gallery.

Indeed, *Peter Morin's Museum* defied easy categorization. In its initial manifestation it had every appearance of a museum, with its familiar elements of art and ethnological displays. Its transformations, however, were meant to subvert visitors' expectations, especially of the now well-established, modern genre of exhibitions featuring carefully selected and spotlighted Northwest Coast masterworks fixed in place. Like many of those exhibitions, *Peter Morin's Museum* spoke to the history and use of Indigenous cultural belongings; yet it simultaneously eluded a focus on the material, using performative strategies to create an alternate experience for the viewer. In the changes he made and the actions he took, Morin—for whom performance art is central to his artistic practice—placed greater emphasis on the intangible and fluid connections between objects, community knowledge, and the land.

The exhibition temporarily inhabited an urban space above a nightclub, on the unceded traditional territories of the Sḵwx̱wú7mesh (Squamish), xʷməθkʷəy̓əm (Musqueam), and Tsleil-Waututh peoples. In that space it sought to transport visitors to the ancestral lands occupied by the Tahltan in northwest British Columbia since time immemorial—not by disguising the gallery's urban context or by mounting didactic panoramas of territories located a thousand miles north, but by restructuring this institution through specific Indigenous concepts and processes.[2] Peter Morin, a member of the Tahltan Tsesk'iye (Crow clan), aimed to activate the

PETER MORIN'S MUSEUM MANIFESTO

1. I invite you to participate in this new museum.
2. There is a possibility to remember.
3. There is a possibility for people to learn.
4. There is a possibility for the sacred.
5. There is a possibility for worship.
6. If you can't laugh or talk in the museum then you are not in the museum.
7. The objects watch us as much as we watch them.
8. There is no urban. There is no reservation. The land is where you are.
9. We are changed when we come into contact with the objects. Our DNA is changed.
10. Knowledge and knowing happen in a circle. There is no beginning. There is no ending.
11. You are welcome to cry. The museum is place of emotion, of laughter, of happiness.
12. There will be no boring tours in Peter Morin's Museum.
13. Children are invited to run around.
14. There will be food for sharing and tea for drinking.
15. This is a place of belonging for the community. Community members, from near and far, come to this place to spend time with their relatives.
16. This space is designed to demonstrate indigenous knowledge.
    Indigenous knowledge is like a river.
17. The Tahltan land is present here. The Tahltan land is present in our hearts.
18. The museum changes like the land changes.
19. Most of the objects speak Tahltan.
20. The objects are philosophy. The objects are the organized structures which support the transfer of Tahltan knowledge. You have to read the objects in order to understand Tahltan history.
21. There is a history of Tahltan ideas. New Tahltan ideas happen every day.
22. The museum is not just for old stuff. People can make new stuff and bring it to the museum.
23. We all have ancestors. These ancestors connect us to a land. These ancestors come with you when you enter into the museum. These ancestors help you to understand.
24. This is a temporary museum. People should feel free to make their own museum.
    People should make a museum wherever they go. Please honour your family, community, and culture.
25. Tradition is also a record of the tools used to make new objects.
26. Indigenous knowledge is made every day.
27. i heart Peter Morin's Museum.

9.2. *Museum Manifesto* by Peter Morin. *Peter Morin's Museum*, 2011. Courtesy of UBC Museum of Anthropology (MOA)/ Satellite Gallery, Vancouver, British Columbia.

presence of his people's knowledge right there at 560 Seymour Street, performing what he envisioned as a Tahltan concept of museum. "The Tahltan land is present here," read the *Manifesto* that Peter Morin mounted inside the entrance of the gallery. "[This] museum changes like the land changes."

> Peter Morin (PM): Tahltan knowledge is specific to an area, a location, a time frame, a historical reference, a historian, a structure, an art form—and it is also portable.[3] You walk into the Satellite Gallery and it reads as an exhibition, and it also feels like it is more than an exhibition because you are feeling Tahltan ways of knowing.
>
> I was wondering how to be away from home and ideas of home and still be a cultural producer—the idea that you can have Tahltan land/ground wherever you are, so that you can still be yourself. I wanted to make a space where I felt safe in the city. I liked the idea, and wondered about the idea, that Indigenous knowledge rearranges Western space/time. I wanted to experiment with how Indigenous knowledge fills a space and also is emptied from a space.
>
> I am choosing to re-locate the word "museum" through the creation of immersive environments that not only highlight the organization of knowledge from Indigenous perspectives, but also illuminate the practice (praxis) connected to these ideas. If there were a Tahltan museum, you would have to swim through the information. The information would envelop you. You would feel changed by the experience.

In this jointly authored chapter, we—the trio who developed *Peter Morin's Museum* at Satellite Gallery—reflect on this experimental exhibition and how it continues not only to inspire our work as artist, curator, or educator but more importantly to unsettle the prevailing discourses about Northwest Coast Indigenous art and its place within institutional display. Indeed, *Peter Morin's Museum* brought viewers face to face with one of the most urgent debates facing contemporary museums that feature collections and exhibitions of Northwest Coast and other Indigenous art: how to address the collision—and intersection—of Indigenous knowledge and museum knowledge that often lies at the center of their institutional practice. It raised the key question, as expressed in Morin's own words: "What would happen if Indigenous objects, and the Indigenous history of knowledge to which they are connected, were defining the museum first—as an Indigenous space?"

Peter Morin's Museum contributed to the multivocal, ongoing mobilizations by Indigenous and non-Indigenous scholars, artists, community members, and museum workers to not only shift but ultimately decolonize the Western knowledge traditions underlying much of the legacy of Northwest Coast and other Native art exhibitions and institutional discourses. These efforts, in turn, are tied to a broad impetus, growing since the early 1990s, to collaboratively develop strategies for upending the power relations between Indigenous peoples and museums and art galleries.[4] Positioning his own practice in relation to his home community as well as urban art and performance-art audiences, Morin does not reproduce the formal qualities and canonical styles of carving and painting in his work as they have come to signify the traditional arts of the Northwest Coast, which characterize the approaches of many Indigenous artists in the Pacific Northwest, including most Tahltan artists today.[5] Morin is more likely to reference or incorporate into his performances his own collection of beaded cloth and skin items of the kind made by his aunts and his other Tahltan teachers that reveal the community's Athabascan heritage and ties to Tlingit neighbors. What deeply implicates his work within Northwest Coast and other Indigenous art, however, is their shared conceptual foundation, whatever the medium. All speak to the process of an object's making and use, the embodiment of a world view within which they function—despite the history of colonial silencing that they have survived—and the relationships with community and narratives of place they represent.

Peter Morin's Museum was temporary, fleeting, changeable, and experiential. There, and in some of his subsequent works, Morin investigated Indigenous knowledge as it is expressed in the activation of objects, whether that activation takes place at the gallery or in ceremony or around the kitchen table. At Satellite Gallery he set out to create a space of cultural sharing where Tahltan and Western frameworks of understanding would intersect—and in the process, where an art gallery could transform into a Tahltan "river of ideas." Through his performative strategies Morin interpreted "museum" as also a Tahltan idea—that is, as a way of not only containing artifacts but of organizing, holding, and exchanging knowledge—to contribute to repositioning institutional practices within Indigenous ways of being and doing. In that repositioning, he called both object permanence and the solidity of familiar institutional structures into question.

Behind the Glass: Looking at Museums and Northwest Coast Art

Often unstated but critical to thinking about Northwest Coast art within museum exhibitions is the reality that the historical objects themselves have little presence in contemporary Indigenous communities. Instead, they are held in museum and private collections around the world and to a far lesser extent in Native-run cultural centres. With the increasing impacts of colonization through the nineteenth century and into the twentieth, thousands upon thousands of Northwest Coast carvings, weavings, and other belongings were sold, traded, destroyed, or otherwise removed from originating communities.[6]

Displaced from family and ceremony, many objects entered these collections and, particularly for items circulating in the art market, their specific histories and makers' names were often lost. More important for Morin, he says: "When I go into the museum I also become a spectator to a history, a cultural identity, a cultural practice. There is also the trauma that we carry in our hearts when we go to the museum; this trauma is a result of the loss of the relations to these objects, the loss of relationship to the makers of these objects, the loss of the record of their making, and the loss of relationship to the teachings of these objects."[7] Central to current shifts in museum methodologies is the possibility for community members to connect, as more than spectators, with historical works created by their ancestors.

> PM: The Western museum holds onto much Indigenous history. And by the nature of its establishment in our shared nation, it has played a role in silencing Indigenous communities. Our people's production of community-based objects was seriously hindered by governmental policies like the potlatch ban of 1885 to 1951. This artistic production included things like carving, sewing, beading, moccasin making, weaving, totem-pole carving, and the making of button blankets.
>
> I consider it my job as a younger Tahltan person to work for the development of Tahltan history. I have to re-imagine my connection to Tahltan ways of knowing. I have to re-imagine the museum as a site within a wider context that encompasses a global range of ideas, and I have to re-imagine my relationship to the museum as a place of experience. I may not be able to hold the Tahltan object, but I can still see the maker. The maker is still talking.

In contemporary Northwest Coast communities, Indigenous regalia—especially recently made masks, headdresses, drums, dance screens, robes, and blankets—is "exhibited" through actual use in the ceremonial house or in family life. The objects' activation in ceremony not only enacts cultural and artistic resurgence in the face of colonial history but asserts ancestral privileges, names, potlatch positions, songs, and other aspects of traditional governance passed down against all odds through the generations, often through lengthy processes of internal research to rebuild knowledge about art forms, genealogical lines of descent, and hereditary ownership of privileges. Most collections of Indigenous historical belongings now held in museums, by contrast—including some of the baskets and sewn regalia made by Morin's ancestors—reside behind glass. Impossible to contain within the display cases are his grandmothers' acts of pouring tea, laughing together, sharing knowledge, and otherwise making the "artifacts" whole that are so easily seen as disconnected from life. Indeed, "Northwest Coast art"—a category of material objects and styles that museums, by possessing the collections, helped to constitute—was born of the forced rupture between art and social function, and between Indigenous people and the land, that was the project of colonization.[8]

English words and discourses have come to mark ways of comprehending Northwest Coast art for particular audiences and institutions, each with their own hierarchies of knowledge and forms of longing: curios and relics, artifacts, primitive art, degenerate or tourist art, Indian art, fine art. Diverse Western intellectual traditions therefore have staked territories but also intersected in this unsettled field, their conditions of inclusion and exclusion adopted, contested, or ignored by Indigenous artists throughout the history of the art's entanglement with outsiders. By the mid-twentieth century, influential exhibitions like the Vancouver Art Gallery's 1967 *Arts of the Raven* proposed the modernist ideal of the autonomous Native masterwork, "freed from ethnology" while isolated on a pedestal.[9] "The notion that art has a social purpose has been sidelined for the last two hundred years or so," observes scholar Charlotte Townsend-Gault, noting that Western art actually has an equally long history of critique of manipulative power structures.[10] Masterworks or belongings? Artifacts or ancestors? All have become fraught categories within an unfinished history of changing ideas.

When Morin reimagines and enacts his connection to Tahltan ways of knowing, he does so in a complex of intersecting, relational sites: walking on the land and performing in the urban gallery; creating in his studio and visiting with his mother; holding ancestral objects in his hands at the museum or singing to them through glass. Working to recenter the object and the institution within Indigenous knowledge structures, artists and scholars like Morin are finding ways of decentering the artifact of the external gaze—through reconnection to community, to voice, to function, to origins, to new stories, to the present. As Morin said, "The maker is still talking."

Where Objects Speak Tahltan (and a Basket Speaks Foucault)

The fluidity of culture, its constant performance and production, was manifested in *Peter Morin's Museum* through movement. On opening, several display cases stood against the walls, silently holding behind glass what Morin called "objects that speak Tahltan": English porcelain teacups and Indigenous pine-needle baskets, cassette tapes of Elders speaking the Tahltan language, rocks painted ochre red. On another wall was a large group of family photographs on loan from the artist's mother, whose living room they normally decorated. Their mix of plastic and wood frames, some adorned with seashells and bits of abalone, held snapshots of Morin's aunts and uncles, grandmothers and grandfathers, variously posing with their Elvis and beehive hairdos, or with a trophy mountain sheep, or outside their homes. Each framed image was completely wrapped in red cloth strips, like a sacred bundle. Visual access would change through their gradual unwrapping; so too would visitors' relationships to the work as the artist revealed their stories.

> PM: The objects are teaching me language. The museum is filled with drumming, singing, speaking, smoke-tanned hide, and laughing. There is no silence.

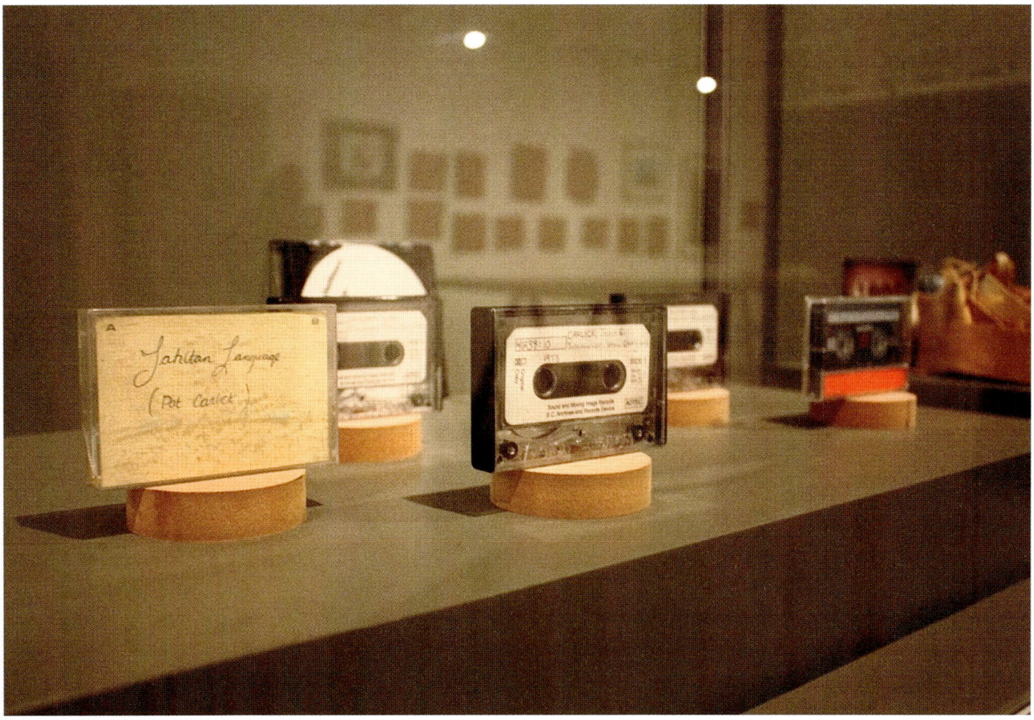

9.3. Display of cassette-tape recordings of the Tahltan language. *Peter Morin's Museum*, 2011. Satellite Gallery, Vancouver, British Columbia. Photograph courtesy of UBC Museum of Anthropology (MOA)/ Satellite Gallery.

The Tahltan Reading Room in the opposite corner offered books and ethnographies, including Morin's recent MFA thesis.[11] These encompassed within their printed pages teachings accumulated by the Tahltan people over time—ideas and philosophical pursuits transferred between generations and sometimes translated through the eyes and words of outside observers. The concept of an archive of Indigenous thought was further represented through a pair of snowshoes, handmade by Morin's grandfather according to traditional methods and hung on the wall. "The Tahltan museum moves on the land," read one of the handwritten labels beside them. There was also a printed version of the story of how Crow got the sun, moon, and daylight, illustrated with children's drawings. And nearby, on an open plinth, was a Coast Salish cedar-root basket—a talking basket. Visitors could lean close and hear a recording, not of an Indigenous language but of French philosopher Michel Foucault and American social critic Noam Chomsky engaged in their 1971 debate, "On Human Nature: Justice vs. Power"; the two Western scholars grappled with the question whether there is a common humanity that underlies our external differences and hierarchies.[12] "Why *wouldn't* this basket speak Foucault and Chomsky?" asks Morin. He describes the basket, his personal possession, as containing

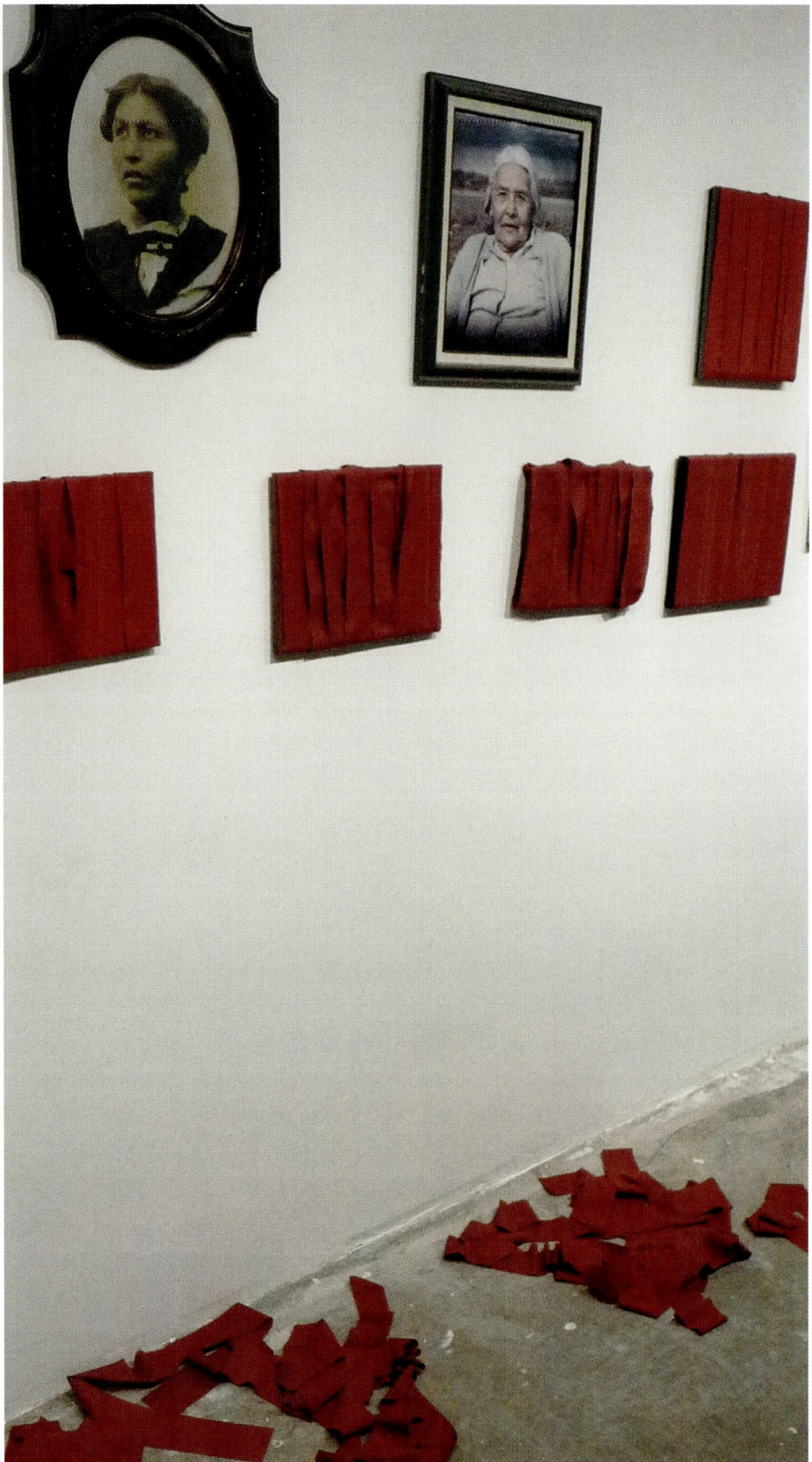

some of the tools he has gathered to help him function in relation to Western institutions. "The basket itself speaks to power in concert with such voices," Morin adds. "It speaks of knowledge systems designed and created by Coast Salish thinkers and makers in their territory, where we now stand."

The rear wall of the gallery was painted to serve as a blackboard for the opening performance—the first of three to take place in the space. In front of it was a tent, sewn of Melton cloth, suspended in the space like a crest-bearing button blanket turned inside out. Beside that was a large cedar-slab table, representing the kitchen table central to Morin's experience of cultural learning. Projected from the ceiling onto the table was a video of a single beaded and embroidered artifact, appearing so real that it could be held yet representing the spirit of Tahltan artwork, its physical form slipping through our fingers. The massive volume of photographs by Edward S. Curtis (1869–1952), *Portraits from North American Indian Life*, lay open beside the projection. With its title altered to read *Portraits of Traditional Knowledge in Practice, by Peter Morin and Edward S. Curtis*, the book's pages had been modified with Morin's ink drawings layered as a "collaborative" act over each portrait, interrupting Curtis's representations of "Indians" as vanishing peoples. Closer to the gallery entrance, Morin mounted his *Museum Manifesto*. Its twenty-seven declarations set the idea of "museum" firmly on the kitchen table: a place of gathering, of his grandmothers' teaching, of Tahltan-specific knowledge. For example, Manifesto #15: "This is a place of belonging for the community. Community members, from near and far, come to this place to spend time with their relatives." And Manifesto #14: "There will be food for sharing and tea for drinking."

In the far corner, Morin hung a display of new, stretched elk-skin drums. Named *This Song Is a Museum*, the assemblage extended the idea of museum to encompass other ways that intangible culture is carried and passed on. The artist had invited Coast Salish singer Hwieumten (Fred Roland) to make a visual record of his song, using a drumstick dipped in black paint. Video monitors allowed visitors to experience, in an endless loop, the beat of the drumstick and the process of "painting" the song onto each drum's resonant surface. "The museum has a tendency to lose the singing," Morin explained. "The voice connected to the objects becomes hard to reach. The drums are a record of his practice of Indigenous knowledge. The record of the practice relates to the environment. And the record will always be different."

That recognition of the ever-changing nature of knowledge-in-practice was primarily revealed through the series of three performances that Morin staged to transform the installation over time and throughout the space. The first performance,

9.4. The family photographs, with some unwrapped (detail view). *Peter Morin's Museum*, 2011. Satellite Gallery, Vancouver, British Columbia. Photograph courtesy of UBC Museum of Anthropology (MOA)/ Satellite Gallery.

about history and Tahltan intellectual traditions, was held on opening night; the second, examining how Tahltan people organize stories and knowledge, took place a few weeks later, when the printed catalog was launched.[13] The third and final performance occurred at the exhibition's closing: a demonstration of knowledge in action. In the process, visitors were invited to witness the transformation of the idea of museum from solid to fluid—that is, from recognizable objects and structures to an evocation of the Tahltan River.

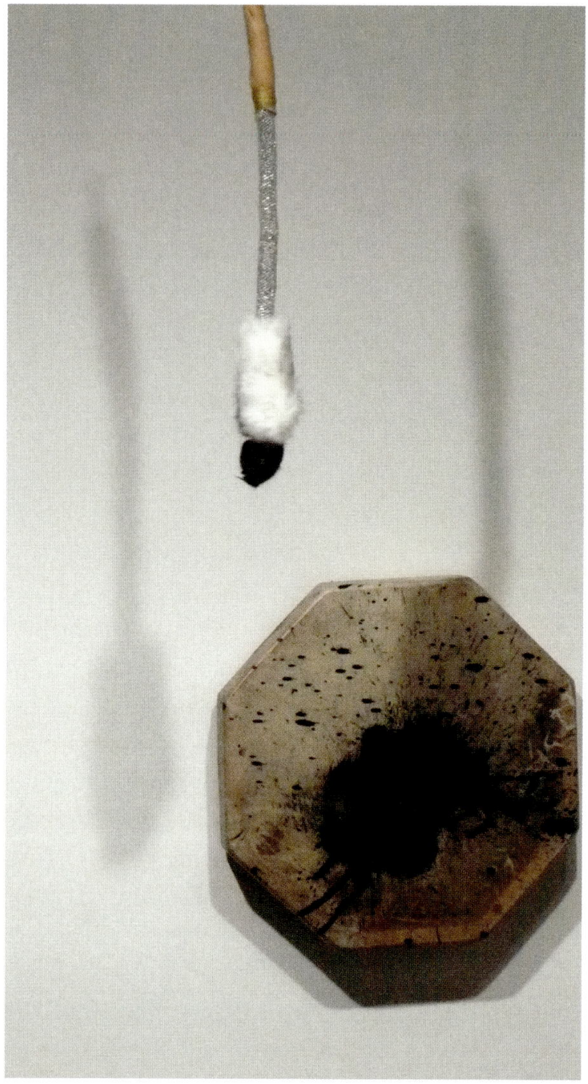

9.5. *This Song Is a Museum* drum installation (detail view). *Peter Morin's Museum*, 2011. Satellite Gallery, Vancouver, British Columbia. Photograph courtesy of UBC Museum of Anthropology (MOA)/Satellite Gallery.

"We have to pour the tea before we can talk about ideas," said the artist, and this was an important element of his first performance. There, at the public opening, he emptied the exhibit case that held the teacups and placed them on the table so that the projected video of the artifact would fall over them like a river of colors and forms. Then he approached the blackboard and began to write, white chalk words flowing over the blackness like a river. Tied to Tahltan memories of residential schools and to one system of knowledge inscribed over another, the blackboard offered a medium for Morin to enact the rewriting of history by writing a genealogy of Tahltan ideas, overwriting any information that might have been missed, writing about the Tahltan creation story as a framework for ways of knowing the world today. Before it had time to settle, Morin took a bundle of black hair and wiped it over the words, partially obscuring them. On completion, he poured tea, filling the cups to overflowing, and it was shared by all.

Several weeks later, at the second performance, the artist's mother, Janelle Morin, gave a "curatorial lecture" about the loved ones represented in the family photographs on the wall. As she chose each photo and spoke about it, Peter laid it on a button blanket on the floor, the arrangement mapping his mother's ideas as knowledge-in-practice.

> PM: For me, these photos became our cosmology: a reflection of our Tahltan environment and a reminder of how we are connected to place. You knew you were in an Indigenous person's home because of those photos. . . . I mean, how they were arranged, how they are celebrated. Consider that some folks don't have any photos as a result of residential school, sixties scoop, foster care.[14] They are more than identity. They are also a rhythm for language, a pacing of knowledge. I keep thinking about how Indigenous folks travel and share knowledge with each other. Those photos, and how my mother talked about them, would be an example of this tradition.

Prints of red spawning salmon were mounted, several each day, by the artist and gallery staff on the blackboard and the now-empty wall where the photos had hung. Finally, in the closing performance, the table was dismantled, a larger tent frame was set up over the cloth tent, and all of the display cases opened. The sweet, smoky aroma of tanned hide released from one case filled the room. The cassette tapes of fluent speakers recording words and phrases of the Tahltan language were

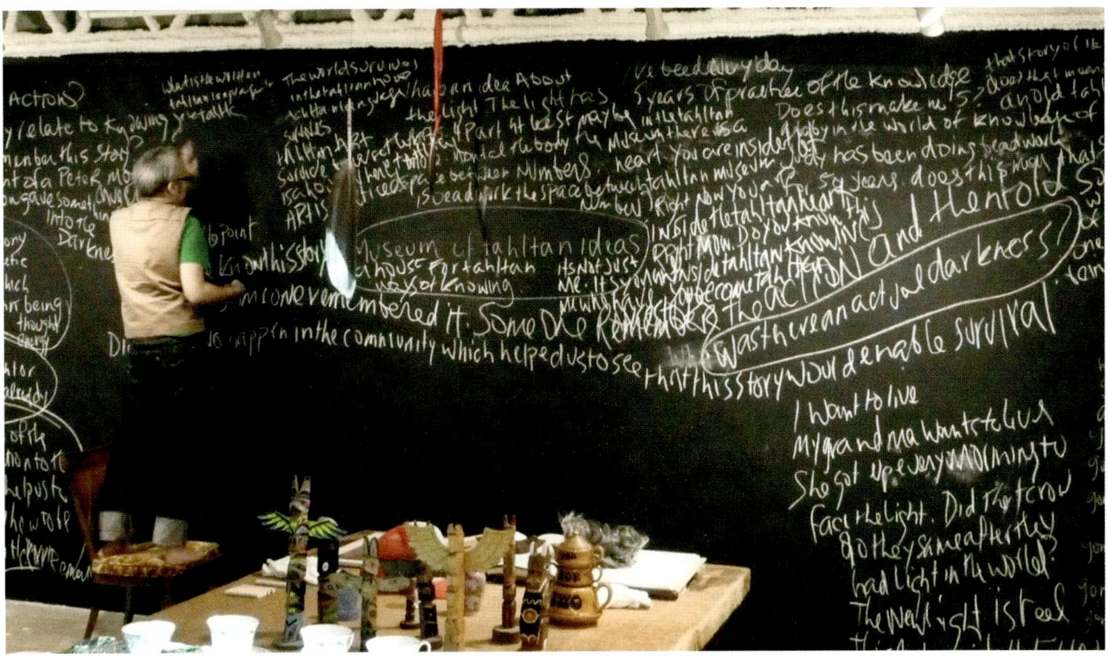

9.6. Peter Morin in performance on opening day. *Peter Morin's Museum*, 2011. Satellite Gallery, Vancouver, British Columbia. Photograph courtesy of UBC Museum of Anthropology (MOA)/Satellite Gallery.

played. Blindfolding himself with the red cloth strips removed from the family photos, a masked Peter Morin began doing beadwork in the darkness, while his cousin Tsēmā Igharas washed the blackboard behind him.

DJ Darwin Frostwing and singer Simon Reece added their voices to the sonic landscape. After making his way around the room, singing to the drums and other objects that remained on display, Morin cut down the small tent and removed his mask and blindfold. The new tent structure offered a framework for the future movement of Tahltan knowledge over the land and through urban spaces; the river of salmon now covered the walls; and Morin's performance invoked the difference between the time before and after the Crow shared light—and knowledge—with the world.

> PM: Tahltan knowledge-in-practice was about lifting the lids of the museum-style cases. They were spewing salmon that were going back to the river to make more knowledge. In my mother's curatorial talk, she spoke about collective knowledge. Survival is collective knowledge. It was important to open up those cases and let the scent of my grandmother's smoke-tanned hide into the space . . . it moves through the space and is the actual Tahltan land. The animal walked on the land, the animal ate from the land. The animal becomes the artwork that carries this knowledge.

Around the Kitchen Table

Morin had been grappling with the idea of museums off and on in the years preceding *Peter Morin's Museum*, at times directly in his work as a visual and performance artist but also as a community educator and advocate for urban Indigenous youth. He would bring youth in Victoria to the Royal British Columbia Museum, where he would introduce them to the collected objects from their communities as "grandparents"—objects intrinsically tied to community knowledge and able to "speak to them in their language."[15] Several decades earlier, as a youth himself, Morin had had his own encounter with a kind of grandparent object, but at a kitchen table in summer fish camp on the Stikine River, Tahltan territory. There, an Elder decided that the young Peter was ready to begin learning something of his culture, so the Elder gave him his first look at a traditional beaded belt. Morin recalls his immediate response: this object belongs in a museum. By holding it in his hands, the belt became Morin's introduction to the continuum of Tahltan art history:

> PM: When Annie Henyu showed me the beaded belt, she changed my life forever. But knowledge does that. Knowing—ideas in practice—does that. The belt was

> built by Tahltan ideas from the foundation upward. Wearing the belt is practice. Making the belt is practice. The belt becomes a teacher of Tahltan ideas and ways of knowing.

Fittingly, the idea of creating *Peter Morin's Museum* at Satellite Gallery emerged through conversation as the three of us shared tea around a table, imagining how we—an Indigenous artist/curator, along with an art educator and a curator, both non-Native—could work collaboratively to realize Morin's vision of a Tahltan museum. The mandate and location of the new Satellite Gallery offered the possibility—indeed, the expectation—of an experimental approach. It was an in-between space in terms of being physically removed from the sites of its partner institutions. While *Peter Morin's Museum* was produced and supported by the Museum of Anthropology (MOA), the project had the potential of functioning less as an institutionally embodied space directly subject to the MOA's logistical and managerial constraints, and more as a shared space for the artist to reimagine the possibilities of "museum" from his own perspective.[16] Indeed, building on the assumption that museum is also a Tahltan idea, Morin resisted having his work seen as an intervention within an engulfing institution. This required an alternative approach to what more commonly are interrogations of the conventional Western "apparatus" through artists' interventions that take aim at (while located inside) its structure.[17]

At the Satellite Gallery, Morin sought to confuse the distinction of what was the preexisting gallery and what was *Peter Morin's Museum*: arguably an act of transformation, both physical and conceptual, rather than of dismantling. He worked to indigenize the space of art—the white cube—in a way that the object might still (temporarily) reside on a pedestal. With such objects on display as cassette tapes of the Tahltan language, or a pile of tanned hides made by his grandmother, Dinah Creyke, a viewer would also experience the absence, and later the presence, of sound, touch, and scent as well as the gradual revelation of knowledge. In this approach Morin made clear that Satellite Gallery was a hybrid space.

> PM: If I was going to apply the English word "museum" to the experience of Tahltan epistemologies, then the museum is a place of movement and sound. And my remembering of this place is a ceremony. But "ceremony" is an English word just like "museum." In this case, I want "museum" to encompass everything before the making of an object, the act of making, and everything that follows the making of that object. This knowledge about the process to create these objects is often missing from the Western museum. I want the word to also include the act of remembering the transfer of knowledge embedded in the object. We need to organize our collective ways of knowing, a project in which the Western museum can play an important role.

In our own process of collective imagining, it became evident that *Peter Morin's Museum* would privilege performance as a central element of its refusal—or perhaps displacement—of the exhibition modes within which the display of Northwest Coast art has become naturalized. Performance was already a central element of Morin's work, offering a way of tying lived experience to displayed objects beyond their institutionalization as material things, or even as art. Underlying Morin's proposition was his intention to unfold the idea of Tahltan knowledge as embodied. He would demonstrate his own relation to the objects and their power to *act*—pedagogically, metaphorically, transgressively—through touch and smell, laughter and song, voice and story. Already in 2005, Morin used performance to challenge the segregation of the object at the site of the museum.[18]

I Grieve Too Much was a work he staged at MOA, beside a glassed-in drawer of materials collected among the Tahltan people. There, blindfolded, Morin acknowledged the members of his community who were being arrested that day for defending their territory from natural-gas drilling. He told a story about an anthropological betrayal of Indigenous people. He cleansed himself and poured tea for his aunties, who had made the objects now behind glass. He sang James Taylor's "Fire and Rain," the song he had repeatedly listened to after his grandmother passed away. The performance was broadcast into a nearby room to be witnessed by the audience. "I wanted to convey the experience of having your relationship to the objects mediated through glass," Morin explains. "I heard these Tahltan objects singing and this singing was beyond my reach. And I felt that these ways of knowledge in the museum were causing continued harm . . . presented as an authority on the aboriginal body."[19]

> PM: Performance is inherently a part of Indigenous art histories—all of them. The purposeful making of objects, the purposeful sitting down with beads and attaching them to fabric or carving—that object is a piece of not just a life of itself, but a life in communion with an action. I think that's really key: that's really important to think about when you're in places like the museum, and you're looking through glass at these things. Making requires you to feel the object. Making well requires you to hold the older pieces. These are things that my auntie made—my metaphorical auntie—and I want to hold them because that's what my auntie would do. She would let me hold them. I would be able to feel her work—or his work, my uncle. That's a lineage. The lineage of artistic work. These are the artists that we have a legacy with. We are connected to them.

Morin's visual, performance, and curatorial work is part of a recent and ongoing history of interventions in and against the Western museum model. Since the 1980s, diverse forms of Indigenous performance and installation art have pointed to the dynamics of knowledge production in (and by) the museum, directly confronting racialized representations and how these are produced and mediated, playing with institutional structures and cultural subjectivities both visible and absent.[20] Works by such artists as Rebecca Belmore and James Luna navigate a colonial history that extends beyond the museum or art gallery, interrogating established representations and policies affecting Indigenous peoples in the past and today. Luna's *Artifact Piece* (1987, 1991) provides a particularly strong counterpoint to Morin's own work with the museum as a site of institutional critique. Set within a period of intense debate and internal shifts around identity politics and decolonization in the United States, Luna's intervention famously involved positioning his own body inside an exhibition case at the San Diego Museum of Man.[21] Luna challenged the notion that Indigenous peoples are objects of display and not authors of their own historical and cultural narratives. The performance contributed importantly to then-emerging critical discourses around Indigenous cultural revival, repatriation, and restitution.[22]

In thinking about performance art as part of a continuum of Indigenous practice, Morin has developed his own distinctive approach in relation to Tahltan knowledge keepers and teachers who belong to his home community. He names as exemplars of Tahltan performance art his aunt, Rosie Dennis, and grandmother, Eva Carlick. As makers of things brought to life in communion with action, their practice includes speaking the Tahltan language: a language Morin struggles to retain when he is away from home. "Words are one of the structures that carry Tahltan thought over the land," he wrote on the wall in *Peter Morin's Museum*. In the kinds of objects with which his ancestors would traverse their landscape—moccasins, clothing, and knife sheaths embellished with symmetrical beaded patterns—he says, "I see the levels of territory conceptually represented in those things, how walking with this symmetry reminds you of your relationship to the cosmos." Here again, Morin returns to the acts of relationality that would define a Tahltan idea of museum: establishing and reestablishing networks among objects, people, and the land. Through performative acts, like writing about Tahltan knowledge on the blackboard or releasing tanned hides from their glass case, he mobilizes institutional and colonial critique—both to strengthen cultural practice for his own community and to rebuild the idea of museum.

Performing the Object

In the days following each of the three performances at *Peter Morin's Museum*, there was always a trace of changes having just happened. The *Museum* appeared static, and yet some things were askew: cases were dismantled, objects had escaped, structures had vanished. Labels describing motion and fluidity remained tacked to the wall, even when the objects they accompanied had settled elsewhere. It felt like the aftermath of an event, where one's relationship to what had been there before had also changed. "I wanted to experiment with how Indigenous knowledge fills a space and also is emptied from a space," Morin said. What was it that now filled *Peter Morin's Museum*? What had been emptied?

> PM: Indigenous knowledge, if we honour it, makes these Western spaces messy and seemingly disorganized. This is partly why I have always thought of our collaboration as brave. It was easy to just do the "normal" thing.
>
> You needed to come to the performances. You needed to experience all of the complexities around this knowledge. You didn't just get to consume it . . . you had to work at it. In the Tahltan story of how Crow got the sun and moon, he/she had to grow, had to do work, had to deserve the light. You don't get the end of the story first. The knowledge is both abstract and experienced. This is like me with the beaded belt. I had to deserve to see that artwork. If releasing the light is a metaphor for knowing, then you have to share it.

In their work with historical collections, Indigenous artists and researchers have made it clear that they require a relationship with objects, and that in turn objects find new meaning in relation to Indigenous communities. This is a reciprocal

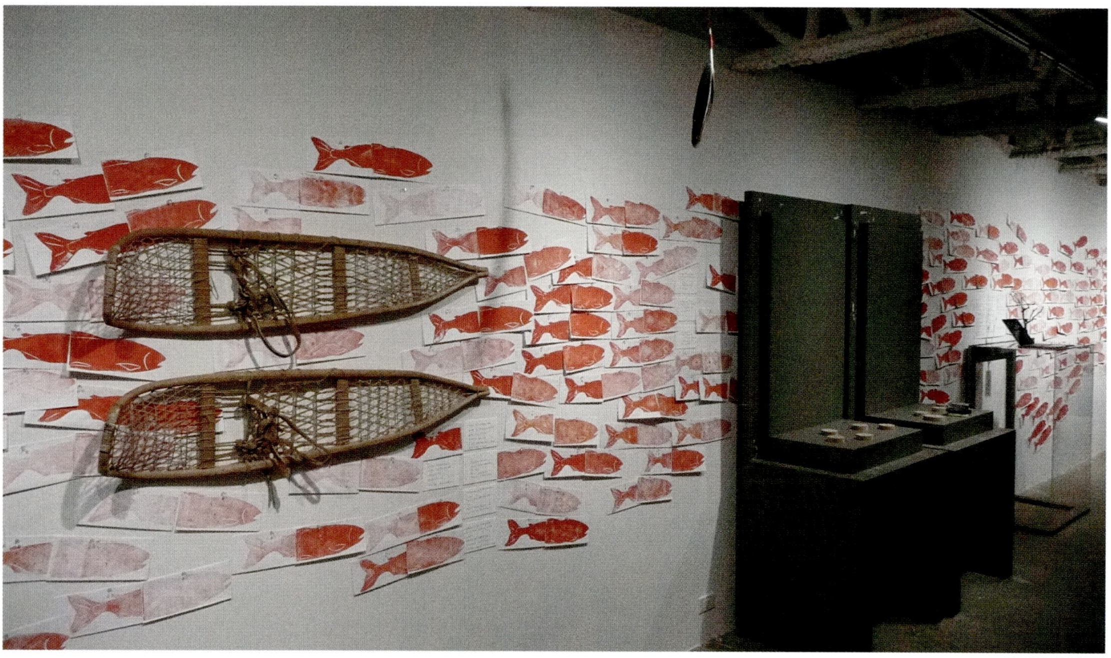

9.7. The cases are emptied and a river of salmon circles the walls. *Peter Morin's Museum*, 2011. Satellite Gallery, Vancouver, British Columbia. Photograph courtesy of UBC Museum of Anthropology (MOA)/Satellite Gallery.

exchange increasingly initiated on the Northwest Coast by originating community members. In this period of cultural resurgence, repatriation, and debates over reconciliation, such reciprocity is critical to the development of meaningful collaborative strategies by museums and Indigenous partners. Reconstituting endangered languages, classifications, protocols, and the community functions of objects that are currently part of museum collections remains a vital and primary challenge. "Make them move," says Nuu-chah-nulth historian and artist Ki-ke-in about museum collections. "Give them life. Inject them into a system that exists outside of that museum and at the same time, inject into that museum some of what exists out here."[23]

What might constitute such motion, however, when the rarity and high insurance value of many Northwest Coast artworks, and concerns about preservation, imply security and stability over reactivation? Indeed, the MOA's established process of loan agreements, object handling, and condition reporting had to be abandoned at the start of *Peter Morin's Museum*, since Morin needed to remain flexible in selecting which of the items from his personal collection he would show and when he would remove or replace them. By contrast, artifacts in a museum's permanent collection that are cataloged, numbered, and mounted on stands appear to be fixed in place. Yet circulating around them remain the questions with which this chapter began: How do we address the collision—and intersection—of Indigenous knowledge and museum knowledge that often lies within institutional practice? Morin asks, "What if Indigenous objects, and the Indigenous history of knowledge to which they are connected, were defining the museum first—as an Indigenous space?"[24] As *Manifesto* #16 says: "This space is designed to demonstrate Indigenous knowledge. Indigenous knowledge is like a river."

While museums and art galleries have, over the past century or more, shifted theoretical positions around providing "context" for their Indigenous collections, Morin's objective was to create a context of relationality: establishing and reassembling social networks around objects and culturally specific knowledge. *Peter Morin's Museum* signaled a shift in Indigenous performance—less toward making the Western museum "disappear" than toward using it as part of cultural recovery from the lasting impacts of colonization. Morin occupied the space of Satellite Gallery completely—immersively—instead of merely intervening in it. His performative process demonstrated agency in representing his understanding of Tahltan culture, his learning what it means to be Tahltan in multiple landscapes, his commitment to ensuring that "Indigenous knowledge is made every day" (*Manifesto* #26). In addition, "There is a possibility to remember," wrote Morin (*Manifesto* #2), as he invited visitors to his kitchen table. "There is a possibility for people to learn" (*Manifesto* #3), and "We are changed when we come into contact with the objects" (*Manifesto* #9).

PM: Indigenous ways of knowing are fluid; they are about process. . . . When we are finally able to reflect on these ways of knowing and on the ways in which Indigenous communities have organized this knowledge, then we can rebuild the museum together.

NOTES

1 Curated by Peter Morin and Karen Duffek, *Peter Morin's Museum* was held at Satellite Gallery from April 20 to July 3, 2011. Gallery director Karen Benbassat Ali managed the space and developed the associated public programs. The three founding partner institutions of Satellite Gallery were the UBC Museum of Anthropology (MOA), the Morris and Helen Belkin Art Gallery (also at UBC), and Presentation House Gallery (now the Polygon Gallery, North Vancouver). Satellite Gallery was a five-year project funded by the Michael O'Brian Family Foundation (2010–15).

2 Tahltan territory is located in northwestern British Columbia, Canada: its northwestern border runs parallel to the Alaska–Canada border and includes part of Yukon Territory, and its southeastern border includes the upper Nass River tributaries and the western half of the Stikine plateau.

3 Peter Morin's contributions in this chapter are set apart as direct quotations (preceded by "PM") to more clearly identify his voice for the reader.

4 See Michael M. Ames, *Cannibal Tours and Glass Boxes: The Anthropology of Museums* (Vancouver: University of British Columbia Press, 1992); Martha Black, "Collaborations: A Historical Perspective," in *Native Art of the Northwest Coast: A History of Changing Ideas*, edited by Charlotte Townsend-Gault, Jennifer Kramer, and Ki-Ke-In, 785–827 (Vancouver: University of British Columbia Press, 2013); Marcia Crosby, "Construction of the Imaginary Indian," in *Vancouver Anthology: The Institutional Politics of Art*, edited by Stan Douglas, 266–91 (Vancouver: Talonbooks, 1991); Haida Heritage Centre, *Gina Suuda Tl'l Xasii: Came to Tell Something* (Skidegate: Haida Gwaii Museum Press, 2014); Laura Peers and Alison K. Brown, eds., *Museums and Source Communities: A Routledge Reader* (London: Routledge, 2003); Ruth B. Phillips, introduction to "Community Collaborations in Exhibitions: Toward a Dialogic Paradigm," in *Museum Pieces: Toward the Indigenization of Museums* (Montreal: McGill-Queen's University Press, 2011), 155–70; Ruth B. Phillips, *Museum Pieces: Toward the Indigenization of Museums* (Montreal: McGill-Queen's University Press, 2011); Task Force on Museums and First Peoples, *Turning the Page: Forging New Partnerships between Museums and First Peoples*, edited by Tom Hill and Trudy Nicks (Ottawa: Assembly of First Nations and Canadian Museums Association, 1992); and Charlotte Townsend-Gault, "The Material and the Immaterial Across Borders," in *Native Art of the Northwest Coast*, edited by Townsend-Gault, Kramer, and Ki-Ke-In, 963–94.

5 The anthology *Native Art of the Northwest Coast*, edited by Townsend-Gault, Kramer, and Ki-Ke-In, offers a critical historiography of the construction of the idea of Northwest Coast art and its contestations. Some of these artists with Tahltan ancestry include Dempsey Bob, Stan Bevan, Dale Campbell, Sheldon Dennis, Ken McNeil, Jamie Nole, and Roberta Quock.

6 Douglas Cole, *Captured Heritage: The Scramble for Northwest Coast Artifacts* (Seattle: University of Washington Press, 1985); Douglas Cole, "Tricks of the Trade: Some Reflections on Anthropological Collecting," *Arctic Anthropology* 28, no. 1 (1991): 48–62; Ira Jacknis, *The*

Storage Box of Tradition: Kwakiutl Art, Anthropologists, and Museums, 1881–1981 (Washington, DC: Smithsonian Institution Press, 2002); and Andrea Laforet, "Objects and Knowledge: Early Accounts from Ethnographers, and Their Written Records and Collecting Practices, ca. 1880–1930," in *Native Art of the Northwest Coast*, edited by Townsend-Gault, Kramer, and Ki-Ke-In, 128–65.

7 Peter Morin, "My Life as a Museum, or, Performing Indigenous Epistemologies," unpublished manuscript, 2011, unpaginated.

8 Kwakwa̱ka̱'wakw educator Daisy Sewid-Smith has argued that it was during the potlatch prohibition period of 1885 to 1951 that "many carvers and painters became well known as 'Northwest Coast artists'"; see Daisy Sewid-Smith, "Interpreting Cultural Symbols of the People from the Shore," in *Native Art of the Northwest Coast*, edited by Townsend-Gault, Kramer, and Ki-Ke-In, 15–25. During this period the Canadian federal government encouraged curio production as a form of economic development and even as national symbol, while criminalizing the making and use of ceremonial regalia.

9 See Wilson Duff, ed., *Arts of the Raven: Masterworks by the Northwest Coast Indian* (Vancouver: Vancouver Art Gallery, 1967). For an analysis of this seminal exhibition, see Marcia Crosby, "Indian Art / Aboriginal Title," MA thesis, University of British Columba, 1994.

10 Charlotte Townsend-Gault, "Let X = Audience," in *Reservation X: The Power of Place in Aboriginal Contemporary Art*, edited by Gerald McMaster, 41–52 (Hull, Quebec: Canadian Museum of Civilization, 1998), 47.

11 Peter Morin, "Circle," MFA thesis, University of British Columbia–Okanagan, 2011.

12 For a transcript of the "On Human Nature: Justice vs. Power" debate, see "Human Nature: Justice versus Power: Noam Chomsky debates with Michel Foucault, 1971."

13 The exhibition was accompanied by a thirty-two-page hand-bound catalog by Peter Morin and Karen Duffek, *Peter Morin's Museum: An Installation with Performances* (Vancouver: Museum of Anthropology at UBC, 2011), available at https://moa.ubc.ca/exhibition/peter-morins-museum/ (accessed June 8, 2019).

14 The "sixties scoop" refers to the practice of social service agents "scooping up" Indigenous children from their families to be placed into largely non-Indigenous homes for fostering or adoption. The practice was especially widespread from the late 1950s to the 1980s.

15 Peter Morin, "My Life as a Museum, or, Performing Indigenous Epistemologies," in *Embodied Politics in Visual Autobiography*, edited by Sarah Brophy and Janice Hladki, 137–52 (Toronto: University of Toronto Press, 2014), 143.

16 Exhibitions and programs at Satellite Gallery were generally created by the individual partner institutions, and occasionally in collaboration with one another. The exhibition and catalog for *Peter Morin's Museum* were produced by MOA.

17 Giorgio Agamben, *"What Is an Apparatus?" and Other Essays* (Stanford, CA: Stanford University Press, 2009).

18 Morin was invited by the MOA to create this performance for a symposium organized by the Vancouver New Forms Festival in 2005.

19 Morin, "My Life as a Museum."

20 For discussions of contemporary Indigenous performance-art practice, see, among others, Greg A. Hill, "Caught . . . (Red-handed)," in *Caught in the Act: The Viewer as Performer* (Ottawa: National Gallery of Canada, 2008), 145–63; *The Medicine Project*, 2008, www.themedicineproject.com/index.html; grunt gallery (accessed June 8, 2019); and Charlotte Townsend-Gault and James Luna, *Rebecca Belmore: The Named and the Unnamed* (Vancouver: Morris and Helen Belkin Art Gallery, 2003).

21 See Richard William Hill, "Remembering James Luna (1950–2018)," *Canadian Art*, March 2018, https://canadianart.ca/features/james-luna-in-memoriam/ (accessed June 8, 2019).

22 Institutional interventions by performance artists continue to be a prominent form of risk-taking necessary to bring public attention to the legacies of colonialism. Morin cites Rebecca Belmore and the late James Luna as especially influential on his practice. See Anna Johnson, "Coco Fusco and Guillermo Gómez-Peña," *BOMB*, January 1993, https://bombmagazine.org/articles/coco-fusco-and-guillermo-g%C3%B3mez-pe%C3%B1a/ (accessed June 8, 2019).

23 Charlotte Townsend-Gault, "A Conversation with Ki-ke-in," in *Nuu-chah-nulth Voices, Histories, Objects and Journeys*, edited by Alan L. Hoover, 203–29 (Victoria: Royal British Columbia Museum, 2000), 208.

24 Morin, "My Life as a Museum," 147.

CHAPTER 10

From Behind-the-Scenes to the Front of the House

HERE & NOW: NATIVE ARTISTS INSPIRED AT THE BURKE MUSEUM

Kathryn Bunn-Marcuse

THIS CHAPTER TELLS TWO INTERTWINED STORIES ABOUT A 2014 EXHIBIT AT THE Burke Museum of Natural History and Culture titled *Here & Now: Native Artists Inspired*. One is the story of how that exhibit shared with the public the dynamics and outcomes of the Bill Holm Center for the Study of Northwest Native Art artist-researcher grant program at the Burke, and the behind-the-scenes work there. That story is the narrative of *what* happened. The other story is *why* that behind-the-scenes work is essential to both the museum and to Indigenous artists and communities—how this work supports both cultural Indigenous revitalization movements and institutional change, processes sometimes categorized as decolonization and reconciliation.

These intertwined stories are important because historically museums have had a bad reputation among many Indigenous communities from which collections were purchased, traded for, or stolen. Over the past 150 years, across North America, salvage anthropology and the market for "primitive art" was implicit in the loss of critical material culture creations in communities that were already under threat from governmental policies, religious persecution, and settler land invasions. For many decades museums were (and some continue to be) elitist places where collections were off-limits except to academics and rich white patrons—places where art and "artifacts" were valued but people were not. The stories of the *Here & Now* exhibit are stories of how Indigenous artists and communities are building new relationships with the Burke and its staff, responding together to these historical realities in an ongoing effort to decolonize the museum.[1]

Historian Amy Lonetree (Ho-chunk), who has written extensively on the processes and histories of decolonizing museums, wrote that developing collaborative exhibits with communities (or in this case, artists) "is about building trust, developing relationships, communicating, sharing authority, and being humble."[2] Her statement reflects the guiding principles behind both the *Here & Now* exhibit and the work of the Bill Holm Center at the Burke Museum. There are many insightful publications on the need to change institutional structures that have upheld colonial practices and contributed to structural inequalities—the theories and calls-to-action are in print.[3] This chapter focuses on the activities and priorities of the Bill Holm Center at the Burke Museum to provide some concrete examples of how this work is done in one institution.

Museums are often accused of being stingy—displaying only a small percentage of what they hold. This is a well-deserved reputation because it's true. At the Burke, where I work as the curator of Northwest Native art, we currently have just 1 percent of our ethnographic collections on public view. Many museum visitors might question why in 2017 we had 460 items on display in the cultural gallery and 51,000 in storage? Why not make it all "visible storage" as some museums have attempted to satisfy the public's desire to see all of the collections? The stories of the *Here & Now* exhibit illustrate why research collections are essential.

Museum Precedents for the Exhibit

The *Here & Now* exhibit did not occur in a vacuum, or without precedent. It was a waypoint on the Burke's longer institutional trajectory. From its founding in 1885, the Burke Museum has progressed from a focus on collecting and preservation to a focus on study and access for the Northwest Coast art collections.[4] During Bill Holm's time as curator from 1968 to 1985, he facilitated the inquiries of many artists and scholars of Northwest Coast art. He always welcomed those with curiosity about Northwest Coast art and set an early precedent of making Burke Museum collections accessible to Indigenous community members during an era when collections access was more commonly limited to scholars and museum professionals, most of whom were not from the communities represented in collections.

In 2003, Holm's successor, Robin Wright, then curator of Native art, established the Bill Holm Center for the Study of Northwest Native Art at the Burke. The center's goals are to be a learning resource to support Native and public access to the Burke collections through research grants, programs, and publications, and to facilitate connections between contemporary Native American/First Nations artists and the cultural heritage material in museum collections. Wright's founding of the Bill Holm Center was a deliberate effort to continue the legacy of access that Holm had begun and to establish permanent resources to ensure that Burke staff would always be able to respond to collections-access requests. Wright remembers that founding moment:

> We needed money to facilitate research on the collections for Native artists and one of the hallmarks of Bill's career here was his door was always open to anybody who would walk in with a question . . . or to Native artists who just

> wanted to see examples of the kind of things that they were trying to make. I got the idea that we could create a center for the study of Northwest Coast and at the same while doing that honor Bill Holm and his legacy here and carry on the work that he did while he was here.[5]

Throughout their careers both Wright and Holm worked closely with artists and cultural researchers on inquiries about Burke collections. Wright employed collaborative curation methods for Burke Museum exhibits in the 1980s and 1990s, most notably working with Roberta Haines (Colville) and a Native advisory board to engage with thirty-nine of Washington's tribes on the exhibit *A Time of Gathering: Native Heritage in Washington State* in 1989.[6] While some museums had been engaging with communities directly since the 1980s, such as Aldona Jonaitis's work with Kwakwa̱ka̱'wakw experts for the *Chiefly Feasts* exhibit in 1991 at the American Museum of Natural History, and numerous exhibits at University of British Columbia's Museum of Anthropology and the Royal British Columbia Museum, institutional policies around these kinds of collaborations were rare before the 1990 enactment of the Native American Graves Protection and Repatriation Act (NAGPRA) in the United States and Canada's 1992 Task Force for Museums and First Peoples.[7] NAGPRA demands and encourages museum engagement with Native American, Alaska Native, and Native Hawaiian communities around issues of repatriation and more broadly for protocols for care and access to their collections.[8]

The Bill Holm Center: What We Do

Since its founding in 2003, the Bill Holm Center at the Burke Museum has connected emerging and established artists through workshops and mentorships, and provided artists and scholars with hands-on learning opportunities to study the museum's collection of historical art. This is important, because while art-marking is flourishing in many Native communities—especially along the Northwest Coast—in other communities there are few teachers and even fewer historical artworks from which to learn. The cultural creations in the Burke's collection are imbued with the knowledge of their makers and can be a catalyst for transferring this knowledge across generations.[9] Examples include how visiting artists Vera Best and Gina Lawrence (Colville) found that the construction technique in an "old-style" pair of Sanpoil moccasins was more efficient to make than the current technique and was sewn to prevent stress at the base of the shoe, which was especially useful in children's shoes; or the revitalization of ancient Salish basketry techniques—long buried in baskets unearthed from two-thousand-year-old sites—which have been renewed through study by Suquamish basketmaker Ed Carrier.

While some contemporary artists are committed to making works faithful to long-standing aesthetic forms, others use the historical artworks as a jumping-off

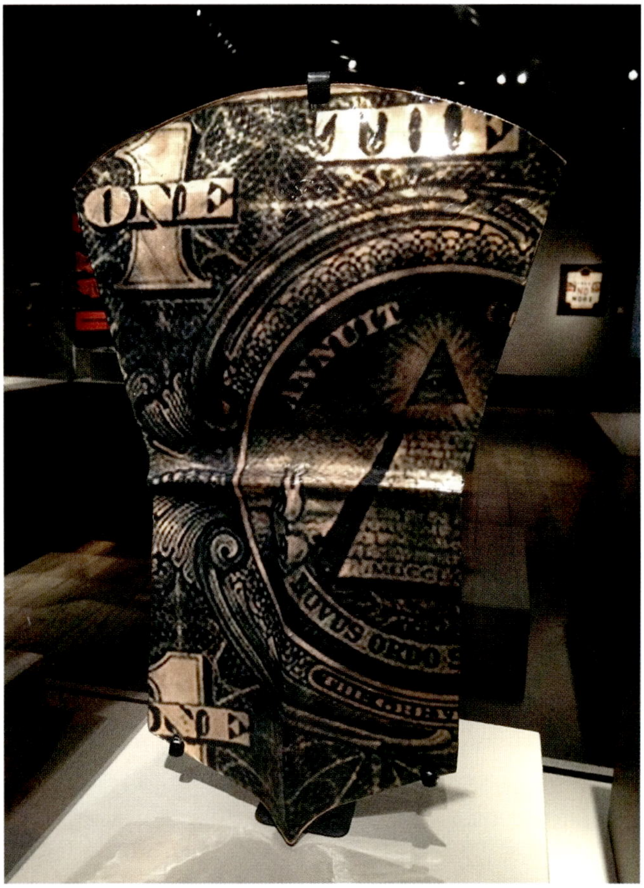

10.1. Alison Bremner, *Big Money*, 2014. Copper, acrylic gel medium, and resin. Burke Museum cat. #2015-77/1. Photograph by Kathryn Bunn-Marcuse.

point for exploring new artistic expressions, such as Alison Bremner's twenty-first-century copper, *Big Money*. In chapter 9 in this volume, Karen Duffek, Peter Morin, and Karen Benbasset Ali's write: "In their work with historical collections, Indigenous artists and researchers have made it clear that they require a relationship with objects, and that in turn objects find new meaning in relation to Indigenous communities." Art historian Lara Evans (Cherokee) noted that part of decolonizing museums "means transitioning to a broader mission, one that focuses on creation in addition to preservation."[10]

This focus on how historical collections can foster new creations has been the driving force for the Bill Holm Center's grant program since its inception in 2003. "Indigenous art is an experience of a future contained in the present," writes Wanda Nanibush, assistant curator at the Art Gallery of Ontario.[11] Supporting the current generation of artists in their connections to and visions of the past, present, and future should be a key value for institutions with cultural heritage collections. The center's advisory board grants fellowships to artists and researchers to work with the collections at the Burke.[12] Connecting with historical creations brings the past directly into conversations that artists are having today and into their planning for the future.

The heart of the center's grant program are artists' visits to collections during which they might spend time with a hundred or more creations over the course of three days. These visits always include close study and analysis but also reveal the personal and familial ties that Indigenous community members have to the cultural creations in collections. Around the table, artists visit with the cultural belongings and share stories, songs, and reminiscences. The collections study space is a site of learning and laughter, a place to connect with past generations. To apply an apt metaphor from art historian heather ahtone (Chickasaw), artworks can be "a pebble to generate ripples of dialogue within the stream of Indigenous consciousness."[13] While artists cannot apprentice with a master from generations back, the artworks themselves can be the teachers. As Nuxalk artist Latham Mack said of his visit to the Burke: "It's great to go and study the old pieces, to look at them, and hold them. You feel their energy. You can't get over the quality, the detail, in the pieces. They're some of the best teachers you get."

The grant program offers travel funding to study Burke collections or conduct workshops at the Burke Museum or in their home communities as well as occasional special project or mentor/apprentice grants. During "collections-based workshops" established artists work with a small group of emerging or beginning artists to study Burke Museum collections then immediately lead a hands-on art-making workshop

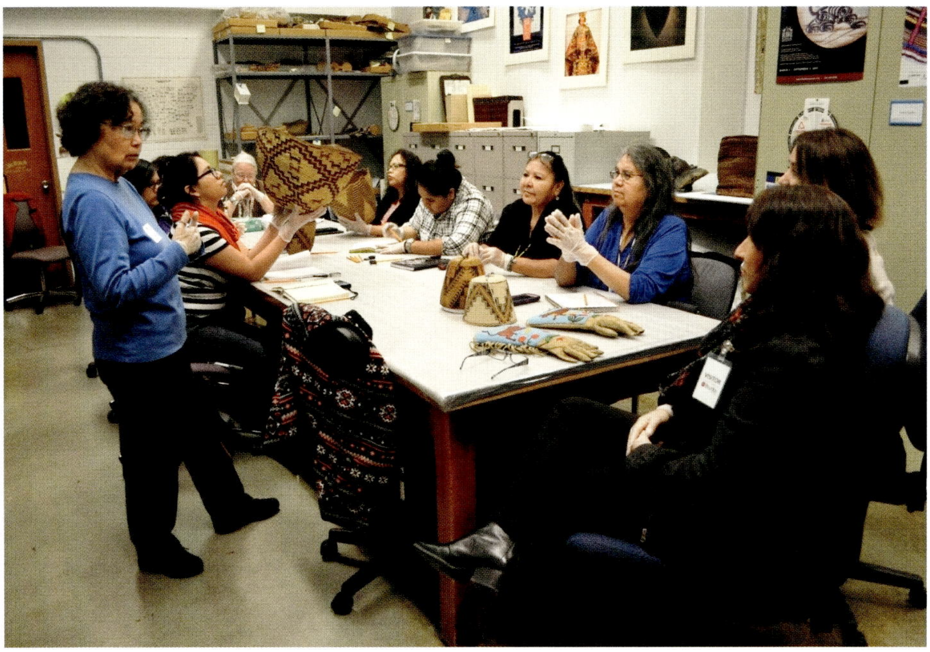

10.2. Columbia River Weaving Workshop with Pat Courtney Gold (Wasco). Burke Museum, 2015.

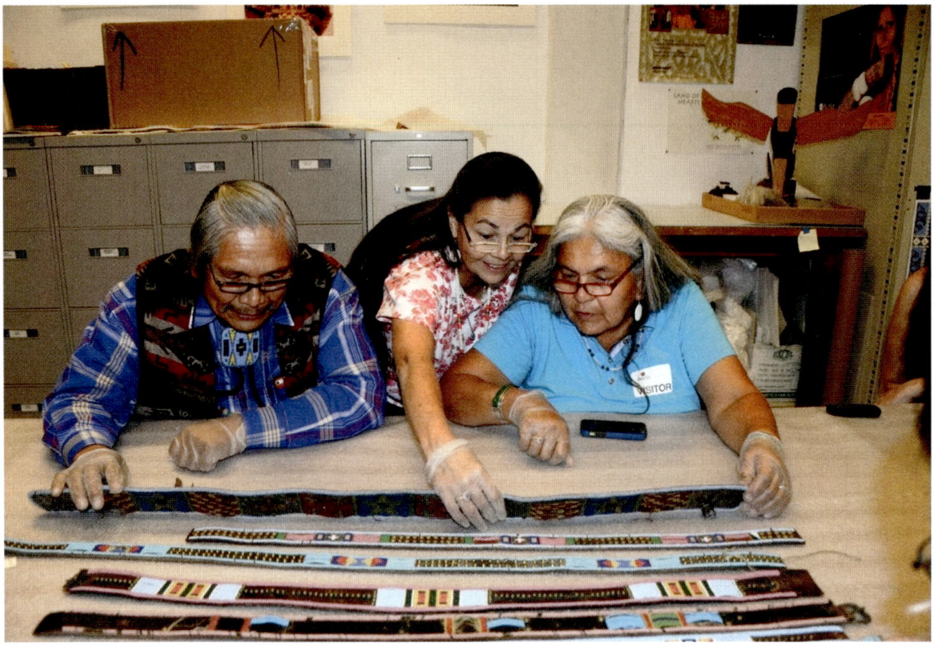

10.3. Plateau Research Group—Rex Buck (Wanapum), Colleen Cawston (Colville), and Angela Buck (Yakama). Burke Museum, 2014.

in the Burke classroom, often with historical collections at hand. Follow-up workshops include the option of requesting artworks from Burke collections be brought out to communities where additional students can join in the workshop. Having historical creations at hand allows artists to discuss techniques, materials, and iconography as well as cultural function or Indigenous-language terms. Discussions often range though these topics and into oral histories, genealogies, and origin stories and lead to plans for new creations or future artistic initiatives for individual artists or communities.

What I have learned from witnessing these collections visits and in talking to artists and community members about their experiences is that historical Native American (and First Nations) art are kin. They want to be functional in service of a new generation—to teach and to reach across generations the way that parents, aunts and uncles, and ancestors do.[14] These creations participate in a cultural web of connection—they are "instrumental for intergenerational transmission of cultural knowledge."[15]

Today, the precedent that Holm and Wright set of working diligently to respond to requests from artists and community members for information and images from the Burke (as well as other far-flung institutions) continues on in the work of Burke curators and staff. As current Burke curator Sven Haakanson has said of Holm, "Bill's impact for me was the importance of giving back. Not necessarily the art, but the importance of what you know and giving back." The mandate to respond to inquiries from artists and cultural researchers fuels the work of current Bill Holm Center outreach staff, who provide robust information including high-resolution photos, collection histories, other published and archival information about artworks or Indigenous technologies free-of-cost to grant recipients as well as to others who inquire. This work, in addition to caring for collections, is one of the most critical roles for Burke staff. While the state tells us that legally as the Washington State Natural History and Culture Museum we own the Burke's collections, our staff recognizes that we are caretakers and that rights to visit, interact, have information about, and assert control over interpretation, exhibition, and use of cultural collections belongs to the communities (and often families) from which the collections originated. Having knowledgeable Indigenous staff members as part of the Bill Holm Center's team has been a critical part of building relationships with artists and communities. The center's staff travels out to visit communities to hear what is needed from the museum and that too has shaped our programs.

These efforts extend beyond the Bill Holm Center to the Burke's broader Culture and Education departments. Staff and curators at the Burke are keenly aware of museums' problematic histories. The Burke's programs and processes are continually being built and improved deliberately to work toward healing the relationships between museums and Indigenous communities.[16] These initiatives often arise as a result of personal relationships between museum staff and Indigenous artists/researchers who engage with the collections and provide feedback on how the museum can better serve them and their communities. These conversations can be kind and gentle or rocky and difficult, but change ensues. Often it is the personal relationships between artist/researchers and Indigenous staff members—relationships strengthened by common ground and personal networks—that result in the sharing of critically important feedback. All these personal relationships, built on respect and reciprocity, can (and have) lead to structural changes in the institution.

This is the background against which the *Here & Now* exhibit came to be. This chapter frames how these institutional programs led to a remarkable exhibit built out of the experiences of artists and museum staff working together.

The Exhibit: Here & Now

In recent years, ever-increasing numbers of artists and cultural researchers have visited the Burke's collections; similarly, there has been substantial growth in the number of public visitors who have wanted to tour the collections, going "behind the scenes." In 2012, as we approached the tenth anniversary of the Bill Holm Center, we wanted to show the public what goes on behind the scenes when collections are actively used; we also wanted to gauge the practical results of the center's grant program for artists' study of historical creations. We contacted each of our grantees and invited them to share how their artistic practices were affected by their visits to the Burke. Taken as a whole, their responses were thoughtful and insightful. While their responses confirmed our prior expectation that artists' visits had been useful to them, we had not fully anticipated how deeply moving those visits were for some artists.

Many told us about new pieces they made that were directly inspired or informed by the historical artworks at the museum. But even more important, many told us in precise, heartfelt, and eloquent fashion how important the visit had been to them personally as well as professionally. Their words and their works, more than any professional public-relations piece or pedagogical narrative, articulated the critical importance and impact of the Burke's "open door" policy and the Bill Holm Center's grant program. In reading the artists' words, and looking at pictures of their new works alongside the Burke's collections, we realized that not only did these artists have a story to tell but that we had an obligation to help that story be told. The *Here & Now: Native Artists Inspired* exhibit arose from that moment, in an effort to showcase their art alongside the pieces from the Burke that artists' identified as being key to their learning, especially to share their "conversations with collections."

The *Here & Now* exhibit shared the outcomes and reflections on artists' time with historical collections. This work, so often deeply embedded in personal conversations between artists, community members, and museum staff—or between these visitors without staff involvement or, even more intimately, between artists and artworks from past generations—can be challenging to present in ways truthful to the process. Public exhibit spaces lack the dynamism and conversational flow inherent in behind-the-scenes work. Sharing the artist's words through text and audio helped to bring this conversational feel into the public space. In preparation for the exhibit, artists engaged with the exhibit team in recorded conversations, during which they described their artwork, their creative process, and the role of the Burke's collections in their learning journey. Excerpts from these conversations became exhibit labels, and audio files accompanied some pairings of historical and contemporary artworks. As is appropriate for such a collaborative process, the participating artists reviewed and approved all exhibit text and audio.

10.4. Participating artists in the *Here & Now* exhibit. Burke Museum, 2014. (a) Sonny Assu (Ligwilda'xw); (b) David A. Boxley (Tsimshian); (c) David Robert Boxley (Tsimshian); (d) Alison Bremner (Tlingit); (e) Shgen George (Tlingit); (f) Pat Courtney Gold (Wasco); (g) Joel Isaak (Kenaitze); (h) Tommy Joseph (Tlingit); (i) Latham Mack (Nuxalk); (j) Lou-ann Ika'wega Neel (Kwakwa̱ka̱'wakw); (k) Aaron Nelson-Moody (Squamish); (l) Lisa Telford (Haida); (m) Evelyn Vanderhoop (Haida); (n) Christian White (Haida); and (o) Rico Worl (Tlingit). Courtesy of the Burke Museum.

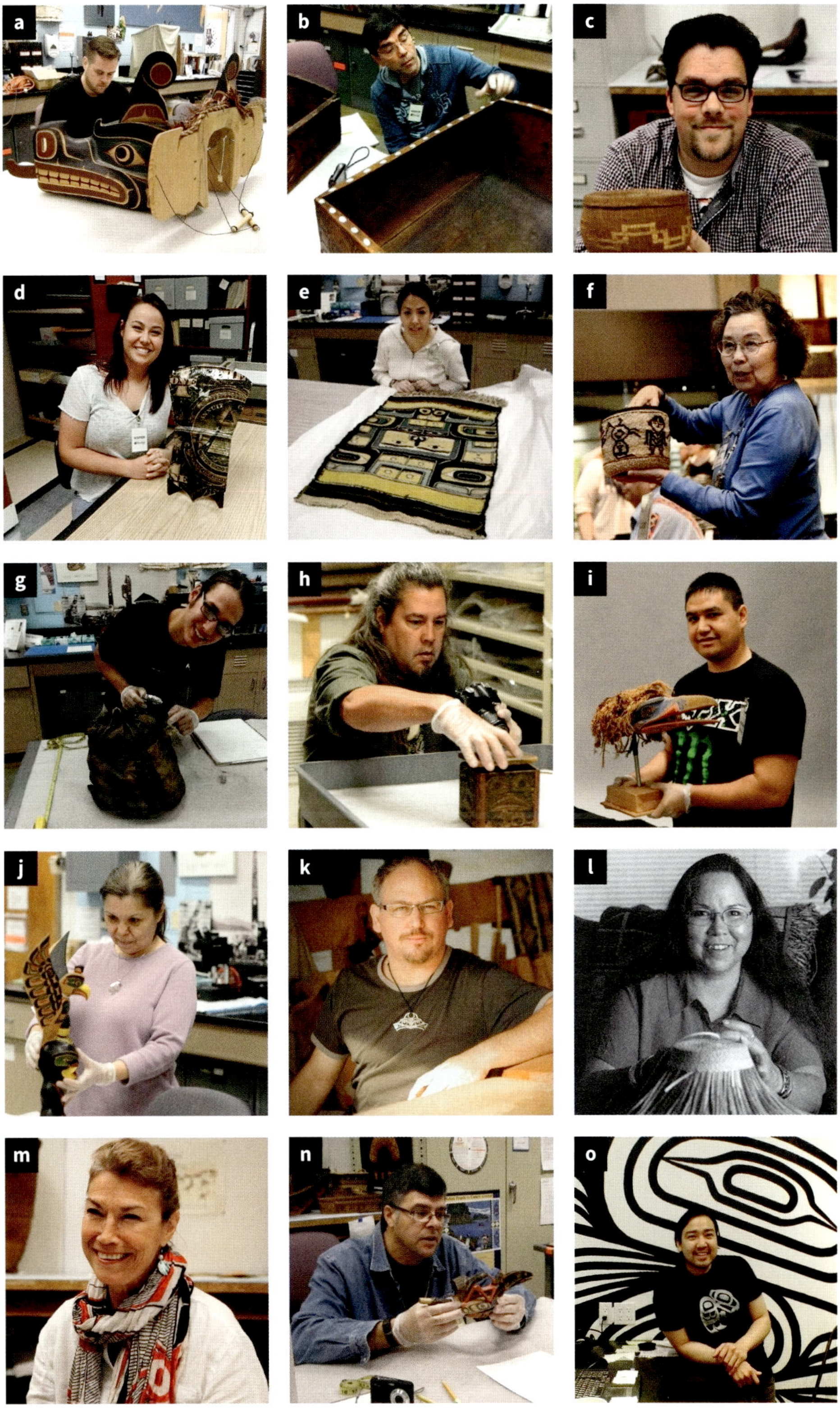
a
b
c
d
e
f
g
h
i
j
k
l
m
n
o

The exhibit reflected the multiple ways in which artists engage with the Burke collections, and conversations with the artists revealed a number of themes that resonated out of this work, including kinship, adherence to nineteenth-century prototypes, and discovery of innovation in past practices that lead to new paths and freedoms for current artists. Many artists discussed how their creations, while inspired by older aesthetic forms, could convey current political and personal concerns.

The fifteen Northwest Native artists featured in this exhibit were Bill Holm Center grant recipients who loaned or sold the museum new works inspired or informed by their research at the Burke.[17] The show included their thirty-four new works paired with twenty-seven nineteenth- and early twentieth-century pieces from the Burke's collection that each artist identified as being key to their learning. Almost unheard of in general showcases of Northwest Coast art, 45 percent of the artists were women. As the curator for the exhibit, I worked with the artists and a museum team to design an exhibit demonstrating why it is so essential to have collections off display but open to researchers in the "back of the house." To that end, we structured the exhibit to focus attention on the artists and their process. Visitors approaching the *Here & Now* gallery were met by a very large (10 foot × 12 foot) photographic fabric scrim close-up of the hands of Haida weaver Evelyn Vanderhoop weaving a Naaxiin robe. This image called attention to the time, materials, knowledge, and labor that contributed to each artwork. Vanderhoop's summary of her time spent at the Burke was displayed in bold three-inch-high letters across the gallery wall: "Studying like this is an extension of our apprenticeship with our ancestors."

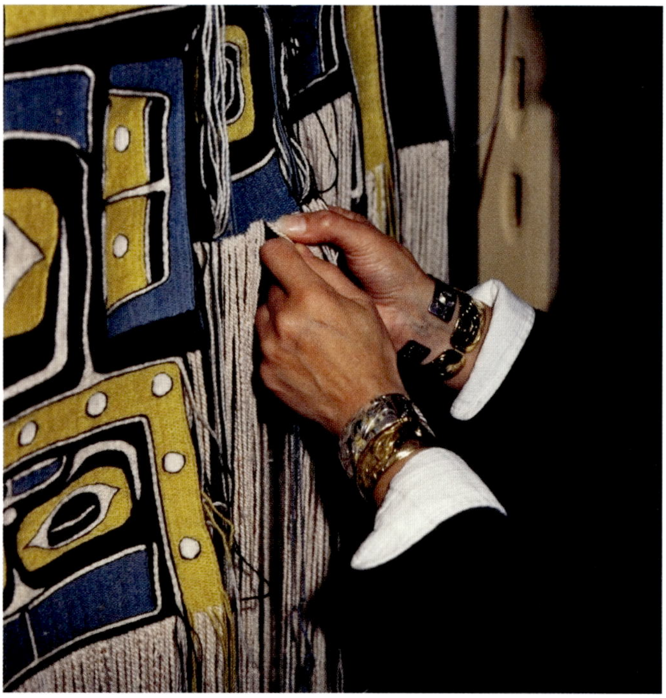

10.5. Evelyn Vanderhoop (Haida) weaving her Naaxiin robe. Photograph courtesy of Helen Carlson.

In the introductory panel to the exhibit I wanted to provide context for visitors to understand the historical collections and their current functions. The primary purpose of the exhibit was to show the artists' works, as well as the historical creations that had inspired them, and to let

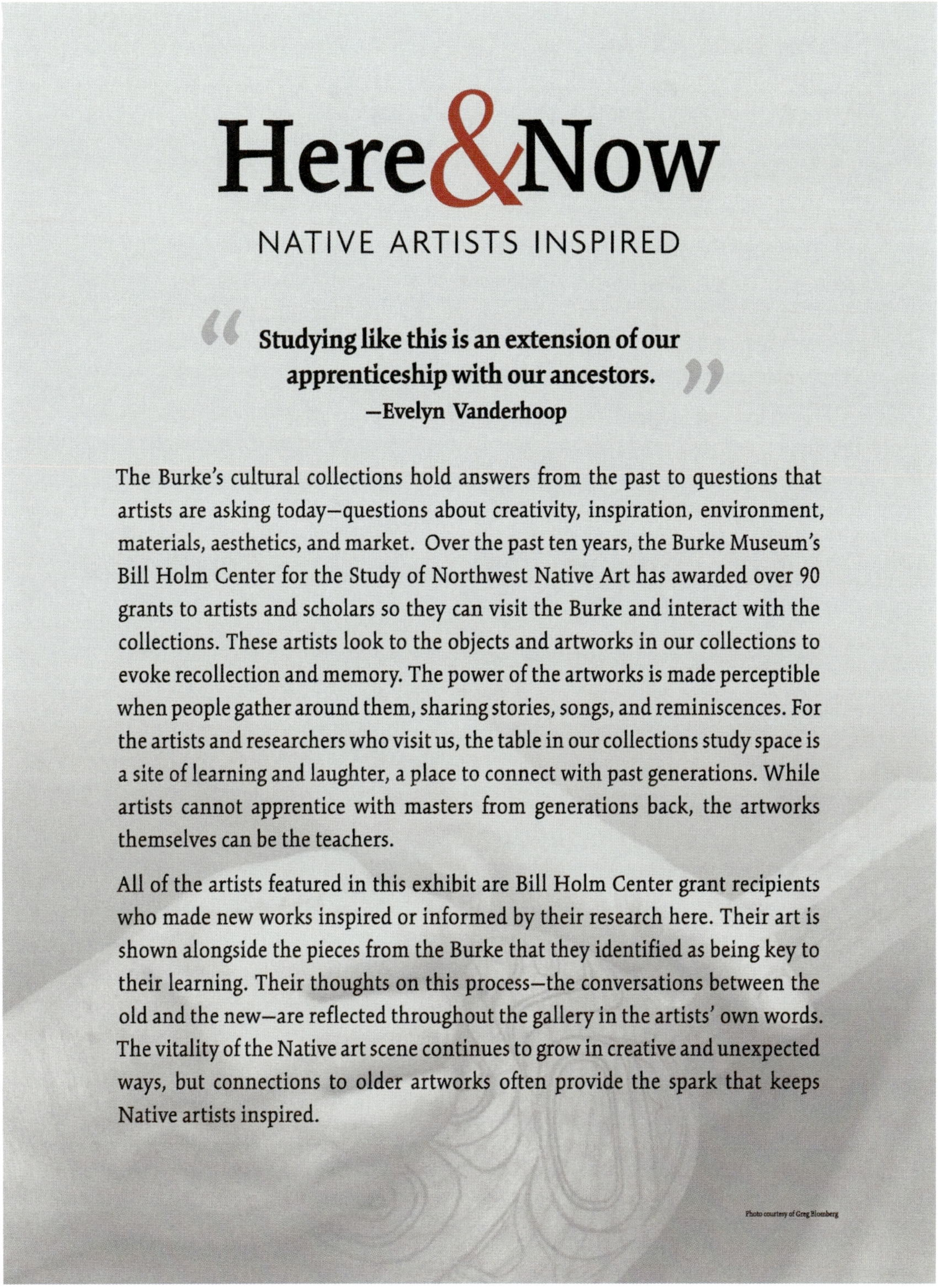

Here & Now

NATIVE ARTISTS INSPIRED

"Studying like this is an extension of our apprenticeship with our ancestors."
—Evelyn Vanderhoop

The Burke's cultural collections hold answers from the past to questions that artists are asking today—questions about creativity, inspiration, environment, materials, aesthetics, and market. Over the past ten years, the Burke Museum's Bill Holm Center for the Study of Northwest Native Art has awarded over 90 grants to artists and scholars so they can visit the Burke and interact with the collections. These artists look to the objects and artworks in our collections to evoke recollection and memory. The power of the artworks is made perceptible when people gather around them, sharing stories, songs, and reminiscences. For the artists and researchers who visit us, the table in our collections study space is a site of learning and laughter, a place to connect with past generations. While artists cannot apprentice with masters from generations back, the artworks themselves can be the teachers.

All of the artists featured in this exhibit are Bill Holm Center grant recipients who made new works inspired or informed by their research here. Their art is shown alongside the pieces from the Burke that they identified as being key to their learning. Their thoughts on this process—the conversations between the old and the new—are reflected throughout the gallery in the artists' own words. The vitality of the Native art scene continues to grow in creative and unexpected ways, but connections to older artworks often provide the spark that keeps Native artists inspired.

Photo courtesy of Greg Blomberg

10.6. Introductory panel to the *Here & Now: Native Artists Inspired* exhibit, 2014. Courtesy of the Burke Museum.

the artists tell the stories of those works in their own words. Here, I have selected a few of the stories from the exhibit. As one example of how contemporary artists make personal connections with past creations, Tlingit weaver Shgen George shared a story of her visit with a textile in the Burke's collection:

> When I was there at the Burke looking at the different robes I felt really connected to the weavers that made them. I found myself wondering who were these women that made these and where did they come from? I came up with a lot of questions and a lot of wondering about where they came from and who they were, and an admiration for their work. Sometimes feeling badly, you know I wish that I had been born earlier to be able to learn from them directly. There was one piece that I was looking at it really closely and you could see a hair woven in and I just thought "there's a piece of the woman who made this," and you could see that it was all woven in like it had just gotten caught while she was making it or maybe spinning the warp. Just seeing that made me feel like that person was there.

Kwakwa̱ka̱'wakw artist Lou-ann Ika'wega Neel had a similar experience during her visit finding literal kinship as well as aesthetic connections to the cultural creations she studied. Neel studied the work of her grandmother Ellen Neel and her great-grandfather Charlie James as well as other Kwakwa̱ka̱'wakw creations during her visit at the Burke. But during her time, she kept coming back to a rattle (Burke cat. # 2010-37/35) that drew her attention over and over—she could not quite let it go back to the storage shelves. When she consulted the catalog information, it turned out to have been carved by her father, John Neel, whom she had never known growing up. She was thrilled to discover that his artistic style resonated with her own. Neel has often repeated this story, demonstrating that familial pieces are very personal documents of history and kinship as well as being incredible artworks.

While many historical creations should have remained within the community to play an active role there, they were often sold to collectors under difficult circumstances. Decolonization of institutions means addressing this history through both the return of cultural belongings through NAGPRA and other return processes and also through making sure that access to the museum's collection is open, supported, and transparent.[18] These efforts are a critical step toward healing the damage that occurred when cultural belongings were improperly sold or traded, or outright stolen out of their original communities. When asked about her opinion on access to museum collections, Neel stated: "I really appreciate being able to go into these collections and know that these pieces have been really cared for, and kept in their original state for a really long time. I wish that there was more opportunity for pieces to come out into the communities, whether it's through our own cultural centers, or through our being able to have those pieces brought back into the community to just remind people of the kind of pride, and care, and love, that the artists of that era put into their work."

Neel was not the first to request that museum pieces travel back home on loan.[19] Conversations like these have shaped Bill Holm Center initiatives, including the offsite collections-based workshop grants where artist choose pieces from the Burke collections that they want to share at workshops in their own communities. Neel looked at model poles and other carvings by her grandmother Ellen Neel and other family members as well as button blankets and other ceremonial regalia from the Kwakwa̱ka̱'wakw and other Northwest Coast communities. Her study revealed a wealth of variety in the techniques that her ancestors used in their sewn creations. As a result, she was inspired to create a wall hanging based on an old Kwakwa̱ka̱'wakw apron in the collection. In preparation for the *Here & Now* exhibit, she explained this experience:

> I came across this one particular dance apron [Burke cat. #4], and it's the one that I modeled my wall hanging after. It had coppers all along the bottom. My eye was drawn to it because it represented such wealth, and richness, and just

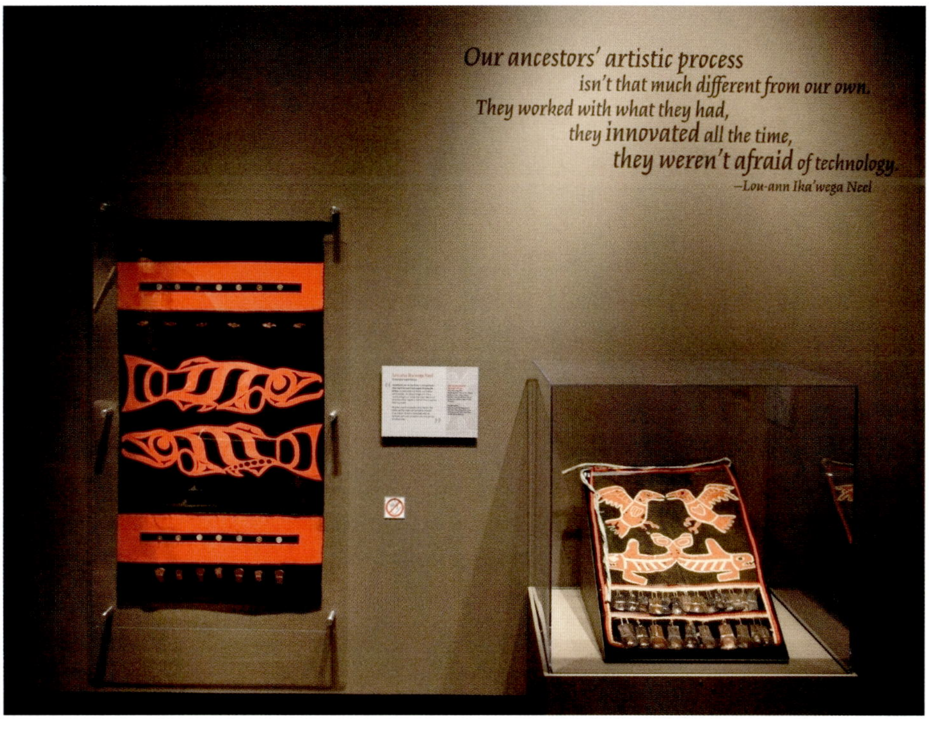

10.7. Lou-ann Ika'wega Neel, *The Wealth of Małik (Sockeye Salmon)*, 2014. Melton wool, ultra-suede, copper, abalone buttons. Burke Museum cat. #2015-17/1. Dance Apron, Unknown artist, Kwakwa̱ka̱'wakw, 1893. Wool cloth, cotton cloth, copper. Burke Museum cat. #4. Photograph by Kathryn Bunn-Marcuse.

> the weight—the physical weight of it was so overwhelming to me as an artist because, I know how long it takes to cut every single one of those coppers, and then to drill all of them, and sew them securely onto a dance apron, and make sure it's going to stay.
>
> When I went to do my wall hanging, I thought about that whole mentor-apprentice relationship that we used to have where someone like me, who is fairly early in my career in textiles, could go to a mentor and learn.

While the nineteenth-century apron has two whales and a row of miniature coppers along the bottom, Neel focused on salmon for her new creation. Again, from the *Here & Now* exhibit:

> Because there is such a strong relationship between our people and the salmon—and salmon has become such a big political environmental issue lately—I thought I'd focus on the salmon. To me, it represented a cycle, the salmon returns every year to its spawning grounds, and to me that really resonated with me what I was trying to convey; that we have this relationship with our territories, we're here all the time, we return every year, just like the salmon does. So I wanted to just create this connection between our people and the salmon, through that wall hanging by also using the same aesthetic and artistic considerations that the person who made that dance apron would've considered.
>
> I also wanted to have that direct relationship that anyone who understands our potlatch culture will see, that having these salmon and these coppers together represent the biggest symbols of wealth of our culture. I wanted to have coppers present. I think there were something like 23 coppers on [the old] apron, and I believe I have five. But I also wanted to show that there is a relationship between the diminishing salmon and the diminishment of our material wealth that is normally represented through copper in our colonized society. I wanted to convey that even though we have these wonderful, incredible connections of symbols and wealth—even though they have deteriorated over time.

Some artists created pieces strongly based on the artwork of previous generations: David Boxley's *Feast Dish* reflects his deep understanding of the northern Northwest Coast formline and the time Boxley spent studying the Burke's nineteenth-century Ts'msyen (Tsimshian) feast dish to create a replica. His son, David Robert Boxley, made a new version of an old Ts'msyen puppet in the collection and wanted to spend time thinking about the possible uses of dramatic props like this one in ceremony. Both Boxleys have spent many hours studying the old pieces in museum collections. David Robert Boxley noted: "One can never be done learning. I want to

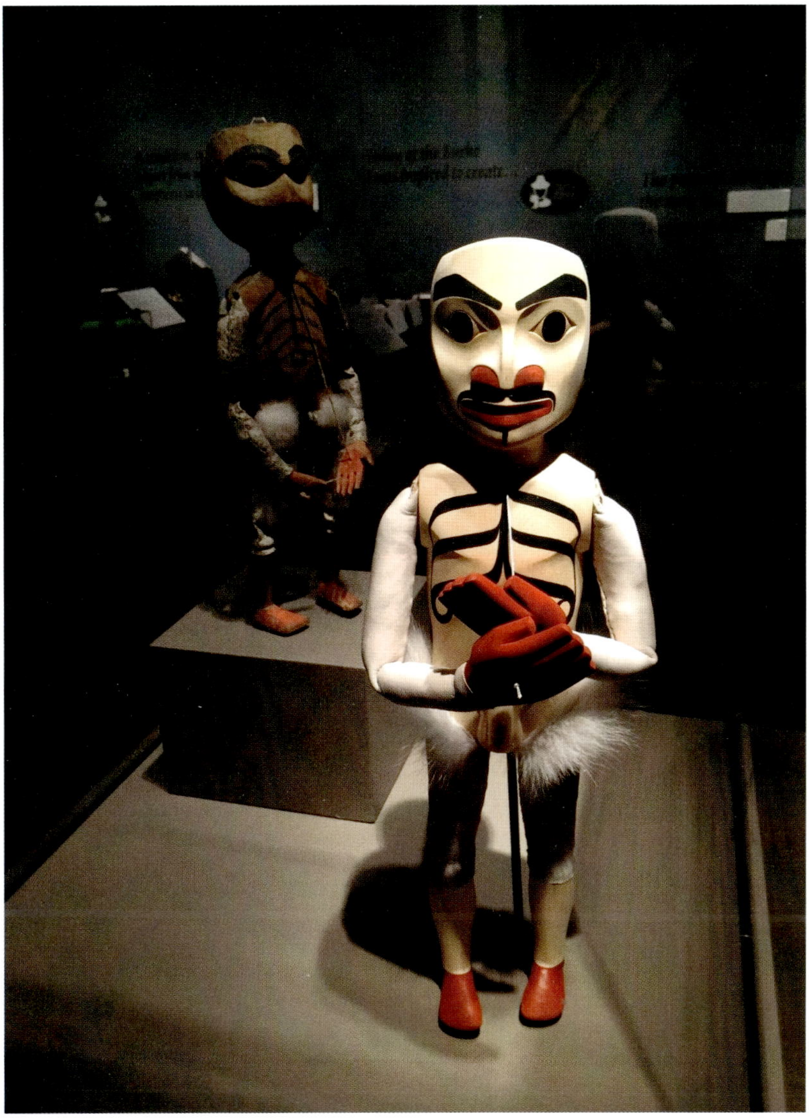

10.8. David Robert Boxley, *Puppet*, 2014. Yellow cedar, paint, fur, leather, string. Burke Museum cat. # 2015-148/1. Unknown artist, Tsimshian, collected in 1954. Wood, leather, nails, string. Burke Museum cat. #1-1653. Photograph by Kathryn Bunn-Marcuse.

see every old piece I can of the old masters. They are my teachers and this is the only way I can learn from them."

Genealogical kinship connections have been recognized by museums through commissions as well.[20] In 2014 the Burke commissioned Christian White to recreate a missing argillite chest front by his great-great-grandfather, Haida artist Charles Edenshaw, following White's 2012 Bill Holm Center research fellowship at the Burke. "It's a very powerful feeling for me to be able to see these pieces, to be able to hold them. As I was carving this chest front I felt like I was reconnecting with my ancestor. I was thinking about the different steps that he had gone through to make this. It was like I had to re-invent that myself."

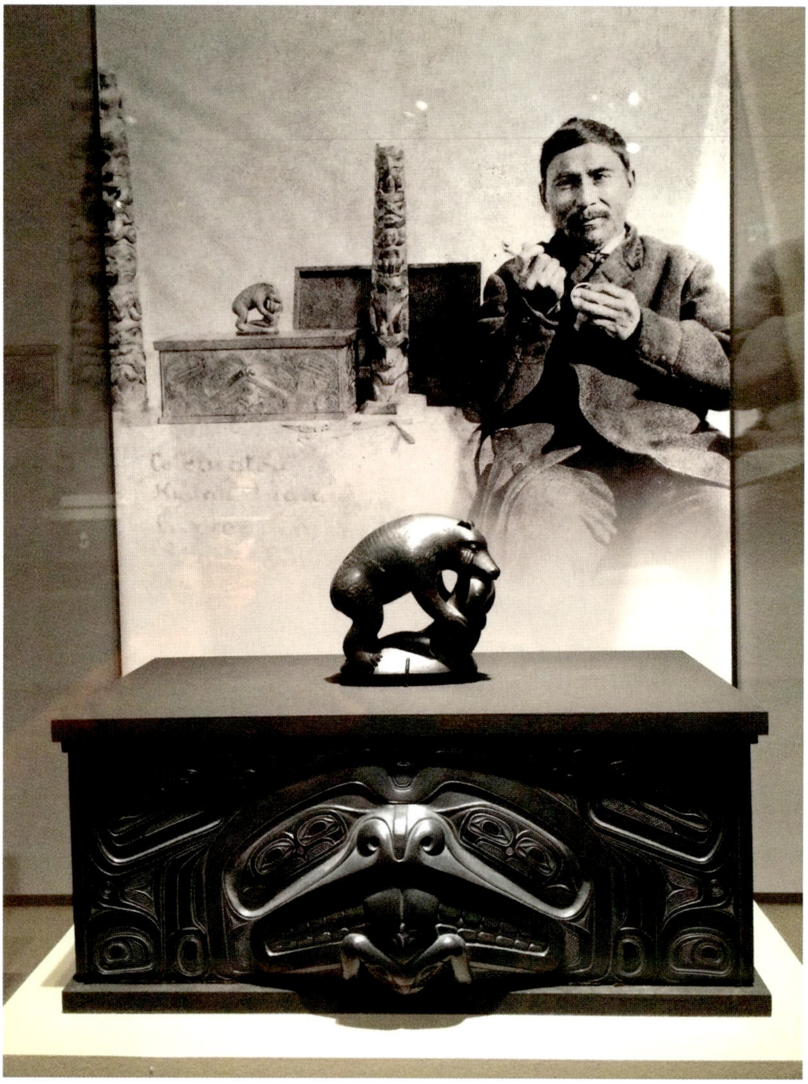

10.9. Christian White, argillite chest panel, 2013. Burke Museum cat. #2014-15/1. Photograph courtesy of the Burke Museum.

White noted that it was a great artistic and historical exercise—and a challenge—to carve something re-creating Edenshaw's style rather than in his own. The missing chest front was bringing him into conversation with his ancestor through their shared artistic endeavors. In the exhibit, White's new chest front was united with a sculptural bear that Charles Edenshaw had carved for the original chest and now the two pieces are together in the Burke's collection. While many of the artists who use the Burke's collections are focused on working in forms and techniques closely tied to long-standing Northwest Coast aesthetic practices, others engage with the

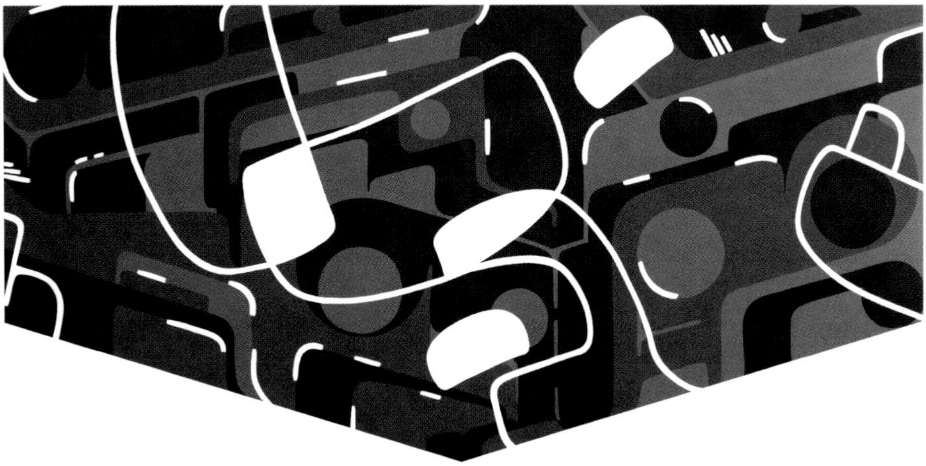

10.10. Sonny Assu, *#potlatchshadesofgrey*, 2014. Acrylic on panel. Burke Museum cat. #2015-62/1. Photograph courtesy of the Burke Museum.

collection to answer a different set of questions they are posing in their current art practice. Making sure that artists know that the collections are there for them—to engage with on their own terms, for inspiration in *whatever* their artistic journey is—is a key part of our mission. Having artists in the *Here & Now* exhibit whose expression ranged from close reinterpretations of past pieces (like the Boxleys) to the abstract paintings of Sonny Assu allowed the public to see that contemporary artists, all of whom engage with the material culture of their heritage, have a vast range of artistic responses to their experience.

Ligwilda'x̱w artist Sonny Assu visited the Burke in July 2012 building on other museum visits that have informed his artistic practice. Assu's large 2013 acrylic on panel piece *#potlatchshadesofgrey* (part of his 2009–15 "Chilkat Series") was inspired in part by a Chilkat pattern board he saw at the Burke. Assu says that in his painting he used the "white lines as language, abstraction or stylistic characters—grafitti-esque, breaking up the formal narrative often found in Northwest work."[21] The formline characteristics of the piece challenge expectations and call into question generalized assumptions about being able to "read" Northwest Coast art. Assu became particularly interested in studying the Chilkat robes and pattern boards after a seminal experience at the Canadian Museum of History, where he visited with the regalia of his great-great-grandfather, Chief Billy Assu: "It was probably one of the most powerful experiences in my career up to date. Having that Chilkat blanket be placed on my shoulders and having the wealth of energy just surge through me brought me to near tears."

Chief Billy Assu's Chilkat regalia reflects the status that chiefs held in Kwakwa̱ka̱'wakw communities based on their roles as stewards of territory and protectors of natural resources and demonstrated through both the wealth of coppers, masks, regalia, and the intangible wealth of songs and dances that were validated at potlatches. Chilkat regalia reflected both tangible physical wealth—the cost in time, labor, and materials of the woven mountain goat and cedar garment—and the intangible weight of responsibility and knowledge that rested on the shoulders of chiefs. Assu's *#potlatchshadesofgrey* queries the role of status and wealth over time and demonstrates how so many contemporary works integrate customary forms with current political discussion. Assu contrasts the Kwakwa̱ka̱'wakw signifiers of status and wealth to how status is acquired in today's online world. "My great-great-grandfather was a very noble person and he was known up and down the coast for all his power and his position as chief. And I put that in contrast to how we formulate our own notions of social status in our modern world through consumerism, branding, pop culture, and social media."

The status of chiefs is contrasted here with references to pop culture through both title and imagery: the title riffs on the book *Fifty Shades of Grey*, and some viewers have seen the white thread of iPhone earbuds running through the piece. Assu has noted that these icons of consumer and pop culture "have become our new forms of totem representation."[22] From the exhibit materials: "The roots of the series really took its shape in social media so that's why I put the hashtag in part of the title of the work . . . to draw connections to platforms like Twitter and Facebook and using those things to talk about our social status. Which is dramatically different than the social status that my great-great-grandfather would have, where he was embedded with the power and knowledge and wisdom of his years as a chief." "Status updates" accrue through today's digital signifiers rather than through the weighty materiality of Chilkat blankets worn by chiefs. Today's signifiers often exist only as waste-accumulating material goods and in the online world of Facebook "likes" and Twitter followers, where one can "update your status" with the click of a button.

This piece seamlessly blends the experiences that Assu had in two separate museums; and it queries the colonial practices that led to the collecting, selling, and forced removal of family treasures while investigating the new uses that cultural heritage collections can have today. Sometimes artists and the public think that museum research can only lead to replicas or careful reconstructions of past artistic practices. Showcasing Assu's piece in the front gallery as visitors entered the exhibit signaled the new creative endeavors that can arise from spending time with historical collections and thinking through how artwork of every time period responded to contemporary needs.

For some artists, the forms and techniques are ancient but the artwork contains explicit messages about current issues. In the *Here & Now* exhibit contemporary Tlingit armor by Tommy Joseph was displayed alongside the older weaponry and armor he had studied. His current works demonstrated his expertise in close replication of older forms and techniques, including helmets, daggers, and slat-and-rod armor bound with copious lengths of sinew. The weaponry of the past fortified Joseph's exhortation to battle against current exploitation of Indigenous lands and waters as symbolized by an armor legging he decorated with the words "Idle No More." Joseph first exhibited this piece in Juneau at the Alaska State Museum, hanging it next to the opening marquee for his solo show, *Rainforest Warrior.* Idle No More is an environmental and social justice movement founded in 2012 in Canada that "calls on all people to join in a peaceful revolution, to honour Indigenous sovereignty, and to protect the land & water." Tlingit people have fought for their rights and territory since time immemorial. Along the Northwest Coast, where Native nations are crossed by national borders, the risks and consequences of oil pipelines and tanker wrecks have ignited a series of protests to safeguard the water and the land. Joseph used this single legging to show his support for the movement.

Taken together or individually, the contemporary works in the *Here & Now* exhibit were enactments of both self-expression and cultural identity, ranging widely in style, materials, and messages. The conversations between the older historical pieces and the creations were reflected throughout the exhibit in the artists' own words. And the public could see that continuum—how historical pieces are a grounding place for artists working in very different genres.

Sharing the Changes in Our Methods

Here & Now: Native Artists Inspired allowed Burke visitors to see the work that goes on behind the scenes at the museum. We hoped to reflect the current relationships between our museum and the Indigenous artists we engage with, and the collaborative support for inquiries about cultural knowledge. These relationships are a conscious reaction to the past, when the collecting practices of museums ranged from relationships based in unequal power dynamics to cases of outright theft. The loss of tangible heritage damaged critical cultural practices, impacting both religion and governance, as well as breaking the chain of aesthetic practices and knowledge in some communities. At the Burke we are working toward healing broken relationships and forging new friendships through accessibility, support, and finding common ground. The days when gatekeeping was the norm and collections were open only to academics should be well behind us.

Slowly, through individual and group visits to the Burke, we hear that attitudes are changing, that museums can foster a reputation for openness and support. As David R. Boxley explains: "That's something that's changed even in my lifetime. When my dad first started researching he could go places and people wouldn't let him touch anything—there was this attitude that it was theirs and you be careful. That's really shifted and we have a lot more freedom to just touch and look and do what we need to do. . . . There's never that feeling that's it's not all right for me to come back and look at these things, it's just when can the doors be open."

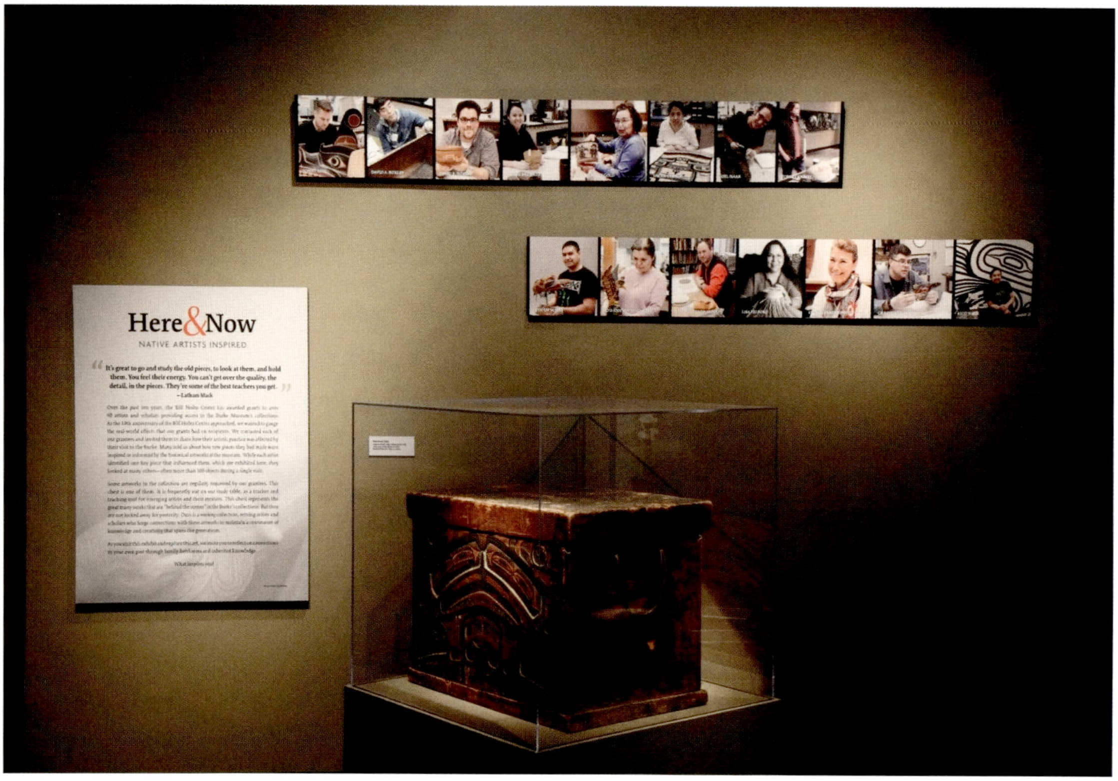

10.11. Chest at the conclusion of *Here & Now* exhibit, 2015. Haida chest, nineteenth century. Burke Museum cat. #1-1593. Photograph by Sven Haakanson.

The *Here & Now* exhibit shared with the public what goes on behind the scenes, bringing to the front of the house the relevance of historic collections and collaborative work to all our stakeholders—artists, communities, scholars, and the public. As curator, I wanted to show the public the work that we do and to reveal the shared authority of a collaborative exhibit model in which artists controlled the selection of artworks on display and provided the interpretive text. But part of what made the exhibit special is what it did *not* do. The exhibit did not include the typical interpretive ethnographic information visitors often expect (especially in natural history museums) such as maps, explanations of cultural heritage, categorization of object type or time period. Neither did it follow what might be thought of as stereotypical art museum practices of spotlighted work on pedestals with the bare minimum of text. My goal was to facilitate what artists wanted to convey about their experiences studying historical creations and how those inspired new creations.

While the exhibit has closed, the work continues. Mentor and apprentices or groups of affiliated artists visit together making artistic and kinship connections to the cultural belongings that currently live far from home. Sometimes the lessons that are learned from these ancestors are concrete, such as Warm Springs artist Marge Kalama reconnecting with the 1 × 1 (spaced beading technique) that exists on the Plateau but hasn't been practiced for several generations; sometimes the lessons are both artistic and personal, such as Lou-ann Neel's connections with the art of her grandmother, Ellen Neel, and father, John Neel; or Sonny Assu's encounter with his grandfather's regalia. There are many more stories of how reconnecting with historical arts through kinship relationships is critical.

This chapter discusses history—what we have done. There is much more to do. We continue to invite instruction and feedback on how best to care for collections, how to improve our grant programs, how to advance still-needed repatriation work, how to best support and value current Indigenous staff members, and perhaps most important, how to actively build or support current education and job-training opportunities for more community members to become museum professionals.

I conclude this chapter the same way that we concluded the *Here & Now* exhibit: with an older northern Northwest Coast chest that we displayed alone, by itself, not paired with any other pieces. It is one of the artworks in the Burke collection that is frequently requested by visiting artists. It is often out on our study table, as a teacher and teaching-tool for emerging artists and their mentors. While the chest is not serving in the capacity for which it was originally created, it has a new role these days as a teacher, as do many other cultural belongings that serve as teachers, guides, and mentors. It is the responsibility of the museum to recognize and support the roles that these ancestors take on. This work is reflected in the 2017 Burke Museum mission statement, which emphasizes the belief that cultural collections be shared so that "people can learn, be inspired, generate knowledge, feel joy, and heal." It is an aspirational statement but one that reflects everyday work at the museum. In the *Here & Now* exhibit, that chest stood for the great many works that are behind the scenes in the Burke's collections. But by bringing it out, we showed that they are not locked away for posterity. Ours is a *working* collection, serving artists and researchers who physically connect with these artworks to maintain a continuum of knowledge and creativity that spans the generations.

NOTES

Thanks to Bridget Johnson, who was the invaluable curatorial assistant for *Here & Now*, and to all the artists in the *Here & Now* exhibit and in the Bill Holm Center grant program who shared their experiences and their guidance on how to change and improve our grant program. Thanks to Sue Rowley, curator of archeology at the UBC Museum of Anthropology for information on *c̓əsnaʔəm, the city before the city*, to Amy Lonetree for sharing some of the latest literature on decolonizing museums, and to Charlotte Basch for critical feedback and suggestions.

1 "Decolonize" as a term is contested in some circles. See the introduction E. Tuck and K. W. Yang, "Decolonization Is Not a Metaphor," *Decolonization: Indigeneity, Education & Society* 1, no. 1 (2012): 1–40, who say it is not a metaphor for education or social programs; and Jane Anderson and Kimberly Christen, "Decolonizing Attribution: Traditions of Exclusion," *Journal of Radical Librarianship* 5 (2019): 113–52, 117, who question "the very possibility of decolonization at all." I see it as the processes of making museums more responsive to priorities set by Indigenous communities whose heritage is in their cultural collections—these priorities include access, ethical exhibitions, collections care, and changes to policies, practices, and staffing.

2 Amy Lonetree, *Decolonizing Museums: Representing Native America in National and Tribal Museums. First Peoples: New Directions in Indigenous Studies* (Chapel Hill: University of North Carolina Press, 2012), 170.

3 A few key texts on this topic include Laura L. Peers and Alison K. Brown, *Museums and Source Communities a Routledge Reader* (London: New York: Routledge, 2003); Ruth B. Phillips, *Museum Pieces: Toward the Indigenization of Canadian Museums* (Montréal: McGill-Queen's University Press, 2011); Bryony Onciul, *Museums, Heritage and Indigenous Voice: Decolonizing Engagement* (New York: Routledge, 2015); Lonetree, *Decolonizing Museums*; Michael M. Ames, *Cannibal Tours and Glass Boxes: The Anthropology of Museums*, second revised edition (Vancouver: University of British Columbia Press, 1992); and Jennifer A. Shannon, *Our Lives: Collaboration, Native Voice, and the Making of the National Museum of the American Indian* (Santa Fe, NM: SAR Press, 2014).

4 For a history of the Burke Museum's earliest and most formative collections, see Bill Holm, *Spirit and Ancestor: A Century of Northwest Coast Indian Art at the Burke Museum* (Seattle: Burke Museum and University of Washington Press, 1987), 22.

5 All quotations in this article are from the 2014 *Here & Now* exhibit interviews unless otherwise noted.

6 See Robin K. Wright, *A Time of Gathering: Native Heritage in Washington State* (Seattle: Burke Museum and University of Washington Press, 1991), 15–27; Phillips, *Museum Pieces*, 94; and Assembly of First Nations and Canadian Museums Association, *Turning the Page: Forging New Partnerships between Museums and First Peoples*, second edition (Ottawa: Assembly of First Nations and Canadian Museums Association, 1992).

7 For history on collaborations between museums and First Nations, particularly in BC, see Martha Black, "Collaboration: A Historical Perspective," in *Native Art of the Northwest Coast: A History of Changing Ideas*, edited by Charlotte Townsend-Gault, Jennifer Kramer, and Ki-Ke-In, 785–827 (Vancouver: University of British Columbia Press, 2013); and Caitlin Gordon-Walker and Martha Black, "Indigeneities and Museums: Ongoing Conversations," *BC Studies* 119 (2018): 11–22.

8 On an institutional level the Burke Museum convened a Native American Advisory Board (NAAB) in 1992 under the leadership of curator James Nason (Comanche). They developed the museum's Native American Collections Policy, which codifies that board advice will be "actively sought on all policy matters concerning the collecting, exhibition, interpretation, and repatriation of Native American materials as well as on any other matters of common interest that arise" (James Nason, NAAB history memo, 2007). The Burke Museum's official Native American Collection Policy states that exhibits with Native content must include consultation with appropriate communities and review by the NAAB.

9 Pieces in museum collections have been called "artifacts" or "objects." In recent years these terms have been rejected as alienating and implicit in breaking the bonds between cultural creations and the communities from which they came. Newer terminology, including "cultural belongings" and "ancestors," deliberately asserts respect for Indigenous ways of

knowing that consider these creations as relatives and ancestors with all the affect, influence, guidance, and nurturance that our human relations might have. "Cultural belongings" is in popular usage in Canada but not as common in the United States. The terms "art" or "artwork" are contested, although many of the artists who come to the Burke use this term. In this chapter I alternate between "artworks" when that seems true to the intention of the artist and "cultural creations" as a broad term.

10 Wanda K. Nanibush, Karen Kramer, Ben Garcia, Tricia Laughlin Bloom, and Lara Evans, "Shared Authority," *Art in America* 105, no. 9: 76–81, 81.

11 Nanibush et al., "Shared Authority," 78.

12 Between 2003 and 2019 the Bill Holm Center awarded grants to 195 individual artists and 22 scholars.

13 heather ahtone, "Designed to Last: Striving toward an Indigenous American Aesthetic," *International Journal of the Arts in Society: Annual Review* 4, no. 2 (2009): 375, https://doi.org/10.18848/1833-1866/CGP/v04i02/35602.

14 See Gordon-Walker and Black, "Indigeneities and Museums," 11.

15 ahtone, "Designed to Last," 375.

16 Karen Kramer, curator at the Peabody Essex Museum, discusses what she calls "presencing Indigeneity," an approach that resonates with current Burke initiatives. She explains that this "means infusing the institution with Indigenous perspectives in many ways, from revealing historical truths and trauma wrought by colonization to celebrating the incredible depth, breadth, diversity, and dynamism of Indigenous creative expression" (quoted in Nanibush et al., "Shared Authority," 78).

17 Many of the artists listed in Figure 10.4 are from the central and northern Northwest Coast, reflecting the regional strengths of the Burke collections and the early years of our grant program (2004–12). Since then, we have focused on supporting Washington and Oregon Indigenous artists.

18 Emily Moore, "Acts of Propatriation: Two Kaats' House Posts by Nathan and Stephen Jackson," in *In the Spirit of the Ancestors: Contemporary Northwest Coast Art from the Burke Museum*, edited by Robin Wright and Kathryn Bunn-Marcuse, 77–86 (Seattle: University of Washington Press, 2013); and Joel Schwartz, "Sculpture Representing First Male Ancestor of the Chilliwacks Returned to Tribe by Burke," *UW News*, University of Washington, last modified October 12, www.washington.edu/news/2006/10/12/sculpture-representing-first-male-ancestor-of-the-chilliwacks-returned-to-tribe-by-burke/ (accessed July 21, 2019).

19 The Burke has loaned artworks in recent years for community celebrations, including the crest hat of Tlingit Chief Shakes in 2007 and the pipe of Chief Shakes, which returned in 2013 for the opening of the Shakes House in Wrangell, Alaska. The contemporary Ravenstail *Damascus Robe* is loaned out for graduations and other events, and kava bowls have been used at Samoan community events.

20 Portland Art Museum purchased Clarissa Rizal's 2014 *Resilience Robe* and commissioned the *Lineage Robe* (2017) by Clarissa's daughter, Lily Hope, to document artistic lineage.

21 Author's personal communication with Sonny Assu, July 17, 2018. In addition to querying "status," Assu notes the painting "is also about the exploration of abstraction and looking at how western artists were influenced and inspired by the Northwest Coast. It's taking their gaze and turning it back onto them by adopting their way of understanding art through abstraction."

22 Sonny Assu, "Sonny Assu: A Selective History," in *Selective History*, edited by Sonny Assu, Candice Hopkins, Marianne Nicolson, Richard Van Camp, Ellyn Walker, and Janet Rogers, 43–211 (Seattle: University of Washington Press, 2018), 54.

CHAPTER 11

Woosh.Jee.Een, Pulling Together

REPATRIATION'S HEALING TIDE

Lucy Fowler Williams with contributions by Robert Starbard

LITUYA BAY IS LOCATED ON THE OUTER NORTH PACIFIC COAST OF SOUTHEAST Alaska within the ancestral territory of the Tlingit T'akdeintaan clan (Raven moiety) of Hoonah.[1] A cherished yet foreboding place of myth and legend, its spirits, great waves, and treacherous tides are remembered in stories, songs, and art.[2] In the nineteenth century, Tlingit Wooshkeetaan (Eagle moiety) artist Ctuwax'ilge was commissioned to allegorize the bay in a garment named the Rock of Lituya.[3] This represented "a last refuge against the onrushing tide of modernity" where T'akdeintaan clan ancestors have sought safety, physically and metaphorically, through hardship and turmoil.[4] This chapter relays a story of the robe's collection in 1924 for the University of Pennsylvania Museum of Archaeology and Anthropology (Penn Museum) by Tlingit curator Louis Shotridge, its repatriation, and finally its reintegration at Hoonah. In relaying elements of this case study, our objective is to highlight the possibilities and potential outcomes of the Native American Graves Protection and Repatriation Act (NAGPRA).[5]

In 1990 NAGPRA was signed into law to correct some of the injustices of past collecting practices in the United States and to reframe the prevailing museum paradigm to acknowledge that Native American objects and human remains carry cultural, religious, spiritual, and social significance that is to be valued as much as, or more than, scientific analysis.[6] Creating a set of legal pathways, the law enables tribes to claim objects of vital importance held in American museums, including human remains, associated and unassociated funerary objects, sacred objects, and objects of cultural patrimony. Sacred objects are "needed by specific religious leaders for the continuance of Native American religious practices." Cultural patrimony held "ongoing, central significance for entire communities at the time of its alienation." An important aspect of NAGPRA, separate from the above definitions, is the right of possession.[7]

As the law is written, claimants must show that the item in question was inalienable at the time of its collection; museums must show that they acquired objects with

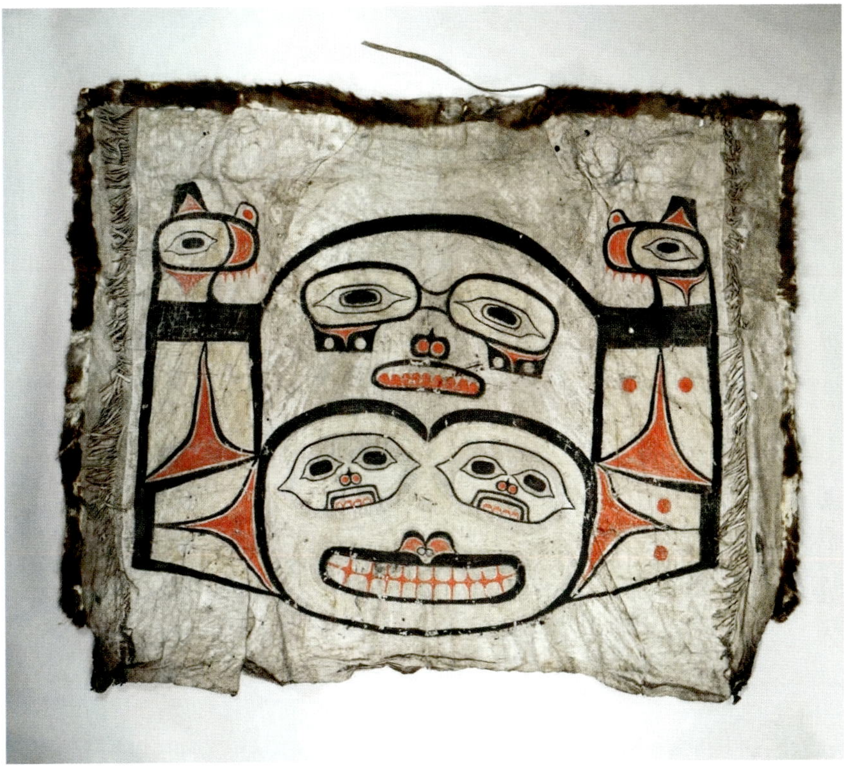

11.1. T'akdeintaan Rock of Lituya robe. Collected by Louis Shotridge, November 22, 1924. Photograph courtesy of the Penn Museum Archives.

the voluntary consent of an individual or group with the authority of alienation. If disputes arise, a NAGPRA board is available to make recommendations. Though complexities and challenges still exist, and work remains to be done by both museums and tribes, museums have developed an improved understanding of Native needs and concerns.[8] The NAGPRA process has created new opportunities for museums and tribes to work together in support of tribal needs and common goals.[9] In that vein, the Hoonah Indian Association (HIA) and the Penn Museum have developed a new partnership that combines their perspectives to address research questions prioritized within the Tlingit community on topics of history, genealogy, and archaeology that potentially move beyond a museum-collections focus.

November 12–22, 1924: Hoonah, Alaska

On the cold Wednesday morning of November 12, 1924, Tlingit Kaagwaantaan Louis Shotridge crossed into Port Frederick.[10] He cut his engine as he entered Hoonah Harbor to take some photographs of the small town from offshore. His stiff hands fumbled for his camera as he scanned the hillside. There was snow in the mountains, and Hoonah's modern clapboard clan houses hugged the shoreline. A bright American flag hung from almost every upstairs window. Seagulls huddled on the

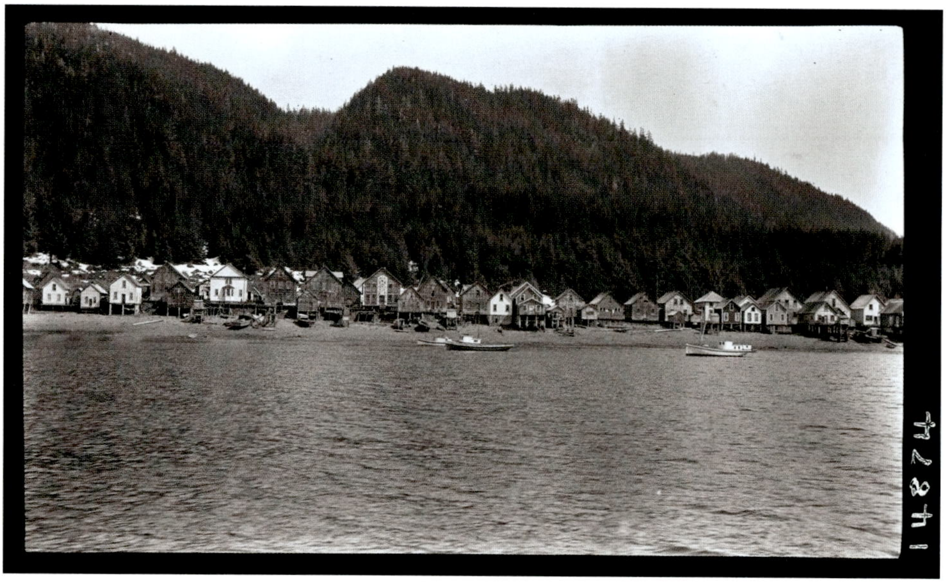

11.2. Hoonah, 1924. Photograph by Louis Shotridge. Photograph courtesy of the Penn Museum Archives.

rooftops, and the flags snapped in the wind (see chapter 14 by Ishmael Hope, in this volume).

As he reached the dock, Shotridge saw that the boardwalk, fresh with wet snow, was decorated with a wrought-iron archway. Draped in evergreens, its words welcomed members to the annual meeting of the Alaska Native Brotherhood (ANB). Wearing long trench coats, spats, and woolen driver's caps against the weather, camp delegates hurried along the boardwalk.[11] The Native Christian organization had been going for over a decade, and its goals of acculturation through education, acceptance of settler religion, and by speaking English had helped ANB members (and Tlingit more broadly) gain American citizenship.[12] Although President Coolidge had just passed the US Indian Citizenship Act, Tlingit people could not own land and were barred from hunting on much of their own territories. Hoonah Camp 12 would host the Grand Camp gathering over the next several days, and Shotridge and his cohort continued the fight, drafting new resolutions for land rights, fishing rights, equal access to education for their children and desegregation.[13]

Louis V. Shotridge, Stoowukáa (ca. 1882–1937), was an elite Kaagwaantaan of the Wolf/Eagle moiety. He grew up north of Hoonah, over the Chilkat Range in the remote and conservative village of Klukwan.[14] Shotridge lived in the era of assimilation, and in many ways his life epitomizes this period of intense transition. His life and career stretch across missionization, beginning with Reverend Sheldon Jackson in 1880, the US Navy bombing of the Tlingit village of Angoon in 1882, the Alaska Organic Act (which established civil government and compulsory elementary education, land allotment, the legislation of fisheries), and segregation (which Tlingit continued to challenge through the 1930s). Shotridge was educated at the strict Presbyterian Mission School in neighboring Haines, where he was trained in English and to succeed in a white man's world.[15] As in most Tlingit towns, "if you did not assimilate you basically went away. There were no other choices."[16] The Christian missionaries in Haines insisted that only after Tlingit families sold off all their old things could they become Christian, and many did so.[17] "Louis saw the assimilation policies as a death knell to [his] culture," said Robert Starbard, tribal administrator. "Watching the regalia, the totems being destroyed. This was quite an affront to his sensibilities."[18]

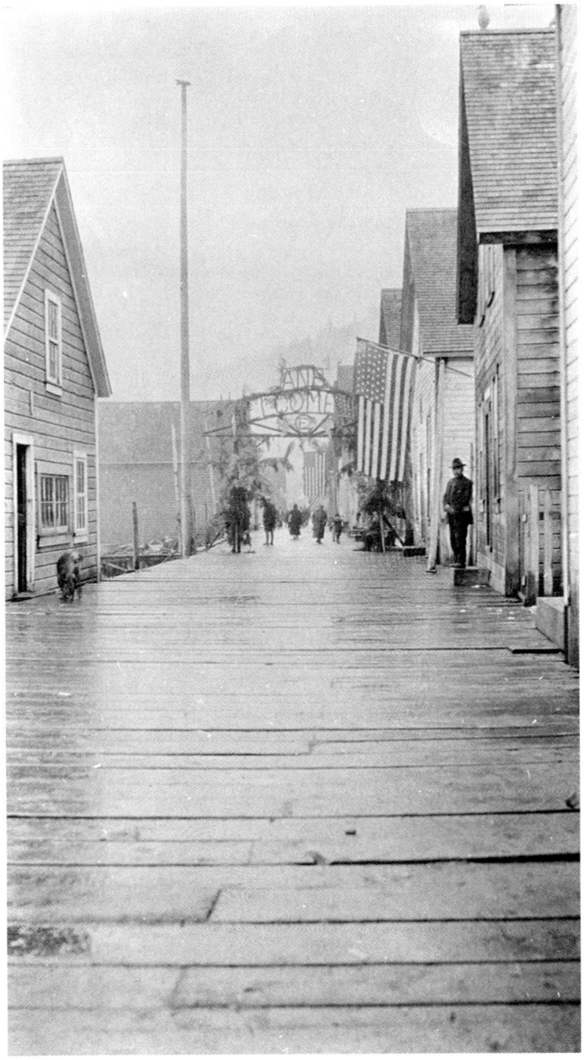

11.3. The boardwalk at Hoonah welcomes Alaska Native Brotherhood members, November 12, 1924. Photograph by Louis Shotridge. Photograph courtesy of the Penn Museum Archives.

Shotridge was no stranger to the market for tribal art; he was exhibiting Tlingit masks at the 1906 Portland Fair when he met George Gordon of the Penn Museum.[19] The two hit it off and in time Shotridge's elite position and knowledge as a Tlingit culture bearer earned him a job at the Philadelphia museum.[20] Gordon hired him in 1912 and, together with Franz Boas in New York City, trained Shotridge in ethnology, museology, and linguistics.[21] After three years, Gordon sent Shotridge back to Alaska to acquire Tlingit collections for his growing Penn Museum.[22] Much has been written about Shotridge—the first Northwest Coast Native to experience long-term employment in a museum, the first Tlingit with academic training in linguistics and ethnography, and the first indigenous transcriber and translator of Tlingit oral literature.[23] Employed for eighteen years, Shotridge assembled a five-hundred-piece collection, which is among the best in the world.

On Shotridge's previous visit to Hoonah, almost ten months earlier, a fellow Kaagwaantaan clanswoman

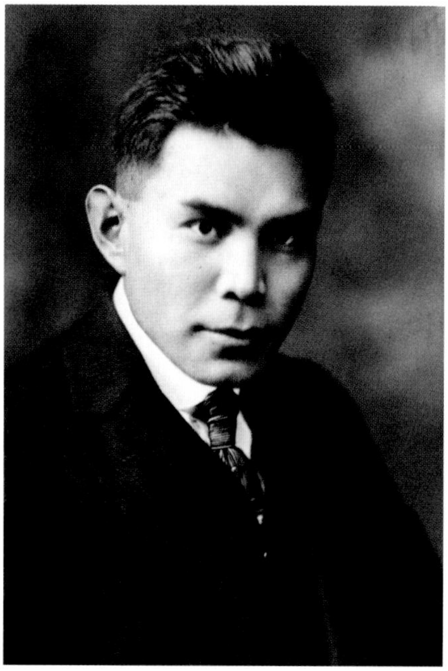

11.4. Louis Shotridge, elected president of the Alaska Native Brotherhood, 1930. Courtesy of the Sealaska Heritage Foundation Archives.

had offered some "old things."[24] In September a T'akdeintaan clan member offered items in his possession for sale.[25] Archie White (Dimitrii Tukk'axaaw, 1859–1939) was the head of the T'akdeintaan Mt. Fairweather House, the most prominent Tlingit clan in Hoonah at the time.[26] White was also the first Tlingit Russian Orthodox priest in all of Southeast Alaska and president of Hoonah's Holy Cross Brotherhood until his death in 1939. At age sixty-five, American citizenship now a certainty, and with his maternal nephews also parish leaders, White seems to have held onto some items and sold many others.[27] Shotridge purchased forty-five objects for $500, half the asking price proposed two months before.[28]

After ten days of meetings in Hoonah, Shotridge cruised home to his winter quarters in Sitka. He set to work on the T'akdeintaan objects, typing up his notes and recording the histories he had been told.[29] Until now, "none of the many collectors and curio buyers had approached that which is most important, the objects that represent the honorable history of the people."[30] To correct this, Shotridge set out to record the histories of the "once great" clans through their clan art.[31] He had already secured good examples from the Kaagwaantaan, L'ooknax.ádi, and Deisheetaan, and the Hoonah pieces strengthened his growing collection. Safely cared for and displayed in the Philadelphia museum, they would "stand as evidence of the Tlingit claim of a place in primitive culture" alongside other world cultures such as Greece, Egypt, and China.[32] One ceremonial garment, the Rock of Lituya robe, heralded the tenacity of the T'akdeintaan especially well, and Shotridge was eager to get the story down. He unfolded the painted robe and set to work.[33]

Shotridge's cataloging system was a microcosm of Tlingit social organization. Hoonah had four resident matrilineal clans (T'akdeintaan Ravens, Chookaneidi Eagles, Wooshkeetaan Eagles, and Kaagwaantaan Eagles) and each held ancestral territory and rights to natural resources around Glacier Bay. All Tlingit were divided into two matrilineal exogamous halves or moieties, Ravens and Eagles (Wolf), which regulated marriage and ritual practices. The T'akdeintaan were Ravens, and Mt. Fairweather House was the leading house at the time. Each clan had heraldic crests and variations. Within each clan were several houses, each with its

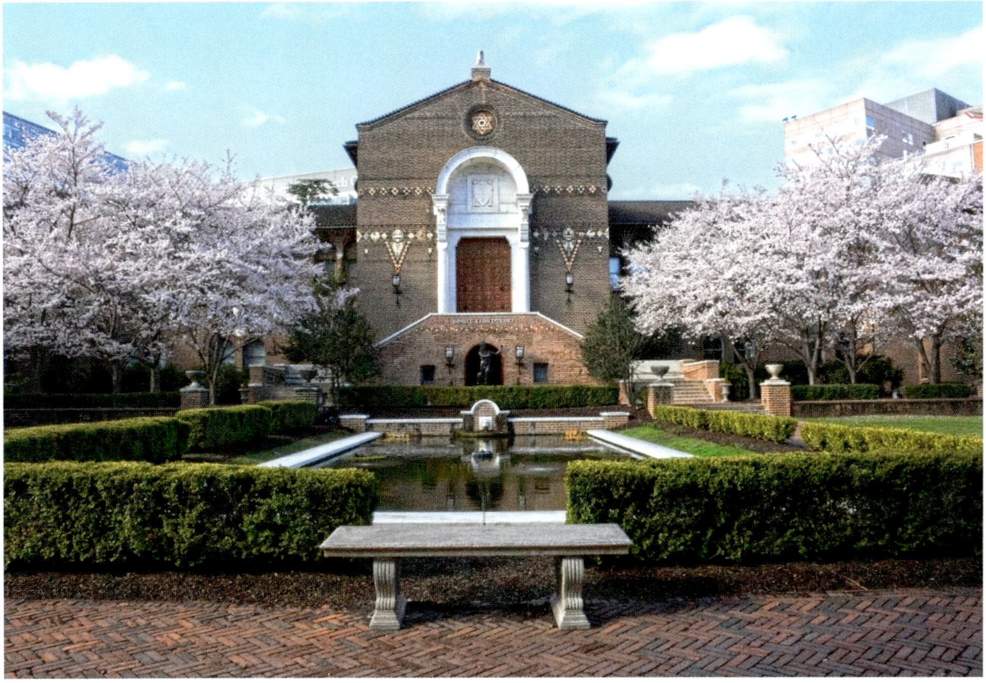

11.5. University of Pennsylvania Museum of Archaeology and Anthropology, Philadelphia. Photograph courtesy of the Penn Museum Archives.

own house leader, personal names, histories, and ceremonial prerogatives or "emblems" called at.óow.[34] At.óow were important clan crests that were owned communally.[35] True crest art was commissioned by clan or house leaders from a craftsman of the opposite "side," named and publicly validated or "brought out" in the ritual context of a "call together" or ḵu.éek' (*potlatch*), an invitation or feast.[36]

Shotridge described the "Rock of Lituya" robe as a ceremonial robe made of finely tanned caribou hide, fringed on two sides, edged with martin fur, and with a painted design on one side.[37] It had been commissioned by the T'akdeintaan (Raven) Mt. Fairweather Snail House Master, Tuqaxawu I, from Ctuwax'ilge, an (opposite) Wooshkeetaan (Eagle moiety) artist for the occasion of a Kaagwaantaan ḵu.éek' (*call together*) in Sitka. The robe had been passed down to two subsequent House-masters, Yakuan and Tukawu II. Shotridge recorded its story: "Amidst the unmerciful waters of Lituya Bay lies a once time-honored reef, 'the last hope of the lost man.' A hunter, more than once, who had been carried away by the out-rushing tide, held on to this rock as the last hold of safety. Such has been the experience of the last of our House Master[s] in this onrush of modern life, which incited him to adopt this rock, of our former home, as an object of reverence for his family."[38]

The robe's painted faces were the double-headed rock of Tltu-ah and on either side the angry waters of the rapids.[39] Of the forty-five objects, only a few were like

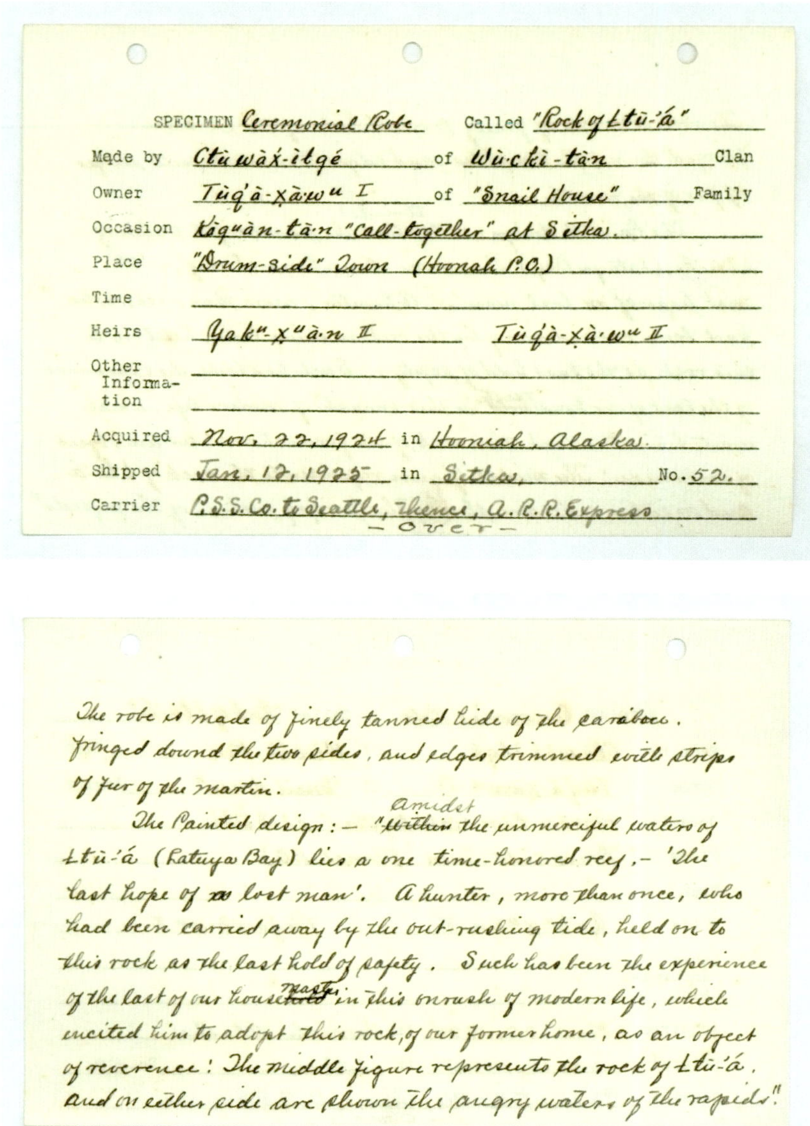

SPECIMEN Ceremonial Robe Called "Rock of Ltū-'á"

Made by Ctùwàx-ìlgé of Wù·ckì-tàn Clan

Owner Tùq'à-xà·wᵘ I of "Snail House" Family

Occasion Kòqᵘàn-tà·n "Call-together" at Sitka.

Place "Drum-side" Town (Hoonah P.O.)

Time

Heirs Yakᵘ-xᵘà·n II Tùq'à-xà·wᵘ II

Other Information

Acquired Nov. 22, 1924 in Hoonah, Alaska.

Shipped Jan. 12, 1925 in Sitka, No. 52.

Carrier P.S.S. Co. to Seattle, thence, A.R.R. Express

— over —

The robe is made of finely tanned hide of the caraboo. fringed down the two sides, and edges trimmed with strips of fur of the martin.

The Painted design: — "~~Within~~ amidst the unmerciful waters of Ltū-'á (Latuya Bay) lies a one time-honored reef, — 'The last hope of a lost man'. A hunter, more than once, who had been carried away by the out-rushing tide, held on to this rock as the last hold of safety. Such has been the experience of the last of our house masters in this onrush of modern life, which incited him to adopt this rock, of our former home, as an object of reverence: The middle figure represents the rock of Ltū-'á, and on either side are shown the angry waters of the rapids."

11.6. Louis Shotridge's catalog card, (a) front and (b) back, for the Rock of Lituya robe, Courtesy of the Alaska State Library.

the robe and held important crests with historic descriptions. Several of these recorded events in the lives of leading shamans in the T'akdeintaan history, including the Box Drum, Owl of the Heavens mask, Raven Head-cover, and Loon Spirit Rattle. Other objects held Raven creation stories, such as the Ravine frontlet, made for a rebuilding of the Mt. Fairweather House when their ancestors lived up north at Dry Bay. The Commander of the Tides dance mask had eyes that opened and closed. Two months after Shotridge's return from Hoonah, President Coolidge declared the Hoonah Natives' homeland Glacier Bay National Monument and Reserve.[40] With the stroke of a pen in Washington, DC, this meant more restrictions on subsistence hunting and fishing at Lituya and Bartlett Cove and on gathering berries, cockles, and "gumboots" (an edible marine mollusk) from their beloved "ice box" of Glacier Bay.[41] As Shotridge carefully packed and shipped the Mt. Fairweather possessions via freighter to Seattle and express train on east, he felt relief knowing the "old things" would be safe and appreciated in Philadelphia.

It is important to note that in some Tlingit communities Louis Shotridge remains a controversial figure to this day because he acquired clan objects considered to be owned communally. Some believe that by sending collections to Philadelphia he turned his back on his culture, selling out to make a profit. But as this and other essays have shown, though there were exceptions, Shotridge's detailed records reveal that he collected from clan and house leaders who during these decades of assimilation had the authority to sell the objects, and that his motivations were on behalf of the Tlingit community rather than for his own gain.[42] Shotridge's goals were to hold up the historical greatness of the clans and to find an institutional sanctuary for Native art objects seen at the time as obsolete, negative, and opposed in a society advocating assimilation to Western norms of patrilineal inheritance and Christianity. As such, his collecting goals were fully compatible with the progressive modernist agenda of the ANB. This was the salvage paradigm of his mentors in anthropology, in tune with Shotridge's own upbringing.[43] Hoonah tribal members have grappled with this history. As Starbard had explained: "Tlingit people of Hoonah for a long time really did feel that he stole them, hoodwinked whomever, and depending on which clan you talked to, it was either Archie White, the House Leader who sold them, or more deviously it was his wife who was of the opposite moiety."[44]

Certainly the reasons for the sales to Shotridge (and others) were due to the ongoing effects of colonialism writ large and its destructive impacts on Tlingit cultural practices. For this reason, Tlingit clans have been active in this area and are using NAGPRA as a means to strengthen and heal their communities from the ongoing and devastating effects of the changing times, specifically the repercussions of the anthropological collection of their material culture.[45]

The Request for Repatriation of These Objects

In 1995 Penn Museum received a repatriation claim for the Snail House objects from the Huna Totem Corporation (HTC). The request transformed into a competing claim between HTC and the Hoonah Indian Association (HIA), a federally recognized tribe. After six years the groups came together and submitted a revised claim by HIA. Early versions of the claims failed to address each individual object as either sacred or cultural patrimony, instead treating them as groups. In 2002 and 2009 the Trustees of the University of Pennsylvania asserted their right of possession to the objects. Though details of the decisions are confidential and thus not available for inclusion in this chapter, the university on both occasions agreed to work outside of NAGPRA to repatriate eight objects that met NAGPRA's definitions of sacred object and/or object of cultural patrimony outright, and to find a way to resituate the remaining objects in Alaska with the clan. A notice of Intent to Repatriate was published in 2010, and the Tribe took possession of the eight objects including the Lituya Bay Robe in 2011.[46]

The university also proposed a new partnership that would focus on educational endeavors into the future. In so doing, Penn recognized the spirit of the NAGPRA legislation, acknowledged the university's ongoing respect for the Tlingit people and its desire to continue a relationship with the Tribe that began with Louis Shotridge, and supported Native American religious and cultural integrity. Unsatisfied with this outcome, the Tribe requested a hearing with the national NAGPRA Review Board; a 2010 meeting found unanimously in the Tribe's favor. With NAGPRA Review Board recommendations nonbinding, Penn remained hopeful the Tribe would accept its offer to resituate the remaining objects in Alaska and consider forming a partnership. Six years later, a discussion, initiated by Robert Starbard, HIA's CEO and tribal administrator, concluded with revisions and compromise by both parties regarding aspects of the language of Penn's proposal. A formal memorandum of understanding (MOU) was signed in October 2017. As Starbard explained:

> You might start to wonder how we might have changed our view of what Louis did. It's more than that assimilation went away and was replaced by self-governance. It is simpler than that . . . June 14, 1944. The community of Hoonah burned to the ground.[47] Every house, every drum, was destroyed, except for what was thrown out the windows. When we rethink Louis today, it's not hard to say, but for this collection and the care Penn Museum did for our T'akdeintaan collection we would not have any of it. It has taken time, taken a lot of meetings with elders.[48]

Until the Hoonah Indian Association completes the construction of its own museum and cultural center in Hoonah (currently in the planning stages), the Tribe requested the remainder of the T'akdeintaan Mt. Fairweather Snail House collection be housed at the Alaska State Museum, Juneau, where they are available for use by the HIA and the T'akdeintaan at any time and in perpetuity. When exhibited at any location, the collection will be labeled as cared for jointly by the Hoonah Indian Association and Penn Museum. The museum may also request use of the objects for future educational purposes as mutually agreed. In addition, in keeping with the "balance" critical to the Tlingit, a partnership was made with both Eagle and Raven clans to work together on future educational projects. As Starbard put it: "The concept of the idea of a relationship stems from a resolution by Penn. Some tribal members were against it. They wondered, what are they wanting to extract from us now? I saw it as a tool, a way to pull together to find a common basis for a relationship. We can't do it, [perpetuate our culture] alone, the challenges are too great."[49]

October 14–15, 2017: T'akdeintaan Clan Memorial K̲ u.éek', Hoonah

I check my phone. It is noon in the gymnasium as the k̲u.éek' (*modern-day "party"*) slowly gets started. Guests trickle in and the leading men huddle together in serious discussion around the at.óow table; their beaded seal fur and deerskin vests show their Raven and Eagle crests, and they dart out of the gym, only to be back again a few minutes later. The white box we packed up at the Penn Museum six years earlier is in pristine condition. With great care, they lift the Rock of Lituya robe and place it underneath the Mt. Fairweather Woman Spirit Hat in the center of the table.[50]

Repatriated in 2011, the robe is reincorporated into the ritual k̲u.éek' context. It is exhilarating to see the Mt. Fairweather Dog Spirit Hat paired with a Chilkat blanket; the Mt. Fairweather Hat, and Kittywake Hat, like dressed relatives, are each paired with robes as well.[51] My Penn colleagues and I carried by hand three more of the forty-five objects for the occasion—Raven the Pilgrim Rattle, the blanket with Chilkat strips, and cedar bark headdress—which are positioned close by.[52] Also prominent are portraits of the honored deceased: Adam Greenwald, Frank O. Williams Jr., Victor Bean, Freda Borchick, Erling Skaflestad, Paul Rudolph, and Irene Lampe.

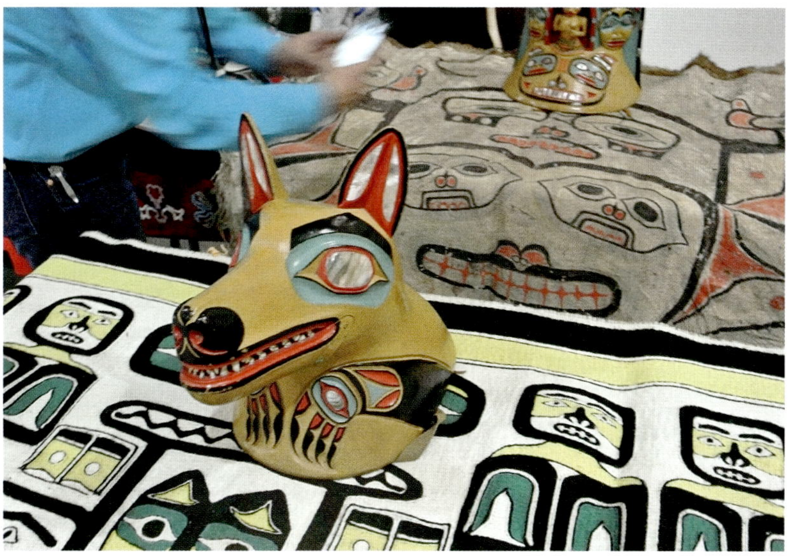

11.7. Hoonah Raven at.óow table showing the Rock of Lituya robe with the Mt. Fairweather Woman Spirit Hat (top right), Hoonah k̲ u. éek', October 14, 2017. Photograph by Lucy Fowler Williams.

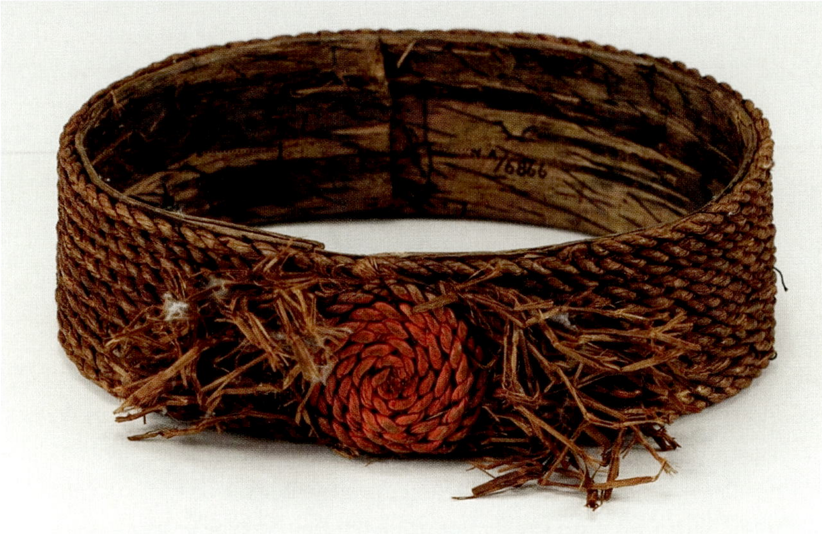

a

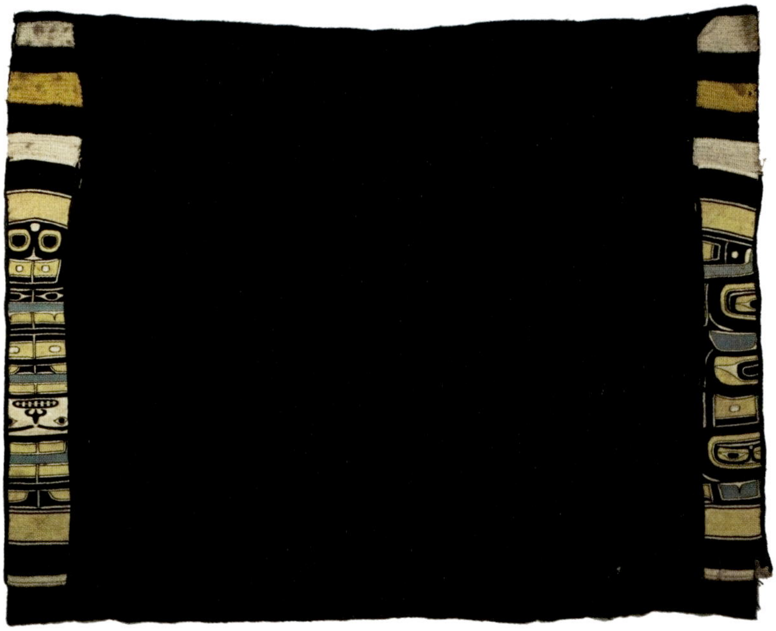

b

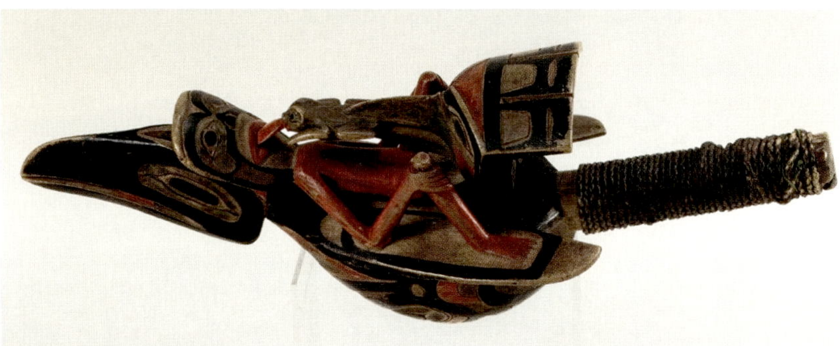

c

"Put this on," whispers clan mother and elder leader Marlene Johnson, as she gently thrusts a red button blanket into my arms. "Stand over there with the others." The wool blanket is heavy, and I feel its warm embrace. I wait patiently for the naa kaanx'i yán (*in-law from the opposite side*) to put the black marks on my cheeks during the initial mourning portion of the ceremony.[53] Harold Jacobs, cultural specialist for Central Council of Tlingit and Haida Indian Tribes of Alaska, had taught us about Tlingit protocol over the years, and I had a good understanding and appreciation of what was happening around me.[54] Two days before, at the Welcome Home Ceremony in Juneau, Penn colleagues Stacey Espenlaub and Wendy White were adopted and I received an honorary name, that of Marlene Johnson's grandmother, Daax Keil Aatch, whose Western name was also Lucy Williams.[55] This was very special for each of us, and it was an honor to participate in the celebration.[56] We stand close together with approximately twenty clan members, robes touching, surrounding the widow and her children at the front of the gym. As the family sings the grieving songs, they quietly wipe away tears, hold each other's hands, and stare at the floor. Though I can't understand the words, I feel the sadness. Slow and solemn. I can still feel it now.

The Raven hosts carefully share their stories with their Eagle guests. Following protocol, the Rock of Lituya is placed on leading Raven elders by their Eagle opposites. It is also placed on family members of the deceased as well as young men as a way of honoring and teaching their grandchildren. On each occasion, they call out the names of their ancestors and effectively gather the people at Lituya Bay. Through song, oratory, and the physicality of the robe itself, they are wrapped in the arms and history of their ancestors, connected physically to the spirit and strength of their homeland, the bay and the rock, and to the spirits of their family members. After much discussion, the blanket, headdress, and rattle brought from the Penn Museum are placed on elder Kenny Grant. Arms stretched, he walks slowly and carefully back and forth, introducing his newly returned ancestors to his guests.

Marlene quietly motions us up again. This time all the Snail House women don heavy red fringes that hang from our ears. Standing closely and swaying back and forth, the T'akdeintaan women sing the wave song, singing the waves into motion; remembering the drownings, the fringes mark the heaviness of the grief. This is what Tlingit art is made and designed to do. In following these traditions, clan members do what their ancestors taught them, and this is the greatest honor they can give them.[57] In this way they also look forward and train their children and

11.8. Mt. Fairweather House (a) cedar bark headdress, (b) blanket with Chilkat strips, and (c) Pilgrim Raven Rattle hand-carried from the University of Pennsylvania Museum of Archaeology and Anthropology for the Hoonah k̲u.éek', October 14, 2017. Photographs courtesy of the Penn Museum.

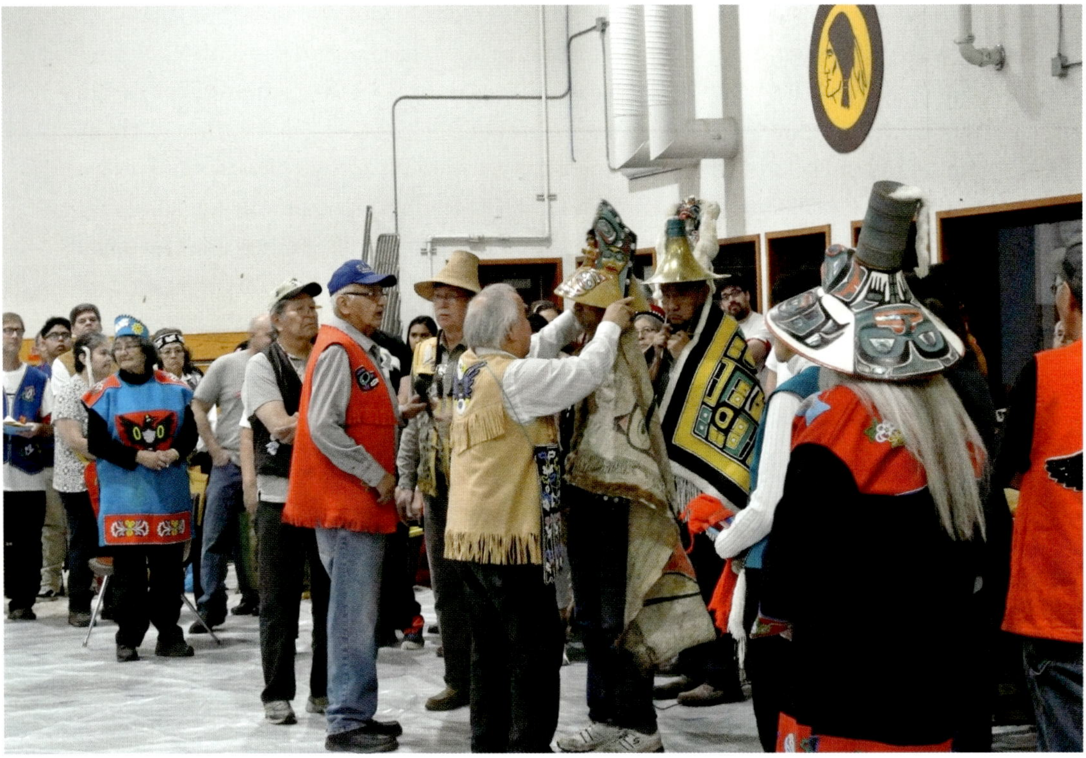

11.9. Eagles dressing their Raven hosts, at the Hoonah ḵu.éek', October 14, 2017. Photograph by Lucy Fowler Williams.

grandchildren to do this in the future. The old Rock of Lituya marks the persistence and tenacity of the T'akdeintaan.

The "party" continues through the night. Now it is the Eagles' turn to reciprocate, and they display their clan art. Each group holds up their named at.óow and, with song and words from the heart, tell the stories of their ancestors' journey. Together with the material objects their words offer comfort, love, and support and sooth the grieving Raven hosts. As they have done for generations, their words and actions strengthen their bonds to the grieving families. As one participant said in a similar ceremony in 1968: "This brother-in law (blanket) has come here for your grief, yes, to remove it from you. And yes, now that blanket: it's just as if it has become a towel in my hand, to wipe away your tears."[58] Tlingit crest art has always been used for spiritual healing. Only by giving comfort to the living of the opposite moiety can symbolic comfort pass over to the clan departed in the spirit world, and in the process, bring spiritual healing and removal of grief to the hosts.[59]

We Ravens work hard through the night to host and comfort our Eagle guests. The party is held by the family to say thank you for the help, love, and support over the previous year. We serve two hundred Eagles coffee, lemonade, and water, and the

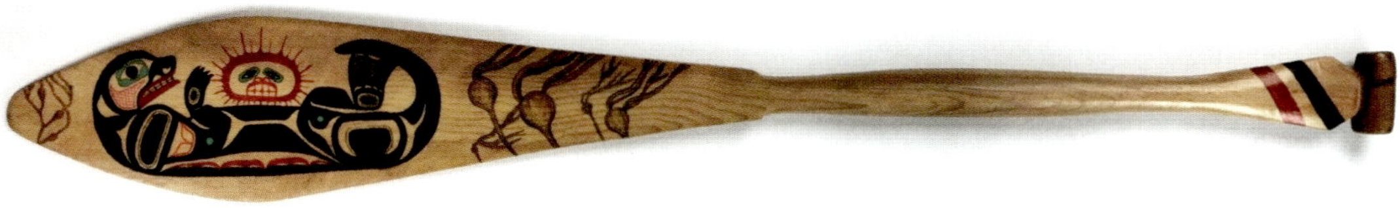

11.10. A T'akdeintaan healing-canoe paddle, gifted to the University of Pennsylvania Museum of Archaeology and Anthropology on October 11, 2017, reminds us that we are in the canoe together and on a new journey. Photograph courtesy of the Penn Museum.

favorite meals of the deceased. Frank O. Williams's family serves ham and fried bread, smoked salmon spread and crackers, and chocolate cake; a few hours later the Greenwald and Rudolph families offer Nayadee (Coho) salmon and potatoes as well as herring egg salad. Still later, Adam Greenwald's family offers deer stew and Sailor Boy crackers. Working in pairs, we literally run distributing enormous sums of gifts—hand-picked apples and berries, oranges and bananas, and hundreds of jars of dry goods, jarred Coho, and sockeye, berries, and fish oil, bath towels, pens and paper, sewing kits, devil's club ointment, dish towels, watches, more salmon, creams, shampoos, clothing, baskets, and blankets. In between gifting and feeding, we entertain our guests with song and dance with open hands to push away the grief. Around 3:00 a.m., Robert Starbard, now in his role as caretaker of the at.óow of the Takdeintaan Tsal Xaan Hit–Mt. Fairweather House aka Tax' Hit–Snail House, publicly thanks and honors the Penn Museum. He introduces us to the crowd and hands me a beautifully carved and painted canoe paddle, a gift that recognizes how far we've come as well as the journey ahead.[60] The party continues until dawn.

Supporting Tribes in New Ways

Since 1990, NAGPRA has brought transformative change to American museums, perhaps most important the practical requirement of consultation, which necessitates dialogue and discussion. Tribal members often say "NAGPRA has no teeth" because museums still hold the controls to make final determinations.[61] In this case study, the University of Pennsylvania followed both the letter and spirit of the law. Even though it held the right of possession to the objects Shotridge collected, with help from the Tribe, it found a way to return the objects to the Tlingit people. As early as 2002, Penn Museum expressed interest in collaborating with the Tribe on mutually beneficial projects such as educational programs, research, and visiting artist and internship programs. Though we ultimately may have differences of opinion, the museum and university are grateful for the respectful leadership and persistence of Ronald Williams, Marlene Johnson, Robert Starbard, and others who have opened this discussion inside the Tlingit community and with us at Penn.

With time and conversation, and by listening and learning about one another's views, we ultimately agreed to combine our efforts with the intention of contributing to the ongoing vitality of Tlingit culture (rather than only preserving historic Tlingit culture). In 2018 the Hoonah Indian Association proposed two joint anthropological research projects with the University of Pennsylvania Museum, which are currently under discussion. The first involves working with early twentieth-century Hoonah census data to corroborate traditional Tlingit names with later English names. A second proposal involves an archaeological study and mapping of Hoonah's graveyard at Pitt Island using LIDAR (light detection and ranging) and ground-penetrating radar. Combining our resources, these projects will enrich Hoonah's understanding of its clan ancestry and history, build traditional and historical knowledge, and support Tlingit cultural revitalization. The full impact of the return of the T'akdeintaan Mt. Fairweather Snail House ancestors through repatriation may be known only to the clan. Starbard says:

> Yes, the return has been healing. The first objects returned have played an important role in memorial ceremonies and there has been a healing. Regardless of the semantics of how our discussions are framed, for the clan elders, it doesn't matter. If not for Shotridge's and Penn's efforts, they would have been lost in the fire of 1944. We equate it to a kind of universal karma that has allowed a healing to take place. We have had some serious incidents in Hoonah in recent years that have embroiled the community, but we are now becoming whole. This healing continues to provide hope and it is crucial for future generations to use and learn from.[62]

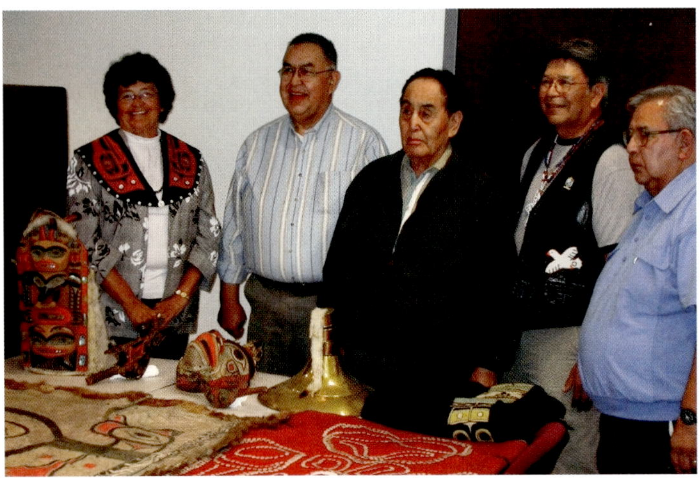

11.11. Consultation visit at University of Pennsylvania Museum of Archaeology and Anthropology, 2005. Photograph by Lucy Fowler Williams.

The NAGPRA process has also been beneficial for the Penn Museum. It has been strengthening for museum staff to talk with Hoonah community members about Louis Shotridge in his own time and to discuss how he adapted like so many Tlingit of his generation, with ambition, hard work, skill, and determination to preserve Tlingit art, history, and culture. Through the lengthy process of this repatriation, we have sensed a softening of understanding of Shotridge's vision and efforts within the Tlingit community. The claim process has reminded the university that the collections we steward in Philadelphia are not passive art objects but often living beings associated with vital communities in real time. Tlingit clan art functions in ritual contexts to remember those who came before and to sooth the grief of the living. Activated through reciprocal dialogue and in balance, it feeds the spirits and eases the grief of those left behind. This story exemplifies the extraordinary ways in which Tlingit communities, and Native Americans more broadly, continue to live with art as containers of knowledge and history that tie them to their ancestors and places on the landscape and forge new pathways to the future. Here, historic emblems hold an enduring life force and, through their unique practices of communicating through balance and reciprocity, hold the community together.

Finally, HIA's interest in collaborating further with the Penn Museum by directing research questions to develop new knowledge about Tlingit history and anthropology has strengthened our bond and gives new direction to our relationship. Rather than focusing on our differences, we are combining our strengths to find common ground on future educational projects to help encourage the young people in the community and to protect and perpetuate Tlingit culture.

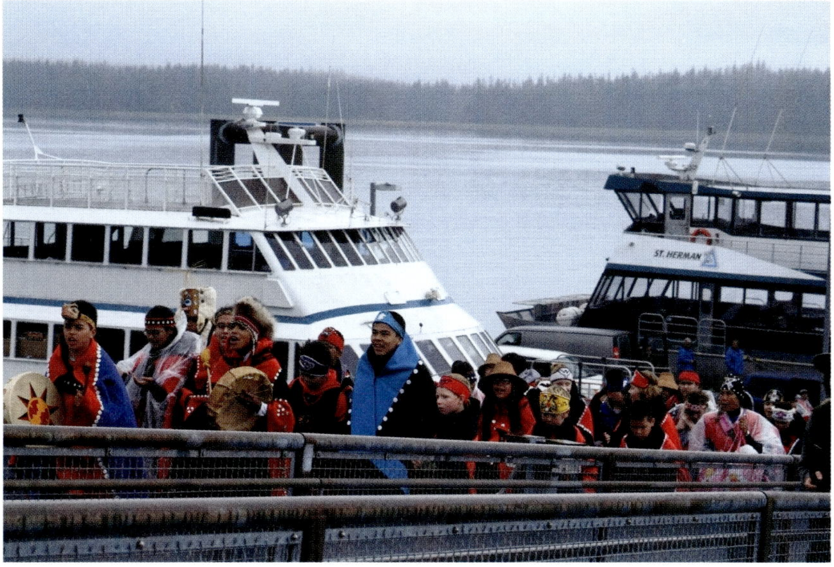

11.12. Children of Hoonah in song as they attend the healing ceremony at Bartlett Cove, August 2018. Photograph by Lucy Fowler Williams.

August 25, 2018: Glacier Bay, Alaska

As the final shipment of Snail House objects arrives from Philadelphia, it travels first to the Xunaa Shuká Hít (Huna Ancestors House) at Bartlett Cove in Glacier Bay to be welcomed by the ancestors.[63] The objects sit quietly inside this magical, peace-filled hand-hewn cedar house, surrounded by a carved house screen and four massive house posts that visualize the origin and migration stories of the four Hoonah clans. Clan leaders, state dignitaries, clan members, and guests gather outside to witness the raising of a new twenty-foot red cedar healing pole to commemorate Hoonah's improving relationships with the National Park, recent healing programs in the community around issues of domestic violence, and the return of the collection and a new partnership with Penn. The new pole honors and promotes a Tlingit copresence inside the park and its symbol of Lituya Bay is one of many visual emblems that tell of the Hoonah clans' journeys and tenacity through time. Like the old art in practice, this new art brings strength and healing to the Hoonah people spiritually.

In describing the artwork, Starbard in effect described the qualities needed for the HIA and Penn Museum to work successfully together:

> The exterior panel of the Xunaa Shuká Hít at Bartlett Cove demonstrates tenacity. On one side, the left side of the tribal house is the Raven opening the box of knowledge. On the right side is the Eagle, in the clutches of the Eagle's talons is the tinaa [*a Tlingit object*], symbolic of wealth, but for us, the wealth we are

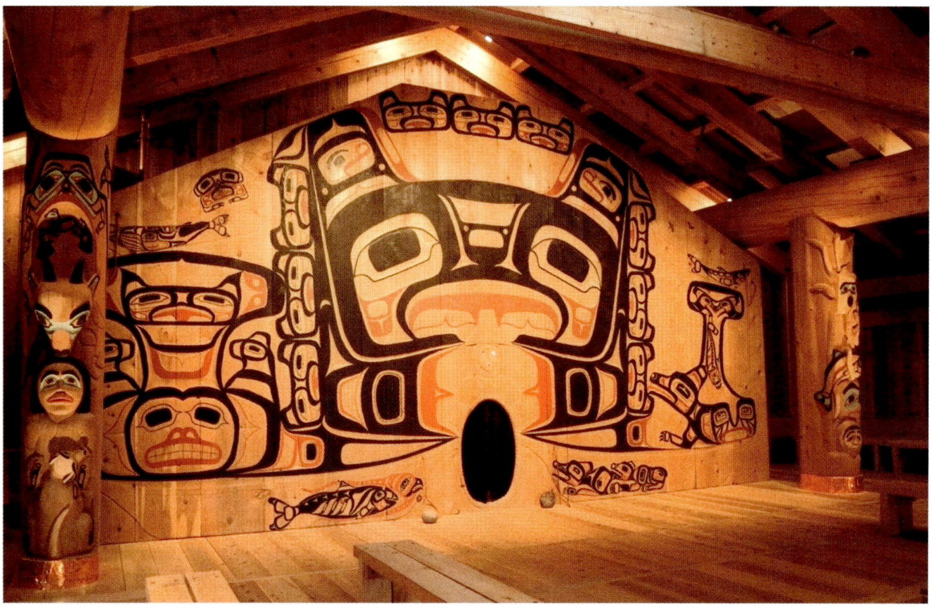

11.13. The Xunna Shuká Hit interior, Bartlett Cove, Glacier Bay. Photograph by Lucy Fowler Williams.

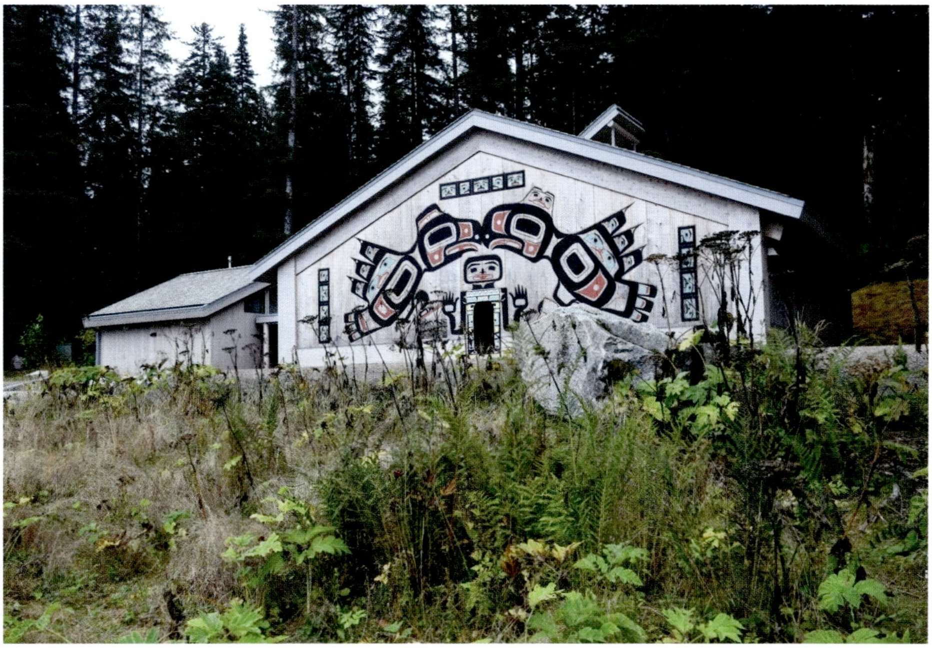

11.14. Xunna Shuká Hit, Bartlett Cove, Glacier Bay. Photograph by Lucy Fowler Williams.

holding on to is our culture. It is not necessarily the tinaa, but the eagle that is clutching the tinaa. For an eagle to release his talons he must release the opposite pressure. If too big he will swim to shore to press down to release his talons. Here the Master carver is trying to depict that we have held onto our culture with the tenacity of the Eagle and we refuse to let it go. . . . Our relationship [with Penn Museum] has grown and has been fostered. We are at the very beginning and we are trying to find out how it might work. If any of you are married, you know a relationship takes work, communication, tenacity, and compromise.[64]

NOTES

Details in this chapter are taken from Louis Shotridge's ethnographic notes, letters, and writings housed in the Archives of the Penn Museum and the Alaska State Library; see Louis Shotridge Digital Archive, University of Pennsylvania Museum of Archaeology and Anthropology (UPM) Archives, www.penn.museum/collections/Shotridge/index.html.

1 Tlingit society is arranged by matrilineal clans of descent. All Tlingit are also organized by matrilineal exogamous moieties, Raven and Eagle (Wolf). Four clans settled Hoonah: the T'akdeintaan (Raven), Wooshkeetaan (Eagle), Chookaneidi (Eagle), and Kaagwaantaan (Eagle). For a good introduction, see Sergei Kan, *Memory Eternal: Tlingit Culture and Russian Orthodox Christianity through Two Centuries* (Seattle: University of Washington Press, 1999); Walter R. Goldschmidt and Theodore R. Haas, *Haa Aani Our Land: Tlingit and Haida*

Land Rights and Use, edited by Thomas Thornton (Seattle: University of Washington Press; Juneau, AK: Sealaska Heritage Foundation, 1998), 196.

2 G. T. Emmons, "Native Account of the Meeting of La Perouse and the Tlingit," *American Anthropologist* 13, no. 2 (April–June 1911): 294–98; Frederica De Laguna, *Under Mt. Saint Elias, the History and Culture of the Yakutat Tlingit* (Washington, DC: Smithsonian Institution Press, 1972), 273; and Rosita F. Worl, "Tlingit At.óow: Tangible and Intangible Property," PhD diss., Harvard University, 1998, 304.

3 Some Tlingit art is produced in balance according to proper clan protocol.

4 Louis Shotridge's catalog description, University of Pennsylvania Museum of Archaeology and Anthropology (UPM) NA6829.

5 This chapter emphasizes outcomes rather than processes of our negotiations.

6 Sangita Chari and Jaime M. N. Lavalee, eds., *Accomplishing NAGPRA: Perspectives on the Intent, Impact, and Future of the Native American Graves Protection and Repatriation Act* (Corvallis: Oregon State University Press, 2013), 8.

7 For details, see NAGPRA of 1990, 25 U.S.C. §3001(2)(3)(C); §3001(2)(3)(D); and §3001(2)(13).

8 Patricia Capone, "Amending Wonder: Museums and Twenty Years of the Native American Graves Protection and Repatriation Act," in *Accomplishing NAGPRA*, edited by Chari and Lavalee, 115–34.

9 See Martha Graham and Nell Murphy, "NAGPRA at 20: Museum Collections and Reconnections," *Museum Anthropology* 33 no. 2 (2010): 105–24; National Park Service, *Journeys to Repatriation: 15 Years of NAGPRA Grants (1994–2009)*, compliance by Sangita Chari and Lauren A. Trice (Washington, DC: US Department of the Interior, 2009); Eric R. Hollinger, Edwell John Jr., Harold Jacobs, Lora Moran-Collins, Carolyn Thome, Jonathan Zastrow, Adam Metallo, Gunter Waibel, and Vince Rossi, "Tlingit-Smithsonian Collaborations with 3D Digitization of Cultural Objects," *Museum Anthropology Review* 7, no. 1–2 (2013): 201–53; and Chip Colwell, *Plundered Skulls and Stole Spirits: Inside the Fight to Reclaim Native America's Culture* (Chicago: University of Chicago Press, 2017), 265.

10 Louis Shotridge itinerary, UPM Archives.

11 Before 1924 the Alaskan Citizen Act of 1915 required strict suppression of the Tlingit language and religious ḵu.éek' were strictly forbidden. A ḵu.éek' is a potlatch or ritual feast held to mark important occasions such as memorials held a year after the death of a clan member.

12 Philip Drucker, *The Native Brotherhoods: Modern Intertribal Organizations on the Northwest Coast*, Bulletin, Smithsonian Institutions, Bureau of American Ethnology (Washington, DC: US Government Printing Office, 1958); and Stephen Haycox, "William Lewis Paul," in *Haa Ḵusteeyi, Our Culture: Tlingit Life Stories*, volume 3 of *Classics of Tlingit Oral Literature*, edited by Richard and Nora Dauenhauer (Seattle: University of Washington Press; Juneau, AK: Sealaska Heritage Foundation, 1994), 506.

13 The ANB is a federation of individual community chapter organizations called camps. Shotridge was a member of ANB Sitka Camp 1 (Maureen E. Milburn, "Weaving the Tina' Blanket: The Journey of Florence and Louis Shotridge," in *Haa Ḵusteeyi, Our Culture*, edited by Dauenhauer and Dauenhauer," 560). Six years later, in 1930, Shotridge was elected ANB grand president. It would be another ten years before the US government would recognize Tlingit land claims, and only then would ANB members begin to focus their efforts on reinstating the Tlingit language and religion.

14 His mother, Kudeit.sáakw, was Eagle Kaagwaantaan, and his father, Yeilgooxi, was Raven Gaanax.teidi (see Maureen E. Milburn, "Louis Shotridge and the Objects of Everlasting Esteem," in *Raven's Journey: The World of Alaska's native People*, edited by Susan Kaplan and Kristin Barsness, 54–77 (Philadelphia: University Museum Press, 1986), 60.

15 Milburn, "Louis Shotridge and the Objects of Everlasting Esteem," 60.

16 Quotation from Robert Starbard in "Woosh.Jee.Een, Pulling Together: Xunaa & Penn Museum in Partnership," the Anthony Paredes Memorial Lecture on Sustainable Partnerships given by Robert Starbard and Lucy Williams at the annual meeting of the Society for Applied Anthropology, April 4, 2018, Philadelphia.

17 Austin Hammong in Dauenhauer and Dauenhauer, *Haa Ḵusteeyi, Our Culture:* 847.

18 Quotation from Starbard in "Woosh.Jee.Een, Pulling Together."

19 Milburn, "Louis Shotridge and the Objects of Everlasting Esteem," 57.

20 Milburn, "Weaving the Tina' Blanket," 553.

21 Gordon arranged for Shotridge to spend two months with Franz Boas in New York City in the winter of 1914. He attended Boas's classes in ethnology at Columbia and worked with Boas on Tlingit phonology. See Franz Boas, *Grammatical Notes on the Language of the Tlingit Indians* (Philadelphia: University of Pennsylvania Museum, 1917).

22 Eleanor M. King and Bryce P. Little, "George Byron Gordon and the Early Development of the University Museum," in *Raven's Journey: The World of Alaska's Native People*, edited by Susan Kaplan and Kristin Barsness, 16–53 (Philadelphia: University Museum Press, 1986), 41.

23 Alden J. Mason, "Louis Shotridge," *Expedition* 2 (1960): 11–16; Edmund Carpenter, "Collecting Northwest Coast Art," in *Indian Art of the Northwest Coast: A Dialogue on Craftsmanship and Aesthetics*, edited by Bill Holm and Bill Reid, 9–27 (Houston, TX: Rice University Institute for the Arts, 1975); Douglas Cole, *Captured Heritage: The Scramble for Northwest Coast Artifacts* (Seattle: University of Washington Press, 1985); Milburn, "Louis Shotridge and the Objects of Everlasting Esteem," 54; Nora M. Dauenhauer and Richard Dauenhauer, "Louis Shotridge and Indigenous Tlingit Ethnography: Then and Now," in *Constructing Cultures Then and Now: Celebrating Franz Boas and the Jesup North Pacific Expedition*, edited by Laurel Kendall and Igor Krupnik, 165–84, Circumpolar Anthropology 4 (Washington, DC: National Museum of Natural History, Smithsonian Institution Press, 2003), 165; Ishmael Hope, "You're Going To Hear about This: Frank Johnson, Louis Shotridge, and Civil Rights," August 24, 2011, www.goldbeltheritage.org/wp-content/uploads/2014/03/24a-Other-Notable-Tlingit-Civil-Rights.pdf; Robert Preucel, "Shotridge in Philadelphia: Representing Native Alaskan Peoples to East Coast Audiences," in *Sharing Our Knowledge: The Tlingit and Their Coastal Neighbors*, edited by Sergei Kan, 41–62 (Lincoln: University of Nebraska Press, 2015); and Lucy Fowler Williams, "Louis Shotridge: Preserver of Tlingit History," in *Sharing Our Knowledge*, edited by Kan, 63–78.

24 Louis Shotridge letter to George Byron Gordon, January 7, 1924, UPM Archives.

25 In a letter of September 29, 1924, Louis wrote to his employer, museum director George Gordon, about his intention to inspect items available in Hoonah (in the UPM Archives).

26 Sergei Kan, *Memory Eternal: Tlingit Culture and Russian Orthodox Christianity through Two Centuries* (Seattle: University of Washington Press, 1999), 490.

27 Kan, *Memory Eternal*, 491. White's motivations are ambiguous. The objects were likely anathema to his position, he may have needed cash, and he may have wanted to find a safe place for the objects.

28 Contents of Package No. 9, Louis Shotridge to GBG; Ethnological Specimens Purchased for the University Museum, Louis Shotridge, UPM Archives. Shotridge paid significantly higher prices than other collectors of his day; see Cole, *Captured Heritage*, 256.

29 Gordon had trained him to document, and Franz Boas had helped him develop a Tlingit orthography system. See Williams, "Louis Shotridge: Preserver of Tlingit History."

30 Louis Shotridge letter to George Byron Gordon, 1924, UPM Archives.

31 For a detailed overview of Shotridge's collections and writings, see the Shotridge Digital Archive, www.penn.museum/collections/Shotridge/index.html.

32 Louis Shotridge letter to George Byron Gordon, January 27, 1923, UPM Archives.

33 Shotridge wrote about the "moods and emotions" of Tlingit people and their art. Louis Shotridge, "The Emblems of the Tlingit Culture," *Museum Journal* 19, no. 4 (1928): 350–77.

34 Kan, *Memory Eternal*, 6. Shotridge translated "emblem" as "at.u" (Boas, *Grammatical Notes on the Language of the Tlingit Indians*, 157). Other scholars, including John Swanton (1909), also used "emblem." See Swanton, *Tlingit Myths and Texts* (Washington, DC: Government Printing Office, 1909).

35 See Nora M. Dauenhauer and Richard Dauenhauer, eds., *Haa Shuká, Our Ancestors: Tlingit Oral Narratives*, volume 1 (Seattle: University of Washington Press, 1987), for the processes of at.óow.

36 Nora M. Dauenhauer and Richard Dauenhauer, eds., *Haa Tuwunaagu Yis, for Healing Our Spirit: Tlingit Oratory*, volume 2 of *Classics of Tlingit Oral Literature* (Seattle: University of Washington Press; Juneau, AK: Sealaska Heritage Foundation, 1990).

37 Louis Shotridge UPM catalog card NA6829.

38 Louis V. Shotridge, UPM Digital Archive, asl_sm37_394_01; and Louis Shotridge catalog card housed in the Alaska State Library Archives, Juneau.

39 Louis Shotridge exhibit label, "Lituya Bay Robe," UPM Archives.

40 Glacier Bay National Park was established in 1924. Sitka National Park was established in 1910, Old Kassan in 1916, and Katmai National Park in 1918.

41 Thomas F. Thornton, *Being and Place among the Tlingit*, Sealaska Heritage Institute (Seattle: University of Washington Press, 2011), 90.

42 Maureen Milburn, "The Politics of Possession: Louis Shotridge and the Tlingit Collections of the University of Pennsylvania Museum," PhD diss., Department of Fine Arts, University of British Columbia–Vancouver, 1997; and Dauenhauer and Dauenhauer, "Louis Shotridge and Indigenous Tlingit Ethnography: Then and Now"; Hope, "You're Going to Hear about This"; and Preucel, "Shotridge in Philadelphia."

43 Dauenhauer and Dauenhauer, "Louis Shotridge and Indigenous Tlingit Ethnography: Then and Now," 168.

44 Starbard, "Woosh.Jee.Een, Pulling Together."

45 Robert Preucel and Lucy Williams, "The Centennial Potlatch," *Expedition* 47, no. 2 (2005): 9–19; Graham and Murphy, "NAGPRA at 20"; and Eric C. Hollinger and Harold Jacobs, "A Killer Whale Comes Home: Neil Kuxdei woogoot, Keet S'aaxw, Mark Jacobs Jr. and the Repatriation of a Clan Crest Hat from the Smithsonian Institution," in *Sharing Our Knowledge*, edited by Kan, 483–95.

46 *Federal Register* 75, no. 239 (2010): 77897–98, Tuesday, December 14, 2010, www.penn.museum/documents/collections/nagpra_Snail_House.pdf.

47 This is a reference to "500 Homeless after Fire Sweeps Hoonah," *Sitka Sentinel*, June 16, 1944.

48 Starbard, "Woosh.Jee.Een, Pulling Together."

49 Starbard, "Woosh.Jee.Een, Pulling Together."

50 The Mt. Fairweather Woman Hat depicts the woman inside Mount Fairweather, just north near Lituya Bay. Her spirit was a vision of a T'akdeintaan shaman (see Dauenhauer and Dauenhauer, *Haa Tuwunaagu Yis, for Healing Our Spirit*, 91).

51 The original Dog Spirit Hat burned in the Hoonah fire of 1944 (see Dauenhauer and Dauenhauer, *Haa Tuwunaagu Yis, for Healing Our Spirit*, 102); and Thornton, *Being and Place among the Tlingit*, 70.

52 Traveling to Alaska on October 10, 2017, to celebrate the new HIA/Penn Museum partnership, Penn staff Lucy Williams, associate curator and keeper, Stacey Espenlaub, NAGPRA coordinator, and Wendy White, Office of General Counsel, returned three more objects in the Snail House collection.

53 Lily White and Paul White, "K̲oo.eex': The Tlingit Memorial Party," in *Celebration 2000*, edited by Susan W. Fair and Rosita Worl, 133–36 (Juneau, AK: Sealaska Heritage Foundation, 2000).

54 Penn Museum loaned clan hats to Tlingit k̲u.éek' in 2003, 2004, 2005, 2006, and 2009 in Sitka, Juneau, and Angoon. See Stacey O. Espenlaub, "Building New Relationships with Tlingit Clans: Potlatch Loans, NAGPRA, and the Penn Museum," in *Sharing Our Knowledge*, edited by Kan, 496–508. To date, all the hats loaned have been either repatriated or are part of a competing repatriation claim.

55 Mary Catharine Martin, "After Almost a Century Absence, Sacred Objects Return to the Tlingit People of Hoonah," *Juneau Empire*, October 13, 2017, http://juneauempire.com/news/local/2017-10-12/after-almost-century-absence-sacred-objects-return-tlingit-people-hoonah. A Welcome Home Ceremony and Celebration was hosted by the Tsal Xaaan (Mt. Fairweather House) Tax' Hit (Snail House) at the Sealaska Heritage Institute Shuka Hit, Juneau, on October 11, 2017. Emceed by Gordon Greenwald, this event involved Raven and Eagle clan leaders, a Welcome Home Ceremony and T'akdeintaan clan welcome, including Raven and Eagle welcome speeches and Spirit Songs, and a formal thank you from the clans to the University of Pennsylvania. Following the transfer, Espenlaub and White were adopted into the T'akdeintaan clan. Since I had been adopted previously by the Kiks.adi, I received an honorary T'akdeintaan clan name. For generations Native Americans have actively named outsiders as a way of marking and strengthen their relationships. NAGPRA has inspired Tlingit clans to adopt or name museum staff. See Sergei Kan, ed., *Strangers to Relatives: The Adoption and Naming of Anthropologists in Native North America* (Lincoln: University of Nebraska Press, 2001); and Aldona Jonaitis, "Tlingit Repatriation in Museums: Ceremonies of Sovereignty," *Museum Worlds* 5 (2017): 48–59, for further discussion on this practice.

56 In my experience Tlingit clan leaders adopt museum colleagues to honor and thank them for their work as individuals, to build alliances, and also for pragmatic reasons such as to keep repatriation activities, procedures, and participants safe and "in balance." Adoption effectively gives outsiders a place or role by making them family. See Kan, *Strangers to Relatives*.

57 Nora Dauenhauer, "Tlingit At.óow," in *Celebration 2000: Restoring Balance Through Culture*, edited by Susan W. Fair and Rosita Worl, 101–6 (Juneau, AK: Sealaska Heritage Foundation, 2000), 102.

58 Austin Hammond's speech at a 1968 k̲u.éek' in Hoonah, cited in Dauenhauer and Dauenhauer, *Haa Tuwunaagu Yis, for Healing Our Spirit.*

59 Richard Dauenhauer and Nora Dauenhauer, "Evolving Concepts of Identity and Clan," in *Coming to Shore: Northwest Coast Ethnology, Traditions, and Vision*, edited by Marie Mauze, Michael E. Haskin, and Sergei Kan, 253–78 (Lincoln: University of Nebraska Press, 2004), 276.

60 The healing canoe is a revitalized traditional form used as a symbol of healing; see Dauenhauer and Dauenhauer, "Evolving Concepts of Identity and Clan," 272.

61 Robert Starbard, personal communication, April 3, 2018.

62 Robert Starbard, personal communication, July 2018.

63 The House was dedicated in 2017 as part of the Return to Homeland Centennial Celebration to strengthen the relationship between the HIA and the National Park Service (NPS). See Mary Beth Moss, "Two Totem Poles Raised in Front of Huna Ancestors' House," *Juneau Empire*, June 1, 2017, http://juneauempire.com/art/2017-05-30/two-totem-poles-raised-front-huna-ancestors-house; and National Park Service, News Release, "Hunaa Shuka Hit: A Collaborative Milestone," September 2, 2016, www.nps.gov/glba/learn/news/a-collaborative-milestone.htm.

64 Starbard, "Woosh.Jee.Een, Pulling Together."

THOUGHTS ON FORMLINE

Iljuuwaas Tyson Brown

To find your place
like an inner ovoid
is to end up
where you should be.
Suspended in balance
but free to express
you settle in
among your kin.
—5/29/17

Ovoid and U
oft embrace
in dance or tussle
on negative space.
—6/2/2017

If we were conscious of
each other's space,
the way positive and negative are,
we'd live beautifully
like them.
—10/26/2018

PART IV

Beyond Art

CHAPTER 12

Soft Robes of Thundering Power

MOUNTAIN GOAT FIBER TEXTILES OF THE NORTHWEST COAST

Evelyn Vanderhoop

WOVEN ROBES OF MOUNTAIN GOAT FIBER SWAYED WITH THE STRIDES OF CHIEFS on the Pacific Northwest Coast long before the arrival of European visitors. Despite the vast changes that came with the eventual colonialism of the First Nation people, the continuum of culture, art, and dance have brought the woven arts forward into the present. To better understand the Northwest Coast textiles, I began in 2000 to look back into their past. That year, I received a study fellowship through the combined program of the National Museum of the American Indian (NMAI) and the National Service Organization for Native American Arts, ATLATL. That year, the NMAI was still in the process of moving into its new location on the Washington, DC, mall, so the Visiting Artist Program scheduled trips to other major museums in New York, Philadelphia, and Washington, DC. I studied all the textiles I could find within the exhibits of the New York Museum of the American Indian and the collections of the Brooklyn Museum, the American Museum of Natural History, the University of Pennsylvania Museum of Archeology and Anthropology, and the National Museum of Natural History. It was eye-opening to see so many historic robes. I knew that each one had a story, a declaration of the identity of the chief that had once owned it, an identity that wrapped in the origins and alliances the ancestors had with the natural and supernatural forces within the Northwest Coast.

Many historic robes—Ravenstail (the northern geometric robe) and the Naaxiin, commonly called the Chilkat blanket—were woven from mountain goat fiber. It is believed that these robes evolved from the earlier cedar bark garments using basketry weaving techniques of two-strand and three-strand twining. The Ravenstail chiefs' robes were constructed with pure mountain goat wool and were predominately rectangular and adorned with geometric designs. In contemporary time, the existence of the geometric robes was obscured from memory and only recently rediscovered. The Naaxiin robe is a polygon with a shallow V bottom that uses advanced techniques to create the iconic formline designing. An inner core of cedar

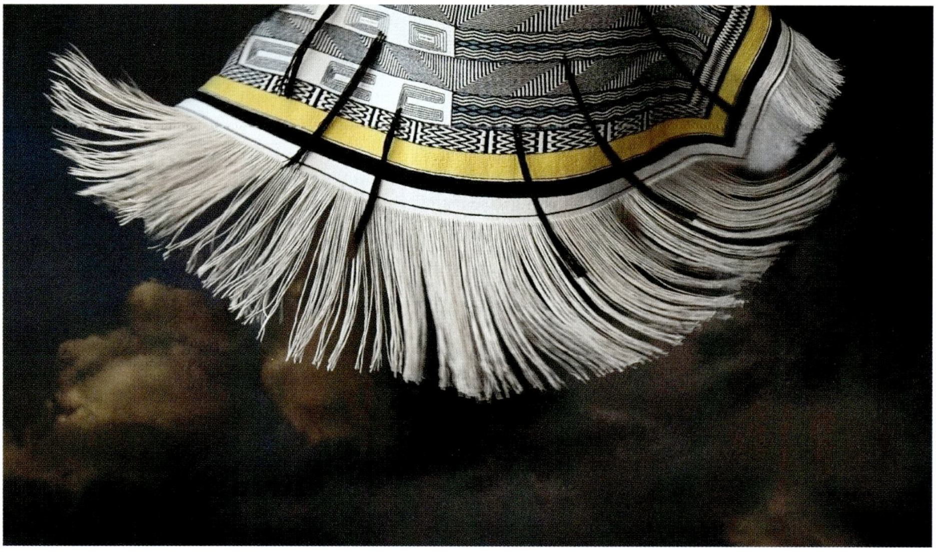

12.1. Evelyn Vanderhoop, Sky Robe, Ravenstail Robe Swaying, 2019. Collection of the Boston Museum of Fine Arts. Photograph credit Bernadette Jarrard.

bark is thigh spun into the mountain goat warps to aid in maintaining the tension required for creating the undulating shapes. The weaving techniques and skill that went into the robes are amazingly complex, and in my own journey to emulate these early weavers, I continue to strive for their perfect forms. The implicit stories seeded my desire to know more about how the mountain goat garments fit into the cultures of the coast. Stories from the forest and the sea, now draped over by the cloak of time, are "written" into garments of cedar, Ravenstail and Naaxiin robes, and later button blankets. Corroborated by elders, artists, and early visitor's documents, the stories have given me new insights into power garments of the past.

The Haida were very fortunate to have an early ethnologist, John Reed Swanton, come to Haida Gwaii and Southeast Alaska in the early 1900s to collect stories from elders of that time. When he first arrived, it had been just twenty-four years since the missionary influence began on Haida Gwaii. Because of their direct memory of witnessing traditional ways of the pre–missionary era and their recollections of clan stories, these elders were able to give Swanton the ancient literature he so earnestly sought. Clues tucked within the language of the ancestors in story and song resonate with the past. Fortunately, Haida translators helped Swanton write down the words that made up the oral stories. I read and reread the Haida words of mystical beginnings, ancestral adventures, and tales of historic epochs within Swanton's three major published works on the Haida: *Haida Texts and Myths, Skidegate Dialect* (1905), *Haida Texts Masset Dialect* (1908), and *Contributions to the Ethnology of the Haida* (1905).[1]

"Sky Blankets" were spoken of in more than one story taken down and translated for Swanton. In Raven's traveling sagas, the ravenous appetite of Raven drove him to tricks of transformation as he slipped into the "skin" of fish, fowl, and mammal. Two "sky blankets" were also a part of his garment arsenal. This intrigued me, and I looked for connections that could help me determine what these robes may have looked like and whether they could be the ceremonial robes currently coined Ravenstail? In one story, Supernatural-Being-Who-Went-Naked, two types of robes are used by the hero—one is referred to as a sky blanket and the other is called a dancing blanket. If the sky blanket is the pure mountain goat wool Ravenstail chiefs' robe, then would the dancing blanket be the Naaxiin chiefs' robe? Knitting the stories with documents from early explorers and fur traders helped me to go back in time to see what I could find.

In the beginning of the story, Supernatural-Being-Who-Went-Naked, the hero, receives qwii'q'al gyaa' ad gisti'n (*two sky blankets*) from his mother: "He asked of his mother, who was weaving near the wall: 'Mother, have you any?' 'Yes, chief, my son when something made you and shut you in the womb I had some made for you. They are here.' Then his mother hunted in a box, brought out two sky blankets, and gave them to him."[2] In the hero's adventures he loses the robes and regains them, and at the end he puts one on his sister: "Then he put a sky blanket upon his sister and seated her on the mainland. And he seated his mother on the Haida country."[3]

The two sky blankets were made especially for Supernatural-Being-Who-Went-Naked and were given to him by his mother after he strengthened himself. What were they made of, and what were their designs? Nowhere could I find the direct answers to these questions, so I searched through the Haida words for any association with the qwe'gal (*sky*). In Haida, Ye xe l' gan means *having clouds around his neck*. How can clouds be around a neck? Could a garment with design representing clouds be the answer? Another Swanton collected story, The One Abandoned for Eating the Flipper of a Hair Seal, has a statement that led me to believe it was the answer: "Then Master Carpenter's daughter brought out a mat with edges like cumulus clouds and they laid his younger brother upon it."[4]

While studying the Northwest Coast textiles at the British Museum in London, I examined cedar robes and capes that had edge designs made from mountain goat wool taken from the soft undercoat of the goat's shoulder ruff. Since the islands off the coast were not a part of the goats' natural habitat, the Island people need to acquire the valuable hanks of roving and mats of the wool by trade. Liis is the Haida word for *soft, white mountain goat fiber spun*. If you were to close your eyes and drop a bit upon your hand, you could not feel it land, it is so soft. Clouds seem like the perfect design to create with it. Clouds crown the mountains where the goats are found. Only hunters with inherited prerogatives could pursue them in their lofty realm. Shamans used their image on carved rattles and amulets to conjure their help within healing ceremonies.

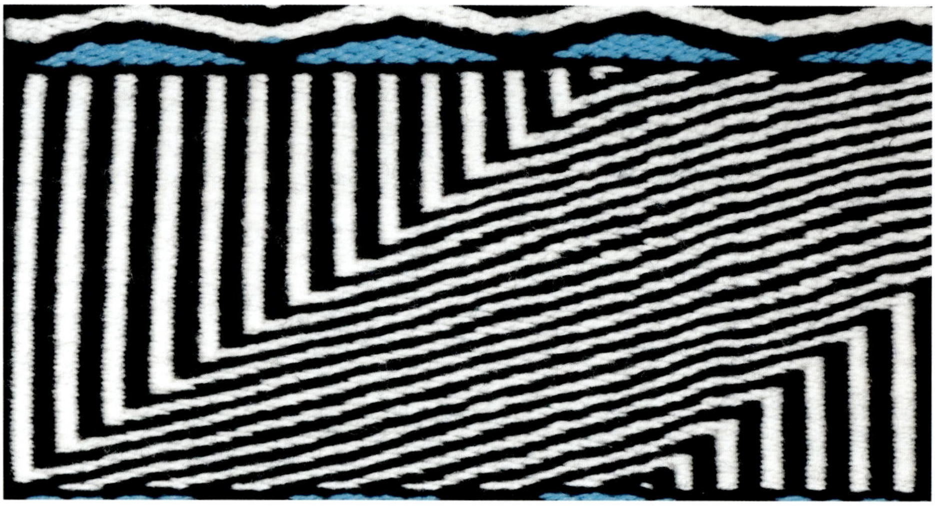

12.2. Lightning design, detail, design pattern woven by Evelyn Vanderhoop. Collection of the Boston Museum of Fine Arts. Photograph credit Bernadette Jarrard.

George Vancouver collected wool-edged cedar garments during his three seasons on the coast between 1792 and 1794. He observed the ways weavers used mountain goat fiber in garments. On his second survey season he was at a region he called New Hanover, midcoast, north of Vancouver Island, and noted in his journal the following observation: "The clothing of the natives here was either skins of the sea otter, or garments made from the pine bark [cedar bark]; some of these latter have the fur of the sea otter, very neatly wrought into them, and have a border to the sides and bottom, decorated with various colours. In this only they use woollen yarn, very fine, well spun, and dyed for that purpose; particularly with a very lively and beautiful yellow."[5]

In 1793, during the time Vancouver surveyed the coast, Sigismund Bacstrom, a surgeon on a fur trade ship, documented in a watercolor portrait a Haida chief wearing a cedar garment. The top edge is obscured by the chief's hair, but the bottom edge shows two white and black diagonal designed borders. Bacstrom's painting illustrates the edging that Vancouver observed and also possibly reflects the designs in Master Carpenter's daughter's "cumulus cloud" edged mat.

Sigismund Bacstrom painted other Haida people in a variety of clothing, Native made as well as European clothing gained in trade. Three of his Haida portraits feature plain green-blue robes. I couldn't help but wonder, were these "sky robes" depicting a clear blue sky? In one painting a blue robe drapes over the shoulders of a chief's wife. It is described in the book *Soft Gold: The Fur Trade and Cultural Exchange on the Northwest Coast of America*: "This drawing was finished in England, but delineates the Indians of Port Rose (southern Queen Charlottes) at the time that Bacstrom visited there in the Three Brothers in 1793; it suggests how they looked at home, rather than in ceremonial clothes."[6] Notations on the preliminary drawing, for this painting, further describe the garment worn by the chief's wife as a "dirty greenish blue cloak." This was his way of remembering the paint mixing for the color, not the state of its cleanliness. Other paintings of Bacstrom's used the same word—"dirty"—to describe a color dulled by a brown paint color.

Bacstrom was a man of science interested in medicine, chemistry, and art. As a surgeon he was most likely trained in a scientific manner of observation and

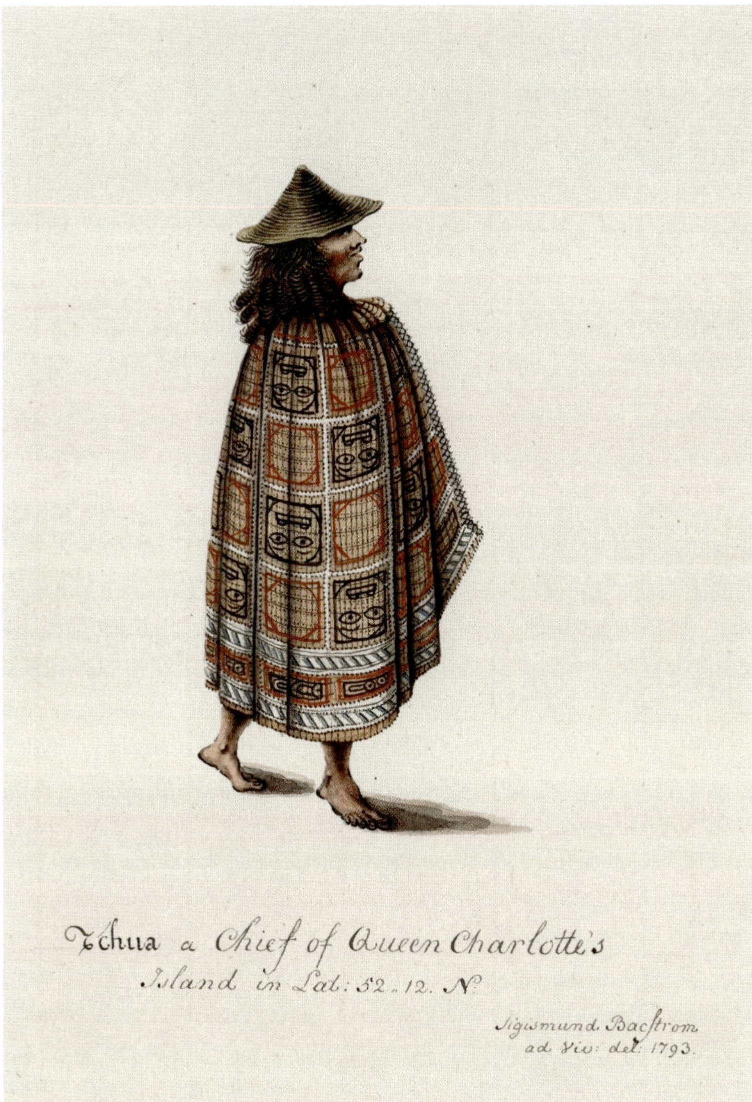

12.3. Sigismund Bacstrom, *T'chua a Chief of Queen Charlotte's Island in Lat: 52, 12 N, 1793*. Watercolor. Franz and Kathryn Stenzel Collection of Western Art, Beinecke Rare Book & Manuscript Library, Yale University.

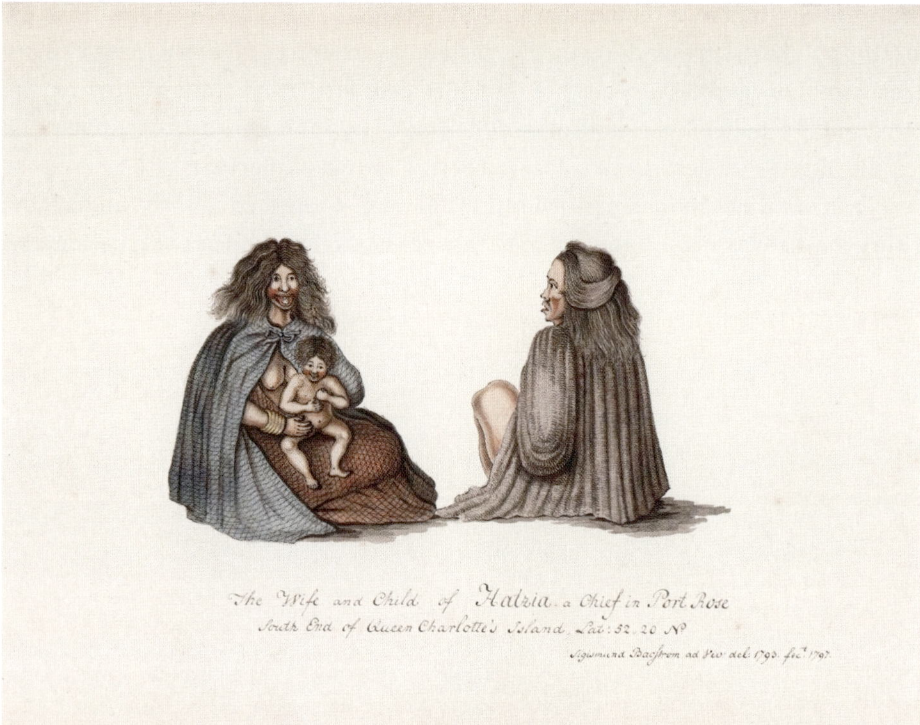

12.4. Sigismund Bacstrom, *The Wife and Child of Hatsia a Chief in Port Rose South End of Queen Charlotte's Island Lat: 52, 20 N;* 1793–1797. Watercolor. Franz and Kathryn Stenzel Collection of Western Art, Beinecke Rare Book & Manuscript Library, Yale University.

drawing. This training makes his paintings more ethnological in their precision, not clouded by the romantic notions of that era or interpreted with artistic license. I applied and received a research fellowship from the Yale University's Beinecke Rare Book and Manuscripts Library to examine Bacstrom's paintings and sketches firsthand. My experience as a watercolor painter as well as a weaver of wool textiles helped in examining his painting techniques of cross hatching and stippling to determine if the single colored blue capes and robes were hand-woven garments or trade blankets. I concluded that the patterns painted for the blue garments indicated twill-twining weaving techniques of the Pacific Northwest coast.

Blue was an expensive color because of its rare dye sources and therefore the prerogative of chiefs and their direct families. A year before Bacstrom painted portraits of Haida in blue robes, the custom of wearing two blue robes was witnessed firsthand by Don Jacinto Caamano, a Spanish explorer to the coast in 1792. Caamano was at Northern Haida Gwaii in the area of North Island between two Haida villages, Kiusta and Dadens, where the Chief Cania (Coneah, Cooneah, Gaanyaa) resided. Caamano notes the clothing that this chief wore during the greeting ceremonies upon his ship:

> Cania came on board at 5 o'clock that evening. He is of very big frame, and stout in proportion, with a handsome face, and is about seventy years old. His clothing, all of sky-blue cloth, consisted of two loose frock coats one over the other, ornamented with Chinese cash, each one strung on a piece of sail-making twine with a large light-blue glass bead the size of a hazel nut, loosely attached to the material, and together forming a button. . . . The trimming of his clothes was formed by the selvage of the cloth; and this made up for the lining, which was altogether lacking.[7]

This passage contains enough clues to determine that the two sky-blue "frock" coats were Haida woven. The single bead button closure and the noted lack of lining for these two outer garments make me suspect they were not trade cloth because in other journal entries the Spanish captain readily notes European trade cloth use by the Haida. But in this observation, Caamano goes further in stating that each "coat" was strung on a piece of twine. Both styles of mountain goat fiber chiefs' robes are constructed on a simple bar loom, where wool warps are strung over a heading cord. The heading cord was traditionally made from leather but evidence from Naaxiin robes, now on museum shelves, reveal that the earliest changes in postcontact robe construction is the substitution of commercial twine for traditional leather heading cords. This description of the coats as "each one strung on a piece of sail-making twine" could mean that the two sky-blue over garments were woven in Haida traditional techniques using European sailor's twine as the heading cord.

Unlike the plain and unadorned blue robes depicted in watercolor by Bacstrom, Caamano's word picture notes that the two sky blue robes of Cania's had Chinese "cash" ornamenting them. Chinese coins, trade beads, and buttons joined the seashell, deer hooves, and bird beaks in the tradition of embellishing garments with distinguishing designs. Designs of identity upon garments were the norm, and cloud patterns that adorned cedar capes, mats, and robes could have been crest designs. Within the Haida Nation, cumulus clouds were crest designs for some Raven clans. Clouds were also designated as the "potlatch dress" of the One-in-the-Sea, ruler of all sea creatures. This monarch of the sea was believed to also rule the weather, so clouds and wind were natural elements that were symbolized in designs affiliated with the supernatural beings of sea and sky.

Alexander Mackenzie, a Hudson Bay factor stationed in the early 1880s at Massett in Northern Haida Gwaii, noted Haida customs and ideas he learned from direct inquiry. He was told about spirit people in the region of clouds and the manner they were depicted in design: "Certain clouds occasionally seen in the western horizon are termed qyow (Kwiiyaaw). It is said qyow clouds indicate good weather. These clouds have the form of a T and the base line of the T is supposed to represent the horizon, spirit people are said to inhabit the region of the qyow. An old medicine man saw the place in a vision. These spirit people's heads were elongated on each

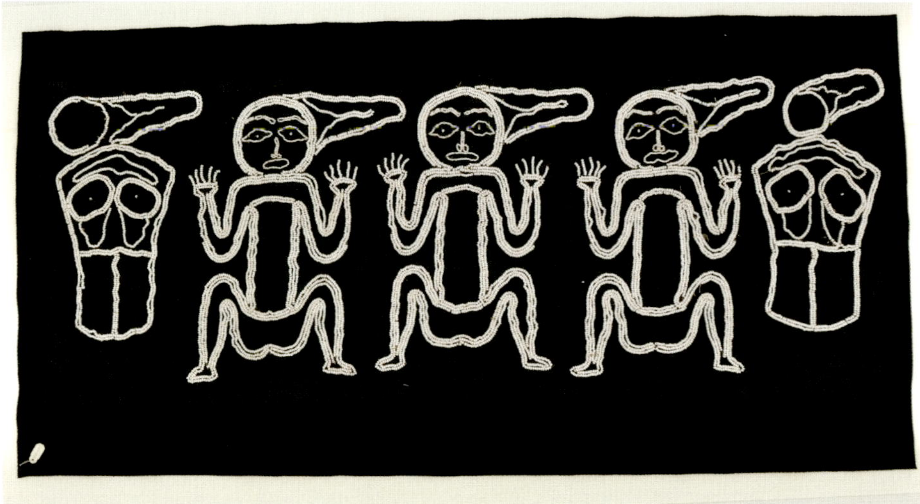

12.5. Beaded cloth with designs of Cloud People (Kwiiyaaw). Alaska State Museum, Juneau.

side like the upper end of the T they were called Qyow people."[8] This button robe design depicting human figures with caps tapering to the side may be illustrating the Cloud people that Mackenzie reported on.

Supernatural-Being-Who-Went-Naked, the hero who received sky blankets, had rescued his brothers who had lost wrestling matches with the Cloud People, the Kwiiyaaw spirit people. His mother's gift of two sky blankets was given to him only after he strengthened himself and was ready to pursue the rescue of his brothers. He had earned the sky robes and with them he was eventually triumphant. Did the robes have supernatural power? Haida world view encompassed the idea that designs could influence elements of the natural world. In How Shining-Heavens-Caused-Himself-To-Be-Born, a story within the Massett dialect texts, designs capable of changing the weather are written about: "He got up and his father said to the child, 'Chief my child, come and let me dress you up.' Then he went to him, and he (Master-Carpenter) put stratus-clouds upon his face. 'Now, chief, my son, go and sit idly by the sea.' And as soon as he did so the weather was fair."[9] Sg̱aaga (*medicine men* or *shaman*) were thought to influence the weather. In the Haida early culture the Sg̱aaga were essential companions for canoe journeys upon the unpredictable seas surrounding Haida Gwaii.

John Wallace, a Haida carver in Southeast Alaska, was interviewed by anthropologist Viola Garfield in the 1940s when he was eighty years old. In the interview John Wallace spoke of designs that related to gestures that may have helped to control the weather. As a young man he had assisted his well-known father, Dwight Wallace, in wood carving. The stories that Dwight shared with his son came from Northern Haida Gwaii where his clan originated. While sharing his father's stories, many details came out that are not commonly known. John Wallace talked about a design depicting Daughter of Cloud: "Hands either side, means no wind. The rain clouds with hands coming down means little rain. Below these are thick clouds right on edge of ocean and it's safe to go from North Island to Massett."[10]

Haida story heroes wrestled the Cloud People and lived to tell of their interaction with the supernatural. Sg̲aaga see the spirit people in visions and describe them in symbols. These and other stories are passed on and continue to be proclaimed in designs of woven robes and garments. The belief that the designs came about from ancestors' interaction with supernatural beings is underscored by a story John Wallace shared with Garfield that speaks to the continuation of blanket designs of ancient origins:

> A Man had only one daughter at North Island [Haida Gwaii]. He was evidently supernatural and he told his daughter to always respect small things. She saw a tiny bullhead in a pool at low tide and picked it up stuffing food into its mouth until its stomach was distended. Then she put it back and the children laughed at its efforts to swim. [She] repeated [the] performance the next day and a man appeared and said "You are invited." She followed him and they went down steps into a beautiful large house. It was split rock under the sea.
>
> The father searched all around the Islands for his daughter and finally a school of whale killers came on the beach. [The] man asked them to help find [his] daughter and he got on ones' back with his [its] face painted in secret design and a blanket. They found the house and the chief said. "Leave her here and take the blanket designs etc. for your family." He did and they have used it since.[11]

The One-In-The-Sea used cumulus clouds as his potlatch dress. Was this potlatch dress a sky robe embellished with cloud designs? Were these the designs given by the undersea chief in the story above? Soft fiber of the mountain goat must have been the base of the sky robes referred to in the clan stories as well as the robes of wool fiber dyed blue, witnessed by Sigismund Bacstrom and Don Jacinto Caamano.

The robes, now coined Ravenstail, made purely from the mountain goat fiber, are said to predate formline-designed weaving. The dyed wool of yellow and black portrayed ancient declarations in the angular geometric patterns. Many designs on the Ravenstail robes are also found on baskets. Some of the designs have names and histories, but most have lost their stories through the ages just as the contemporary weavers had lost touch with unique techniques and knowledge of the existence of the pure mountain goat robes. The collector and ethnographic photographer George Thornton Emmons described the ancient robe in a few paragraphs in his 1907 monograph, *The Chilkat Blanket*.[12] It wasn't until Cheryl Samuel, while doing research into her own book on the Chilkat Blanket, noticed Emmons's descriptions and broadened her research to include the geometric patterned robe. Her book, *The*

Raven's Tail (1987), brought the knowledge back to contemporary weavers and a textile weaving revival began.[13]

One of the most prevalent border designs on the ancient Ravenstail robes is the same predominant pattern on the edges of cedar robes, capes, and skirts. Of the fifteen robes found and featured in *The Raven's Tail*, ten have a border that is now identified as "lightning" design variations. Thunder accompanies lightning, and names found in the Swanton documented stories speak of garments that "thundered": Supernatural-Woman-The-Edge-of-Whose-Skirts-Thunder and Thunder-in-Your-Own-Dress-as-You-Sit. These names refer to garments of power with sky-inspired designs. If Ravenstail robes were the story sky robes, then their patterns might be displaying cloud, sky, and rain motifs. Designs that edge the Ravenstail may possibly surround it with this "sky" power.

At the end of the story Supernatural-Being-Who-Went-Naked, the hero gives the sky robes away and puts on a dance robe to accomplish a transformation: "Now, he put on a dancing blanket and dancing leggings and started along on land near his younger brothers (who were going along in their canoe). He bent over as he ran, and farther off he stood up straight. In that way Supernatural-Being-Who-Went-Naked became the Swamp-robin."[14] Swanton footnotes that the robin is probably a varied thrush (*Zoothera naevia*). The varied thrush has a wide black band across his orange/yellow breast and a blue/gray upper back. The black and yellow bands

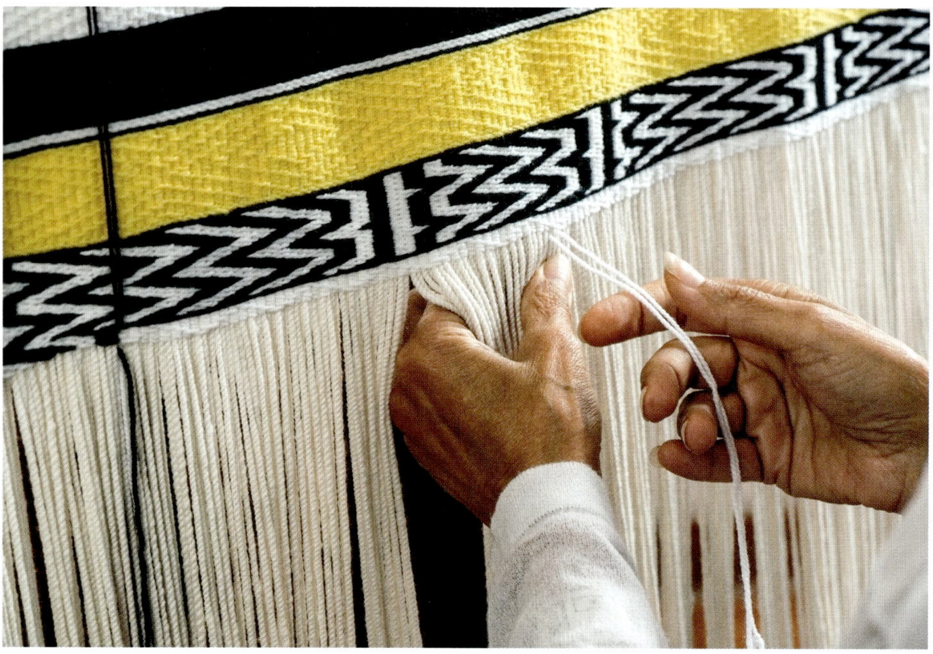

12.6. All My Ancestors, detail, an ancient pattern being woven by Evelyn Vanderhoop. Photograph credit Bernadette Jarrard. Now in the Collection of the Boston Museum of Fine Arts.

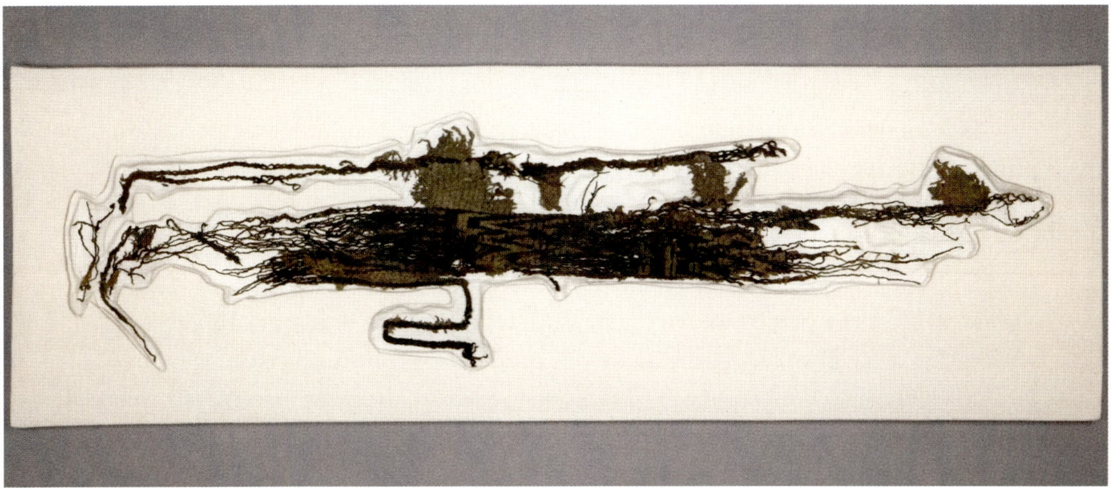

12.7. Ravenstail fragment. Alaska State Museum, Juneau.

that surround the inner design of the Naaxiin robe could be the reason for the association of the thrush to the dancing blanket. Robes that were intended to dance would have been constructed with mountain goat wool fiber because they would have the flexibility to sway with dance movements. The pentagonal five-sided Naaxiin robes, worn by chiefs today as well as in the past, must have been the "dancing blanket" referred to in the story. Advancing techniques of joinery and back-and-forth weaving gave the Naaxiin weavers the ability to create the flowing formline images of supernatural beings as well as crest-inspired designs.

The Naaxiin robes have been described by George Emmons, Franz Boas, Bill Holm, Cheryl Samuel, and other authors and researchers concerned with the textile art of the Pacific Coast. They have written and illustrated the techniques and descriptions of the Naaxiin chiefs' robes in object-centered analysis. Pattern subjects have been guessed at by identifying symbolic designs. For example, Beaver always have two large front teeth and crosshatched tails; Eagle's beak bends more angular than Raven's; Killer Whale has a dorsal fin; supernatural beings exhibit human hands along with talon, flipper, or wing. These figurative symbols can help name the crest or being in the complex, bilateral, and abstract patterns of the Naaxiin robe but do not tell its complete story. The above-mentioned researchers all had Native informants, and still their interpretations on some Naaxiin robe designs are conflicting.

The stories were intellectual property of clans, and individuals did not have the right to tell them to others. Tlingit have designated treasure keepers who hold the at.oow (*clan property*). They are trained for this position and are knowledgeable about the object and story histories. Matriarchs within Haida clans are expected to learn and pass on the history of clan stories and property. These clan treasure keepers are copyright holders. Retelling of these histories outside of clans is taboo and thought to be identity theft. Informants can explain another's crest pattern only in a very vague manner. Even the stories shared with John Swanton were probably infringement-avoiding *Reader's Digest* versions.

After initial contact and the fur trade era, a swiftly dominating, non-Native culture imposed upon the Indigenous people and caused many cultural activities to drop by the wayside. Some elements were forgotten, like the weaving of the Ravenstail. Yet the persistent survival of the Naaxiin robe is extraordinary and within this story of survival, the history of contact and continuing culture is contained. Wool robes were observed in 1774, when Spanish explorer Juan Perez came to Northern Haida Gwaii. This was the first documented European contact for the Pacific Northwest Coast of Southeast Alaska down to the Oregon coast. Leaders on canoes, danced, sang, and encircled the large frigate, the *Santiago*. These chiefs wore wool robes and sea otter garments. After British explorer James Cook's journal of his 1778 expedition to this coast was published, news of sea otter garments spurred outsiders to return to the coast as fur trade partners. Because the royal pelt garments were traded away for the shoulders of Tsars and Mandarins across the ocean, it was the woven Naaxiin robe that remained to adorn chiefs in ceremonials throughout the uncertain and turbulent times beyond the era of sea otter trade.

In 1874, a century after Perez's initial visit to Haida Gwaii, Alexander McKenzie described the way he saw the Haida use Naaxiin garments in ceremonies within the clan houses of Massett: "On occasion of an arrival whom it was desirable to honour, the settlement of an individual quarrel, healing a tribal feud, making a treaty of friendship or peace or celebrating a potlatch or 'house warming' an indispensable adjunct to the ceremony was the dance with the Tsilk and Na-hung [Naaxiin] and scattering of eagle down. Sometimes a number of persons thus attired performed at once, and the costume was considered quite appropriate for either male or female dancers."[15] Tribal feuds and peace treaties were prevalent during the time when "Old World" diseases wiped out whole villages and clan chiefs jostled for hierarchical positions in the resulting aggregate villages of Massett and Skidegate. The continuation of ceremony expressed the Haida attempts to balance their swiftly changing world. This continuance of ceremony encompassed the continual use of ceremonial objects and the Naaxiin, through the vast changes, endured.

The many majestic Naaxiin robes tucked into museum shelves and drawers outnumber the robes that remain within clan treasure holdings. This discrepancy speaks volumes about the changes within cultures of the coast. Waves of disease epidemics left robes without chiefs and heirs. Then curiosity seekers began to collect the iconic art of the coastal people thought to be on the demise. Surviving clans and family members began to give up ancient riches to survive a new alien economic system. The Northern Tlingit in the Chilkat River Valley area began to weave robes for tourists and museum collectors in addition to the ceremonial clan robes. The shared respect of the sea for the coastal people dependent on canoe transportation is one important element of history revealed in museum textile collections. The prevailing design on Naaxiin robes in these collections is the Diving Whale. I believe it is not a crest design. Crest designs, like the stories that accompany them, were protected clan treasures. The conventionalized Diving Whale designs could transverse cross-cultural groups as they did in ancient times when southern area chiefs traded for the prestige's northern formline robe. This shared design proclaiming the canoe peoples' collective respect for the spirits of the sea would have been used for the new economics of bartering with outsiders.

While studying at the Beinecke Library, I found an unusual design drawn by Johnny Kit Elswa, a Haida informant and travel guide for James Swan in 1883. The ink-on-paper sketch titled *Tekul or cirrus clouds* appears to follow the Naaxiin convention of triptych and bilaterally splayed designing. The subject is T'kul and the artist in his explanation refers to wind spirits: "Above are the wings, and side are the different winds, each designated by an eye, and represented by the patches of

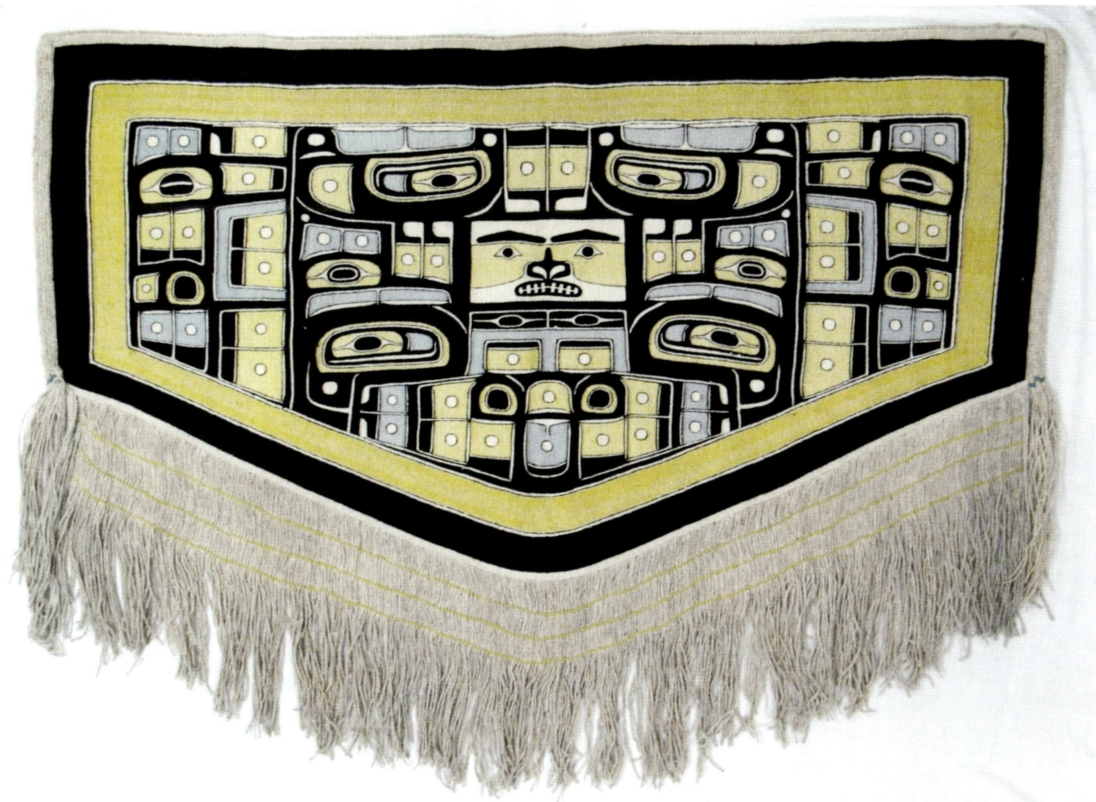

12.8. Diving Whale–patterned Naaxiin robe. Alaska State Museum, Juneau.

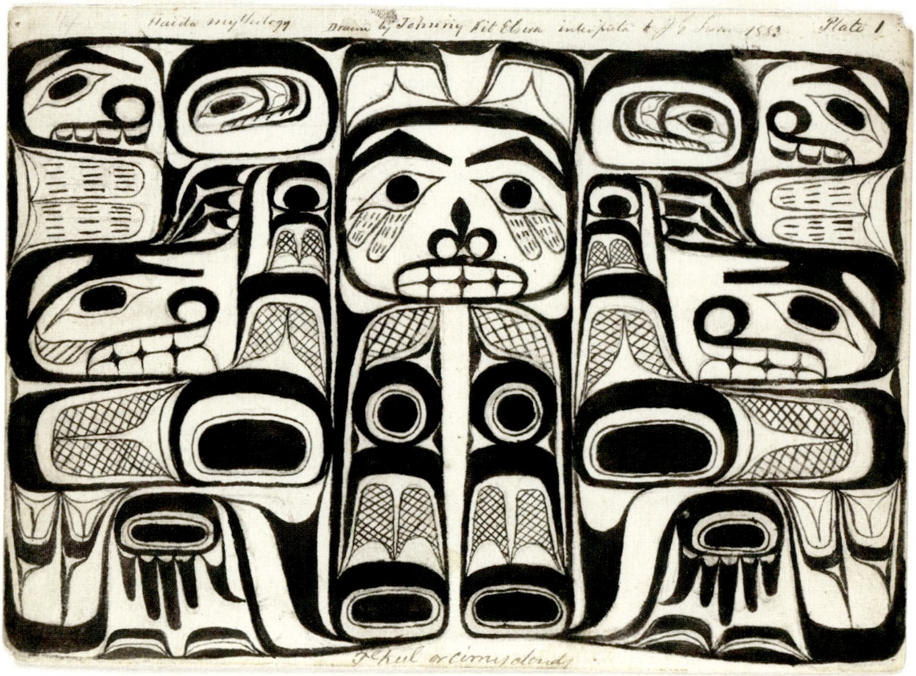

12.9. Johnny Kit Elswa, *Tekul or cirrus clouds,* 1883. Ink on paper, 17.9 × 25.5 cm. Franz and Kathryn Stenzel Collection of Western Art, Beinecke Rare Book & Manuscript Library, Yale University.

cirrus clouds. When T'kul determines which wind is to blow, he gives the word and the other winds retire. The change in the weather is usually followed by rain, which is indicated in the tears which stream from the eyes of T'kul."[16]

After reading Viola Garfield's interview notes on John Wallace, I can add to the description that the hands also indicate "little rain" as they turn down on the lower sides of the central figure of T'kul. Johnny Kit Elswa's explanation of the eyes symbolizing the different winds provide for the possibility of the wind spirits in other Naaxiin patterns. John Wallace carved a replica of an Eagle post that originally stood in Howkan, Alaska. On this carving he painted the front of the Eagle chest and wings with a Naaxiin robe design. His explanation was that it represented mountain, cloud, and whale, as told to Viola Garfield:

> John Wallace, who made the copy, interpreted the design as symbolic of mountains, clouds, and creatures that live in the mountains. The face in the center section, with very large eyes, round nostrils, and prominent teeth, is the mountain itself, and above it are three faces symbolizing clouds. The center one is a fair-weather cloud, those on either side with darkened upper half are light rain clouds on the mountain top. Below the mountain face is another, symbolizing

the homes of animals living on the slopes. On either side of the lower face are whale tails, symbolizing the whales brought to the mountains by thunderbirds.[17]

These two examples of natural elements made into symbolic form within designs that follow the conventional layout of Naaxiin robes offer more clues for understanding the interpretations of formline patterned chiefs' robes.

The power to influence the weather was transferred to Haida chiefs and Sgaaga through designs gifted in supernatural adventures of the Ancestors. Ravenstail sky robes that have geometric cloud designs, cedar garments with thundering lighting border patterns, and Naaxiin formline-designed robes all could have wrapped The-One-In-The-Sea with cloud power. Pulling out the drawers in museum textile collections and tracing the undulating formline will not lead me to the detailed story lines of the mountain goat textiles, but clues from early visitor's journals, sketches, clan art and stories all help me to read between the "lines" and get me closer to understanding how and why they were used in the past. History evolves, change is inevitable. Mountain goat fiber is now predominately replaced with domestic sheep's wool. The once extinct Ravenstail robes now contemporarily woven outnumber the scant remnants and rare robe examples held in museums around the world. Naaxiin robes, new and historic, may not be thought to dance a chief into transformation any longer, but they are still worn by leaders to declare prestige, identity, and power in the new social hierarchies of a people and culture that has endured with evolving traditions. As time marches on, new stories emerge and contemporary artists take the ancestor's techniques and twine them into story garments of today. Swaying with the energy of this enduring spirit, the textiles of the Pacific Northwest coast will hopefully dance into future centuries.

NOTES

1 John R. Swanton, *Haida Texts and Myths, Skidegate Dialect* (Washington, DC: Smithsonian Institute Bureau of American Ethnology, 1905); Swanton, "Part Two Haida Texts, Masset Dialect," in *Memoir of the American Museum of Natural History* (New York: American Museum of Natural History, 1908); and Swanton, *Contributions to the Ethnology of the Haida* (Leiden: E J. Brill, 1905).

2 As cited in Swanton, *Haida Texts and Myths*, 212.

3 As cited in Swanton, *Haida Texts and Myths*, 224.

4 As cited in Swanton, *Haida Texts and Myths*, 181.

5 George Vancouver, *A Voyage of Discovery to the North Pacific Ocean, and Round the World: In Which the Coast of North-West America Has Been Carefully Examined and Accurately Surveyed: Undertaken by His Majesty's Command, Principally with a View To Ascertain the Existence of Any Navigable Communication between the North Pacific and North Atlantic Oceans, and Performed in the Years 1790, 1791, 1792, 1793, 1794 and 1795, in the Discovery Sloop of War, and Armed Tender Chatham, under the Command of Captain George Vancouver,* volume 2 (Piccadilly, UK: John Stockdale, n.d.), 280–81.

6 Thomas Vaughan and Bill Holm, *Soft Gold: The Fur Trade and Cultural Exchange on the Northwest Coast of America* (Portland: Oregon Historical Society, 1982), 207.

7 Jacinto Caamano, "The Journal of Don Jacinto Caamano," *British Columbia Historical Quarterly* (1938): 217.

8 Alexander Mackenzie and George Mercer Dawson, *Descriptive Notes on Certain Implements Weapons, &c., from Graham Island, Queen Charlotte Islands, B.C.*, section 2 (Montreal: Royal Society of Canada, 1891), 48.

9 As cited in Swanton, *Haida Texts and Myths*, 286–87.

10 John Wallace in the unpublished notes of Viola Garfield, University of Washington Library, 1945.

11 John Wallace in the unpublished notes of Viola Garfield, University of Washington Library, 1945.

12 George Thornton Emmons, *The Chilkat Blanket* (New York: American Museum of Natural History, 1907), 341.

13 Cheryl Samuel, *The Raven's Tail* (Vancouver: University of British Columbia Press, 1987).

14 As cited in Swanton, *Haida Texts and Myths*, 224.

15 Mackenzie and Dawson, *Descriptive Notes on Certain Implements Weapons*, 48.

16 As cited in George A. Miles, *James Swan Cha-tic of the Northwest Coast* (New Haven, CT: Yale University Press, 2003), 34.

17 Viola E. Garfield and Lynn A. Forrest, *The Wolf and the Raven* (Seattle: University of Washington Press, 1948), 97–99.

CHAPTER 13

Sayach'apis and the Naani (*Grizzly Bear*) Crest

Denise Nicole Green

FOR MANY NUU-CHAH-NULTH PEOPLE THE CONCEPT OF HILTH (*LOCATION* OR *TO be located in a place*) is an important foundation for wider social relationships and creative expression. Part of this understanding is that since iikmuut (*the time before time*), Kuu-as (Nuu-chah-nulth *people*) have been engaged in making temporally designated places within their territories to mark important transitional events.[1] These ceremonies, known as n'uushitl (*potlatch*), are a space of contradiction between the ephemeral and the stable.[2] They are what feminist spatial theorist Doreen Massey would describe as "spatio-temporal events"—that is, a place which arises from a dynamic entanglement of time and space.[3] Haa'yuups, an important Hupacasath maker and knowledge-keeper, explained to me: "We're in a heightened state and spiritual things are being done. People are showing representations of their ancestors and talking about the relationship between themselves and specific places on the land."[4] Places come into being through their visual representations and through the physical bodies and spaces that carry these representations.

In this chapter I examine the textiles and regalia used in one particular potlatch to analyze how the body, memory, and material culture intersect to make the potlatch ceremony as a site of creative, spiritual, and cultural production. This specific potlatch was a Yaxmalthit (*cleansing potlatch*) held by Sayach'apis (Walter Thomas) in February 2010. It resulted in the production of new ha'wilthmis (*chiefly wealth treasures*)—specifically, the addition of a visual representation of a near-death experience onto the thliitsapilthim (*ceremonial curtain*) belonging to Walter, and the creation and claim of a new family crest that was rendered onto women's dance shawls and men's vests. I focus specifically on the thliitsapilthim and huulthin (*ceremonial dance shawls*) as articulations of family rights and privileges, as communication devices, and active entities that produce sacred space. During the potlatch, entanglements of people, places, and the ha'wilthmis (*masks, headdresses, ceremonial curtains, rattles, drums* etc.) transform and partition space, and the presence of family treasures and their role in the invitation of ancestors make the space sacred. Bodies adorned in huulthin travel through spatial delineations, follow protocols that regulate movement, and all the while engage the mind, memory, and "historical imagination" in the making of a new place.[5] Amid this means of place-making, potlatch participants connect their experiences to the wider landscape, which must be imagined and evoked through visual representation on the thliitsapilthim.

N'uushitl (Potlatch) and Yaxmalthit (Cleansing Potlatch)

A n'uushitl (Nuu-chah-nulth *potlatch*) is a ceremony held to mark important transitional life events, such as birth, puberty, naming, seating (chieftainships), marriage, cleansing, and ending grief. In a potlatch ceremony, family and community members are called to witness the business that takes place and is therefore an important part of Nuu-chah-nulth oral history tradition. A potlatch is also a venue for redistribution of wealth across diverse tribal communities that have access to different kinds of resources.[6]

The Canadian government attempted to suppress Nuu-chah-nulth ceremonial life—and that of other First Nations of the region—by outlawing the potlatch for nearly a century through legislation that became known colloquially as the Potlatch Ban. This legislat was originally written as an amendment to the Canadian Indian Act in 1876, deemed unconstitutional, and revised in 1884 (and again in 1895, 1906, and 1927). Despite these laws, potlatching flourished in the Alberni Valley after 1880 and, despite threats, Nuu-chah-nulth people continued potlatching.[7] To make the ceremony more secret, the ha'wilthmis shifted in form, as did some practices.[8] The strategies employed by Nuu-chah-nulth people to continue potlatching are visible in the contemporary forms of material culture that shape the spatial layout of the n'uushitl. The thliitsapilthim is a cloth partition, typically eight to ten feet high and twenty to thirty feet long, which depicts the crests of the most prominent chiefly families in Nuu-chah-nulth haahuul thii (*traditional territory*). Previously, these crest paintings adorned large cedar board partitions and were called kiitsaksuu-ilthim (*"marked on in a meaningful way" ceremonial partition*). With the Potlatch Ban, kiitsaksuu-ilthim were replaced by thliitsapilthim, which could be folded up and hidden away.[9]

The legacy of the Potlatch Ban is preserved in the contemporary potlatch where the thliitsapilthim's use continues and functions as a disciplinary marker of spatial and social boundaries. By drawing the thliitsapilthim across a trolling wire hung the width of the gymnasium, the space becomes delineated between the host family and guests, the sacred space of the floor and backstage, and what is public and what is private.[10] The thliitsapilthim not only acts as a spatial partition but also as a mode of communication by declaring the rights, resources, territories, and histories of the chiefly families. There are many kinds of Nuu-chah-nulth feasts and potlatches, but in this chapter I focus on a Yaxmalthit. Yaxmalthit translates as *brushing off* or *sweeping off* and is a cleansing potlatch, usually held if someone has endured a near-death experience and the kahmis (*deathness*) still lingers around the body. The literal translation of *sweeping off death* reveals how people think and act spatially. Past traumas linger in the spaces surrounding the body: this space, as much as the body itself, requires public cleansing. Memories of the near-death experience become semitangible (as kahmis) and linger in a spatial way around the bodies to which they have become attached. Kahmis is perceived as polluting and dangerous, and the Yaxmalthit ritual functions as a mechanism to spatially contain and control the deathness—and becomes the liminal state of being in-between life and death.[11]

Historical Context: From Tom Sayach'apis to Walter Thomas Sayach'apis

The name, Sayach'apis, like other important Nuu-chah-nulth names, has many generations of owners. Sayach'apis is Walter Thomas today, but Sayach'apis was also the late Tom Sayach'apis, a primary informant to linguistic anthropologist Edward Sapir (from 1910 through 1914) and Franz Boas (in 1889).[12] Sapir used the distinct life of Sayach'apis to illustrate broader social and cultural themes, while alluding to the impact of colonialism and new economic systems on Native life. He was enthralled by the specificity of Nuu-chah-nulth cultural practices—particularly family tuupatii (*rites*)—and this cultural trait made it increasingly problematic to write about *the* Nuu-chah-nulth (or the Nootka, as he referred to them). Sapir chose instead to focus on individual life histories as vessels to illustrate nuanced cultural attributes, social traits, and ethnological realities.[13]

Douglas Thomas was the eldest son of Tom Sayach'apis, and Douglas's eldest son was Yaayuukwii-a (Alex Thomas). Yaayuukwii-a, like his father and grandfather, proved invaluable to Sapir as an informant. While I sat next to Thlotiismayak (April Thomas) at the 2010 Yaxmalthit, she beamed while telling me stories about Alex Thomas, and particularly noted his talent for song composition. Walter also fondly remembered his grandfather, Alex Thomas: "He knew a lot. He got a lot for the reserve, here. There's a piece on the curtain about him, how he traveled to Ottawa to get our fisheries going down in the river here. He had a lot to do with it. A lot to do with our language." Walter continued: "He was a Chief, too, and I guess I'd call it a passion. [He] wanted to do something for our people so we could fish. Over the years a lot of band members have made a lot of money over it, and it's because of him."[14] While Walter was not the eldest brother in his generation, his father (who was the eldest son of Alex Thomas) requested that Walter be seated as head of the family. Walter now holds the name Sayach'apis.[15]

Walter is a man of few words. He is reserved and contemplative with a smile in his eyes, and speaks with a singsong voice that brings to mind his Ditidaht ancestry. I have only known him after his near-death experience, after his sobriety, after his commitment to being at home and serving as head of his family. Walter comes from a long line of highly regarded men, and now in his sixties he commands respect by playing an active role in ceremonial life, hosting potlatches, and thus increasing the prestige of his family. He did not always play an active role in ceremonial life. "It was later on in my years that I started going," he explained to me. "When I started going a lot of times I was asking myself why I didn't start earlier, cause there is a lot of important stuff that's brought out, eh?" Walter struggled with alcoholism throughout his youth and adulthood. "In my teenage years I was in jail quite a bit. So I lost out on a lot of teachings," he said.[16]

Walter also spent a lot of time away from home, working in the logging industry, living away for weeks at a time in logging camps and shake block cutting camps. Today he is fulfilled and content to be at home, to be sober, to be an example of strength and leadership among his family and community. His grandfather and father are now deceased, so Walter looks to other people of knowledge to seek out information and advice. He consults his cousin, Haa'yuups, and aunt, Kathy Robinson, about cultural protocols and history. He has asked me to keep him updated if I find anything in my research related to his family. In continuing the ceremonial practices enacted by his ancestors, Walter is consciously and meticulously educating himself. He has faced very real challenges in his life and these trials have made Walter a stronger leader of his people. He is relatable, admired for his sobriety and dedication to cultural practices. He, like his great-great-grandfather Tom Sayach'apis, has hosted numerous feasts and potlatches. Sapir wrote of Tom Sayach'apis: "The many feasts he has given and the many ceremonial dances and displays he has had performed have all had their desired effect—they have shed luster on his sons and daughters and grandchildren, they have 'put his family high' among the Ts'isha'ath [Tseshaht] tribe, and they have even carried his name to other, distant Nootka tribes, and to tribes on the east coast of the island that are of alien speech."[17]

Walter Has a Supernatural Encounter

The event that brought about the need for a Yaxmalthit and resulted in the new crest for Walter's family and additional imagery to his thliitsapilthim was both a near-death and supernatural encounter.[18] A naani (*grizzly bear*) attacked Walter, who communicated with it and survived with one arm maimed. His thliitsapilthim, which was originally painted by Haa'yuups, was modified to include a representation of the event.[19] Aa-aatsiknuk (Ray Sim), a member of the Musqueam First Nation, living in Port Alberni, designed the grizzly bear crest that was later silkscreen printed onto T-shirts distributed at the potlatch and appliquéd onto dance shawls and printed onto men's vests, which were worn by family members at the Yaxmalthit.

In November 2008, Sayach'apis was employed in the logging industry, which brought him to a remote site in midcoast British Columbia (near Bella Bella). "All it could have taken was a few seconds for that thing to end my life, eh?" he told me. "Because I was face to face with it [the grizzly bear]. Like that [points to image on curtain, Figure 13.1]. Before it took off it was just not even a foot from my face. And that's when I figured if my head goes in his mouth, I'm gone." He was walking in the woods and mistakenly stepped into the bear's den. He had a fish sandwich in his backpack and assumed the bear had smelled it (the last he saw of the bear, it had grabbed his backpack and ran away). Before taking off, the bear pinned him down. Walter explained what happened next:

> I was thinking, "I'm not that old, eh? This is too soon for me to go see Harvey [his brother] and Dad." Cause we had their memorial that February [2008] and this happened in November [2008], and I was thinking, "This is too early for me to go." . . . One thing that I remember too is when at the time when I thought it was going to kill me, I figured, I'm dying anyway so I'm going to start yelling at this thing, just to, not a defensive thing, but I started screaming, "Why are you doing this to me?" And it stopped. And that's when, like I didn't sit there and dwell on it, but it got to mind about thinking about Harvey and Dad. Like just a split second thing, but like I said after a while I started thinking about it. Then I thought about it when I was screaming and yelling and swearing at it . . . and after I asked him the question "Why are you doing this to me?" he stopped, and took off down the hill.[20]

This story from Walter is of great consequence because it is a firsthand account of a contemporary encounter of spiritual, emotional, and supernatural significance. In the future he plans to add wolves to his thliitsapilthim (at least two), around the image of the naani attacking him "to signify that something was watching that day over me." Walter, like other Nuu-chah-nulth people, considers the thliitsapilthim a living, unfinished document that visually represents the family's ongoing history. The creation of the new crest and mnemonic representation on the thliitsapilthim was a result of Walter's encounter. Wanting the image as large as possible, he had it tightly placed between the mouth of the whale and a sealskin float (see Figure 13.1).

It is not out of the realm of possibility that a person working in the woods of midcoast British Columbia might encounter a grizzly bear. What is extraordinary, and what makes Walter's experience one of the supernatural realm, was his ability to communicate with the bear while simultaneously thinking of his recently deceased family members. It was only after Walter asked the bear why he was attacking him that the bear stopped, thought about it, and abandoned the fight. At this same moment, Walter's mind went to his father and elder brother, and he consciously thought that it was not his time to travel home to Ta'winisim (*the world*

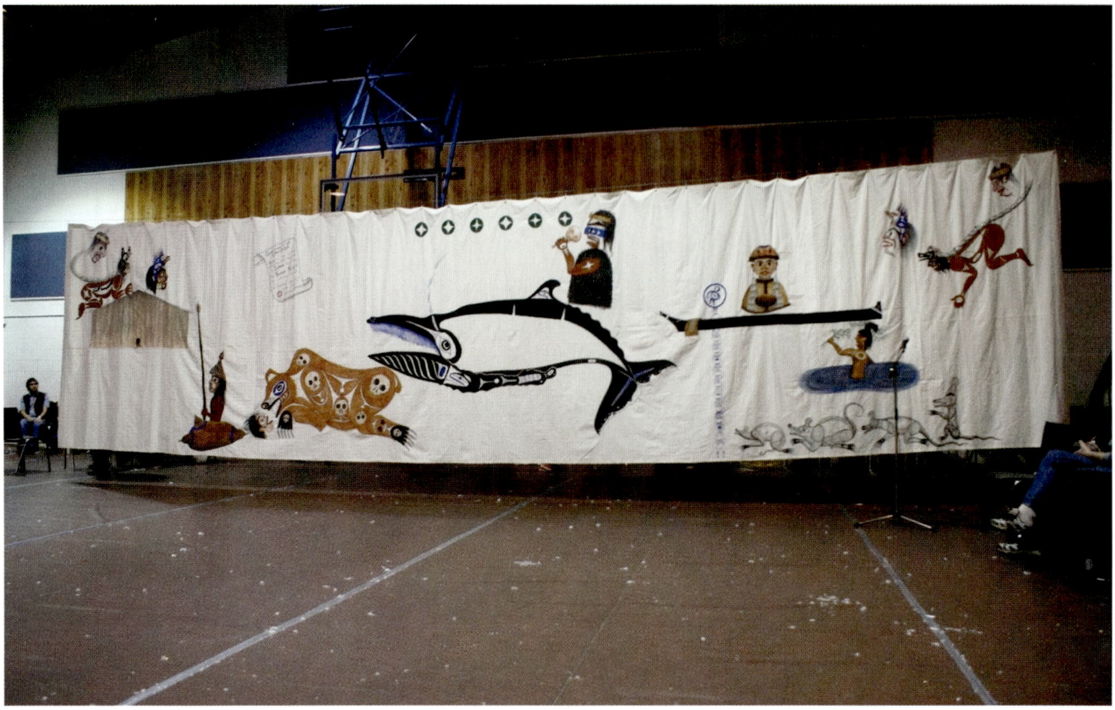

13.1. Walter's thliitsapilthim on display at his February 2010 Yaxmalthit. Eagle down on the floor indicates sacred space. Photograph by author.

beyond the horizon). This moment transformed an encounter of the natural world into an encounter of the supernatural.

The Yaxmalthit: Display of the Thliitsapilthim and the Naani Crest

Supernatural experiences are believed to elevate the prestige and power of Nuu-chah-nulth families.[21] Some of these experiences are considered secret and known only by the family (or a select few within a family), whereas other supernatural encounters are shared publicly and ultimately declared in visual form. In the case of Walter's great-great-grandfather Tom Sayach'apis, who had three supernatural encounters, he kept amulets—that is, physical affirmations—of these experiences very close to his body. Keeping these talismans nearby enabled wealth accumulation, and in Sapir's recounting of these supernatural events, he ended each story by concluding that the encounter had made Tom Sayach'apis "favored in the accumulation of wealth."[22] Walter's encounter was also made public through an anthropologist's text (here, and in my 2014 dissertation), but more importantly through ha'wilthmis: he chose to work with artists to visually represent his encounter both on his thliitsapilthim and as crests on the garments worn by his family during this potlatch (and those to follow).[23] Next I outline the proceedings of the Yaxmalthit, with emphasis on, and interpretation of, the new forms of ha'wilthmis depicting his supernatural experience.

For oral histories, cultural knowledge, and ceremonial business to unfold appropriately at a n'uushitl, a great deal of prior planning occurs. There are many months of dance practices and family meetings, however the family meeting the night before a potlatch is most crucial: Haa'yuups, Sayach'apis, his sister Florence, and the potlatch floor manager met the prior night to confer about the logistics.[24] As we shared the meal, the appropriate order of events were outlined, spatial layout discussed, and the particulars of the Yaxmalthit ritual summarized.

Walter's Yaxmalthit took place at the Maht Mahs Gymnasium on the Tseshaht Reserve and began around 10 a.m. on February 6, 2010. Before the space of the floor was made sacred, the first order of business was to present cash to grieving families, something known as a ta-althma (*a cane to hold up those grieving*).[25] Though each family has unique ceremonial rights and practices, the protocol of acknowledging grief is shared among all Nuu-chah-nulth tribes and families.[26] Acknowledging those grieving at the very start of the potlatch visually identifies grieving families to the other Ha'wiih (*heads of families*) and members of the host family. This knowledge will shape people's behaviors toward those grieving throughout the potlatch; it will help the wider public understand why those grieving might not fully participate. Some grieving families are acknowledged even though they are not present—precisely for that reason, as they may have declined the invitation to the potlatch because their family practice is isolation during periods of grief.

Following the presentation of ta-althma, the maamaatl'e (*security guards*) are introduced. These "security guards" monitor space and enforce proper movement. Their position of authority is made visible through shawls they wear, which are pinned with cash. Following these announcements, the potlatch floor is "fixed," which marks the most important spatial transformation of the entire potlatch. Fixing the floor is a process of making boundaries—that is, of dividing space into the sacred and profane. Interestingly, this is a process of taking spaces that have been shaped by colonial forces—whether the government of Canada, the United Church, or other settler spaces—and transforming them back into Indigenous spaces.[27] "A lot of our tribes don't have big houses," Haa'yuups explained to me. "This means we have to host potlatches in all kinds of different places. But we can make spaces sacred: a gymnasium, a house, the Port Alberni Italian Hall."[28]

Like most spatial transformations in the potlatch, a song signals this change. The song genre is called ts'iiky'ak, which are chants used to call ancestors into the space and are the most ancient songs known to Nuu-chah-nulth people. These chants are believed to be produced through contact between human and spiritual beings (i.e., supernatural encounters that typically take place in the woods). The chant is accompanied by the sound of a rattle, which is moved in a counterclockwise direction. Two men proceed around the floor in a counterclockwise direction, moving through the larger circle in a series of smaller counterclockwise circular movements while dropping handfuls of ts'iilthaen (*eagle down*).

This ritual follows Michel de Certeau's contention that space is dynamic and includes intersections among "mobile elements" that brings the space alive through bodies.[29] The bodies performing the rite move in a counterclockwise direction, replicating Nuu-chah-nulth beliefs about birth and death. When a person's physical body dies, their thliitmaktlstii (*spirit*) moves counterclockwise from the horizon down into the Undersea World, back up into the On-The-Land World to the In-The-Sky World, and flies away into the Up-In-The-Sky World, known as Ta'winisim (*the world beyong the horizon*). When ancestors are invited to be present, those making the invitation embody and enact this spatial-spiritual understanding. A place is being made through the ceremony and the corporeal intention of the embodied subject is to use the body to enter into another world.[30]

After the ts'iikaa is completed and ancestors are present, the Ha'wiih are named and acknowledged with taana (*money*) for their attendance and role in witnessing.[31] A second ts'iikyak indicates another significant spatial transformation: the thliitsapilthim is pulled across the trolling wire upon which it is hung, revealing the history, rights, and responsibilities of the Sayach'apis family. Recently added to the now visible thliitsapilthim is the depiction of a vicious naani with razor sharp claws, staring down at the face of Sayach'apis. In the moment of revelation when the thliitsapilthim is exposed, the landscapes, memories, and histories that are depicted become part of the place that emerges through the potlatch. The imagery on Walter's thliitsapilthim declares the histories, privileges, and rights that belong to his family. The genesis of Walter's thliitsapilthim began with Walter's father, Bob Thomas, in the summer of 2003. Bob Thomas called his nephew Haa'yuups to his home to bear witness to his wishes for his son Walter to be seated in his position one day as head of their family. Walter's thliitsapilthim was painted in the mid-2000s to be shown first at the Thlaaktuulthaa (*end-of-grief potlatch*), which was held for Bob Thomas in February 2008.

The original crests were decided upon through a consultation between Walter's father and Haa'yuups, and later between Walter and Haa'yuups. Walter wanted to use the thliitsapilthim to display the history of his family broadly and left space on the thliitsapilthim for the unknown events of the future. Some of the images on the curtain correspond with artifacts, stories, and sound recordings that were collected by Edward Sapir and are now in the Canadian Museum of History: the large talking stick that belonged to Tom Sayach'apis (on the far right side of the thliitsapilthim), the mice along the bottom right, which represent a song owned by Walter's family and recorded on wax cylinder by Sapir ("Mouse dance song," Canadian Museum of History # VII-F-79), and the house post that would have been inside Tom Sayach'apis's *ma-as* (big house), which is represented at the top left of the thliitsapilthim (Canadian Museum of History # VII-F-425a-d).

In addition to the ha'wilthmis held by the Canadian Museum of History, the thliitsapilthim also includes images as mnemonics, used for recounting different aspects of the family's history. The central image is of a whale, meant to foreground the family's whaling history, with a man above using a rattle and a ts'ikyak to communicate with ancestors. The practice of uusimch (*ritual bathing*), which would have taken place before an important hunt or ceremony, is depicted to the right of the whale and above the mice. A declaration is painted to the upper left of the whale and represents the important work of Alex Thomas, Walter's grandfather, who traveled to Ottawa and fought for their Indigenous fishing rights. The declaration reads: "Government of Canada: Know all men by these presents, that the group of Indians living along the Somass River + its estuary shall not be molested while they pursue their livelihood fishing."

In addition to the declarations and histories depicted visually, the thliitsapilthim also creates spatial regions within the potlatch—in other words, the production of places that are "bounded to some degree by barriers of perception."[32] The thliitsapilthim conceals the preparations and wealth of the host family and is a "barrier of perception" guarded by the maamaatl'e: only the host family and significant others invited by the host have authority to go behind the curtain. In a Nuu-chah-nulth nuu'shitl the passage from behind to in front of the thliitsapilthim, while closed to the audience, is highlighted visually. As Haa'yuups explained to me: "The headdress, the robe, and the human being in it come out, and they turn a full circle to the left at the edge of the thliitsapilthim and they go from this getting ready place to this place where real things happen. So thliitsapilthim are places of transition in that case where one world turns into another world for a brief moment."[33]

The first business of the potlatch was to yaxshitl (*sweep off*) Walter, an embodied process in which Walter stood on a wool blanket, women covered him in ts'iilthaen (*eagle down*), and men brushed him with tuuhmapt (*spruce* or "*scare bush*"). Tuuhmapt is called "scare bush" because it is believed to scare away any negative or sad feelings, and the sharpness of the spruce needles reinforces this physically and phenomenologically. Once sweeping was completed, four women took hold of Walter to lead him off the blanket. The men dropped their spruce branches onto the blanket, which was subsequently folded up and taken down to the river, where it was immediately burned and the ashes left to travel away to the ocean.

The thliitsapilthim, audience seating, and the architectural structure of the gymnasium combined with the ritual "fixing the floor" created a kind of differentiated space within which mobility could occur. In this situation, power was harnessed as "external power" to eliminate kahmis (*deathness*).[34] The deathness that lingered on the body of Walter was considered dangerous but could be controlled through the ritual.[35] This is, in part, why Walter requested that the two men who helped him after the naani encounter—a helicopter pilot and foreman—also be brushed. Their closeness to Walter immediately after the attack means that they were likely exposed to the kahmis as well. Through this ritual, danger was controlled by disciplined movements that are believed to vanquish the kahmis spatially and materially.

After the business of cleansing, the potlatch underwent numerous spatial transformations throughout the remaining twenty hours. As coauthors Helen Roberts, Edward Sapir, and Morris Swadesh have noted, Nuu-chah-nulth ceremonial life is punctuated by use of song, and singing generally marks potlatch transitions.[36] During meals, the thliitsapilthim was drawn back and the host family sang feast songs and served their guests. During what is typically considered the "entertainment" portion of the potlatch, which lasted nearly sixteen hours, the thliitsapilthim was opened to its full length and various families gifted the host with taana to use the potlatch floor to perform imchaapyak (*entertainment songs*), dances, and to a'tikshitl (*give a formal, public acknowledgment of gratitude*) the host family.

The longer the entertainment portion of the potlatch lasts, the more the prestige of the host family is heightened. Other families—often relatives of the host—invest in the potlatch by performing and giving support in the form of gifts, goods to be redistributed, and money. This is part of a process of "holding up" and "making high" the host and host family. When a family takes the floor, it is common that the first explication is of the kinship ties to the host. If cultural forms—like songs, dances, names, crests, legends, or oral histories—strengthen these roots, the details are publicly pronounced and sometimes displayed. The thliitsapilthim often guides these explications as a mnemonic device. Today, as in Tom Sayach'apis's time, "the threads of the genealogical past are wound tight around the North West Coastman."[37]

After the entertainment portion of the potlatch finished at 6:15 a.m. the following day, the host family took the floor to begin their final business: they displayed ha'wilthmis (*chiefly wealth possessions*), declared ownership of a new crest for the family, the naani (*grizzly bear*) (Figure 13.2), and, after acknowledging his maa'miiksuu (*elder lines of descent*), seated Walter Sayach'apis as the head of the Nash'asat-h. Walter's family performed their haatshuulthaa (*chiefly wealth songs*)—the first was a hinkiits, a dance involving a male and female serpent headdress. Hinkiitsim are representations of serpent messengers for Nuu-chah-nulth deities, and their performance brings these spiritual creatures to life. All of these dances were performed by dancers wearing new huulthin depicting the naani crest. By performing their most highly treasured and prestigious songs in these shawls, Walter's family solidified their declaration of a new crest and elevated its status. Following this dance, the Ha'wiih in attendance were acknowledged through presentation of cash for witnessing this ch'ihamis (*spiritual wealth*) and the display of their new crest.

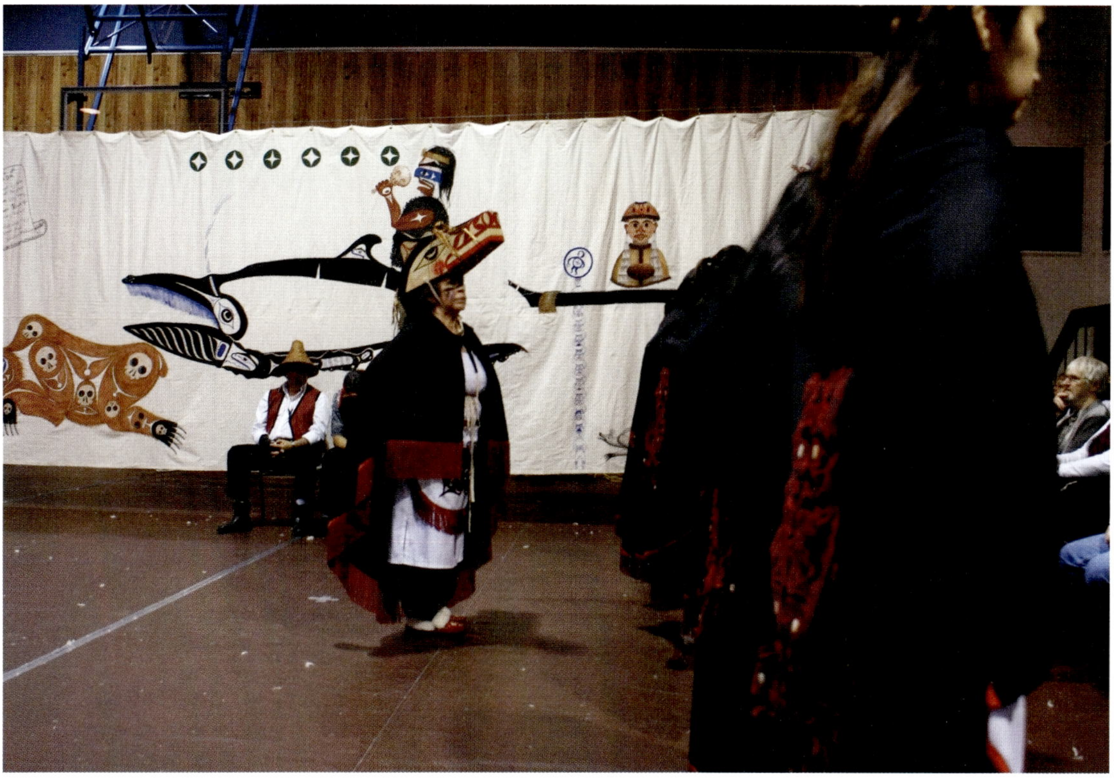

13.2. Women of Walter's family made twenty shawls with an appliquéd grizzly bear crest. Walter (seated) wore a vest that was silkscreen printed with the same design. The shared crest visibly identified the members of Walter's family and served as a declaration of their new crest. Photograph by author.

Prior to his official seating, Walter Sayach'apis acknowledged the son of his elder brother, who is maamee-ux (*elder*) to Sayach'apis. He addressed his nephew's position by giving him the name held by his nephew's grandfather, Bob Thomas, and great-grandfather, Alex Thomas: Yaayuukwii-a. Only after elder male lines of descent were acknowledged, did it become appropriate to move ahead with the seating of Sayach'apis who, at the behest of his father, bypassed an elder male line in taking the seat as the Head of the Nash'asat-h. Haa'yuups spoke on behalf of Sayach'apis: "We came here today to acknowledge that Sayach'apis had an encounter with a naani [. . .] Finally we have come to what we have been waiting for, to see someone seated where his father was." At this point, dressed in garments passed onto him from his father, Sayach'apis was physically, metaphorically, and socially seated as the Head of his family, his House, and the Nash'asat-h subdivision of the Tseshaht (Figure 13.3).

To complete their business, the host family acknowledged all witnesses to the passing of the hereditary tikuu-ilth (*seat/position*). The family pulled the thliitsapilthim back to reveal their wealth: an enormous mountain of gifts to be presented

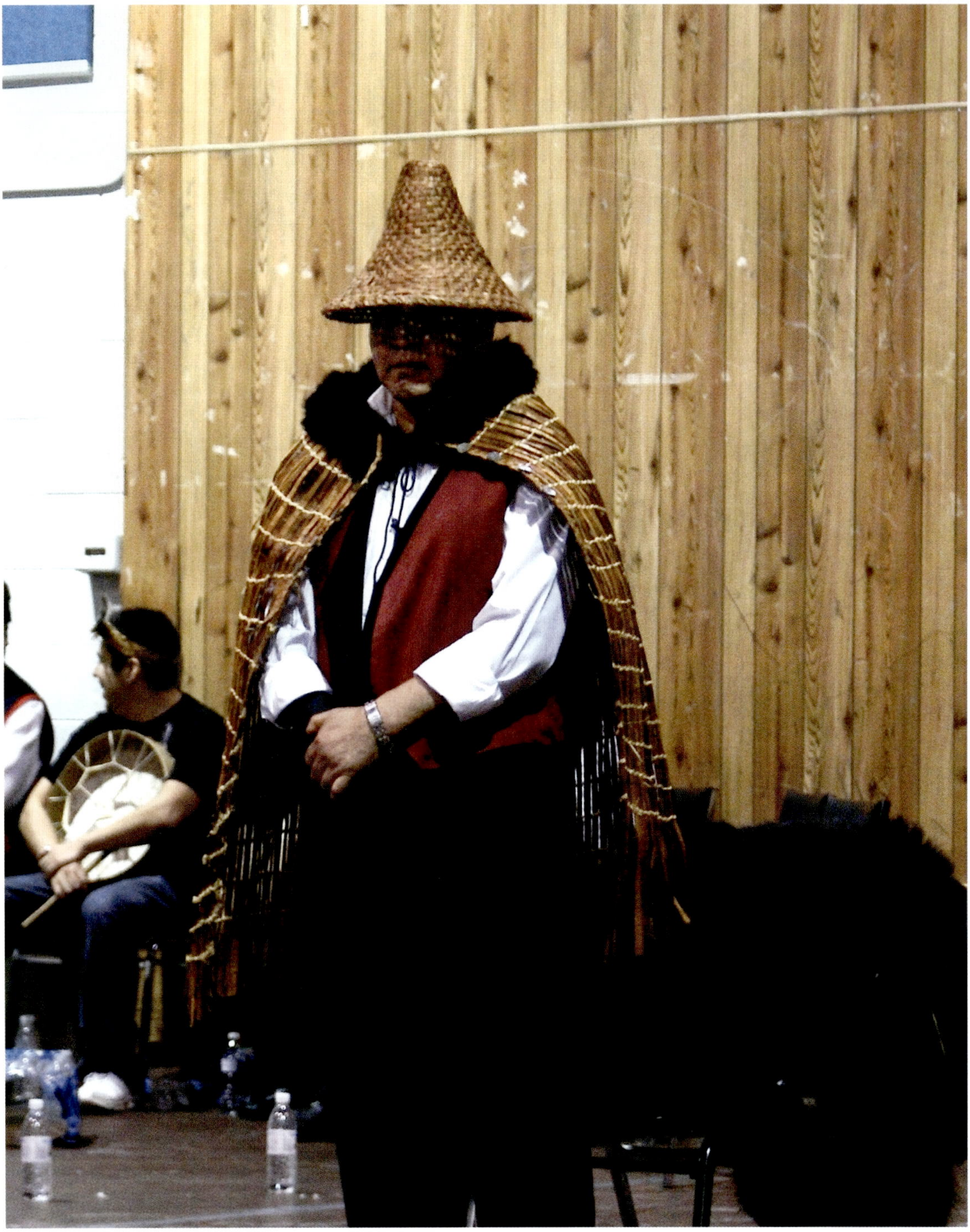

13.3. Walter is seated as the head of his House. Photograph by author.

to witnesses. This signaled another powerful function of the thliitsapilthim: to simultaneously conceal yet convey the wealth of the family. As anthropologist Eric Wolf has argued, the material embodiment of power and wealth come to life at the end of a potlatch through redistribution.[38] A Haatshuulthaayak song signaled the moment of wealth distribution, and the space transformed as "runners" (often young male members of the host family) began carrying cash to witnesses in a highly structured distribution; later, female "runners" moved between the pile of material goods and the guests, delivering gifts in a seemingly random fashion. At about 10:00 a.m. these networks expanded into the world outside of the potlatch as a huulthlwachitlyak (*song used to bring about "storm blowing up"*) signaled to guests that it was time to exit the gymnasium.

Witnessing Transformation

Potlatching is a way of publicly creating and addressing social debt. The family creates a debt in asking the broader community to attend as witnesses. In this case, witnesses observed the cleansing ritual, saw the thliitsapilthim and were informed of the new grizzly bear crest, and witnessed naming and the seating of Walter. These witnesses were acknowledged with food, cash, and material goods bestowed upon them at the conclusion of the event. Walter acknowledged the debt of his life, giving gifts to the people who helped him during his attack and later healing.

A contemporary Nuu-chah-nulth potlatch is a dynamic place of creative expression and declaration, punctuated by spatial transformations. While a potlatch may at first appear temporally and spatially contained, boundaries of time and space are perforated by the visual imagery on the thliitsapilthim, the crests worn on bodies, and the movement of material culture within the space. The thliitsapilthim connects potlatch attendees to family histories through mnemonic imagery; the addition of the grizzly bear is a new mnemonic, which was added to affirm the event and declare the right to a new crest. Walter's family danced new shawls, all with the naani crest and performed their most prestigious songs, haatshuulthaa, adding prestige to the new imagery. These materials, which adorn both spaces and bodies, are the bedrock of a Nuu-chah-nulth potlatch ceremony and aid in the perpetuation of long-standing family histories. The potlatch itself is an unbounded encounter between structures of power, embodied subjectivities, entangled histories, and memories. The convergence of these forces is articulated through ha'wilthmis, like the thliitsapilthim and huulthin, which produce a sacred place for contemporary ceremony to unfold.

NOTES

1 The direct translation of Kuu-as (Nuu-chah-nulth *people*) is "real, living human being."

2 Henri Lefebvre, *The Production of Space*, translated by D. Nicholson-Smith (Oxford: Blackwell, 1991), 163.

3 Doreen Massey, *For Space* (London: Sage, 2005), 130.

4 Author, interview with Chuuchkamalthnii (Ron Hamilton), October 24, 2009. Haa'yuups is the name currently used by Chuuchkamalthnii.

5 Keith Basso, *Wisdom Sits in Places: Landscape and Language among the Western Apache* (Albuquerque: University of New Mexico Press, 1996), 7.

6 Eugene Y. Arima and John Dewhirst, "Nootkans of Vancouver Island," in *Handbook of North American Indian*, vol. 7, *Northwest Coast*, edited by W. Suttles and W. Sturtevant, 391–411 (Washington, DC: Smithsonian Institution Press, 1990); Franz Boas, "Second General Report on the Indians of British Columbia," *British Association for the Advancement of Science*, 60th meeting (1890) 572–715; George Clutesi, *Potlatch* (Sidney, BC: Grey's Publishing, 1969); Alan L. Hoover, ed., *Nuu-chah-nulth Voices: Histories, Objects, and Journeys* (Victoria: Royal British Columbia Museum, 2000); and Franz Boas and Helen Codere, *Kwakiutl Ethnography* (Chicago: University of Chicago Press, 1966).

7 Susan Golla, "He Has a Name: History and Social Structure among the Indians of Western Vancouver Island," PhD diss., Columbia University, 1987, 60–61.

8 For example, the popular practice in the early 1900s of using an older, female proxy in an Aaytstuulthaa to stand in for the young girl who would have been away at the Alberni Mission school (later called the Alberni Indian Residential School).

9 Denise N. Green and Chuuchkamalthnii, *Histakshitl Ts'awaatskwii (We Come From One Root)*, documentary film (67 minutes), Ethnographic Film Unit at the University of British Columbia–Vancouver, 2010; and Charlotte Townsend-Gault and Chuuchkamalthnii, *Backstory: Nuu-chah-nulth Ceremonial Curtains and the Work of Ki-ke-in* (Vancouver: Belkin Art Gallery, 2010).

10 Erving Goffman, *The Presentation of Self in Everyday Life* (Garden City, NY: Doubleday, 1959).

11 Mary Douglas, *Purity and Danger* (London: Routledge, 1966), 116.

12 For clarity, throughout this chapter I use the English name Walter to refer to Sayach'apis Walter Thomas. This is done to remove confusion between Walter Thomas and his great-great-grandfather, Tom Sayach'apis.

13 Edward Sapir, "Sayachapis: A Nootka Trader," in *American Indian Life by Several of Its Students*, edited by Elsie Clews Parsons, 297–324 (New York: Viking Press, 1922).

14 Author, interview with Sayach'apis/Walter Thomas, October 13, 2011.

15 Walter assumed the name Sayach'apis at the Thlaaktuulthaa held for his late father and older brother, Harvey, in February 2008.

16 Author, interview with Sayach'apis/Thomas.

17 Sapir, "Sayachapis: A Nootka Trader," 297.

18 In the days leading up to the February 2010 Yaxmalthit, Walter and I spoke informally about the event; he gave me permission to keep a detailed record in my field notebook of the potlatch and to take photographs. It was not until the fall of 2011 that I formally interviewed Walter over the course of two days. During this formal interview he shared with me, in detail, his near-death experience.

19 At the time the thliitsapilthim was painted, Haa'yuups was primarily using the name Ki-Ke-In. When the thliitsapilthim was modified in 2009, Haa'yuups was using the name Chuuchkamalthnii. Since 2017, he has primarily used the name Haa'yuups. Aa-aatsiknuk (Ray Sim) helped with the painting of the thliitsapilthim.

20 Author, interview with Sayach'apis/Thomas.
21 Sapir, "Sayachapis: A Nootka Trader."
22 Sapir, "Sayachapis: A Nootka Trader," 310–11.
23 Denise Green, "Producing Materials, Places and Identities: A Study of Encounters in the Alberni Valley," PhD diss., University of British Columbia, 2014.
24 The floor manager is responsible for use of the potlatch "floor." It is their job to oversee that everything runs smoothly throughout the event. I was also in attendance at this meeting in my role as the anthropologist keeping record of the event.
25 Each family has a unique proprietary practice of making the floor sacred—some use eagle down, others use paint, some use a special dance or prayer chant, and many use some combination of the aforementioned. Filming, photography, or recording of any kind (including written), in my experience, is never allowed during this portion of the potlatch.
26 Where families differ is in particular observances of grief and in how grief is thrown away in a Thlaakt'uulthaa (*end-of-grief potlatch*).
27 The Mat-Mahs Gymnasium, the location of Walter's potlatch, was the gymnasium of the Alberni Indian Residential School (until 1973).
28 Author, interview with Haa'yuups/Chuuchkamalthnii, February 6, 2010.
29 Michel De Certeau, *The Practice of Everyday Life*, translated by S. Rendall (Berkeley: University of California Press, 1984), 117.
30 Arnold Van Gennep, *Rites of Passage* (London: Routledge, 1960), 20.
31 Upon discussing the order of events to unfold on the floor in the organizing meeting the evening prior, everyone acknowledged that "the floor belongs to the Ha'wiih before anyone else."
32 Goffman, *Presentation of Self in Everyday Life*, 106.
33 Author, interview with Haa'yuups/Chuuchkamalthnii, November 22, 2009.
34 Douglas, *Purity and Danger*, 119.
35 Douglas, *Purity and Danger*, 116.
36 Helen Roberts, Edward Sapir, and Morris Swadesh, *Songs of the Nootka Indians of Western Vancouver Island* (Philadelphia: American Philosophical Society, 1955).
37 Sapir, "Sayachapis: A Nootka Trader," 300.
38 Eric R. Wolf, *Envisioning Power: Ideologies of Dominance and Crisis* (Berkeley: University of California Press, 1999), 89.

CHAPTER 14

Tlingit Art

Ishmael Hope

I HAVE BEEN TRYING TO GET CLOSER TO EARLY TWENTIETH-CENTURY TLINGIT writer Louis Shotridge's writings since I first heard about him from my father, Andy Hope III (1949–2008), when I was a teenager. In Tlingit writer and current Alaska Writer Laureate Ernestine Hayes's Native literature class, my father said that Shotridge possessed a "classic, classic Tlingit worldview." Andy, Xhaastánch of the S'iknaxh.ádi clan, first stumbled across Shotridge's writings when he was a teenager in Sitka, looking through the archives of Sheldon Jackson College. Shotridge worked for many years at the University of Pennsylvania, collecting Tlingit cultural treasures and writing thousands of notes on the objects, and much else, such as genealogy and Tlingit history and culture, and frequently publishing finely penned articles in the university's journal.[1]

My dad grew up in Sitka in the 1950s and 1960s. He frequently commented to me and others about how there had been so little going on culturally, how one couldn't find any published resources on Tlingit culture, how there was almost no cultural curriculum in the schools, how young people were not being taught their traditions and customs. My dad turned to Shotridge "for guidance, for strength." And, indeed, Shotridge's writings provide enormous guidance and strength, especially if you are equipped to receive the gifts. Nora Marks Dauenhauer (1927–2017), K̲eixwnéi, also turned to Shotridge's writings during a time, in the 1960s and 1970s, which she called "the Tlingit renaissance." During these years, Tlingit writers, artists, and scholars worked with Elders to revive the arts and traditions of the people and to form new paths of cultural identity. Through the likes of Nora Dauenhauer and my father, Louis Shotridge directly inspired Tlingit cultural, literary, and artistic revitalization.[2]

Shotridge as Tlingit Storyteller in English

Nora Dauenhauer noted that she could hear Tlingit "at the backside" of Shotridge's "Ghost of Courageous Adventurer" (1920), a magnificent telling of a Shangukeidí clan history in which iron and copper were discovered by the Tlingit. When I first tried reading through the story as a youngster, I could barely make heads or tails of it. It was hard to get through the "thees and thous," the Victorian archaism that Shotridge employed to capture—to great effect, I later realized—the sonority and grandiloquence of classic Tlingit storytelling. Moreover, I was lost in all the movements, all the little gestures one makes in scaffolding a story, all the particular patterns of thought a story follows, all which spring from a direct, specific tradition, just as *all stories are told*. We are fooled into thinking that there is a "universal" way to tell stories, which conveniently and strictly employ structures invented and *defined entirely by Westerners*.

Nora once contended that "you have to know the [Tlingit] language" in order to *get* Shotridge's stories. This may strike one as odd given that he wrote them down in English. However, she felt that the stories were written down very consciously in a *Tlingit thought structure*, even bending the English language to mirror Tlingit patterns. For example, in his "Ghost of Courageous Adventurer," Shotridge writes: "With the turn the sky like gray, through loops of packstraps faces passed. Heavy they were, those packs of food. Steep it was that Trout Creek Mount. Thitherward that journey moved, without eating for the tongue was yet coated. Different is he the man of this moment. Eat first and his work next, but the man of long ago with him was his work first and with the rise of sun comes his time to eat. Food eaten before the tongue was cleared, they say, was to the stomach unwholesome. It was then the sun was sliding."[3]

Here Shotridge writes of the traditional practice of abstaining from food until the day was well under way, after much work was done, because in the morning the tongue was coated and it was considered unhealthy to eat at that time. It is a delightful aside, in the mode of traditionalist Elders tinged with nostalgia over the rugged and great past. Not only does such a passage evince traditional practices, the sentence structure is consciously *Tlingit in form*. Phrases such as "With the turn the sky like gray, through loops of packstraps faces passed" can be converted, practically word for word, and in order, into the Tlingit language and sound quite felicitous to an Elder's ear. As I gain some level of fluency in the language, and as I deepen my studies into my own culture and now have years of listening directly to many Elders behind me, it is a tremendous joy to discover and savor some of those patterns.

My friend linguist Roy Mitchell some time ago made a great comment on Facebook that has stuck with me. He wrote about how if we "chunk" a large cache of phrases in our language learning, carefully memorizing all the sounds to competently say aloud on command, at least a few hundred sentences, then the language starts to enter our subconscious, where the real learning happens, where it does the work. I got to thinking how the language has been entering into my consciousness. It gets me thinking about how language works in real time. When we compose sentences, we start with the thought and not quite the words. *Something*, the meaning-making part of the mind, *captures* the words and then words start coming out, formed from the storage cache of lexicon and grammatical structures embedded by practice and memory, which is then ignited by the spontaneous part of the subconscious which marries meaning to language.

With plenty of listening, and plenty of practice, those words can come out beautifully and in a rich, complex, pleasing form. Every language has a specific structure and logic born in grammar, yet within that linguistic structure there is *mind.* The mind of language that was born and fostered in a specific place, and which is much older than all of us. My friend and mentor, poet Robert Bringhurst, says that "language is a living thing," and I fully agree. I am intensely grateful to be reaching a point in my Tlingit language acquisition in which I can almost sense the ancestral presence, the "thought world of the ancestors," which the Yup'ik scholar Angayuqaq Oscar Kawagely observed was embedded in our heritage languages.[4] Shotridge's "The Ghost of Courageous Adventurer" has become a revelation to me as I deepen my language studies.

Art from a Tlingit Point of View

Louis Shotridge left behind a richly detailed, incisive, and brilliantly written corpus that illuminates Tlingit art and oral literature, conveying their intellectual and cultural traditions. Just as I was first bewildered with his stories, many of the cues, gestures, reference points, and trail markers he gave us are embedded in Tlingit cultural contexts and thus can potentially be misunderstood or entirely glossed over. A problem—or opportunity, depending how look at it—with standing on the fault lines of two very different cultures is that there are multiple spaces to contend with: the spaces that are distinct and particular to a culture, and the spaces where there is seemingly accessible common ground, such as storytelling motifs of the "hero's journey" or the "eternal return," say, or Northwest Coast art's resemblance to calligraphy, which feed into the relentless Western universalist drive.

In a colonial setting, only the common ground, the spaces already familiar to the colonial culture, are privileged, acknowledged to be real, to be seen and heard as a tangible thing, and to be accorded authority and meaning. While the legion of masterworks of Northwest Coast art that pepper galleries and museums across the world continue to beguile, mystify, and elicit awe in viewers—as they indeed *are* aesthetically pleasing in a universal sense—few have bothered to *ask Native people* how they view and experience the art, and fewer still have learned much from those interactions, unconsciously shackled as they are to their own constructs.

Scholars often bemoan the lack of available material to truly understand Native art as it was conceived and composed by Native peoples. Anthropologist Frederica de Laguna, for example, in her editing comments for George T. Emmons's *Tlingit Indians* (1991) regrettably noted the lack of a "precontact Native view" regarding

Tlingit art.[5] Surely de Laguna was familiar with the detailed notes Shotridge left behind in the University of Pennsylvania Museum archives, and without a doubt she closely read Shotridge's published journal articles.[6] While de Laguna should be lauded for the monumental ethnographies she left behind, what she was looking for was in plain sight. It was in Shotridge's writings. Shotridge brilliantly elucidated a way to understand Tlingit art, to understand *Tlingit aesthetics,* by thoroughly investigating and illuminating its deep cultural context.

For many artworks, Shotridge begins, in his notes and his articles on the art, by identifying the previous caretaker of the art, the clan leader who kept it under his care. Then he provides details about how the clan acquired the object: by commission, trade, warfare, and so on. He goes on to tell, whenever he knows it, the history behind the crest of the object, such as how the Kaagwaantaan acquired the G̱ooch (Wolf crest) or how the Kiks.ádi obtained the Xíxch' (Frog crest) and so on.[7] Then Shotridge explains the process of how the artist was commissioned, any details about their artistic process that he knew, and the ceremony in which it was brought out and paid for to be witnessed at a ḵu.éex' (*potlatch*).

The Whale House

Louis Shotridge was not only curating museum objects and writing notes and articles about them—he was a master storyteller and a major art critic and historian. It is worthwhile to fully quote his story of how the G̱aanax̱teidí clan of Klukwan, Shotridge's father's clan, established the Yáay Hít, in the early part of the nineteenth century. The Whale House, as a significant clan house, whose leader X̱'eits'óow commissioned Ḵaajisdu.áx̱ch of the Kiks.ádi clan of Wrangell, to carve the house posts. I quote the whole story (interpolated with some of my thoughts) to demonstrate both his conception of Tlingit art criticism and history and a bit of his capabilities as a storyteller, transcribed by me from the Louis Shotridge Digital Archive, with Tlingit words edited for modern orthography.

> X̱'eits'óow II was a man to be admired as a leader of men. He possessed a thinking power that none of his successors approached; he was the outstanding figure among the Chilkat patriots, and to his magnanimous policy was credited the foundation of the G̱aanax̱teidí power. The G̱aanax̱teidí, as the composition of its name implies, [From within the G̱aanax̱teidí] was a party, only a small one to begin with, which wandered away from the G̱aanax̱teidí at Tongass, the main body to which had been a part, and during its immigration up along the coast a number of other small groups joined it, and these came on to the head of the Lynn Canal in its company. Among themselves the immigrating groups referred to one another by certain names, each of which had derived from the geographic position whence the bearer had come.

For a time, after the G̱aanax̱teidí made its settlement at the place which is now known as Klukwan, on Chilkat River, no one ever thought of forming the various small groups in one body, until X̱'eits'óow II stepped into the leadership of the leading group, and it was with him the most important part of the G̱aanax̱teidí history began.[8]

Here Shotridge ties in the ancient connections the clan had, from its traditional split from its connected clans, from the Tongass and Prince of Wales Island. By drawing upon that ancient history, it raises the stature of the leader in showing the clan's ancient ties and enterprising abilities. Shotridge continues:

Eventually the leading group grew to such a body of men that it was necessary to build another house. This move was made, however, not only because of increase in number, but the members developed into different ranks. Such is the motive of the foundation of the Whale House. The foundation of the new house was an opportunity for X̱'eits'óow II to put to test his great plan—to strengthen his own party by making the other small groups combine with it, so that this new division will have a defensive power. The members of the other groups, then, did not know enough to appreciate the meaning of organization, until the time came for them to realize the danger of an attack by other comers to the region.[9]

For readers unaccustomed to oral traditions around the world, the establishment and building of houses may seem marginally important. However, from Homer's tales to *Beowulf* to many Native American stories, a primary concern is the *honor of the house,* which includes genealogy, lineage succession, and tangible and intangible property. In Tlingit culture, lineages were accorded by house, organized by matrilineal descent. The house was the container of at.óow and even at.óow itself, including the carved house posts that hold up the house and the painted wall screen that partitions the leader and his wife from the rest of the house. To the canon of house lineage stories Shotridge adds the one of the illustrious Whale House, which, it should not be lost on the reader, was made all the more illustrious due to the mastery of its art possessions.

The foundation of the Whale House in Chilkat, indeed, set an example not only for the division, but for many others as well. The whole thing was operated in such a magnanimous manner that the different groups were not at all aware of the astute man's intention until each became part of the great G̱aanax̱teidí Clan. As already stated, it was thought that the Whale House was to be built only as an annex to the Raven House, to commemorate the incident from which

> the clan had adopted the Whale as its emblem, and to accommodate the different classes of members, but, as was learned later, there was a deal more than that to the founder's plan.
>
> In carrying out his plan X̲'eits'óow II began by holding a council with the different groups that lived in company of his own. When they all were seated, he laid before them his plan: "Shaka K̲wáan; T'íx'eidí; Laawayikeidí, and G̲aanax̲teidí." Addressing the different groups. "Together we came to the land of our choice, and here we are destined to remain. By our own making we may enjoy our lives together, or we might prefer to remain indifferent of one another's company. But, should we not all be friends? Before us flows Chilkat; together we drink of it and together partake of its bounties, in peace. Indeed, the good goddess of Fortune has looked upon us with favor. But to maintain this peaceful life we must create some sort of defense, lest someone else will take from us that which we enjoy. We should stand together, each man in place like a timber of a well-constructed stockade; unless we form such a defense the inmates of Klukwan are still exposed to the danger of an attack.[10]

The genius and ingenuity—or "cleverness" in the parlance of Shotridge's times—was an admired trait of aayátx'i (*Tlingit noble people*). By being able to peaceably expand the population and reach of his clan house by including other clan houses in its domain, X'eits'óow expands his clan's political and economic power and embodies the most admired traits among traditional Tlingit.

> The foregoing is all that was remembered of X̲'eits'óow's address at the first council of the G̲aanax̲teidí Clan. The members of the three allied groups were not educated enough to appreciate the gist of the idea, but it seemed that there was none else to do but to accept the proposal of the chief; in a half-hearted manner the elders of the groups acceded—they had no more to do than to follow the leader.
>
> In his own native way X̲'eits'óow II was educated—he was well versed on conditions of affairs of the Tlingit worlds, and he knew all the persons of importance in the various divisions, and in turn the astute man was well known. Therefore, he was in a position to call on anyone from most any Tlingit town.[11]

Perhaps Shotridge is implying here that X̲'eits'óow is doing things slightly unorthodox yet fitting within traditional frameworks. Traditionally, a closely connected relative on the opposite moiety is called on to make at.óow. However, they picked someone from a faraway village who was also of the Raven moiety. Shotridge notes here that because of X̲'eits'óow's "importance" and other positive attributes that he was able to make this unusual commission.

> K̲aajisdu.áx̲ch II, of Shtax'héen Kiks.ádi, was well known, in the Tlingit world, for his unusual skill in carving wood. Shax'héen [Stikine River] was a great paddling distance from Chilkat, but K̲aajisdu.áx̲ch was the only one then who could fill well the requirements of the G̲aanax̲teidí project in Chilkat; hence, distance was no obstacle to X̲'eits'óow, when he requested the service of the great carver.
>
> It was in the Spring of the year when the messengers, from Chilkat, arrived in K̲aas'el'a.aan, an old town now known as "Old Wrangell." The mission of the party was, of course, well known to the Shtax'héen K̲wáan, for the news of the G̲aanax̲teidí Chilkat affairs were then far-reaching in the Tlingit worlds, therefore the messenger party was received in a manner that befit a representative of the great chief, but in order to avoid unnecessary delay the customary receptions were made brief, for the travelers were taking advantage of the fair condition of weather. K̲aajisdu.áx̲ch himself had been informed that his services were to be called from Chilkat; therefore he was prepared, and awaited only the arrival of the message, so immediately following the brief reception the party set out on its return voyage to Chilkat.
>
> From the moment the messenger party left the shore of K̲aas'el'a.aan, an elder, who had come along for just such purpose, began to relate to the chief of wood carvers "The Journey of the Raven," that noble old legend which stands as a foundation to all that pertains to the creation of important things in the Tlingit world. At each camp, all the way, K̲aajisdu.áx̲ch whittled away at the thick pieces of bark of the cottonwood, as he listened to the narrator. Thus, by the time the small party approached Chilkat the master carver had fashioned the models of the four house pillars that were to be the masterpieces of all carved wood in the country.[12]

This type of artistic inspiration, with the commissioning clan telling the full history that they wish to depict on the crest object, is consistent with the stories of modern Elders. For example, Paul Marks, Nora Dauenhauer's brother and a culture bearer himself, has frequently told me about such visits, in which an Elder or clan leader cordially invites a carver into their home, has coffee, and then the Elder tells of the clan's plans for at.óow to be dedicated at a party. Paul tells me that they do not outright ask for the object to be made, but the suggestion is clear. They will also not negotiate a fee; it is to be paid at the k̲u.éex' when the object is dedicated. Then the Elder tells the long clan history to elicit the appropriate artistic inspiration.

> One year, thence, in Chilkat Whale House stood K̲aajisdu.áx̲ch II, the greatest carver of wood in the history of the Tlingit people: passing around, in course of the sun, pronounced the names of the four pillars that he had just finished; starting with the one placed on the Northern corner: "This, oh chief, is the

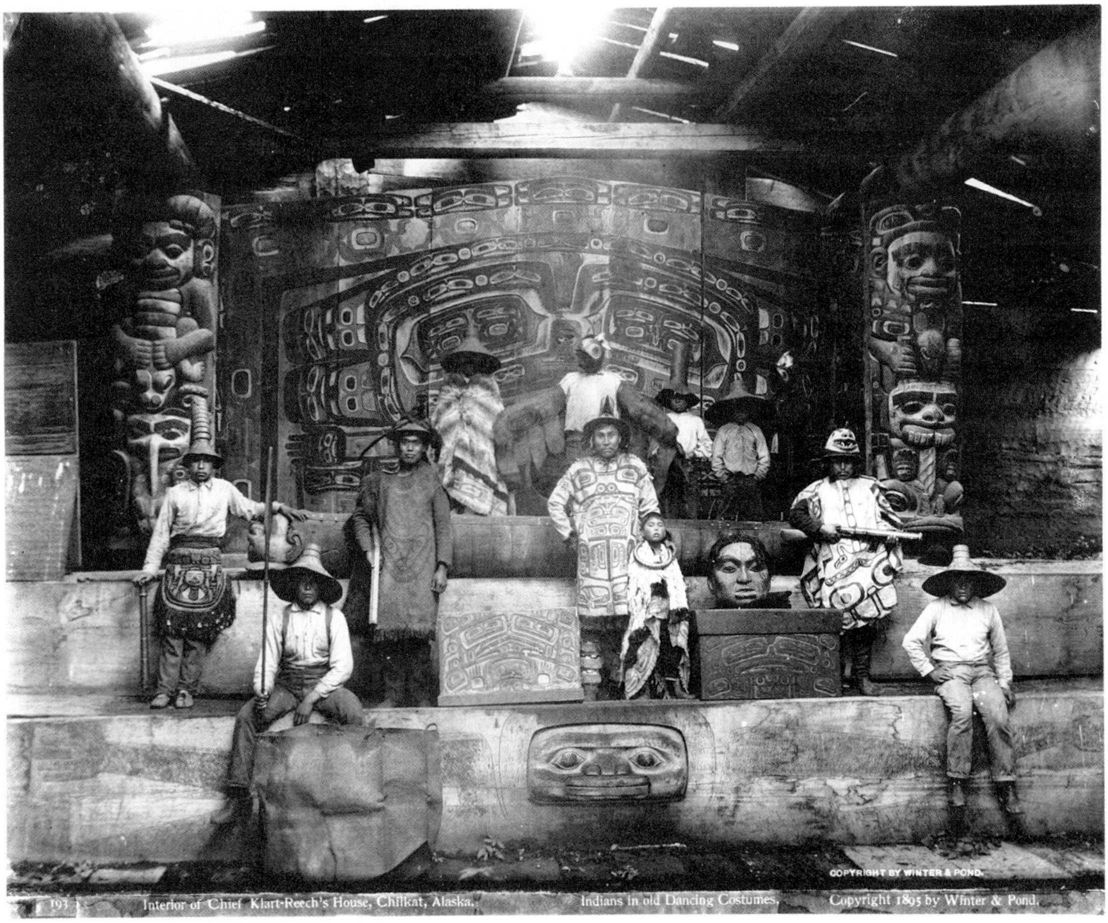

14.1. Interior of the Klukwan Whale House, ca. 1895. P87-0010, Alaska State Library, Winter & Pond Photograph Collection.

'Tree of Worm.'" Then he passed on to the one on the Eastern cover "This is the Raven—for the sake of justice the creator of things deceived the gods." And again he passed on to the one on the Southern corner: "This one is the Whale, when the Raven flew into the stomach of the great chief of the sea." At last he passed on to the front of the one on the Western corner: "This one is the Black-skinned Giant, the Champion of Physical Strength." K̲aajisdu.áx̱ch then turned to face the chief, and said, "Oh chief, no genius lives who can do justice to the working power of a noble mind, yet withal I offer to thine hand these, the result of a humble attempt, but because of their owner I should have a hope that these posts shall serve their purpose." Thence, these few modest words remained in company of the greatest pieces in history of the Tlingit art in wood carving.

> During the ceremony of the dedication of the Whale House, the four different groups that were to form the G̱aanax̱teidí were each assigned its place in the new council house: the Laawayikeidí was allotted its place by the Tree of Worm; the Shaka Ḵwáan by the Raven the Artificer; the G̱aanax̱teidí proper took its place by the Whale post, and the T'íx'eidí was assigned its place by the Black-skinned Giant.
>
> Thus, the different groups became as one body, regardless of origin. Though each resided in its own house, to the last, they were all represented in the Whale House, and looked to this in a manner something like a state does it capital home. This was the manner in which the G̱aanax̱teidí of Chilkat acquired the reputation of being the most successful party in the region.[13]

There is so much going on here. I encourage the reader to view the narrative, in part, as *art history and criticism*. Shotridge details how a major patron of the arts, X̱'eits'óow, accumulated the appropriate political and economic authority to acquire four monumental sculptures that have been immensely admired first by the Tlingit and their neighbors in Ḵaajisdu.áx̱ch's own time and then by viewers the world over, since famous pictures of the clan house have circulated for more than a century. Shotridge details the artistic process of the master carver, Ḵaajisdu.áx̱ch. The main form of artistic inspiration is the "Journey of the Raven" story, a long cycle of Raven stories that detail how the world was shaped into its present form, which was specified to intertwine with the clan migration history of the G̱aanax̱teidí clan.

It is interesting to note that an Elder storyteller was brought on the journey to elicit the appropriate artistic inspiration, so the artist could capture the essence of their history in the form of four monumental house posts. Is one not amazed with wonder when picturing the great carver whittling away at model totems while an Elder of the commissioning clan captivates with a long epic, as paddlers pull and pull their paddles from the southern end of Tlingit country back to the great Chilkat River? That is a lovely sight to behold in the mind's eye.

Barbecuing Raven Hat

Since Shotridge did not actually acquire the Whale House posts and screen, he did not write the same kind of notes he wrote for other objects, objects that may not have the same luxury of a detailed history as shared above, but that nonetheless demonstrate a rich methodology. To examine such methodology, let us turn to Shotridge's writings on the Barbecuing Raven Hat, an object owned by the L'uknax̱.ádi. As seen with the Whale House, Shotridge tells the history of the hat:

> The name given to this old piece is from one of the episodes in the "Raven-traveling," a Tlingit myth of Creation.

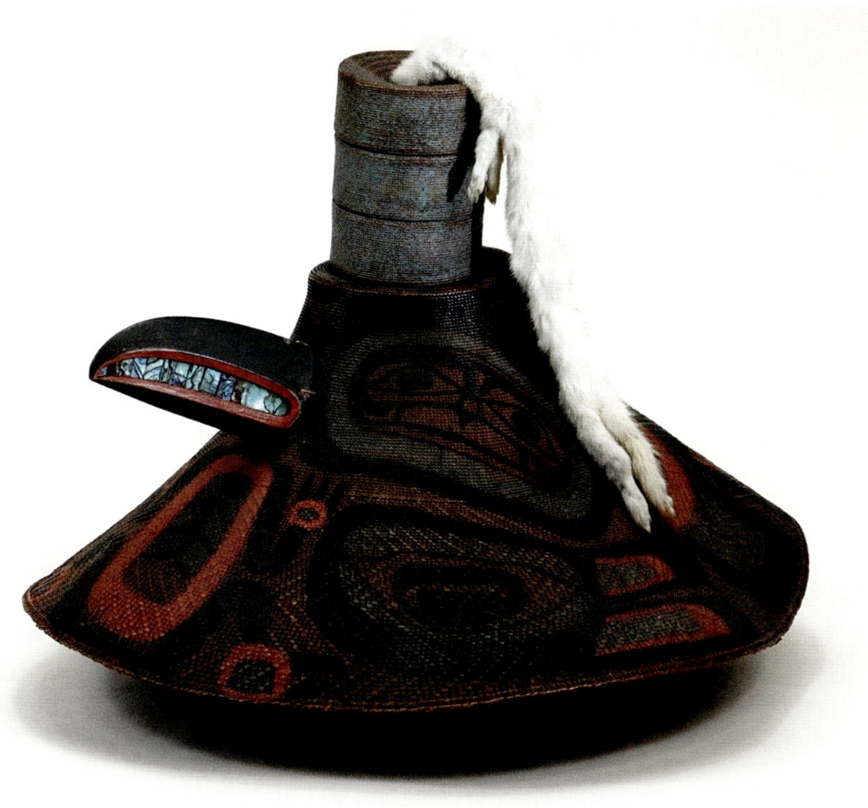

14.2. Barbecuing Raven Hat, Tlingit Sea Lion House, Tluknaxadi, Sitka, collected in 1918. University of Pennsylvania Museum, NA8504.

When the Raven killed the king salmon a large crowd of small birds and squirrels rushed to the scene. Raven saw that one salmon was not sufficient for the crowd. He thought of a scheme. He made the crowd dig a hole in the ground large enough for the salmon to go in, and after this was done, he sent them after some skunk cabbage leaves to wrap around the salmon for the barbecue. They packed in a pile of this, but Raven said that what they brought was unclean because it was gathered where his mother was cremated, and he instructed them to go beyond two mountains for the kind he wanted, so they all went.

In the meantime, Raven cooked the salmon in the leaves that were brought, and ate it all before the crowd returned. When they came with what he ordered, Raven sat like a virtuous person pretending to look like he was awaiting the cooking of the salmon, This is the part chosen for the name of the L'uknax̱.ádi helmet, and the interpretation is, "No other [clan] has a right to lay claim to a man's own achievement." The story, of course, went on.

> The old helmet is the same one which tells us the years of struggle between the G̱aanax̱teidí clan of Chilkat and the L'uknax̱.ádi. In the dispute between these two powerful clans to determine which held the legal claim on the popular raven crest, the G̱aanax̱teidí is said to have shown most evidence. This dispute resulted in an internecine conflict, and not until Shkoowuyéil, chief of the G̱aanax̱teidí party, had taken to wife Yaku-hu-dayd-saku [name in modern orthography currently not known], daughter of Yéil Tlein, "Big-Raven," a war lord of the rival party, did the intense anger abate.
>
> The helmet was carried through only two ceremonies, and before it was brought up to the standard of recognition, it fell into the hands of the rival clan during one of the conflicts. It remained there until Yéil Tlein, the father-in-law of the rival chief, entered his office as a head chief of his own clan, when his daughter was in a position to make an appeal to her husband for the return of the helmet to her father, which was immediately carried through. It was through the influence of this woman also that the persistence of her husband's party gradually subsided.
>
> Although the L'uknax̱.ádi admitted defeat, after it was returned, the Barbecuing Raven was kept in the bottom of the clan chest. It never saw real service. It was called a helmet because it was made preceding the war, and it was brought out during the councils to be pointed to as the goal of the clans' efforts.[14]

A Tlingit person familiar with their history would see in the hat some of the rich history of the Yéil Ḵutláakw, the Raven stories that tell of how the world came together. They would consider Tsalx̱aan, Mt. Fairweather where the story took place. They would remember how the Raven first tricked the salmon and then the birds to help prepare the food, who are then sent off across mountains while the Raven basked in the delicious salmon. Then one would consider the great war between the G̱aanax̱teidí and the L'uknax̱.ádi over the right to use the Raven as a clan crest. In traditional times, such rights would be earned not only by bloodshed but by the amount of wealth that is "killed," either by giving out to the opposite clans or by literally killing a number of their poor slaves. All of these considerations would percolate in the mind of a traditionally raised Tlingit, as it does to this day.

In addition to getting the story down, Shotridge would write notes on the object, such as here where he notes that K'ooḵlaa, a Chookaneidí carver, was the maker of the Barbecuing Raven Hat. Additional notes Shotridge wrote include the date of acquisition (1918), the clan house that owns it (Taan Hít), and the materials it was composed of (wood, spruce root, ermine skin, hide, pigment, brass, or copper). All of this history and note compilation would be set in the backdrop of a large body of Tlingit knowledge documented by Shotridge, including his richly told "Journey of the Raven" and his numerous notes and articles on Tlingit ceremonies, cultural objects, stories, and the clan system.[15] This type of examination of the large body

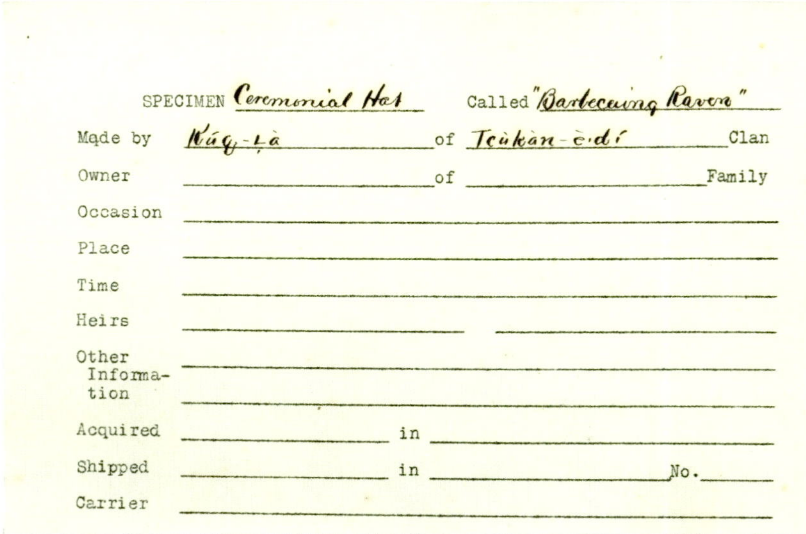

SPECIMEN Ceremonial Hat Called "Barbecuing Raven"

Made by Kúq-ɬà of Tcùkàn-è·dí Clan

Owner ____ of ____ Family

Occasion

Place

Time

Heirs

Other Information

Acquired ____ in ____

Shipped ____ in ____ No. ____

Carrier

14.3. Louis Shotridge catalog record for the Barbecuing Raven Hat. Louis Shotridge Digital Archives, Penn Museum Archives.

of meanings, histories, places, objects, and cultural confluences is precisely a "total social phenomenon," which scholar Marcel Mauss has elucidated when examining the potlatch.[16] Such objects could only be experienced in their true meaning through their uses in Tlingit potlatches.

The story of the Barbecuing Raven Hat happily does not end with Shotridge's acquisition and documentation of it. In the fall of 2017 the object was reobtained through the Native American Graves and Protections Repatriation Act and displayed at the Clan Conference, a gathering of Tlingit clans and scholars that my father founded in 1993. Harold Jacobs, the tribe's cultural specialist and highly knowledgeable Tlingit historian, presented the object back to the L'uknax̱.ádil clan and told some of the history of the hat, a good amount of which he knew from Shotridge's writings. It was dressed on the head of L'uknax̱.ádi clan leader Herman Davis (L'eiwtu Éesh, Yéil Tlein). It should not be lost on the reader the historical dimensions powerfully present with Davis: the L'uknax̱.ádi clan leader carries the name of Yéil Tlein, who factors large in the war for which the hat is known. Before dancing in the hat, as would be appropriate, Davis, true to the beautiful heritage of Tlingit oratory, delivered a short and heartrending speech, here transcribed and then translated.[17]

Ax tuwáa sigóo gunalchéesh yéi yax̱wsak̲aayí
yáa aadéi haa een yéi jeeyaneiyi yé,

yáa haa at.óowu.
Yéil S'áaxw áwé a yáadáx̱ ḵuwateen.
Á áyá has du g̱aax̱í áyá wutuwa.áx̱.
"Eesháan xát dé.
Eesháan x̱át dé.
Neildé x̱at tuwatee.
Neildéi x̱at tuwatee.
Ax̱ tuwáa sigóo x̱át tsú.
Ax̱ yatx'usáani has du x̱oot ax̱walg̱einí, x̱át tsú.
Dei eesháan x̱át dé, eesháan x̱át dé.
Neildé x̱at tuwatee."
Ách áyá a daa ax̱ toowú yak'éi
yáa ax̱ yát yeewudlaag̱í
yáa Yéil S'eeg̱i S'áaxw,
Ganká Yéili.
Gunalchéesh áyá
yá aadéi haa een yéi jeeyaneiyi yé.
Ḵa yeewháan tsú yáax' yéi yee wuteeyí.
Ax̱ léelk'w hás, Kaagwaantaan.
    Anaxóots: Áawé.
Ax̱ tláa yá du éesh Kaagwaantaanx̱ wusitee.
S'iknax̱.ádi,
    Jix̱éik': Áawé.
gunalchéesh.
Dak̲l'aweidí,
    Wóochx̱ Kaduhaa: Áawé.
gunalchéesh.
Yéi áyá ax̱ tundatáani yéi yatee.
Yéi áyá ax̱ tundatáani yéi yatee.

And in English translation:

I would like to say thank you
for how you have worked with us
for our at.óow.
The Raven Hat left from here.
And so we heard its cry.
"Pity me.
Pity me.
I want to go home.
I want to go home.

I would also like
to look among my precious children's faces, me too.
Already pity me, pity me.
I want to go home."
That is why I feel good about it
for bringing to my face
the Barbecuing Raven Hat,
Smokehole Raven.
Thank you
for how you have worked with us.
My grandparents, Kaagwaantaan.
Andrew Gambel: Áawé.
My mother's father was Kaagwaantaan.
S'iknax̱.ádi,
Gerry Hope: Áawé.
thank you.
Dak̲l'aweidí,
Edwell John: Áawé.
thank you.
That is how I am thinking.
That is how I am thinking.[18]

Aesthetics

Tlingit art has, appropriately, been admired by many non-Native writers. So too Shotridge took great pleasure in identifying artists he particularly admired, such as the Dak̲l'aweidí woman weaver Taakw Shaatk'í, who wove the Yáay Shaadakóox, the Whale Headcover-stock, a hat with so-called "potlatch rings," which he called "the greatest object of its kind that existed in Tlingit history," or K̲aajisdu.áx̱ch, "the greatest carver of wood in the history of Tlingit people" (see Shotridge's history of the Whale House quoted earlier in this chapter). Other artists of note included Naakushtáa, the Dak̲l'aweidí carver who carved, among other attributed objects, the Xíxch' Hít gáasx', the Frog House posts (Tlingit Elder Johnny Marks told me he thought these posts were so good because it looked like the frogs "were about to jump out at you"); and Shkeedlik̲áa, a G̲aanax̱teidí leader and artist who specialized in painting. The other part of the Yáay Hít that has enchanted viewers for generations is the Séew X̲'éen, the Rain Screen, which was created by Shkeedlik̲áa. Shotridge details its composition:

> There was gradual improvement upon everything which had been created to represent our own culture. Among our own household it was X̲'eit'idus'óow II

> who brought about ideas each of which in its turn developed into something of importance. At the time this providential man founded the Whale House he placed in it a wooden screen or partition which was painted to represent the "Rain Storm." The man at that timc must have been satisfied with the creation which appeared to have been the outcome of a longevous daydream, and there lived no genius then who would dare to criticize the "masterpiece." But then Shkeedliḵáa III, who succeeded the famous lord of Klukwan, found the house-screen in place, like many other objects, in an unfinished manner.
>
> The new master, who himself was a noted carver of wood, was never at ease about the crude form from which the object of family pride was represented, until, at last, he had it taken down. In a manner of a gifted artist the critical master began to arrange his bark patterns over the surface of the screen. Thus it was in accord with such skillful mind that the Rainstorm design was carved on the screen. And to this day there has appeared no artist who is gifted enough to criticize Shkeedliḵáa.[19]

This restless artist who is "never at ease" with a work that is anything less than a "masterpiece" finally creates a work "in accord with such skillful mind." It is impossible to overlook the intense artistic discernment and refinement that pervaded the Tlingit community.

This demonstrates that while Shotridge's approach isn't purely formal or aesthetic, he does not omit aesthetic appreciation, wonder, and dazzlement. He frequently comments on the "greatness" of artists of high esteem and of the aesthetic appreciation he and his Elders felt for special objects. Shotridge outlined, in a sense, a classification system, a flexible yet fairly hierarchical structure that assigned more "weight" for certain objects over others. There were some objects that were "purely aesthetic," meaning some crests the clan possessed, often obtained by trade, were not used for sacred treasures; they were not at.óow--objects that Nora Dauenhauer defined as "an owned or purchased thing."[20]

Then he discussed the added value Tlingits held for major objects, such as house screens, house posts, Chilkat blankets, clan hats and staffs—all richly endowed with clan crests. Shotridge appraised higher value to the objects of antiquity and special historical significance, whether they were aesthetically masterful or not. After thorough, multiple readings of his writings and notes, one senses a weighted scale of value that Shotridge—and, by extension, the people whose ideals he is attempting to articulate—attributed to Tlingit art, with aesthetic achievement ranking with high importance but not as high as the historical value, the esteem held for the clan and the previous caretakers, and the cost for which the crest was won, often by the loss of life. The Western context that privileges *art for art's sake* demeans and completely ignores the deep ties Native people have to their history and traditions.

Its pleasing aesthetic quality, never too far from our minds, is inseparable from the contextual appreciation of its history, its ties to a clan and its ownership, how it was made, the crests it embodies, and its deep connection to our lands and waterways.[21] As Dauenhauer has written: "For a traditional Tlingit person, art ties many components of folklife together. History (the stories of covenants among people, animals, spirits, and the land), song and dance, visual art, and the ritual use of an art object are inseparable."[22] While Tlingit people never had a word for *art*, Europeans never had a word for at.óow.

The deep spiritual, place-based, ceremonial, historical, and other inseparable contextual elements attached to the experience of Tlingit art only *adds to, rather than subtracts or limits,* our enjoyment. Fine aesthetic appreciation is a pivotal but not-quite-overriding aspect to how the works are regarded. To truly contend with the works, as the likes of Shotridge and Nora Dauenhauer demonstrate, after an appreciative visual-conceptual encounter, one takes in the great stories tied to it, often told by master storytellers as equally gifted in oral form as visual artists are gifted in visual form. Then one carefully learns any details culled from it, beginning with the attribution of the great artist who composed the material, and the people who commissioned and cared for the works, and anything else regarding the material, such as how it was brought out at a ḵu.éex' (*potlatch*). Then you get a chance to see the art come alive during the ḵu.éex'. Oratory that reaches the heights of poetry is molded out of metaphors connected to the art, metaphors used to remove grief, to elicit joy, to protect the people from potentially harmful spirits. And in the background, past the thin wooden slat coverings of the clan house, are the inimitable and monumental rainforest and waterways where the art, stories, and people were born. The art is at.óow. It is alive. It is infused with soul, spirit, and meaning. I like to think that it is the best possible destiny an artist could hope for their art, even what a work of art would want for itself.

Louis Shotridge: A True Kaagwaantaan

Louis Shotridge was raised, as he noted, to be "a true Kaagwaantaan," one of the eminent clans in Tlingit country.[23] His writings are told clearly enough and can be universally appreciated on its surface levels, yet the depth of meaning may not be grasped without carefully learning Tlingit cultural contexts, especially as it is understood in the original language. There is joy in such learning, as one senses how Shotridge savors so many moments and details, perhaps being stilled with wonder as many of us are when visioning Ḵaajisdu.áx̱ch whittling away at his model totems, on his canoe journey to his patrons' homeland. Nora Dauenhauer and Andy Hope also spoke with visceral joy and deep admiration whenever they talked of Shotridge and his stories. As Nora said to her Elder George Davis of Angoon:

> His work is real good, so I could go back and read, and understand some of what he was doing. You can't understand it without knowing the language. You have to know the language. Some of us, like me, even if I know the language, I don't know the intellect, yáa kháa yaa khusgéiyi [*the intelligence of the person*] And all the history that weaves into every day of our lives. Like when our people die, and when we're happy, when we joke together, who do we joke with? When we sing together, who do we sing to? All these things are a big question mark, because the people that wrote about it didn't understand us. And it's going to be that way if we don't do anything about it. It's just going to stay that way forever. Except that man that worked there, that's Louis Shotridge. But he didn't finish it. Maybe he didn't live long enough, I don't know.[24]

Such joy and recognition encouraged Nora Dauenhauer to begin *translating* Shotridge's profoundly Tlingit-yet-English rendering of the "Ghost of Courageous Adventurer" back into Tlingit, what she heard in her mind's eye at the "back side of it." One senses that an old-timer would be bewildered by the strained separation of aesthetics and context discussed in modern art circles. Yes, *you can* simply enjoy Tlingit art by just looking at it. But why not experience the whole thing? This is one reason why it is so odd to us that much of our at.óow is lifelessly displayed in museum cases, as Nora noted that such displays can be "disconcerting for Native people." She notes that "in Tlingit tradition, visual art is displayed in action as part of a ritual process that confirms its mythic and spiritual context. Museum display in Western tradition is by nature more static and decontextualized, at best like a movie without a sound track."[25]

This is the kind of art that touches on the *total experience* of humanity in contact with nature, its histories, and its communities. Teachers like Louis Shotridge and Nora Dauenhauer show us that our art becomes whole and is best appreciated in its context, in its multiple layers of meaning and histories.

NOTES

1 For these essays, see Louis Shotridge, "My Northland Revisited," *Museum Journal* 8 (1917): 105–15; "War Helmets and Clan Hats of the Tlingit Indians," *Museum Journal* 10, nos. 1–2 (1919): 43–48; "A Visit to the Tsimshian Indians," *Museum Journal* 10 (1919): 49–67, 117–48; "Ghost of Courageous Adventurer," *Museum Journal* 11, no. 1 (1920): 11–26; "Tlingit Woman's Root Basket," *Museum Journal* 12, no. 3 (1921): 162–78; "Land Otter-Man," *Museum Journal* 13, no. 1 (1922): 55–59; "The Emblems of Tlingit Culture," *Museum Journal* 19, no. 4 (1928): 350–77; "The Bride of Tongass: A Study of the Tlingit Marriage Ceremony," *Museum Journal* 20, no. 2 (1929): 131–56; "The Kaguanton Shark Helmet," *Museum Journal* 20, nos. 3–4 (1929): 339–43; and "How Ats-ha Followed the Hide of His Comrade to Yek Land," *Museum Journal* 21, nos. 3–4 (1930): 215–26. Also see Louis Shotridge and Florence Shotridge, "Indians of the Northwest," *Museum Journal* 4, no. 3 (1913): 71–100.

2 For more on this revitalization, see the introduction to this edited volume.

3 Shotridge, "Ghost of Courageous Adventurer," www.penn.museum/collections/Shotridge/pdfs/CourageousAdventurer.pdf.

4 Robert Bringhurst, "What Is Language For?" November 12, 2009, www.youtube.com/watch?v=26fwWUIi_70&t=1525s; and Oscar Kawagely, *A Yupiaq Worldview: A Pathway to Ecology and Spirit* (Fairbanks: University of Alaska Press, 1995).

5 George T. Emmons and Frederica de Laguna, *The Tlingit Indians* (Seattle: University of Washington Press, 1991).

6 See the Louis Shotridge Digital Archives, www.penn.museum/collections/Shotridge/.

7 Louis Shotridge, "The Founder of Chilkat Whale House," University of Pennsylvania Museum (Id: Shot0525.jpg), www.penn.museum/collections/Shotridge/display.php?type=documents&id=Shot0525.

8 Shotridge, "Founder of Chilkat Whale House," 1.

9 Shotridge, "Founder of Chilkat Whale House," 2.

10 Shotridge, "Founder of Chilkat Whale House," 2–3.

11 Shotridge, "Founder of Chilkat Whale House," 3–4.

12 Shotridge, "Founder of Chilkat Whale House," 4–5.

13 Shotridge, "Founder of Chilkat Whale House," 5–7.

14 Shotridge, "War Helmets and Clan Hats of the Tlingit Indians," 45–46, www.penn.museum/collections/Shotridge/pdfs/War_Helmets_and_Clan_Hats.pdf.

15 Shotridge digital archive, see www.penn.museum/collections/Shotridge.

16 Marcel Mauss, *The Gift* (1954; reprint, London: HAU Books, 2016).

17 Herman Davis, unpublished oral recording during the Tlingit Clan conference, recorded by Sarah Betcher, shared by Peter Metcalfe of the Clan Conference organizing committee, 2017.

18 Davis, unpublished oral recording during the Tlingit Clan conference.

19 Shotridge digital archive, see www.penn.museum/collections/Shotridge.

20 Nora Dauenhauer, "Tlingit *At.oow*: Traditions and Concepts," in *the Spirit Within: Northwest Coast Native Art from the John H. Hauberg Collection* (Seattle: Seattle Art Museum, 1995), 21.

21 The preeminence of a view, on the part of Tlingit peoples, which is "functional and contextual" rather than "formalist," as articulated by Dauenhauer, "Tlingit *At.oow,*" likely contributes to the pervasive misunderstanding of Tlingit aesthetics.

22 Dauenhauer in Steven C. Brown, ed., *The Spirit Within: Northwest Coast Art from the John H. Hauberg Collection* (Seattle: Seattle Art Museum, 1995).

23 Maureen Milburn, "The Politics of Possession: Louis Shotridge and the Tlingit Collections of the University of Pennsylvania Museum," PhD diss., Department of Fine Arts, University of British Columbia, 1997.

24 Nora Dauenhauer Oral Literature Collection, William L. Paul Sr. Archives, Sealaska Heritage Institute, Juneau, AK.

25 Dauenhauer, "Tlingit *At.oow,*" 21.

Conclusion

FIFTY YEARS STUDYING NORTHWEST COAST ART: A PERSONAL VIEW

Aldona Jonaitis

I HAVE BEEN STUDYING NORTHWEST COAST ART SINCE 1970 AND HAVE EXPERIenced firsthand the profound changes in its scholarly discourse.[1] Like other members of my generation, the choice to pursue what was then infelicitously termed "primitive art"—African, Oceanic, and Native American—was in part inspired by the liberation movements of the 1960s and 1970s, which sought to empower Indigenous people and demonstrate their multifaceted achievements, including art.[2] In other words, it was a political choice for me to study Northwest Coast art and has remained so. But, as new perspectives and cultural values have entered the field, scholars like me learned from and responded to the ever-changing landscape of Native art studies, modifying our own positions accordingly. In this brief historiography of Northwest Coast art, I reveal my personal odyssey as a Northwest Coast art historian discovering how a non-Native scholar can ethically support the political, intellectual, and artistic sovereignty of Indigenous people as well as usefully contribute to knowledge.

Why in a book of innovative explorations into Northwest Coast art does the concluding chapter examine previous sources, some decades old? Knowledge does not emerge de novo, without precedent, and years in this field continue to enrich my understanding and appreciation of new perspectives. This genealogy of scholarship from which recent studies descend reveals that useful past literature maintains its influence, outdated ideas of others are virtually ignored, and some—adhering to a disputed paradigm—are actively contested. As the contributions in this book demonstrate, scholarship advances knowledge upon a foundation of previous works that can harmoniously enhance and augment or dissonantly contradict and disprove. Intriguing, impressive, and sometimes perplexing, Northwest Coast art has inspired a considerable body of literature.[3] Over the decades, wide-ranging analyses, evaluations, and interpretations extolled its aesthetics, ascribed to it a deeply mystic essence, deciphered its unique visual language, reevaluated earlier historical reconstructions, and more recently embraced decolonization.[4] The broad social, political, and intellectual movements of the twenty and twenty-first centuries influenced the myriad endeavors to comprehend Northwest Coast art, each of which was a product of its time.[5] An example of this appears in the introduction by Kathryn Bunn-Marcuse demonstrating that the more widespread contemporary Indigenous struggles for Indigenous authority and sovereignty inspire many essays in this volume.

Analyzed from a twenty-first-century perspective, a good deal of historic literature reveals colonialist underpinnings. Working within the paradigms of their time, their authors would have unlikely imagined such later criticisms, appropriate as they may be today. In the first half of the twentieth century, authors expressed their admiration of Native art by equating it to European and Euro-American traditions and celebrating its intellectual sophistication. Such arguments advocating the value of Indigenous creations disrupted the prevalent culture of discrimination and racism. As Indigenous people began asserting their autonomy, scholars gradually became less focused on parallels with the West—which still privileged traditions derived from Europe—and began analyzing the art's intrinsic cultural value as well as critiquing the colonial biases of their predecessors. Later in the twentieth century, scholars worked—and continue to do so—toward more egalitarian, sensitive, and collaborative works, such as those described in this book.

Northwest Coast Art History: From Franz Boas to the 1960s

Art historical scholarship of the Northwest Coast begins with Franz Boas, whose essays addressing art dating from 1890 to 1916 culminated in his 1927 study *Primitive Art*.[6] One of his major contributions to anthropology—and to the dismemberment of evolutionism, a theory that races existed in a hierarchy at the apex of which were white Anglo-Saxons—was his insistence that cultural differences resulted not from a group's position on an evolutionary ladder but instead from historical factors contributing to its culture. Boas substituted history for evolutionism and by so doing promoted the equality of races, no matter how different their cultures. He was therefore the first major intellectual who contested the widespread belief of the supposed intellectual and cultural inferiority of Indigenous people; as the "father of American anthropology," he produced several generations of ethnologists, many of whom shared his values.[7]

In the years before World War II, Northwest Coast art began to be recognized as an impressive and valuable tradition. In 1927 the National Gallery of Canada installed a significant exhibition of First Nations art in Montreal, Ottawa, Paris, and Toronto.[8] Totem pole restoration projects were initiated in both British Columbia and Alaska in the 1920s and 1930s.[9] The Roosevelt administration reversed earlier discriminatory governmental policy and endeavored to enhance Native

American economic well-being and to promote their culture. The Indian Arts and Crafts Board, a governmental agency, supported a historic 1941 exhibition, *Indian Art of the United States*, that filled all four floors of the Museum of Modern Art (MoMA).[10] At MoMA, Northwest Coast art, along with other Native American art traditions, was installed as "art" as opposed to the artifacts of anthropology. By equating Native art with other worldwide art traditions, and presenting it according to the most up-to-date aesthetic standards of museological display, curators Frederic Douglas and René d'Harnoncourt sought to elevate its status in the public's mind.[11]

A group of refugees from Europe who were in New York during the war found Northwest Coast art fascinating. In 1943 anthropologist Claude Lèvi-Strauss poetically contemplated the aesthetic value and symbolic meaning of totem poles, masks, Chilkat blankets, and other items on exhibit in the American Museum of Natural History's Hall of Indians of the North Pacific Coast, equating them to the arts of Egypt, Persia, and medieval Europe. Lèvi-Strauss even suggested that Northwest Coast artists had created cubist images years before Picasso.[12] Surrealists including Max Ernst, Andre Breton, Kurt Seligman, and Wolfgang Paalen discovered in Northwest Coast art qualities they believed inherent in their own art, such as an exploration of the subconscious, participation in universal mythology, and unification of the dualisms of life and death, past and future, high and low.[13] Other contemporaneous artists praised Northwest Coast art but for different reasons. Abstract Expressionist Barnett Newman, for example, indicated that the abstraction of Northwest Coast art was "the normal, well-understood, dominant tradition"—something he wanted his own culture to understand.[14]

Yet of course it is clear to us today that the highly subjective interpretations of mysticism and abstraction credited to Northwest Coast art reveal more about the artistic agendas of the Surrealists and Abstract Expressionists than they do about inherent qualities in the art. The aestheticization of Native art in the 1941 MoMA exhibition and Lèvi-Strauss's suggestion that Northwest Coast art should soon leave the ethnographic institution to take its rightful place in the art museum, its exaltation by Surrealists, and its praise by Abstract Expressionists all share one essential feature: they praised the art by equating it to non-Native art traditions ancient and modern. The impositions of non-Native templates onto Native culture—at that time honest indications of admiration—would over time come to be disparaged as colonialist. What these approaches to Northwest Coast art overlooked (or more precisely, had no access to) is that, as Ishmael Hope illustrates in his chapter, Indigenous people have long appreciated own their art.

Despite the enthusiastic promotion of Northwest Coast (and other) Native art by government agencies, artists, and anthropologists, during the 1950s and early 1960s most literature on Northwest Coast focused from an anthropological perspective on its social function rather than its aesthetic merits.[15] It is noteworthy, however, that during that time Audrey and Harry Hawthorn at the Museum of Anthropology

(MOA) in Vancouver, Wilson Duff at the British Columbia Provincial Museum (BCPM) (now the Royal British Columbia Museum), and Victoria and Erna Gunther at the Burke Museum in Seattle all promoted the art and culture of the Northwest Coast. Perhaps most significant, the MOA and the BCPM hired Mungo Martin to publicly carve totem poles, initiating a more public understanding of the ongoing vitality of Northwest Coast culture.

Breakthroughs of the 1960s and 1970s

Attitudes toward Native art began to change dramatically in the 1960s and 1970s, when liberation movements worldwide, including the American Indian Movement, fought vigorously for Native rights. Energized interest in Indigenous cultures inspired growing numbers of publications on Northwest Coast art and that of other First Nations. Instead of the kinds of comparisons cited earlier in this essay, the style and symbolic significance of the art itself attracted increasing attention.

The most significant achievement of this period was Bill Holm's codification of the formal elements of northern Northwest Coast art. As art historian and curator Kathryn Bunn-Marcuse has pointed out, this focus on form paralleled intellectual trends in contemporaneous European and American Modernism, which favored art style over meaning.[16] Not inconsequentially, by concentrating entirely upon the actual art object, this focus bypassed the kinds of problematic interpretations and comparisons of previous decades. In 1965 the young artist Bill Holm, scholar and later professor of art history at the University of Washington, published *Northwest Coast: An Analysis of Form*, which became the most influential and widely read book on the topic. He meticulously documented the methods artists employed to create the distinctive, two-dimensional images of historic art. Holm defined the language now universally used—formlines, ovoids, U-forms, and the like—which interacted to constitute the elegant northern style.[17] Pursuits of even deeper formal understanding of Northwest Coast art continue and include *The Transforming Image*, *Raven Travelling*, and *Northern Haida Master Carvers*.[18]

A quarter century after the 1941 MoMA exhibit, scholars and artists were again praising the aesthetic accomplishments of Northwest Coast art.[19] In 1967, Holm, along with Haida artist Bill Reid and anthropologist Wilson Duff, curated the Vancouver Art Gallery's *Arts of the Raven*, which represented itself as the first time Northwest Coast art had been exhibited *as art* as opposed to anthropology.[20] Then, in 1972, in *Form and Freedom*, Holm and Reid considered in acute connoisseurial detail an assortment of Northwest Coast artworks. The deep understanding Holm had pioneered now formed a framework for a genuine art criticism.[21]

As historic Northwest Coast art achieved increasing public recognition as a style of considerable merit, the contrasts between the "classic" arts of the eighteenth and nineteenth centuries and later productions became accentuated.

According to the views held at the time, settlement and acculturation had reduced and sometimes eliminated art production. "Authentic" Native art had been produced by cultures believed, by and large erroneously, to have been untouched by "civilization." By the early twentieth century, if artists made anything, it was considered "tourist art" such as model totem poles and baskets, which, in the words of anthropologist and art specialist Peter Macnair, had become "artistically and intellectually moribund," sharing nothing with the great tradition of Northwest Coast art from the previous century. Now, however, artists could return to that great tradition.[22]

As Holm was working on deciphering Northwest Coast style, Reid began producing art that adhered to his Haida ancestors' canons and quickly became recognized as a master northern Northwest Coast artist. Reid and Holm began training younger artists, who in turn educated others in formline traditions. Interest in this new artistry expanded, as the 'Ksan School of Northwest Coast art opened in 1970 in Hazelton, BC, and the British Columbia Provincial Museum (now the Royal British Columbia Museum) in Victoria commissioned new works for the 1971 exhibit *The Legacy: Continuing Traditions of Canadian Northwest Coast Indian Art*.[23] In 1976 the Museum of Anthropology at the University of British Columbia opened its new building with exhibits that highlighted the aesthetics rather than the anthropological significance of Northwest Coast material.[24] The impressive flurry of artistic activity during the 1970s resulted in abundant numbers of new Northwest Coast artworks, leading to this era being characterized as the "Northwest Coast Renaissance." Although some communities used these new creations during ceremonies, commercial galleries transformed most of them into commodities purchased by enthusiastic non-Native consumers.[25]

Whereas style took center stage in this period, some ventures into symbolic analyses sought to penetrate the inner meaning of Northwest Coast art. Like the earlier interpretations of the Surrealists, these inquiries emerged from contemporary cultural movements. Fueled in part by societal interest in altered states of consciousness, mysticism, and the occult, the "Spiritual Indian" became celebrated by members of the counterculture. Shamanism seized the imagination of many, including scholars of Northwest Coast art. Though formalism continued to dominate, shamanic interpretations made their way into the literature. A shamanistic world view was seen as responsible for the "mysterious . . . supernatural . . . esoteric" qualities of the art.[26] Shamanic experiences along with cosmic models were thought to underlay much art.[27] Experiences of shamanic metamorphosis inspired motifs of merged animals and humans as well as Kwakwa̱ka̱'wakw transformation masks.[28] The shamanic tree of life was said to have developed into the totem pole.[29] In my late twenties, I too was fascinated by shamanism and chose to research for my dissertation the Tlingit, who arguably produced the largest number of shamanic artworks on the Northwest Coast.

In New York, thousands of miles from the place where the art we studied was made, and where the descendants of its makers lived, my mentor, Douglas Fraser, encouraged us to analyze art from theoretical rather than formal perspectives. It is worth stating directly that at that time, in a department of art history, fieldwork was not a requirement nor was soliciting information from contemporary Indigenous people. A perfectly acceptable research project could be based in museums and libraries. Moreover, the still-prevalent paradigm of salvage anthropology and its partner, salvage Native art history, by focusing on the "authentic" creations of eighteenth- and nineteenth-century artists, ignored later works that diverged from the refined canons of "classic" northern Northwest Coast art.

Shortly after I entered graduate school, Fraser became an advocate of structuralism.[30] To simplify an immensely complex theoretical system, in Levi-Straussian structuralism, since the minds of all humans share the same binary structure, no culture was superior to any other.[31] The structural principles were apparent in the art itself when analyzed along with mythology, social structure, and other ethnographic information available in museums and libraries. My own interest in shamanism and my mentor's new enthusiasm for structuralism became the theoretical foundations for my dissertation, which compared the art used by shamans in their rituals and that used by clans to present their histories and express their rankings. This became the basis for my first book, *Art of the Northern Tlingit*, which addressed the binaries of sacred and secular.[32] By concentrating only on nineteenth-century art and ignoring works created in the twentieth, I was tacitly accepting the then prevalent judgment that until the 1960s, modern Northwest Coast art was of little value since it so strongly reflected cultural damage inflicted by settlement. But even more problematic with my position at that time was the notion that I could understand art by employing theoretical constructs developed by non-Natives and ignore the actual belief systems and ongoing cultural strength of those whose ancestors created these artworks.

It is relevant to point out that the Holmian concentration on style bypassed this problem by focusing solely on the concrete—what the art looked like—not applying any theory fashionable or otherwise, not attempting to interpret, and not comparing Northwest Coast art to other traditions. It is for these reasons, I think, that it has had a longer scholarly duration and far greater influence than the various interpretive methods I've mentioned. My own work was soon to change when, observing and supporting activities of Indigenous groups, I started critically reflecting on the nature of my scholarship.

The 1980s: Challenging Stereotypes

Deciphering Tlingit iconography began to seem wrong as I read exciting new works in postcolonial studies such as Edward Said's *Orientalism* (1978) and Gyatri Spivak's

"Can the Subaltern Speak?" (1988).[33] I reflect back to that time when I read Ishmael Hope's words: "In a colonial setting, only the common ground, the spaces already familiar to the colonial culture are privileged, acknowledged to be real, to be seen and heard as a tangible thing and to be accorded authority and meaning" (see chapter 14 in this edited volume). Seeing myself as an academic "expert" who, unwittingly, silenced Indigenous voices and recognizing my lack of authority to interpret Native art, I decided to pursue topics I could legitimately analyze: instead of suggesting what art meant to historic Indigenous communities (a project for which I had no authority), I would focus on my own culture as it engaged with that art, studying non-Native analyses, collections, and appropriations.[34]

I had worked on my dissertation in the American Museum of Natural History, which had abundant quantities of Tlingit art; similar objects were also found in other museums across the country. How did they find their ways to distant institutions? Douglas Cole's *Captured Heritage: The Scramble for Northwest Coast Artifacts* (1985) revealed actions both honorable and questionable of those who procured Northwest Coast art for museums; the work influenced me deeply and in part inspired the 1988 publication *From the Land of the Totem Poles: The Northwest Coast Art Collection at the American Museum of Natural History.*[35] This kind of cultural biography of Native art, tracing its trajectories from the hands of those who made and used it to major Euro-American institutions, struck me as an appropriately self-reflective project for a non-Native scholar. The era was ripe for reassessing how non-Native scholars had defined Native art from a Euro-American perspective. For example, many students of Northwest Coast art—including me—had ignored art made for sale, since we had been inculcated with the standard judgment that it was not "authentic."[36] One type of "tourist art," argillite carvings, which had previously been interpreted as expressions of postcontact cultural disintegration, now became prized as commodities that adhered to classic canons and equaled so-called "fine arts" of totem pole and mask carving.[37] The serious study of argillite produced books and art historian Robin Wright's impressive analyses.[38]

Another earlier bias proved wrong was the concept that Native artists lacked individual creativity and slavishly followed established models.[39] Once scholars understood the elements of Northwest Coast style, variations that signified different artists' hands became evident, and individual Northwest Coast artists finally became acknowledged and appreciated. The Kwakwa̱ka̱'wakw had never ceased making art of considerable aesthetic merit and starting in 1959, when Wilson Duff wrote the enthusiastically titled article "Mungo Martin, Carver of the Century," publications on other Kwakwa̱ka̱'wakw artists including Willie Seaweed, Ellen Neel, and Charlie James made their names familiar to the public.[40]

Charles Edenshaw, who had worked with Boas, Swanton, and others, was early recognized as a great master of Haida art. Reid, Holm, and Duff so admired him they installed an entire room of Edenshaws in Vancouver Art Gallery's *Arts of the*

Raven, though eventually it was recognized that not all were by him.[41] Using the connoisseurial skills developed from his deep understanding of formline art, Bill Holm asked in 1981: "Will the Real Charles Edenshaw Please Stand Up? The Problem of Attribution in Northwest Coast Indian Art." This initiated a series of careful studies by Wright, Steve Brown, and others identifying individual Haida and Tlingit artists.[42] Edenshaw has remained the most admired and well-known historic artist, as evidenced by *Charles Edenshaw*, a major retrospective of his work at the Vancouver Art Gallery (2013).[43]

On the heels of the civil rights movements of the 1960s, the rise of feminism in the 1970s eventually brought greater attention to the overlooked art of women. Little had been written on this subject since the anthropological monographs of the first decade of the twentieth century on Tlingit baskets and Chilkat blankets.[44] Once again, Bill Holm forged the way to new understanding of textiles in "A Wooling Blanket Neatly Wrought: The Early Historic Record of Northwest Coast Pattern-twined Textiles" (1982) by identifying the prototypes of Chilkat, twined cedar bark, and Ravenstail robes. Concurrently, weaver Cheryl Samuel analyzed large numbers of textiles in museums, publishing books on the Chilkat blanket (1982) and the Ravenstail robe (1987). As Samuel and the so-called "last Tlingit weaver" Jennie Thlunaut trained women, new textiles were created, paralleling the reenergization of men's art. The most notable celebration of female creativity was Tsimshian artist Doreen Jensen's and Polly Sargent's groundbreaking exhibit *Robes of Power: Totem Poles on Cloth* in 1986, the first presentation of button blankets as significant expressions of cultural identity.[45] Unfortunately, these contributions exerted little influence in the field, and women's art inspired little serious scholarship until recently.

The 1990s: Collaborations and Reevaluations

Anticolonialist movements begun in the 1960s intensified by the 1990s as Native people more vociferously sought independence from white authorities, confronted discourses that they had "disappeared," and worked toward correcting the consequences of colonialism. Within Northwest Coast art studies the most ardent statement on this is Marcia Crosby's 1991 "Construction of the Imaginary Indian" in which she accuses scholars of "dominating or colonizing First Nations people, our cultural images and our land, as well as salvaging, preserving and reinterpreting material fragments of a supposedly dying native culture for non-Native 'art and culture' collections."[46] In Crosby's judgment one of the most egregious activities on the part of non-Natives has been museum presentations, which imposed non-Native classifications and interpretations of Native American culture. Indigenous people were no longer going to accept the products of the colonial project but instead would enthusiastically embark on paths of resistance and replacement.

In the mid-1980s I had proposed to the American Museum of Natural History an exhibition on the Kwakwa̱ka̱'wakw potlatch. This experience once again changed my approach to Northwest Coast art by revealing the pleasures of collaboration. During my first trip to visit the Kwakwa̱ka̱'wakw on Vancouver Island, I stopped at UBC's Museum of Anthropology to discuss the exhibit with director Michael Ames. Then the most articulate non-Native proponent of collaboration, Ames in the 1970s had forged innovative partnerships with First Nations.[47] I remember him advising me to collaborate with Gloria Cranmer Webster, director of the U'mista Cultural Centre in Alert Bay, BC.[48] I did so, and together we assembled a group of "Old People" (as Webster preferred to call the Elders) who transformed my understanding of Native art by revealing how significant historic objects were to their living culture.[49]

Chiefly Feasts: The Enduring Kwakiutl Potlatch (1991) represented one of several museum exhibits succeeding Ames's groundbreaking work, including the Burke Museum's *A Time of Gathering* (installed in 1989, catalog published in 1991), curated by Robin Wright, the Seattle Art Museum's Northwest Coast installation, curated by Steve Brown in 1995 and the Royal British Columbia Museum's *Ḥuupuḵʷanum·Tupaat—Out of the Mist: Treasures of the Nuu-Chah-Nulth Chiefs*, curated by Martha Black in 1999.[50] The paradigm had changed from patronization to partnerships. During the 1990s it became undeniably evident that those who sought to exhibit Native American art had to abandon non-Native curatorial authority to welcome collaboration and Indigenous authority.[51]

Another change in Northwest Coast art studies concerned Salish art. In contrast to the unremitting focus on the northern and central Northwest Coast, most publications had dismissed art from the southern region as a remnant of the earlier pan–Northwest Coast geometric style that more aesthetically advanced northerners had replaced with formline creations.[52] Franz Boas found Salish art "much cruder" and more archaically "pictographic" than that of northern groups; moreover the Salish produced less art than their northern neighbors.[53] Wayne Suttles, a well-respected anthropologist who energetically resisted such devaluation, argued that cultural constraints prevented the production and public display of their artworks.[54]

Archaeological excavations of the 1970s and 1980s stimulated more research when, by revealing the existence of ancient southern formlines different from those in the north, they demolished any notion of Salish artistic inferiority.[55] Brown even convincingly argued that in the nineteenth century the southern tradition influenced the northern style, further complicating yet enriching Northwest Coast art history.[56] Exhibits began to feature Salish art, such as the Burke Museum's 1989 exhibit *A Time of Gathering*, art from Washington state, including Salish works. Then, in 2008 the Seattle Art Museum opened *S'abadeb. The Gift: Pacific Coast Salish*

Art and Artists, a historic presentation at a major institution entirely dedicated to the heretofore overlooked body of Northwest Coast art.[57] A fitting celebration of this revelation of aesthetic value, *S'abadeb* firmly established the significant achievements of artists from the southern Northwest Coast.[58]

The Twenty-First Century

The trajectory of late twentieth- and early twenty-first century Northwest Coast art scholarship has paralleled the many increasingly powerful voices of Indigenous authority in the academy, which insisted on institutionalizing the collaborative paradigm for museum exhibits, dismantling Western-imposed judgments about Native art, critiquing former practices and scholarship as colonialist, encouraging Indigenous participation in the academy, and in general promoting sovereignty and autonomy. Activities promoting sovereignty are evident in numerous arenas. Indigenous groups use art, materials, and localities to communicate their ownership of culture and land, as in Kaitlin McCormick's account of the Haida controlling their argillite (chapter 2), Denise Nicole Green's discussion of Indigenizing place (chapter 14), and Emily L. Moore's history of the three different Seward Shame Pole versions (chapter 1).

Museums closely collaborating with Native artists and communities have assumed a leadership position among institutions as described in several chapters in this volume: in the Northwest, Karen Duffek, Peter Morin, and Karen Benbassat Ali on the Museum of Anthropology (chapter 9), Sharon Fortney on the Vancouver Museum (chapter 8), and Kathryn Bunn-Marcuse on the Burke Museum (chapter 10); and in the East, Lucy Fowler Williams on the Penn Museum in Philadelphia (chapter 11). Jisgang Nika Collison describes the impressive achievements of her Native-run Haida museum (chapter 5). But Emily Moore demonstrates that in Juneau, Alaska—right in the middle of Tlingit territory—the public needs more targeted education about the unacceptable continuation of a colonial narrative (chapter 1).

It is useful to remember that correcting past biases does not imply rejecting all research conducted within the colonialist paradigm, for some information acquired—principally by anthropologists but in some cases art historians, explorers, tourists, even missionaries—has proved invaluable for contemporary art and ceremony. Boas's vast publications on and extensive collections of Kwakwa̱ka̱'wakw material remain central to contemporary scholarship conducted in collaboration with communities, such Aaron Glass, Rainer Hartoum, and Judith Berman's work with the Kwakwa̱ka̱'wakw on Boas's 1897 book on ceremonialism and Bunn-Marcuse's with the Kwag'uł on Boas's 1930 films.[59] In her scholarly and masterfully researched decipherment of certain textile motifs, Evelyn Vanderhoop relies in part on the early twentieth-century work of John Swanton, whom she admires and appreciates (chapter 12). Denise Nicole Green describes the relevance of Edward Sapir's recordings and collections to Nuu-chah-nulth art and ceremony (chapter 13). Ishmael Hope's enthusiasm for the contributions of Louis Shotridge (chapter 14) as well as Lucy Fowler Williams's dependence on Shotridge's information (chapter 11) demonstrate a stunning reconsideration of a man many previously condemned. Bill Holm has been subjected to criticism over the years, but as Janet Catherine Berlo and I demonstrate (chapter 4), many Indigenous people admire and value his contributions to Northwest Coast art.

The increasing numbers of publications on Northwest Coast art written by Native scholars, artists, and culture bearers are challenging the sole authority of non-Native scholars and often approaching material from an Indigenous perspective. While a handful of books and essays by Indigenous authors appeared over the years, since 1990 increasing numbers of Northwest Coast Native writers have presented their own perspectives on art history. An important First Nations contributor to the literature is Ki-Ke-In (who along with Charlotte Townsend-Gault and Jennifer Kramer coedited the masterful 2013 volume *Native Art of the Northwest Coast: A History of Changing Ideas*.[60] As part of museums' efforts to be more inclusive, early on exhibition catalogs initiated the now well-established practice to publish contributions by Indigenous writers, including Gloria Cranmer Webster, Nora Dauenhauer, Robert Joseph, Robert Davidson, and Don Yeomans.[61] In addition, editors of volumes on various themes have invited Indigenous contributors such as Mique'l Askren Dangeli, Debra Sparrow, Delores Churchill, and Larry McNeil.[62] We welcome in this edited volume the unique perspectives on art that Ishmael Hope (chapter 14), Jisgang Nika Collison (chapter 5), Lou-ann Ika'wega Neel (chapter 7), and Evelyn Vanderhoop offer (chapter 12).

Some contemporary artists have, through their artwork, critiqued colonialism and expressed Indigenous sovereignty. It is interesting that on the Northwest Coast, perhaps more than most other North American groups, much art remains deeply connected to nineteenth-century canons and addresses artistic rather than political issues. The often strikingly original creations by Robert Davidson, Susan Point, Doug Cranmer, and others tend to focus respectfully on artistic and cultural history while they invent new visual statements.[63] But other Northwest Coast artists, such as Lawrence Paul Yuxweluptun, Marianne Nicolson, Stephen Jackson, and several artists discussed in chapter 10 by Kathryn Bunn-Marcuse, apply familiar formal elements as they address the multifaceted consequences of colonization.[64] Some Northwest Coast artists, such Da-ka-xeen Mehner, Larry McNeil, Tanis S'eiltin, and Nicholas Galanin, have all but abandoned their ancestors' style as they participate in the broader sphere of contemporary Native art that innovatively assesses the situation of First Nations in the modern world.[65] As Duffek, Morin, and Benbassat Ali illustrate in chapter 9, Morin's installations are revolutionary. Although the formline canon no longer singularly defines Northwest Coast art, some more conservative critics disapprove of innovations. Like those who in the past dismissed souvenirs and ignored women's art, these critics are imposing their concepts of "tradition" upon the definition of an ever-changing Northwest Coast art and ignoring political messages so relevant to Indigenous sovereignty.

Recent scholarship of has responded to the intensification of Indigenous determination to control their own history by more energetically correcting past misunderstandings, misrepresentations, and colonialist biases. One important example is the reexamination of the so-called Northwest Coast Renaissance, which was said to have represented a brilliant rebirth following the death of the great nineteenth-century Northwest Coast artistic tradition—an evaluation, as Christopher Green points out (chapter 3), James Schoppert challenged in the 1980s. It became clear that art did not "die" in the early twentieth century, as I argued in an essay on Haida art history and Ronald Hawker proved in his study of the extensive artistic production in British Columbia between the 1920s and early 1960s.[66] In some cases the government, missionaries, and museums played major roles in this productivity, but the resulting artworks were in fact declarations of cultural pride, self-determination, and resistance to the hegemony of their colonizers. Twentieth-century Northwest Coast art differed from and did not share the precise canons of its nineteenth-century predecessors—but that did not signify death. A notable early opponent to the supposed "disappearance" of Northwest Coast art was anthropologist Margaret Blackman, who argued that the pejorative notion of "acculturation"—which is what led to the precipitous "decline" of their art—denied Native people their clearly evident artistic and cultural creativity.[67] According to anthropologist Aaron Glass, the renaissance discourse positively identified growing cultural strength on the Northwest Coast but nonetheless contained elements of colonialist judgment.[68]

Today, Native and non-Native people participate in a dramatically transformed, globalized world that extends beyond the colonizer/colonized division. Expressions of authority, sovereignty, and cultural ownership have vital importance to Indigenous people worldwide but do not inevitably deny a focus on elements that recognize and welcome mutually beneficial cultural exchanges and understandings. As Plains Cree artist and curator Gerald McMaster asserts, some "Indigenous artists explore . . . varying forms of interculturality—the mutual exchange of ideas and forms between Indigenous people and settlers. Their projects investigate opportunities to connect with the so-called Other."[69] Instead of the disempowering concept of acculturation and its inaccurate allegation of cultural demise, indications abound that Native people have long devised ways of appropriating and indigenizing cultural elements from their interlopers, even as they appeared to accommodate to them.

Encounters between colonizers often ignorant of their impacts and colonized exercising subtle yet empowering agency engendered creative artistic responses. For example, nineteenth-century works in the collection of the American Museum of Natural History, acquired during the age of salvage anthropology, reveal appropriations and indigenizing transformations of non-Native culture.[70] The results of intercultural encounters have become fertile arenas for innovative research on the history of the totem pole, Alaskan totem pole restoration projects, commodification of Native culture, and appropriation and indigenization of European motifs in Haida and Kwakwa̱ka̱'wakw art.[71] Essays in this book address various manifestations of the intercultural, including C. Green on Schoppert's early example of combining Western modernism and historic Northwest Coast art (chapter 3); Lou-ann Neel's account of Ellen Neel's Royal Albert Bone China Totemware (chapter 7), which, while primarily intended for a non-Native market adhered in its imagery to Kwakwa̱ka̱'wakw rules of ownership; and Morin's unique use of a gallery space for his installation (chapter 9). While these examples illustrate the positive artistic consequences of intercultural encounters, Berlo and Jonaitis discuss the fakes and forgeries that disempower Native artists (chapter 4).

At the outset of this conclusion I presented the concept of Northwest Coast art historic genealogy that acknowledges certain scholarly continuities. Sovereignty and decolonization, while immensely strengthened in the twenty-first century and assuming far more central positions in the discourse on art than ever before, are logical enhancements of earlier liberation movements and postcolonialism. Recent museum collaborations enrich and intensify initiatives standardized in the 1990s. Contesting the negativity of acculturation discourse of white domination, interculturality provides an empowering perspective on Native and non-Native encounters.

Much art that was overlooked in the past has become the focus of new scholarship. For years men's arts of painting and carving attracted almost all curatorial and scholarly attention, but now women's art has become entrenched within the narrative of Northwest Coast art history, as the contributions by Megan Smetzer (chapter 6), Lou-ann Neel (chapter 7), Evelyn Vanderhoop (chapter 12), and Jisgang Nika Collison (chapter 5) admirably demonstrate. Greater attention is being directed toward previously ignored artistic traditions, such as Sharon Fortney on Salish art (chapter 8) and Peter Morin on his Tahltan heritage (chapter 9). What is surprising, however, is the absence of new scholarship in this book based on Holmian formalism.[72] While Berlo and Jonaitis refer to Holm's historical position in the field (chapter 4), and C. Green utilizes elements of the formline system in his analysis of Schoppert (chapter 3), neither essay advances insight on style.[73] While understanding the system remains important for numerous Northwest Coast artists, such as Robert Davidson's masterful analysis of Charles Edenshaw's art, its Euro-American formal foundation, as Ishmael Hope has asserted, ignores the profound Indigenous meaning within art.[74] It may be that the Holmian formal lineage is lying fallow until new considerations revive it.

I conclude with a few thoughts about the nature of academic scholarship, which, with its research in archives and/or the field, extensive footnotes, and references to previous literature, is a Western mode of approaching subject matter. Most essays in this volume adhere to that respected and worthwhile tradition that complements and enhances their authors' sensitivities to Indigenous history. However, some Native contributors embrace a different paradigm, relying on customary knowledge, oral history, and cultural ways of knowing. The same is true of the poetry published here. I am not certain such approaches would have been enthusiastically accepted twenty or perhaps even fifteen years ago by the university press reviewers of a book such as this. But Native art studies today accept as equally valid, and valuable, approaches that diverge from academic conventions. And that indicates an even brighter future for understandings of Northwest Coast art.

As an observer of and participant in the history of Northwest Coast art scholarship, I feel humbled and gratified by the current vitality of research, the enhancement of collaborative projects, the investigation of previously overlooked aspects of the art, and the increasing involvement of Native writers in fostering knowledge, creating understanding, and contributing unique perspectives that emerge not from Western scholarship but from their own heritage. Most striking for me about this collection of essays is the conscious inclusion of sovereignty and rejection of Western biases as interconnected leitmotifs; while these do have intellectual ancestors, today they are central, dominant, and comprehensive. Regardless of the topic, scholarship today acknowledges Native authority, strives to Indigenize cultural narratives, and disrupts the colonialist legacy vigorously. By continuing and enhancing these actions, and developing previously unimagined projects based on ethical foundations, Northwest Coast art scholarship will continue to thrive.

NOTES

I wish to take this opportunity to express my deepest appreciation for all the Indigenous and non-Native friends, scholars and teachers who have guided me through my wonderful journey learning about Northwest Coast art. I also thank Janet Catherine Berlo, Kathryn Bunn-Marcuse, Megan Smetzer, Aaron Glass, and Ruth Phillips (who also are friends, scholars, and teachers) for their comments on earlier drafts of this chapter.

1 For decades Columbia's Department of Art History and Archaeology, like most other universities at the time, focused on non-Native art, only grudgingly accepting the "primitive art" that Paul Wingert taught there from 1932 to 1966, succeeded by his student Douglas Fraser, from 1955 to 1982. While PhDs were conferred in African and pre-Columbian art at Yale, and a scant few other places, to my knowledge only five doctoral degrees were conferred in Native American art history in the 1970s: Joan Vastokas, Lee Anne Wilson, and myself at Columbia, and Carol Kaufmann and Zena Pearlstone at UCLA. The two most accomplished Native American art historians received their PhDs in other fields, Ruth B. Phillips in African art history at University College London and Janet Catherine Berlo in pre-Columbian art at Yale.

2 When I discussed this with my two closest friends, distinguished Native American art historians Janet Catherine Berlo and Ruth B. Phillips, they too selected their research fields for similar reasons.

3 See Ira Jacknis, "Regional Surveys of Northwest Coast Native Art: Review Essay," *BC Studies* 155 (2007): 129–36, for a useful review of literature on Northwest Coast art.

4 As is the case with many intellectual movements, "decolonization" is used broadly and has varying meanings for different people. In some cases "sovereignty" and "Indigenization" are useful terms for contemporary liberation movements of Native people.

5 The publications featured in this chapter are not necessarily the first or sole examples of the approach they take to art. Those to which I refer have been particularly important, interesting, and/or influential to me personally.

6 For Boas's contributions to art history, see Aldona Jonaitis, *A Wealth of Thought: Franz Boas on Native American Art* (Seattle: University of Washington Press, 1995).

7 Boas actively collaborated with Kwakwa̱ka̱'wakw-raised George Hunt and during his career trained many distinguished women, including such anthropologists of the Northwest Coast as Frederica de Laguna, Erna Gunther, and Viola Garfield.

8 Leslie Dawn, "Northwest Coast Art and Canadian National Identity, 1900–50," in *Native Art of the Northwest Coast: A History of Changing Ideas*, edited by Charlotte Townsend-Gault, Jennifer Kramer, and Ki-Ke-In, 317–21 (Vancouver: UBC Press, 2013), 304.

9 Aldona Jonaitis and Aaron Glass, *The Totem Pole: An Intercultural Biography* (Seattle: University of Washington Press, 2001), 85–94; and Emily L. Moore, *Proud Raven, Panting Wolf: Carving Alaska's New Deal Totem Parks* (Seattle: University of Washington Press, 2018).

10 Frederic Douglas and René d'Harnoncourt, *Indian Art of the United States* (New York: Museum of Modern Art, 1941).

11 They also presaged later challenges to unchanging "authentic Indian" stereotypes; see Douglas and d'Harnoncourt, *Indian Art of the United States*, 10.

12 Lèvi-Strauss had high regard for the intellect of Northwest Coast and other Indigenous people and challenged the diffusionists' concept that artistic motifs traveled from high to low cultures; see Claude Lèvi-Strauss, "The Art of the Northwest Coast at the American Museum of Natural History," *Gazette des Beaux-Arts* 24 (1943): 175–88.

13 Marie Mauzé, "Surrealists and the New York Avant-Garde, 1920–60," in *Native Art of the Northwest Coast*, edited by Townsend-Gault, Kramer, and Ki-Ke-In, 270–303.

14 Barnett Newman, foreword to *Northwest Coast Indian Painting* (New York: Betty Parsons Gallery, 1946).

15 Robert B. Inverarity, *Art of the Northwest Coast Indians* (Berkeley: University of California Press, 1950), the first major book dedicated to this material, initially reviews the regional environment, Native culture, and identification of animal images and then presents an overview of objects. This became the standard framework for later anthropological works.

16 Kathryn Bunn-Marcuse, "Form First, Function Follows: The Use of Formal Analysis in Northwest Coast Art History," in *Native Art of the Northwest Coast*, edited by Townsend-Gault, Kramer, and Ki-Ke-In, 404–13. This was not the first time that art's formal qualities had been considered, as Herman Haeberlin had discussed them; see Herman Karl Haeberlin, "Principles of Aesthetic Form in the Art of the North Pacific Coast: A Preliminary Sketch," *American Anthropologist* 20 (1918): 258–64.

17 Bill Holm, *Northwest Coast: An Analysis of Form* (Seattle: University of Washington Press, 1965). See more about Holm in chapter 4 by Janet Catherine Berlo and Aldona Jonaitis, this volume.

18 Bill McClellan and Karen Duffek, *The Transforming Image: Painted Arts of the Northwest* Coast (Vancouver: UBC Press; Seattle: University of Washington Press, 2000); Peter Macnair, in *Raven Travelling: Two Centuries of Haida Art*, edited by Daina Augaitis (Vancouver: Vancouver Art Gallery; Douglas & McIntyre, 2006); and Robin K. Wright, *Northern Haida Master Carvers* (Seattle: University of Washington Press, 2001).

19 In the 1950s and 1960s the Burke Museum under Erna Gunther and Audrey and Harry Hawthorn at the Museum of Anthropology had paved the way for this "transformation" of Northwest Coast material into "art" although they did not explicitly promote it as such in the way Duff, Holm, and Reid did in 1967.

20 It was also in 1967 that Canada presented its First Nations art at Expo 67. See Ruth Phillips, *Museum Pieces: Towards an Indigenization of Canadian Museums* (Quebec: McGill-Queens University Press, 2011), 27–47.

21 Bill Holm and Bill Reid, *Form and Freedom: A Dialogue on Northwest Coast Indian Art* (Houston, TX: Institute for the Arts, Rice University, 1972).

22 Peter Macnair, "Trends in Northwest Coast Indian Art, 1880–1959," in *The Shadow of the Sun: Perspectives on Contemporary Native Art*, edited by Canadian Museum of Civilization (Hull, Quebec: Canadian Museum of Civilization, 1993), 52.

23 In 1980 a catalog of this exhibit was published; see Peter Macnair, Alan L. Hoover, and Kevin Neary, *The Legacy: Continuing Traditions of Canadian Northwest Coast Indian Art* (Victoria: British Columbia Provincial Museum, 1980).

24 I thank Megan Smetzer for this insight.

25 Karen Duffek, "Authenticity and the Contemporary Northwest Coast Indian Art Market," *BC Studies* 57 (1983): 99–111; and Karen Duffek, "A Guide to Buying Northwest Coast Indian Arts," *Museum Note* 10 (Vancouver: UBC Museum of Anthropology, 1983).

26 Christian Zervos, preface to *Masterpieces of Indian and Eskimo Art* (Ottawa: National Gallery of Art, 1969).

27 George MacDonald, "Cosmic Equations in Northwest Coast Indian Art," in *The World Is as Sharp as a Knife: An Anthology in Honour of Wilson Duff*, edited by Donald Abbott, 225–38 (Victoria: British Columbia Provincial Museum, 1981). The fascination with shamanic art did not end with this period; see Alan Wardwell's lavishly illustrated *Tangible Visions: Northwest Coast Indian Shamanism and Its Art* (New York: The Monacelli Press, 1999).

28 See Peter Furst, "Roots and Continuities," *Arts Canada* 184, no. 87 (1973): 33–60, as well as Kwakwa̱ka̱'wakw transformation masks in Deborah Waite, "Kwakiutl Transformational Masks," in *Many Faces of Primitive Art*, edited by Douglas Fraser, 266–300 (Englewood Cliffs, NJ: Prentice-Hall, 1966).

29 Joan Vastokas, "The Shamanic Tree of Life," *Arts Canada* 183, no. 87 (1973): 125–49.

30 Starting in the 1920s and continuing as late as the 1950s, diffusionists argued that the uniquely complex style of Northwest Coast art, so different from that of neighboring cultures, did not develop in situ in North America but instead originated in Asia and diffused eastward. See Aldona Jonaitis, ed., *A Wealth of Thought: Franz Boas and Native American Art History* (Seattle: University of Washington Press, 1995).

31 An enthusiastic adherent to structuralism, University of British Columbia anthropologist Wilson Duff promoted the sophisticated intellectual qualities of the art; see Wilson Duff, *Images: Stone B.C.* (Saanichton, BC: Hancock House Publishers, 1975).

32 Aldona Jonaitis, *Art of the Northern Tlingit* (Seattle: University of Washington Press 1986).

33 Edward Said, *Orientalism* (New York: Vintage 1979); Gyatri Spivak, "Can the Subaltern Speak," in *Marxism and the Interpretation of Culture*, edited by Carey Nelson and Larry Grossberg, 271–313 (Chicago: University of Illinois Press, 1988). I wish to acknowledge the profound influence of my then-husband and still close friend, French historian Herman Lebovics, who first introduced me to this literature.

34 My first endeavor in this regard was my article "Creations of Mystics and Philosophers: The White Man's Perceptions of Northwest Coast Indian Art from the 1930s to the Present," *American Indian Culture and Research Journal* 5, no. 1 (1981): 1–45. In 1992 in my chapter "Franz Boas, John Swanton and the 'New' Haida Sculpture at the American Museum of

Natural History," I proposed that the museum's late nineteenth-century Haida art exhibit could have been a vehicle for the social education of New Yorkers. See Aldona Jonaitis, "Franz Boas, John Swanton and the 'New' Haida Sculpture at the American Museum of Natural History," in *The Early Years of Native American Art History: Essays on the Politics of Scholarship and Collecting*, edited by Janet Berlo, 3–66 (Seattle: University of Washington Press, 1992).

35 Douglas Cole, *Captured Heritage: The Scramble for Northwest Coast Artifacts* (Seattle: University of Washington Press, 1985); Aldona Jonaitis, *From the Land of the Totem Poles: The Northwest Coast Art Collection at the American Museum of Natural History* (New York: American Museum of Natural History; Seattle: University of Washington Press). Ira Jacknis also contributed significantly to the literature on museums; see Ira Jacknis, *The Storage Box of Tradition: Kwakiutl Art, Anthropologists, and Museums, 1881–1981* (Washington, DC: Smithsonian Institution Press, 2002).

36 This is of course ironic since much art made during the "renaissance" was—and still is—made for the non-Native market.

37 Erna Gunther, "The Social Disorganization of the Haida as Reflected in Their Slate Carving," *Davidson Journal of Anthropology* 2, no. 21 (1956): 149–53; Marius Barbeau, *Haida Myths Illustrated in Argillite Carvings* (Ottawa: National Museum of Canada, 1953); and Carole Kaufmann, "Changes in Haida Indian Argillite Carvings, 1820 to 1910," PhD diss., University of California, 1969.

38 Leslie Drew and Douglas Wilson, *Argillite: Art of the Haida* (Vancouver: Hancock House Publishers, 1980); Carol Sheehan, *Pipes That Won't Smoke, Coals That Won't Burn* (Calgary: Glenbow Museum, 1981); Peter Macnair and Alan Hoover, *The Magic Leaves: A History of Argillite Carving* (Victoria: Royal British Columbia Museum, 2002); Robin K. Wright, "Haida Argillite Ship Pipes," *American Indian Art Magazine* 5, no. 1 (1979): 40–47; Wright, "Haida Argillite Pipes: The Influence of Clay Pipes," *American Indian Art Magazine* 5, no. 4 (1980): 42–48, 88; Wright, "Anonymous Attributions: A Tribute to the Mid-Nineteenth Century Haida Argillite Carver, the Master of the Long Fingers," in *Box of Daylight: Northwest Coast Indian Art*, edited by Bill Holm, 139–42 (Seattle: University of Washington Press, 1983); Wright, "Nineteenth Century Haida Argillite Pipe Carvers: Stylistic Attributions," PhD diss., University of Washington, 1985; Wright, "The Depiction of Women in Nineteenth Century Haida Argillite Carving," *American Indian Art Magazine* 11, no. 4 (1986): 36–45; and Wright, "Two Haida Artists from Yan: Will John Gwaytihl and Simeon Stilthda Please Step Apart?" *American Indian Art Magazine* 23, no. 3 (1998): 42–57, 106–107.

39 Boas and Haeberlin did suggest that individual artists could be distinguished by their unique signatures; see Franz Boas, *Primitive Art* (Oslo: Instituttet for Sammenlignende Kulturforskning, 1927); and Haeberlin, "Principles of Aesthetic Form in the Art of the North Pacific Coast: A Preliminary Sketch."

40 Wilson Duff, "Mungo Martin, Carver of the Century," *Museum News* 1, nos. 3–8 (1959); Bill Holm, *Smoky-Top: The Art and Times of Willie Seaweed* (Seattle: University of Washington Press, 1983); and Phil Nyutten, *The Totem Carvers: Charlie James, Ellen Neel and Mungo Martin* (Vancouver: Panorama Publishers, 1982).

41 Wilson Duff, Bill Holm, and Bill Reid, *Arts of the Raven: Masterworks by the Northwest Coast Indian* (Vancouver: Vancouver Art Gallery, 1967).

42 See Robin K. Wright, "Kadashan's Staff: The Work of a Mid-Nineteenth Century Argillite Carver in Another Medium," *American Indian Art Magazine* 17, no. 4 (1992): 48–55; Wright, "Anonymous Attributions"; Wright, "Nineteenth Century Haida Argillite Pipe Carvers"; and Wright, "Two Haida Artists from Yan." See also Steven C. Brown, "From Taquan to Klukwan: Tracing the Work of an Early Tlingit Master Artist," in *Faces, Voices and Dreams:*

A Celebration of the Centennial of the Sheldon Jackson Museum, 1888–1988, edited by Peter Corey, 157–75 (Sitka: Division of Alaska State Museums and the Friends of the Alaska State Museum, 1987); Steve Brown, "In the Shadow of the Wrangell Master: Photo Documentation of the Work of Two Nineteenth Century Tlingit Artists," *American Indian Art Magazine* 19, no. 4 (1994): 74–75, 104; and Steve Brown "A Tale of Two Carvers: The Rain Wall Screen of the Whale House, Klukwan, Alaska," *American Indian Art Museum* 30, no. 4 (2005): 48–59.

43 Daina Augaitis, Jim Hart, Robin K. Wright, eds., *Charles Edenshaw* (Vancouver: Vancouver Art Gallery, 2013).

44 George T. Emmons, "The Basketry of the Tlingit," *Memoirs of the American Museum of Natural History*, volume 3 (1903), part 2; and George T. Emmons and Franz Boas, "The Chilkat Blanket," *Memoirs of the American Museum of Natural History*, volume 3 (1907).

45 Bill Holm, "A Wooling Blanket Neatly Wrought: The Early Historic Record of Northwest Coast Pattern-twined Textiles," *American Indian Art Magazine* 8 (1982): 34–47; Cheryl Samuel, *The Chilkat Dancing Blanket* (Seattle: Pacific Search Press, 1982), and *The Raven's Tail* (Vancouver: University of British Columbia Press, 1987). Doreen Jensen and Polly Sargent, *Robes of Power: Totem Poles on Cloth* (Vancouver: University of British Columbia Press, 1986).

46 Marcia Crosby, "The Construction of the Imaginary Indian," in *Vancouver Anthology: The Institutional Politics of Art*, edited by Stan Douglas, 266–91 (Vancouver: Talon Books, 1991).

47 See Michael Ames, *Museums, the Public and Anthropology* (Vancouver: University of British Columbia Press, 1986). It is worth noting that some of the earliest and most important exhibits on Northwest Coast art had Indigenous involvement: for example, Kwakwa̱ka̱'wakw-raised George Hunt at the American Museum of Natural History and Tlingit Louis Shotridge at the University of Pennsylvania Museum.

48 This project would never have been successful without the dedicated involvement of Peter Macnair, who expertly guided me through the collaborative processes.

49 See Aldona Jonaitis, *Chiefly Feasts: The Enduring Kwakiutl Potlatch* (New York: American Museum of Natural History; Seattle: University of Washington Press, 1991), for an essay on how this experience profoundly affected me. My work with the Kwakwa̱ka̱'wakw collection at AMNH inspired my edition of Boas on art and a book on the remarkable Nuu-chah-nulth Whaler's Shrine also at AMNH; see Jonaitis, *Wealth of Thought*, and *The Yuquot Whaler's Shrine* (Seattle: University of Washington Press, 1999). The research on the Shrine and the involvement of the Mowachaht in that project was immensely enhanced by Richard Inglis's dedicated involvement.

50 The exhibit *Chiefly Feasts: The Enduring Kwakiutl Potlatch* opened at the American Museum of Natural History in 1991. Although I urged the museum to use the more preferred designation "Kwakwa̱ka̱'wakw," they insisted that "Kwakiutl" was a more familiar term. When the exhibit traveled to the Royal British Columbia Museum, the title changed to include the preferred name. See Martha Black, "Collaborations: A Historical Perspective," in *Native Art of the Northwest Coast*, edited by Townsend-Gault, Kramer, and Ki-Ke-In, 785–827.

51 Another major victory for Native people in relation to museums was repatriation.

52 See Paul Wingert, *American Indian Sculpture: A Study of the Northwest Coast* (New York: J. J. Augustin, 1949). That this book has been overlooked is indicated not only by its absence in the otherwise all-inclusive bibliography in Townsend-Gault, Kramer, and Ki-Ke-In, eds., *Native Art of the Northwest Coast*, but also by the lack of any mention of Wingert that I found in the entire book.

53 Franz Boas, "Art of the Thompson Indians" (1900), reprinted in Jonaitis, *Wealth of Thought*, 151–53.

54 Wayne Suttles, "Productivity and Its Constraints: A Coast Salish Case," in *Coast Salish Essays* (Vancouver: Talon Books, 1987), 100–33.

55 Bill Holm, "Art," in *Handbook of North American Indians*, volume 7, *The Northwest Coast*, edited by Wayne Suttles, 602–32 (Washington, DC: Smithsonian Institution Press, 1990); and Steven C. Brown, ed., *The Spirit Within: Northwest Coast Art from the John H. Hauberg Collection* (Seattle: Seattle Art Museum, 1995).

56 Steven C. Brown, "Turning the Tables: The Influence of Nineteenth-Century Southern Design Styles on the Northern Northwest Coast," *American Indian Art Museum* 25, no. 3 (2000): 48–55.

57 Barbara Brotherton, ed., *S'abadeb, the Gift: Pacific Coast Salish Art and Artists* (Seattle: University of Washington Press, 2008).

58 When I wrote the survey *Art of the Northwest Coast*, I made every effort to include as much women's and Salish art as I could, although Megan Smetzer, appropriately, chided me for not including enough beadwork. See Aldona Jonaitis, *Art of the Northwest Coast* (Seattle: University of Washington Press, 2006).

59 Aaron Glass, Judith Berman, and Rainer Hatoum, "Reassembling the Social Organization: Collaboration and Digital Media in (Re)making Boas's 1897," *Museum Worlds* 5 no. 1 (2017): 108–32; and Kathryn Bunn-Marcuse, principal author and contributing editor, *Ka̱ ns Hiłile ("Making It Right")—A Collaborative Reframing of Kwakiutl Film and Audio Recordings with Franz Boas, 1930* (Seattle: University of Washington Press, 2020).

60 Charlotte Townsend-Gault, Jennifer Kramer, Ki-Ke-In, eds., *Native Art of the Northwest Coast: A History of Changing Ideas* (Vancouver: UBC Press, 2013).

61 Gloria Cranmer Webster, "The Contemporary Potlatch," in *Chiefly Feasts: The Enduring Kwakiutl Potlatch*, edited by Jonaitis, 227–48; Nora Dauenhauer, "Tlingit *At.óow*: Traditions and Concepts," in *The Spirit Within*, edited by Brown, 21–20; Robert Joseph, "Behind the Mask," in *Down from the Shimmering Sky: Masks of the Northwest Coast*, edited by Peter Macnair, Robert Joseph, and Bruce Grenville, 18–35 (Vancouver: Douglas & McIntyre, 1989); Robert Joseph, ed., *Listening to Our Ancestors: The Art of Native Life Along the North Pacific Coast* (Washington, DC: Smithsonian Institution Press, 2005); Robert Davidson, "Da. A xuugang, Charles Edenshaw, 'Master Carpenter,'" in *Charles Edenshaw*, edited by Daina Augaitis et al. (Vancouver: Vancouver Art Museum, 2013); and Don Yeomans, "The Impulse to Create," in *Raven Travelling*, edited by Augaitis, 155–69.

62 Mique'l Askren (Dangeli), "Memories of Fire and Glass: B. A. Halden, 19th Century Tsimshian Photographer," in *Visual Currencies: Reflections on Native American Photography*, edited by Henrietta Lidchi and Hulleah J. Tsinhnahjinne, 90–107 (Edinburgh: National Museum of Scotland, 2008); Debra Sparrow, "A Journey," in *Material Matters: The Art and Culture of Contemporary Textiles*, edited by Ingrid Backman and Ruth Scheuing, 148–56 (Toronto: YYZ Books, 1998); Dolores Churchill, "Weaving Stories of Art," in *On Aboriginal Representations in the Gallery*, edited by Lynda Jessup and Shannon Bagg, 217–20 (Hull, Quebec: Canadian Museum of Civilization, 2002); and Larry McNeil, "*Fly by Night Mythology:* An Indigenous Guide to White Man, or How to Stay Sane When the World Makes no Sense," in *Alaska Native Reader*, edited by Maria Shaa Tl'aa Williams (Durham, NC: Duke University Press, 2009).

63 Karen Duffek, ed., *Robert Davidson: The Abstract Edge* (Vancouver: Museum of Anthropology at the University of British Columbia, 2004); Gary Wyatt, ed., *Susan Point: Coast Salish Artist* (Seattle: University of Washington Press, 2000); and Jennifer Kramer, *K'esu': The Art and Life of Doug Cranmer* (Vancouver: Douglas & McIntyre, 2012).

64 Karen Duffek and Tania Willard, *Lawrence Paul Yuxweluptun: Unceded Territories* (Vancouver: Museum of Anthropology at the University of British Columbia, 2016); and Lisa Baldissera, ed., *Marianne Nicolson: The Return of Abundance* (Victoria, BC: Art Gallery of Greater Victoria, 2008).

65 Aldona Jonaitis, "Da-ka-xeen Mehner: Looking into Himself," in *Conversations: Eiteljorg Contemporary Art Fellowship 2015*, edited by Jennifer Complo McNutt and Ashley Holland, 75–100 (Indianapolis, IN: Eiteljorg Museum of American Indians and Western Art, 2015); McNeil, *"Fly by Night Mythology"*; Mique'l Askren (Dangeli), "Larry Tee Harbor Jackson McNeil: Visual Myth Maker," in *Diversity and Dialogue: The Eiteljorg Fellowship for Native American Fine Art 2007*, edited James H. Nottage, 77–94 (Indianapolis, IN: Eiteljorg Museum of American Indians and Western Art; Seattle: University of Washington Press, 2008); Veronica Passalacqua, "Tanis Maria S'eiltin: Coming Full Circle," in *Into the Fray: The Eiteljorg Fellowship for Native American Fine Art 2005*, edited by James H. Nottage, 97–110 (Indianapolis, IN: Eiteljorg Museum of American Indians and Western Art; Seattle: University of Washington Press, 2005); and Nicholas Galanin, *Nicholas Galanin: Let Them Enter Dancing and Showing Their Faces* (Seattle: Minor Matters Books LLC, 2018).

66 Aldona Jonaitis, "Traders of Tradition: The History of Haida Art," in *Robert Davidson: Eagle of the Dawn*, edited by I. Thom, 3–23 (Vancouver: Vancouver Art Gallery, 1993); and Ronald Hawker, *Tales of Ghosts: First Nations Art in British Columbia 1922–61* (Vancouver: University of British Columbia Press, 2003).

67 Margaret Blackman, "Totems to Tombstones: Culture Change as Viewed through the Haida Mortuary Complex, 1877–1971," *Ethnology* 12 (1973): 47–56; Blackman, "Creativity in Acculturation," *Ethnohistory* 2 (1976): 387–413; and Blackman, "Ethnohistoric Changes in the Haida Potlatch Complex," *Arctic Anthropology* 14 (1977): 39–53.

68 Aaron Glass, "History and Critique of the 'Renaissance' Discourse," in *Native Art of the Northwest Coast*, edited by Townsend-Gault, Kramer, and Ki-Ke-In, 487–94.

69 Gerald McMaster, "Under Indigenous Eyes," *Art in America* 105, no. 9 (October 2017).

70 Aaron Glass, ed., *Objects of Exchange: Social and Material Transformations on the Late Nineteenth-Century Northwest Coast* (New York: Bard Graduate Center, Decorative Arts, Design History, Material Culture, 2011).

71 Jonaitis and Glass, *Totem Pole*; Moore, *Proud Raven, Panting Wolf*; Solen Roth, *Incorporating Culture: How Indigenous People Are Reshaping the Northwest Coast Art Industry* (Vancouver: UBC Press, 2018); and Kathryn Bunn-Marcuse and Nika Collison, "Gud Gii AanaaGung: Look at One Another," *ab-Original: Journal of Indigenous Studies and First Nations and First Peoples' Cultur*es 2, no. 2 (2018).

72 Formal analysis continues to be useful in some publications such as the Charles Edenshaw catalog; see Augaitis, *Raven Travelling*, and Ronald Hawker, *Yakuglas' Legacy: The Art and Times of Charlie James* (Toronto: University of Toronto Press, 2016).

73 The primacy of the nineteenth-century canon remains apparent in work by contemporary artists whose perfection of past forms continues to impress.

74 Davidson, "Da. A xuugang, Charles Edenshaw, 'Master Carpenter.'" Author's personal communication with Ishmael Hope, 2017, 2018.

CONTRIBUTORS

KAREN BENBASSAT ALI is a writer, educator, and previously the director of Satellite Gallery, an institutionally experimental programming and exhibition space in downtown Vancouver, British Columbia. She holds an MA from the University of Toronto and has worked across the areas of education and curatorial at the Vancouver Art Gallery and the Museum of Anthropology at the University of British Columbia.

JANET CATHERINE BERLO, professor of art history and visual and cultural studies at the University of Rochester, holds a PhD from Yale University. She is coauthor of the influential *Native North American Art* survey with Ruth B. Phillips (second edition 2015). Berlo has collaborated on publications with many Native scholars and artists and has received grants for her work on Native art history from the Guggenheim and Getty Foundations.

ILJUUWAAS, TYSON BROWN, is a Haida artist from Skidegate, Haida Gwaii. He is a member of the K̲aay'ahl Laanas clan of Ts'aahl. His artistic focus is on creating a relevant body of work, while preserving and perpetuating classical Haida design principles. He is inspired by his people's history, culture, and world view. A lifelong student, Brown has completed an apprenticeship with renowned Haida artist Robert Davidson. He works in various mediums, including design, paint, and sculpture.

KATHRYN BUNN-MARCUSE, PhD, is the curator of Northwest Native art and the director of the Bill Holm Center for the Study of Northwest Native Art at the Burke Museum. She is also assistant professor of art history at the University of Washington. Her publications focus on the indigenization of European-American imagery, nineteenth-century Northwest Coast jewelry and other body adornment, and the filmic history of the Kwakwa̱ka̱'wakw. In her role as curator, Bunn-Marcuse collaborates with First Nations communities and artists to identify research priorities and to activate the Burke Museum's holdings in ways that are responsive to cultural revitalization efforts.

JISGANG NIKA COLLISON belongs to the K̲aay'ahl Laanas X̲aaydaG̲a (nee Ts'aahl clan) of the Haida Nation. She is executive director and curator of the Haida Gwaii Museum at K̲ay Llnagaay and has worked in the field of Indigenous language, arts, and culture for more than twenty years. Deeply committed to reconciliation,

Collison is a senior repatriation negotiator for her Nation, pursuing reparation and relationships with mainstream museums on a global scale. She is a lifelong Nation-based scholar of all things Haida.

KAREN DUFFEK is curator of contemporary visual arts and the Pacific Northwest at the Museum of Anthropology at the University of British Columbia. Collaborating with originating community members to document and activate historical belongings—both inside and outside the museum—is a passion, as is working with contemporary art and artists across cultural and disciplinary borders. In her recent and current exhibitions and publications, Duffek has continued to engage with historical Northwest Coast art and contemporary Indigenous knowledge holders as well as to examine the relationships between Northwest Coast art, modernity, and modernisms in the early to mid-twentieth century.

SHARON FORTNEY, PhD, is curator of Indigenous Collections and Engagement at the Museum of Vancouver (MOV). She holds an undergraduate degree in archaeology from the University of Calgary and graduate degrees in anthropology from the University of British Columbia. Past writings have focused on Coast Salish cedar root basketry, First Nations Cultural Centres in British Columbia, and Coast Salish communities and museums. Fortney honors her Klahoose (Northern Coast Salish) ancestry in her role as curator by working hard to ensure MOV is always an accessible, welcoming, and responsive place for Indigenous community members to visit, explore, and work.

CHRISTOPHER GREEN is a PhD candidate in art history at the Graduate Center of the City University of New York (CUNY). His research focuses on modern and contemporary Native American art, digital cultural modes, the representation and display of Indigenous culture, and primitivisms of the historic and neo-avant-garde. Green's scholarly essays and critical writings can be found in *Art in America*, *frieze*, *The Brooklyn Rail*, *ARTMargins*, *Winterthur Portfolio*, and *ab-Original*, among other publications. His present contribution originates from his dissertation research, which considers the interplay between Euro-American modernism and Northwest Coast Native art. He was a 2018–19 Smithsonian Institution Predoctoral Fellow at the Smithsonian American Art Museum and National Museum of the American Indian.

DENISE NICOLE GREEN, PhD, is assistant professor of fiber science and apparel design and faculty member in the American Indian and Indigenous Studies Program at Cornell University, where she also serves as the director of the Cornell Costume and Textile Collection. She uses ethnography, archival research, design practice, and documentary film production to explore textiles and dress as sites of cultural production. On the Northwest Coast she works with Nuu-chah-nulth First

Nations to understand how ceremonial curtains, dance shawls, and other forms of regalia articulate with territory, natural resources, and ongoing histories.

ISHMAEL HOPE is an Inupiaq and Tlingit poet, storyteller, actor, and playwright living in Juneau, Alaska, with his wife, Lily Hope, and five children. Notable recent projects include his second poetry collection, *Rock Piles Along the Eddy*; serving as the lead writer for *Kisima Ingitchuna: Never Alone*, produced by the Cook Inlet Tribal Council and E-Line Media; and codirecting, with Scott Burton, *Lineage: Tlingit Art Across Generations*, a documentary produced by KTOO Public Media. Hope received his MFA at the Institute of American Indian Arts and bachelor of liberal arts at the University of Alaska Southeast.

LILY HOPE (Tlingit) belongs to the Raven T'akdeintaan clan in Southeast Alaska. Traditionally trained by her mother in Chilkat and Ravenstail weaving, Hope teaches and demonstrates nationally and internationally, often presenting on the spiritual commitments of being a Chilkat weaver. She serves as president of Spirit Uprising, a nonprofit dedicated to perpetuating Chilkat and Ravenstail techniques with classes and annual collaborative weavings. Her robes are housed in the Portland Art Museum, Sealaska Heritage Institute, and with private collectors.

ALDONA JONAITIS, director emerita, University of Alaska Museum of the North, holds a PhD from Columbia University. She has been a professor and administrator at Stony Brook University and vice president at the American Museum of Natural History. Her many books include *Chiefly Feasts* (1991), *Art of the Northwest Coast* (2006), and *The Totem Pole: An Intercultural History* (2010, with Aaron Glass). She is currently working on a book with contemporary Tlingit artists.

KAITLIN MCCORMICK is curator of Western Ethnology at the Canadian Museum of History. She received her PhD in Canadian studies from the University of Edinburgh (2016) and completed three years of postdoctoral training in anthropology and museum studies at Brown University and Yale University. She specializes in the artistic expressions of Northwest Coast artists and the histories of collecting in this region. In her research, teaching, curatorial work, and writing, McCormick is committed to better understanding the ways that Indigenous and non-Indigenous people documented and interpreted their experiences with each other.

EMILY L. MOORE, PhD, is associate professor of art history at Colorado State University and associate curator of North American art at the university's Gregory Allicar Museum. Raised in Ketchikan, Alaska, she is author of the book *Proud Raven, Panting Wolf: Carving Alaska's New Deal Totem Parks* (2018).

PETER MORIN is a Tahltan Nation artist and curator. Through his visual and performance art he investigates the impact zones where Indigenous practices collide with Western-settler colonialism. Morin's artworks are shaped by Tahltan epistemological production and often take the form of performance interventions. Exhibiting and performing in Berlin, London, New Zealand, and Singapore as well as across Canada and the United States, Morin has curated exhibitions for the Museum of Anthropology at the University of British Columbia, Western Front, the Bill Reid Gallery, and Burnaby Art Gallery. He was longlisted for the Brink and Sobey Awards in 2013 and 2014, respectively, and in 2016 received the Hnatyshyn Foundation Mid-Career Award for outstanding achievement by a Canadian artist. Morin is an associate professor in the Faculty of Arts at the Ontario College of Art and Design University, Toronto.

LOU-ANN IKA'WEGA NEEL, descendant of the Mamalillikulla, Da'nax'daxw, Ma'amtagila, 'Namgis and Kwagiulth tribes of the Kwakwa̱ka̱'wakw people, is the granddaughter of Ellen Kakasolas Neel and is also a practicing visual artist, which includes wood carving, jewelry-making, textiles, and digital design. In addition to her work as an artist, Neel is the repatriation specialist at the Royal British Columbia Museum in Victoria. Her work involves reconnecting artists with the treasures created by their ancestors and assisting First Nations communities to ensure the safe return of their ancestors' remains to their respective homelands.

DUANE NIATUM has been writing poems, stories, and essays for more than sixty years. He earned a BA from the University of Washington, an MA from Johns Hopkins University, and a PhD in American culture from the University of Michigan. His writing is deeply connected with the Northwest Coast landscape, its mountains, forests, water, and creatures. The legends and traditions of his ancestors help shape and animate his poetry. Niatum's more current books of poetry are *The Crooked Beak of Love* (2000), *The Pull of the Green Kite* (2011), *Agate Songs on the Path of Red Cedar* (2011), and *Earth Vowels* (2017).

MEGAN A. SMETZER, PhD, is an independent art historian based in Vancouver, British Columbia, on the traditional and unceded territory of the Musqueam, Squamish, and Tsleil-Waututh people. She has taught, published, and lectured on historical and contemporary Northwest Coast Indigenous cultural expressions, focusing primarily on work made by women. She has written essays for several museum catalogs as well as the *Journal of Material Culture* and *American Indian Art Magazine*. Smetzer is currently working on her book, *Painful Beauty: Tlingit Women, Beadwork, and the Art of Resilience*.

ROBERT STARBARD, T'akdeintaan (Raven).Tsaixaan Hit (Mt. Fairweather house), is tribal administrator of the Tlingit Hoonah Indian Association, the tribal government of the Xunaa Tlingit living in Hoonah, on the north shore of Chichagof Island on Icy Strait near Glacier Bay, southeast Alaska. Skilled in both business and communications, he works closely with community members to protect and support tribal health and welfare, and to develop educational and economic initiatives that preserve and perpetuate Tlingit culture.

EVELYN VANDERHOOP, Gaw Gitanee clan, Haida, is an artist of traditional Northern Northwest Coast textiles. Her art is in private, municipal, and museum collections internationally. Among the museums that hold her weaving art are the Burke Museum, Seattle; Canadian Museum of History, Gatineau, Quebec; the Haida Gwaii Museum, Skidegate, British Columbia; and the Museum of Fine Arts, Boston. Teaching and perpetuating techniques and cultural knowledge of Naaxiin and Ravenstail techniques is a legacy she received from her mother and grandmother, which she has passed to her daughters as well as other students. Researching and sharing cultural knowledge of Haida history is an important goal Vanderhoop strives for in her travels to institutions and museums. She holds a BA from Western Washington University, Bellingham.

LUCY FOWLER WILLIAMS, PhD, is associate curator and Jeremy A. Sabloff Senior Keeper of American Collections at the University of Pennsylvania Museum of Archaeology and Anthropology in Philadelphia (Penn Museum). A cultural anthropologist, she received her PhD from the University of Pennsylvania. Recent projects include the Louis Shotridge Digital Archive about the work of the Tlingit Alaskan curator and the 2014–21 Penn Museum exhibition *Native American Voices: The People Here and Now.* Her research interests include issues of Indigenous identity and revitalization, histories of collecting and representation, textiles, and material culture.

INDEX

D

L

M

N

O

P

Q

R

S

T

X

Y